The Civic Foundations of Fascism in Europe

The Civic Foundations of Fascism in Europe

Italy, Spain, and Romania, 1870–1945

Dylan Riley

VERSO
London · New York

This paperback edition published by Verso 2019
First published by The Johns Hopkins University Press 2010
© 2010 The Johns Hopkins University Press
© Dylan Riley 2019

1 3 5 7 9 10 8 6 4 2

Verso
UK: 6 Meard Street, London W1F 0EG
US: 20 Jay Street, Suite 1010, Brooklyn, NY 11201
versobooks.com

Verso is the imprint of New Left Books

ISBN-13: 978-1-78663-523-5
ISBN-13: 978-1-78663-524-2 (UK EBK)
ISBN-13: 978-1-78663-525-9 (US EBK)

British Library Cataloguing in Publication Data
A catalogue record for this book is available from the British Library

The Library of Congress Has Cataloged the Hardback Edition As Follows:

Riley, Dylan J., 1971–
        The civic foundations of fascism in Europe : Italy, Spain, and
Romania, 1870–1945 / Dylan Riley.
            p. cm.
        Includes bibliographical references and index.
        ISBN-13: 978-0-8018-9427-5 (hardcover : alk. paper)
        ISBN-10: 0-8018-9427-1 (hardcover : alk. paper)
        1. Fascism—Europe—History—19th century. 2. Fascism—Europe—
History—20th century. 3. Europe— Politics and government— 19th
century. 4. Europe—Politics and government—20th century. I. Title.
D726.5.R48 2010
320.53'3094—dc22   2009020309

Printed in Great Britain by CPI Group (UK) Ltd, Croydon CR0 4YY

Ad Emanuela con amore

Contents

Acknowledgments

This book grew out of my studies at UCLA and has consumed much of my life for the past ten years. But its core idea has a more precise origin: a warm August day in 2001 in the foothills of the Italian Alps in a small town called Torre Pellice. There, in a sunlit room with no books and only a laptop, it struck me that fascism had developed precisely in the dense, culturally rich, and politically sophisticated zones of north-central Italy. These were the same regions in which the seeds of modern civilization, especially the idea of popular sovereignty, had been preserved and then "reborn" in the fifteenth and sixteenth centuries. Further, it was here that dense webs of cooperative societies, chambers of labor, and mutual aid societies had developed in the early twentieth century. Was there any connection between these facts? Did fascism grow from a civic soil? This question immediately raised others. What was the real nature of fascism? To what extent were fascist movements "antidemocratic," as they are widely presented in both historical and sociological accounts? How should fascism be understood comparatively? These questions have occupied at least some of my waking hours, and sometimes all of them, every day since.

I have incurred many debts in the process of writing this book. I would like to thank my extraordinarily patient, helpful, and supportive advisers: Perry Anderson, Rebecca Jean Emigh, Carlo Ginzburg, and Michael Mann. Each contributed in both obvious and subtle ways to the book's conception. All of them read and commented on parts or all of the book.

I also thank Victoria Bonnell, who has been an unfailingly supportive faculty mentor and who encouraged me to make a crucial reorganization of the book and extend the analysis to Eastern Europe. This helped immensely in framing my comparative approach. I am grateful to Giovanni Arrighi, Irene Bloemraad, Michael Burawoy, Georgi Derlugian, Peter Evans, Neil Fligstein, Marion Fourcade, Paul Ginsborg, Marco Santoro, Sandra Smith, Cihan Tugal, and Zulema Valdez, who all commented on various drafts of the project. I owe an enormous debt to the staff of the Fondazione Ugo Spirito in Rome for their wonderful combination of warmth and professionalism. My book benefited substantially from the work of three outstanding research assistants: Ryan Calder, Juan Fernandez, and Nicholas Hoover Wilson. My son, Eamon, was patient enough to let me finish the book, and for this he richly deserves his Lego set. Finally, I thank my wife, Emanuela Tallo, who has been unfailingly supportive and loving during the writing of this book and who has taught me an enormous amount about her own amazing country. It is to her that I dedicate the work.

I have been fortunate to be able to present pieces of my argument to a variety of audiences. I thank audiences at the Johns Hopkins University, the Central European University, UCLA, and UC Davis for challenging me and forcing me to think more clearly about my ideas. I would also like to thank my students at UC Berkeley, especially those in my comparative and historical methods seminar, whose relentless critical intelligence has often prompted me to reformulate and rethink my approach to historical sociology.

Research for this book was supported by a Fulbright grant from the Institute for International Education. In addition, the University of California at Berkeley's Institute for East European and Eurasian Societies, Institute for European Studies, Institute for Industrial Relations, and Committee on Research all provided financial support for the project.

Abbreviations

aA	agrarpolitisch Apparat
ACNP	Asociación Católica Nacional de Propagandistas
ACS	Archivio Centrale dello Stato, Rome
AF	Archivi fascisti
AfA	Allgemeine frei Angestelltenbund
ANI	Associazione Nazionalista Italiana
CDI	Centralverband Deutscher Industrieller
CEDA	Confederación Española de Derechas Autónomas
CGL	Confederazione Generale del Lavoro
CGT	Confederación General del Trabajo
CNCA	Confederación Nacional Católico Agraria
CNT	Confederación National del Trabajo
DAF	Deutsch Arbeitsfront
DC	Democrazia Cristiana
DDP	Deutsch Demokratische Partei

DGPS	Direzione generale pubblica sicurezza
DN	Direttorio nazionale
DNVP	Deutschnationale Volkspartei
DVP	Deutsche Volkspartei
ÉME	Ébredö Magyarok Egyesülete
EOA	Ente Opera Assistenziali
ERC	Esquerra Republicana de Catalunya
FET	Falange Española Tradicionalista
FET-JONS	Falange Española Tradicionalista y de las Juntas de Ofensiva Nacional-Sindicalista
FIOM	Federazione Italiana Operai Metallurgici
FISA	Federazione Italiana dei Sindacati degli Agricoltori
FNR	Frontul Renaşterii Naţionale
FNTT	Federación Nacional de Trabajadores de la Tierra
GdA	Gewerkshaftsbund der Angestellten
Gedag	Gesamtverband Deutscher Angestelltenwerkshaft
IRA	Instituto de Reforma Agraria
JAP	Juventud de Acción Popular
JONS	Juntas de Ofensiva Nacional-Sindicalista
LAM	Legiunea Arhanghelul Mihail
LANC	Liga Apărării Naţional-Creştine
MAIC	Ministero di Agricoltura, Industria e Commercio
MI	Ministero dell'Interno
MOVE	Magyar Országos Véderö Egyesülete
NSDAP	Nationalsozialistische Deutsche Arbeiterpartei

PCI	Partito Comunista Italiano
PNF	Partito Nazionale Fascista
PNL	Partidul Național Liberal
PNR	Partidul Național Român
PNȚ	Partidul Național-Țărănesc
PPI	Partito Popolare Italiano
PSD	Partidul Socialdemocrat
PSI	Partito Socialista Italiano
PSOE	Partito Socialista Obrero Español
PȚ	Partidul Țărănesc
RLB	Reichslandbund
SA	Sturmabteilung
SP	Segreteria Politica
SPD	Sozialdemokratische Partei Deutschlands
SPEP	Situazione politica ed economica nelle provincie
TPȚ	Totul pentru Țară
UGT	Unión General de Trabajadores
UIL	Unione Italiana del Lavoro
UMN	Unión Monárquica Nacional
UNCC	Unión Nacional de Cooperativas del Campo
UP	Unión Patriótica
USI	Unione Sindacale Italiana

Introduction to the Second Edition

The Civic Foundations of Fascism in Europe was written in dialogue with two main theoretical traditions: Marxism and Tocquevillian analysis. The book argues that the most well-established Marxian arguments lack an adequate account of fascist organizations, and that these were key in determining the character of fascist regimes. At the same time, the book rejects the Tocquevillian notion that fascism was based on social atomization. As an alternative, I employ Gramsci to argue that fascist regimes drew on organizational resources in civil society to construct their distinctive party institutions. What is the significance of this claim? This introduction seeks to explain the book's intellectual and political significance. Accordingly, it is divided into two parts. The first locates *Civic Foundations* within Marxian and Tocquevillian discussions about fascism, while the second develops hypotheses about contemporary politics on the basis of the book's analyses.

The Marxist and Tocquevillian Discussion of Fascism

Perhaps the central division between Marxist and Tocquevillian analyses of fascism is whether they consider fascism to be a revolutionary or counterrevolutionary phenomenon. For the most part, Marxist theories of fascism have offered a clear answer: fascism was a counterrevolution.[1] Arrayed against this claim, a varied group of broadly Tocquevillian analyses hold that fascism was a revolutionary regime that aimed to create a "new man."[2] Therefore, Tocquevillians tend to draw parallels between fascism and other revolutionary regimes of both the left and the right. Which of these accounts is more convincing?

The Marxist tradition, when considered carefully, contains two quite different substantive theories of fascism. The first account explains fascism as the consequence of a political crisis in which a weakly developed industrial bourgeoisie allies with a landed elite in the face of a revolutionary threat from an alliance of workers and peasants. In this scenario, the owners of land and capital are too weak to rule by themselves, but the proletariat and the peasantry are not yet strong enough to seize power. Thus, the dominant class delegates authority to a rising fascist party, often seen as sociologically rooted in the "petty bourgeoisie."[3] In this scenario, fascism is seen as a political apparatus that gains relative autonomy from both the dominant social classes and direct producers, establishing a political framework within which the transition to a higher stage of capitalist exploitation can occur. The central argument from this perspective is that fascism is understood as a phenomenon of backwardness.

In the second version of the argument, closely associated with Trotsky, fascism appears as an open dictatorship of capital in decline. As Ernest Mandel points out while summarizing Trotsky's view, "fascism is a product of a severe crisis of monopoly capitalism ... in which the normal valorization of capital under conditions of bourgeois democracy is being increasingly undermined."[4] From this perspective, the problem is not that capitalism is underdeveloped, but that it can no longer achieve an adequate rate of return for its investments in a context of parliamentary democracy.[5] Fascism thus represents an alliance between heavy industry and the state in the imperialist search for markets and resources to shore up sagging rates of profit.[6]

Both versions of the Marxist argument have two main strengths. First, each correctly emphasizes that fascism conserved and extended capitalist property relations rather than undermining them. As a slew of work has shown, business gained a great deal from these regimes.[7] Indeed, it is at least arguable that the greatest long-term economic impact of fascism was to strengthen and stabilize, not eliminate, capitalist relations of production in Italy, Germany and perhaps also Japan. The second great strength of the Marxist arguments is that they correctly identify two of fascism's core bases of support (capital and the landed elite). This is true not so much in the sense that the Marxian argument offers an adequate sociology of fascist parties, but rather in the sense that it emphasizes that without the collaboration of these powerful social elites, fascism would not have come to power. As Robert Paxton, certainly no orthodox Marxist, writes, "the fascist route to power has always passed through cooperation with conservative elites."[8] Thus, the behavior of elites, particularly major owners of property, has to be a central part of any explanation of fascism. The Marxist focus on the behavior of dominant classes deals with this quite effectively.

However, there are major theoretical and empirical problems with what might be called the "classical" Marxist approach. First, it is not clear exactly how the two accounts described above are compatible. While both relate fascism to the dynamics of capitalism, they correlate it with different stages of development of this mode of production. The first account links fascism to an immature capitalism, the second (to continue the analogy) links fascism to a rotten capitalism.

This ambivalence mirrors Marx's own about Bonapartism. In the *Eighteenth Brumaire of Louis Bonaparte*, a text that forms the basic conceptual background for all subsequent Marxist explanations of fascist regimes, Marx develops two sharply different explanations of Napoleon III's rise. Marx's dominant argument focuses on the backwardness of French society. French capitalism in this scenario is peculiarly backward, dominated by small peasant proprietorship (the "Napoleonic" form of property) and a parasitic rent-seeking bourgeoisie.[9] From this perspective, it is the combination of an authoritarian peasantry and a weak parasitic bourgeoisie that allowed for Napoleon III to come to power. This suggestion is compatible with the theoretical logic of Barrington Moore Jr., Palmiro Togliatti, and Angelo Tasca.

Marx combines this focus on backwardness with a second, proto-Trotskyist account. He suggests that only the urban working class could carry out the establishment of a "bourgeois republic" in the mid-nineteenth century because the overall historical period of bourgeois revolution had come to an end.[10] In the context of these claims, Marx tended to emphasize the capitalist character of nineteenth-century French society, including it in the category of "long civilized countries with a developed class structure [and] modern conditions of production."[11] In sum, like his followers would do for fascism, Marx put forward two contrasting accounts for the rise of Napoleon: the overripeness of French society, and its immaturity. Subsequent Marxists would then draw on one or the other of these interpretations to explain fascism.

This inconsistency should not be glossed over. It indicates a basic problem in the Marxist framework for explaining fascism and Bonapartism, and more generally a problem with the theory of the state. The difficulty is that Marxist political theory has never successfully clarified the relationship between state forms and the social property relations of a capitalist economy. (However, this is far from a peculiarity of the Marxist tradition. Weberian sociology has been equally unable to account for the relationship between "modern rational capitalism" and the "modern state.") Thus, authoritarian states can be interpreted either as expressions of capitalism's "latest stage" or as indexes of its immaturity. The real question, broached but not completely resolved by Poulantzas, is how two such similar regimes could appear in economic circumstances that were sharply different?

What of the second position—fascism as revolution? This position has a long pedigree. Hannah Arendt famously argued that both fascist and communist movements were produced by structurally atomized "masses" that emerged out of the pulverization of secondary associations in Western Europe in the nineteenth century.[12] A. James Gregor, in a less lofty and philosophical vein, and drawing exclusively on Italian sources, insisted that fascism was a modernizing revolutionary regime entirely analogous to Bolshevism.[13] A later, classic expression of this position is Renzo De Felice's 1983 preface to *Le interpretazioni del fascismo*. De Felice, in distinguishing fascist regimes from conservative and authoritarian ones, writes:

> The conservative and authoritarian regimes have always tried to demobilize and exclude the [masses] from active participation in political life, offering them a familiar social model and values to which are ascribed the capacity of impeding the inconveniences and errors of some recent revolutionary experience. In contrast fascism has always attempted to create in the masses the sense of being constantly mobilized, of having a direct relationship with the leader ... and of participating and contributing not to a mere restoration of the social order of which everyone feels the limits and historical inadequacy, but rather to a revolution from which a new social order, more just and better than the pre-existing one, will gradually emerge, and which has never been experienced before.[14]

This position has been widely adopted. For example, Michael Mann argues that both Stalinism and Nazism were "regimes of continuous revolution," while Finchelstein defines fascism as a "modern revolutionary phenomenon."[15]

Most of the accounts that interpret fascism as a revolution argue that Marxism has been unable to grasp this dimension of the regimes because of its restricted, economistic view of revolution as a transformation of property relations. For these scholars, fascism was a revolution not of property but of identity. It aimed at creating a "new man" (and a new woman). Frustrated with the split between political institutions and the mass population, fascists sought to overcome the opposition between the "bourgeois" and the "citizen" to establish a new type of political identity: the citizen-producer linked to the state through participation in mass organizations.[16]

The basic strength of this interpretation is that it recognizes the extent to which fascist regimes aimed at altering the relationship between the underlying population and state institutions. In particular, the work from this perspective emphasizes how these regimes built a complex belt of institutions, in which fascist parties were central and which linked classes to states in ways did not exist in their prior liberal histories. But the "fascism as revolutionary" interpretation has two serious weaknesses. First, and most obviously, it deploys no clear theoretical notion of revolution. Since no serious scholarship argues that the fascist regimes transformed private property, this line of reasoning is left with a definition of revolution that is quite empty. Second, none of this work has been able to provide much in the way of an explanation of fascist regimes. Instead, empty tautologies reign. One example comes from the very well-regarded work of Emilio Gentile, who writes:

> The choreographic, liturgical and ludic aspect of the party that absorbed a large part of its activities and of its energies was, in the totalitarian logic of fascism, one of the principle functions for the fascist socialization of individuals and masses, a function carried out with full consciousness of its political objectives.[17]

In short, for Gentile, the "totalitarian logic" of fascism explains its totalitarianism. Or as Michael Mann writes more briefly and clearly, "Revolutionary goals involved a wholesale transformation of society."[18] In other words, fascism was revolutionary because it was revolutionary. Both explanations are reminiscent of

Moliére's joke about a group of doctors who explain the sleep-inducing properties of opium by its dormitive principle.

Civic Foundations intervenes in this debate. It largely takes for granted the correctness of the Marxist idea that fascism was a regime that reinforced the position of existing dominant classes. But it attempts to build a more satisfactory explanation by focusing on the organizational dynamics that set fascist regimes apart from other forms of rightist authoritarianism. Its central thesis, that fascism required a densely organized civil society in order to build its distinctive party institutions, is increasingly recognized in political sociology. Indeed, the book was part of a wider body of literature that challenged the neo-Tocquevillian consensus in the late nineties and early aughts. However, *Civic Foundations* was distinctive in two ways with respect to revisionist civil society literature.

First, unlike much of the critical literature on civil society, my work explicitly rejected any attempt to distinguish between "democratic" and "non-democratic" types of associations. On empirical grounds, I rejected the idea that the nationalist associational sphere out of which fascist parties emerged could be understood as antidemocratic. In their own terms, the fascists did not propose to undermine the democratic foundations of their states in either Italy, Germany, Romania or Spain; rather, they sought to establish a fundamentally new type of representative relation—one that would go through the fascist party rather than elections. They were of course ferociously antiliberal, as well as being antisocialist, but it is simply a misunderstanding to see them as antidemocratic.

I also rejected the distinction between democratic and non-democratic associations on methodological grounds. The attempt to differentiate between good, "democratic" associations, and bad, "antidemocratic" ones smacked to me of a retrospective and ad hoc attempt to save a theory; especially since no one has ever provided any convincing criterion to distinguish between "democratic" and "antidemocratic" associations. If theories of civil society were to be explanatory, I thought, they should retain the *structural* claim that voluntary organizations promote democracy regardless of their character.

The second distinctive claim I made in *Civic Foundations* was that fascist regimes were best understood as authoritarian democracies. This notion, predictably, created howls of protest, especially among political scientists and historians. As Pinto put it, "Riley's definition of 'authoritarian democracy' … is a conceptual problem—he does not use a procedural definition of democracy."[19] Or, as David Art stated,

"Riley's definition is virtually guaranteed to provoke storms of protest [since it is] hardly compatible with any reasonable conception of democracy."[20] Stanley Payne chimed in, correctly surmising that "[t]he most controversial aspect will be its definition of fascism, which he calls an 'authoritarian democracy.'"[21] This response speaks more to the crypto-ideological agenda of political sociology and political science than it does to my book. The question that no proceduralist account of democracy, from Schumpeter onward, can answer is why a particular set of political institutions or procedures should be equated with the term "democracy," which is an essentially contested principle of legitimacy, never a neutral description of existing political realities.[22] The term "authoritarian democracy" means simply that the fascists used a democratic claim to legitimacy to justify a project of nationalist single-party rule. Distinctively, and particularly in comparison to Leninism, fascist "authoritarian democracy" presented itself as a definitive solution to the problem of political representation that had arisen with the establishment of parliamentary regimes, not as a transitional dictatorship destined to disappear along with the state itself.

This discussion is important for two reasons, one more academic and the other more political. To take the academic concern first, by labeling fascist regimes antidemocratic, their distinctive political institutions—the mass parties and the corporatist organizations—are rendered mysterious. But these were central to what made fascist regimes fascist. There was an attempt on the part of the leadership to *incorporate* the mass of the population into the state. In this way the fascist state was to possess a popular basis that the liberal regime preceding it lacked.

There is also a political concern relevant to this discussion. From the perspective of the left, it is important to remember the "authoritarian democratic" features of fascism, because, at least from the perspective of the left-wing resistance, the struggle against fascism was not a struggle to reestablish a preexisting liberal democracy that had manifestly failed; rather, it was an attempt to replace the highly mobilized authoritarian democracies of the fascist period with an equally mobilized non-authoritarian democracy of a new type. Fascism, especially in Italy, changed the institutional conditions for politics in ways that created very high levels of political participation. The transitions-to-democracy literature has largely failed to grasp this fact because of its fundamental commitment to the equation of democracy with liberalism.

These points, however, relate primarily to the work's analysis of historical fascism. What is perhaps much more important today is to position the theses of *Civic Foundations* in relation to the current world turn to the right. This will help both to clarify the argument of the book and perhaps to shed some light on our contemporary circumstances. I will explore these issues as a series of contrasting theses.

Fascism/Trump[23]

Many pundits and scholars, at least in the US, seem to want to draw a parallel between the interwar right-wing dictatorships and Trump. Timothy Snyder's claim, "our political order faces new threats not unlike the totalitarianisms of the twentieth century," is somewhat typical of this idea. The idea appears on the center-right, the center-left and the far-left, although these various political camps draw somewhat different conclusions from the supposed parallel. For the centrists, the lesson is to avoid "extremism" and rally support for a broad coalition in support of a restoration of the "rule of law" or "democracy." For the far left, the conclusion is to combat fascism in the streets through direct action. Obviously, these analyses are simply lightly refurbished versions of the debates of the twenties and thirties on how to effectively resist the interwar dictatorships. All of these interpretations, however, overlook a profound difference between the interwar period and today. Fascism, as I point out in *Civic Foundations*, could arise only in conditions of a highly mobilized civil society. But one of the weaknesses of the text is that it provided no explanation for this level of mobilization: it took it as its task to document the strength of civil society and to show how that strength related to fascist mobilization. In what follows I would like to provide a brief sketch of the causes of civil society development in interwar Europe, as well as to suggest some important contrasts with the contemporary world.

The general thesis I would suggest is that an intense process of inter- and intra-class struggle took place in both domestic and international arenas, and this produced and politically formed the highly organized civil societies of the period that runs from about 1880 to about 1930 across Europe. These struggles began in the 1880s with the formation of the first mass socialist and peasant parties. They then intensified with the imperialist conflicts that led up to World War I, and finally reached a fever pitch with the outbreak of the Russian Revolution. These processes created an impressive set of mass organizations with associated locals, cooperatives and newspapers that engaged the mass population in politics on an unprecedented scale on both the far left and far right.

"Trumpism" and its various European correlates have arisen, in contrast, in the context of a fragmented and depoliticized civil society: the product of the long historical ebbing of the socialist project, and of basically pacific relations in the capitalist core. As a result of this fundamental difference at the level of civil society, which itself is connected with the dynamics of national and international class struggle in the contemporary period, Trumpism paradoxically shares much more with nineteenth-century Bonapartism—in which a charismatic figure emerges in the context of a fragmented and weak civil society—than it does with twentieth-century fascism.

To demonstrate the difference, I will present a set of contrasting theses on fascism and Trumpism. I will then pull together the implications of these for the different forms of rule characteristic of these two forms of right-wing regime. Both fascism and Trumpism can be located in four key relationships:

1. National and international class struggle and the structure of civil society
2. National and international class struggle and the politics of the middle class
3. Structure of the dominant class and class struggle
4. Structure of civil society and the character of regimes

National and International Class Struggle and the Structure of Civil Society

Fascist regimes arose in the period of imperialism—something that *Civic Foundations* did not sufficiently emphasize. Nicos Poulantzas put it best when he wrote, "he who does not wish to discuss *imperialism* should also stay silent on the subject of fascism."[24] In all capitalist countries there was a shift toward "organized capitalism" between 1871 and 1914. This was associated with the saturation of domestic markets and created enormous pressure for war within the core of the world capitalist system over the first couple of decades of the twentieth century. This increasingly turned states into rivals on the global stage; this switch to imperialism affected every advanced capitalist country and led to demands for a greater role for the state. It was also the structural fact behind the outbreak of World War I, which in turn produced the Russian Revolution that further radicalized both the right and the left. It is no accident indeed that fascism, again to quote Poulantzas, arose in the "second two weakest links" in the chain of imperialist countries after Russia (Italy and Germany). Italy and Germany were cut out of the imperial game, and their social elites were profoundly weakened by the postwar crisis.

Imperialism had implications for civil society. The bourgeois politics of the period immediately prior to the outbreak of the war in both Italy and Germany were characterized by the proliferation of a series of pressure groups demanding an end to the nineteenth-century politics of notables, and clamoring for aggressive geopolitical policies, often linked to strident attacks on socialism and the left. Among the most important of these in Germany were the Navy League, the Defense League, and the Pan-German League.[25] In Italy the group around Enrico Corradini's *Il Regno* agitated for a kind of Marxism in reverse: an open class offensive by the bourgeoisie, and at the same time a break with internationalism in favor of an assertion of Italian greatness.[26]

In both Germany and Italy this bourgeois politics had to face a challenging reality: the existence of mass socialist party organizations that were not only anti-capitalist but also explicitly internationalist. In Italy the PSI (Italian Socialist Party) formed a "state within a state"; its members were drawn into party elections, deliberations at party congresses and subjected to intense political education efforts.[27] In Germany the SPD (Social Democratic Party) was by far the most important political mass organization in the country by 1912. These were the first—and consequently the model for—mass party organizations on the European continent.

World War I and the Russian Revolution only exacerbated the dramatic difference in organizational capacity between the left and right. Of course, the Russian Revolution had a contradictory impact on these movements. It radicalized one wing of the labor movement (the communist parties), but at the same time split the movement after 1921. In any case, there was a huge challenge from below that both threatened the social elite and provided an organizational model of mass politics that the fascists adopted. (In the Italian case, many of the political leaders had previous experience in the parties of the left).

Fascism arose not only in the context of a mass anti-capitalist party, but more specifically out of a defeated revolution. Although an objectively revolutionary situation had existed from 1918 to 1920 in Italy and from 1917 to 1923 in Germany, the revolutionary breakthrough failed. Socialists retreated to defending a set of economic demands within capitalism, thereby weakening their hold over the middle strata (the petty bourgeoisie) and the peasantry, who then became available for fascist mobilization.

The result of this conflict, pitting both a socialist and an internationalist working class against an antisocialist and nationalist bourgeoisie, was an organizational explosion in civil society both among workers and the bourgeoisie. It was this intertwined national and international class struggle that largely created the dense of civil societies of the late nineteenth and early twentieth centuries in Europe.

Trumpism, in total contrast to interwar fascism, arises in a low-pressure geopolitical environment. It's perhaps easy to forget this with the constant stream of inane provocation pouring forth from the White House, but the fact remains that the main military conflicts shaping the contemporary world are between the advanced capitalist countries and rather minor border threats. These are of two types: so called rogue regimes, and "terrorism." There are zero pressures toward military conflict within the core of the capitalist world. It is possible that China may seize the moment, but for now the Middle Kingdom remains geopolitically stunted.

As a consequence of this difference, Trumpism has not arisen after a mass mobilizing war. Instead it has emerged in the long aftermath of an economic collapse, and the subsequent response, which has done nothing to address the underlying issues that caused the collapse. As such, this is part of wider pattern of revolt that has been roiling Europe, and also Turkey. These revolts, which have taken both rightist and leftist forms, are a consequence of the etiolation of the material basis of consent to capitalist rule in the advanced capitalist world.

Furthermore, Trumpism, and "right-wing populism" more broadly, does not face anything like a mass socialist political party, and as a result has not been forced into constructing its own form of mobilized right-wing infrastructure. Across the United States and Europe, there has been a steady decline since the seventies in electoral turnout, union density and participation in all sorts of political activities. In Europe the mass political parties that structured many polities only a few decades ago (social democracy, communism, and Christian democracy) have shrunk and weakened.

The dynamics of the political crisis that produces right-wing populism and Trumpism thus involve a disintegration of existing parties rather than a threat from new or rapidly developing parties. Crucially, this means the organizational dynamics that created fascism—as, in Juan Linz's words, late-comers to the political space—are not in operation here.[28] These different patterns of political contestation mean that Trumpism completely lacks a mass party organization in the fascist sense. The contentious dynamics that could produce such organizations are missing.

Trumpism in particular does not emerge from a revolutionary threat, but from the failed reformism of the Obama years. The bailout of large financial institutions with no significant prosecutions, combined with a health care plan premised on massive handouts to private insurance companies, fatally weakened progressive initiatives during Obama's time. The situation bears a faint but instructive resemblance to the years 1918–1920 in Italy, and 1917–1923 in Germany. Obama's economic recovery, meanwhile, was meek. Therefore, while remaining personally popular, he left the Democratic Party in shambles. Again, the specifically counterrevolutionary energy so characteristic of fascist movements is impossible for Trumpism to reproduce.

There is therefore a profound difference between interwar fascism and the contemporary turn to the right. While during the first period the right had to compete in a highly structured and politicized civil society, in which a highly organized national middle class faced a highly organized international working class, in the second it is operating in a much more fragmented and de-politicized context. I return below to the implications of this difference.

National and International Class Struggle and the Politics of the Middle Class

A second limitation of *Civic Foundations* is its treatment of the middle class, petty bourgeoisie, or "middle strata." The implicit class analysis of the book rested on the idea of a basic opposition between the "social elite," comprised of landowners and capitalists, and all direct producers, whether agrarian or industrial. Of course, a considerable part of the cadre of fascist parties was made up of groups between these social classes; likewise, a large part of the political struggle after World War I was focused on winning the allegiance of these groups either to the camp of the national bourgeoisie or the international proletariat. In this struggle for the hearts and minds of the middle classes the left faced a basic problem. The middle classes, because they were linked to national systems of education, because their professional and interest associations were national, and because they made up the lower-ranking officers of national armies, were basically supportive of imperialism, and profoundly hostile to internationalism.

In contrast, despite the betrayal of the SPD (but not the PSI) leadership, nationalism had quite limited purchase, at least on the industrial working classes of Italy and Germany. This limitation was most evident in the defeat of the fascist left (the Strasser brothers in Germany, and the revolutionary syndicalists in Italy). These "left-fascist" attempts—comparable with Peronism—to pull the working class to a politics of national prestige and imperialism ultimately collapsed; that failure is absolutely central to understanding the subsequent course of fascism in both countries. It also shows clearly how the class and national divides reinforced one another in the interwar period.

As a result of this particular configuration of class conflict and nationalism, fascist movements were able to weld together salaried employees and small shopkeepers as well as petty agrarian direct producers into a paramilitary party organization aimed primarily against *international* socialism. (The political sociology of these movements is somewhat controversial. Italian fascism was never primarily an electoral movement, unlike German National Socialism [NS], which had a longer electoral history. One finding that is fairly common is that fascist movements did well among state employees.)

How does the international and national class struggle affect the politics of the middle classes in the age of Trump? Trump's core social support comes from a combination of relatively affluent southern white voters (traditional petty bourgeoisie) and a small sliver of working-class swing voters in the Upper Midwest. The material interests of these groups can at least plausibly be cast in nationalist terms. It is clear that to the extent that Trump's "nationalist" economic agenda has any popular basis, it rests on workers and middle-class groups who fear international competition and immigrants.

In contrast, the highly educated—people whom Poulantzas would call the "new petty bourgeoisie," and Bourdieu would term holders of "cultural capital"—are cosmopolitan in orientation. A considerable quantity of survey evidence now shows that in both Europe and the United States, the working class is increasingly organized in national terms, while the middle class is internationalist in outlook. Because of this, the class basis of Trumpism differs from that of classic fascism. The basic class configuration that produces Trumpism, and right-wing populism more broadly, pits a nationalist working class against an internationalist middle class: a structure that is almost opposite to that of interwar fascism.

Structure of the Dominant Class

Fascist regimes arose in a context of serious intra-dominant class conflict. One line of conflict arose between export-oriented and globally competitive industries, and less internationally competitive heavy industries requiring state support. Another line divided the relatively unproductive and indeed only partly "capitalist" agrarians in the east (Germany) and south (Italy) and industrial capitalists as a whole. For specific historical reasons, in neither Germany nor Italy could the various wings of the dominant class in the postwar period be unified either in a single political organization or in a functioning system of party alternation. Nevertheless, agrarians in both Italy and Germany retained an organizational link to the rural masses, a link that proved crucial to the rise of fascism.

One of the most important services that agrarian elites provided to fascist parties was their insulation of large parts of the rural population from socialist propaganda; in some cases the agrarians transferred these populations into more or less open alliances with the fascists. The Nazi party always had a strong base of support among peasants in Schleswig-Holstein, Mecklenberg and East Prussia, whereas the Italian fascists found support among smallholders and sharecroppers in Emilia-Romagna, Tuscany, Lombardy, Piedmont and the Veneto.

Another very important service that the agrarians performed was to pave the way for fascist movements to take power. In both Italy and Germany fascist parties were invited into power by conservative elites with ties to agrarian circles. Victor Emmanuel III named Mussolini prime minister, just as Hindenburg named Hitler chancellor. In neither case did fascist parties win governmental power by winning a majority of the vote. The NSDAP's (Nazi Party's) electoral high-water mark was July 1932: 37 percent. The PNF (Italy's National Fascist Party) was always more of a paramilitary than electoral organization. Its greatest electoral success came in 1921 as part of the "national bloc" in which it took thirty-six out of 535 parliamentary seats. The fascist movements then had direct access to the state, through the landed upper classes, which formed their social cores.

Trumpism also arises in the context of serious intra-dominant class conflict. In a context of structurally stagnating rates of return, the owners of money and means of production demand increasingly direct handouts from the state, which leads to the immediate politicization of their economic interest conflicts. This leads to dominant class fragmentation rather than cohesion as conflicts develop over which industries and sectors will receive state largess. One of the most remarkable developments over the past couple years is the politicization of intra-dominant class conflicts: fossils fuels and extractive industries back Trump, health insurance companies defend the massive corporate handout known as the Affordable Care Act. All these interest conflicts are carried on with great sound and fury, even though the class terrain on which they are currently waged is relatively narrow.

But Trumpism, unlike fascism, lacks support from a precapitalist agrarian elite; there is neither a Hindenburg nor a Victor Emmanuel and related agrarian-court institutional complex that could install him in power. Consequently, Trump was elected with 46 percent of the popular vote, better than either Mussolini or Hitler. But he still lost the popular vote by 3 million. Of course he did have other institutional advantages. Trump received an eleven-percentage-point boost from the electoral college, whereas this institution penalized Clinton by six percentage points. But Trump's relationship to the state is much more fraught than either Mussolini or Hitler's because he lacks support among an old regime social group.

Structure of Civil Society and the Character of Regimes

How does interwar fascism and contemporary right-wing populism (including Trumpism) differ as a form of regime? Fascist regimes were marked by a dualism of state and party. Leaders such as Mussolini and Hitler balanced party activists pushing for a "second revolution" against bureaucrats lodged in the old regime. Thus, the politics of fascist regimes were shaped by a tendency toward incipient or actual Frondist movements and led by true believers of various sorts: in the Italian case, Edmondo Rossoni and Roberto Farinacci exemplify leaders of these party revolts. In Germany, the establishment of an NS state was partially due to pressure from the NSDAP after the March 1933 elections. Of course, both Mussolini and Hitler largely succeeded in disciplining and weakening their parties. But the struggle between party and state never entirely disappeared, and reemerged as the fascist regimes plunged into crisis after 1941–1942.

There are eerie similarities between Trump's leadership style and Hitler's in particular: the laziness, the emphasis on loyalty, and the anti-bureaucratic structure of the cabinet, with its lack of clearly defined spheres of competence. Furthermore, like both Mussolini and Hitler, Trump faces a Fronde under Bannon, who reminds one of Farinacci.

These superficial similarities, however, only serve to highlight the basic differences between interwar fascism and Trumpism. Both Hitler and Mussolini remained party leaders; they could never fully extricate themselves from the organizations to which they owed their power. Trump is not a party leader; he is a patriarch. He has no organization, and while he rules from the extreme right, he personally lacks a political ideology. Furthermore, comparing Bannon and Farinacci demonstrates Bannon's weakness—he cannot draw on a mass of organized followers to pressure Trump from below. Instead he remains dependent on personal patronage.

This difference matters because it gives fascism and Trumpism very different developmental tendencies. Party pressure was a major source of "radicalization" in fascist regimes. It was the party demand for posts and positions that largely explains the expansion of party control over economic and social life. In the German case, the party was the major institutional force behind the Final Solution. In the Italian case, it was party pressure that forced Mussolini's hand in seizing control of the unions and professional organizations.

Trumpism, in contrast, is marked by a conflict between the bureaucratic state and the Trump organization as a patriarchal family. This is the underlying issue behind the Mueller investigation, for example. At the time of writing, the ultimate outcome of this struggle is unpredictable, but it will not lead to the expansion of the "prerogative state" as occurred under fascism.

In sum, while interwar fascist regimes came to power on the basis of fascist parties and movements that gestated within strongly organized and highly politicized civil societies, Trump came to power on the basis of a fragmenting traditional party system and a largely passive electorate. Trumpism's organizational form is not the political party but rather the family.

Conclusion

I would like to now draw the threads of the analysis together. There are four clusters of factors that distinguish fascism from Trumpism. While the first arose out of an experience of mass-mobilizing war, the second arose in the long aftermath of a financial crisis. While the first emerged out of a quasi-revolutionary situation, the second emerged in the absence of an organized left. While the first galvanized the middle strata behind it, the second did not. While the first was a project both to discipline and to build state power, the second aims to dismantle the "administrative state." Out of this set of contrasts, I would particularly like to emphasize one general feature that distinguishes the two cases. While fascism was a product of intense civil society and associational development, Trumpism is an expression of the etiolation and weakening of civil society. That is why Trump is more similar to Bonaparte, particularly Bonaparte II, than to the interwar fascists. This difference is particularly evident in the basic institutional conflict that characterizes the dynamics of each form of right-wing regime. Fascist regimes were plagued by struggle between the state and the party. Their leaders sat atop these two competing organizations and played them against one another. Mussolini and Hitler's families, however, played very little role in the power politics of their regimes. In contrast to Mussolini and Hitler, the institutional conflict that characterizes Trumpism is what Weber would have called the "logic of the household" and the "logic of bureaucracy." All of Trump's supposed "violations of democratic norms" are not that at all. Instead they are violations of "bureaucratic norms." Trump is constantly reviled in the media for failing understand the difference between loyalty to the person and loyalty to the objective order of the state. The threat that Trump poses, therefore, is not that he might establish a neo-totalitarian nationalist regime, but rather that he might build a neo-patrimonial Bonapartist regime based on the logic of the household.

Having pointed out the differences between the two experiences, I want to nonetheless suggest that there are parallels between the contemporary situation and the interwar period. Trump, (and even more so) Mussolini and Hitler are commonly presented as "antidemocratic" leaders. That is a profound mistake. In fact, these leaders arose, both in the thirties and today, by articulating a demand for a profound renewal of political institutions that would render the state more responsive to the populace than it had been previously. Their rise to power is closely linked to the political left's failure to fully embrace a plausible project of democratization in both cases, but for very different reasons. The key task for the left is to lead a democratic revolution while avoiding the technocratic project of "defending existing institutions," which are to a large degree antidemocratic.

This suggests a second, more institutional, parallel among the cases. Interwar Germany and Italy, as well as the contemporary US, are all varieties of what Arno Mayer famously called persistent "old regimes." There are then two points to emphasize. First, the US Constitution is not so much a system of "checks and balances" as a systems of checks on the power of the one body that somewhat imperfectly reflects the popular will: the House of Representatives. This is the explicit purpose of the Senate, the judiciary, and the executive. Second, the presidency—and this has become abundantly clear under Trump—is an intrinsically Bonapartist or Caeserist institution. The US cabinet is, structurally speaking, a claque; normally, these features are obscured by what are often euphemistically called "norms," which as pundits endlessly state "give the appearance of independence." But Trump's assumption of the position of a unitary executive goes with, not against, the basic setup of the American capitalist republic. His neo-patrimonial style of rule fits the intrinsically patrimonial structure of the executive branch.

This creates both a strategic opening and a strategic trap for the forces of the left. With the strategic opening, the goal should be to democratize institutions. Robert Reich's call for a National Popular Vote Interstate Compact is one good suggestion for a starting point here. But this should be followed by broader discussion aimed particularly at reducing the outsized influence of the judiciary. The trap is the obverse of this: the temptation to appear as the responsible defenders of the indefensible. This rises to the most absurd levels when commentators and pundits speak of the intelligence agencies in terms of a Montesquieuan division of powers. The choice, then, is clear: either to extend the democratic revolution that began in the 1930s but was disastrously checked, or to bind oneself to the defense of institutions that are rapidly and rightly losing popular support. In figuring out a way forward, one could do worse than return to the interwar period in Europe to figure out how fascist regimes organized themselves, so as to better combat the quite different turn to the right today.

The
Civic Foundations
of Fascism
in Europe

1

Civil Society and Fascism in Interwar Europe

Between 1890 and 1914 an organizational revolution occurred in Europe as mutual aid societies, rural credit organizations, and cooperatives blossomed.[1] Indeed, scholars have identified the last decade of the nineteenth century and the first decade of the twentieth century as a period of intensive development of civil society, especially in the countryside.[2] Such developments, according to a widely held "Tocquevillian" thesis, should have produced vibrant liberal democracies across the continent.[3] Yet, in roughly half of Europe, fascism followed this intense wave of associational growth. This outcome is especially puzzling in countries such as Italy, Spain, and Romania (the empirical focus of this book), which had well-established liberal institutions by the late nineteenth century. Associational growth should have strengthened their already existing parliamentary regimes but appears instead to have undermined them, for, rather than shifting from liberal oligarchies to mass democracies, Italy, Spain, and Romania developed as fascist regimes in the interwar period. Explaining why this happened is the central goal of this book.

Investigating the connection between the development of civil society and fascism is by no means of purely academic interest. Contemporary political culture is suffused with civil society romanticism: the term itself is now treated as virtually equivalent to liberal democracy.[4] There is, however, a relative absence of comparative and historical research focused on the political consequences of associational development. Instead, most exponents of the Tocquevillian thesis, and their critics, investigate the relationship between associationism and the quality of democracy in already consolidated liberal democratic regimes.[5] I believe that investigating the effect of associationism on the emergence of interwar European fascism raises serious issues about the political consequences of civil society development and suggests the need for a rethinking, although by no means rejection, of the Tocquevillian thesis.

My argument, in brief, is that the consequences of associational development for regime outcomes, rather than being direct, depend on the presence or absence of hegemonic politics. Civil society development facilitated the emergence of fascism, rather than liberal democracy, in interwar Italy, Spain, and Romania because it preceded, rather than followed, the establishment of strong political organizations (hegemonic politics) among both dominant classes and nonelites. The development of voluntary associations in these countries tended to promote democracy, as it did elsewhere. But in the absence of adequate political institutions, this democratic demand assumed a paradoxically antiliberal and authoritarian form: a technocratic rejection of politics as such. Fascist movements and regimes grew out of this general crisis of politics, a crisis that itself was a product of civil society development.

This argument suggests two important conclusions, to which I return more fully below. The first is that the impact of associational or civil society development depends heavily on the preexisting structure of political conflict, or what I call, following Gramsci, the presence or absence of hegemonic politics. The second is that fascism, far from being the opposite of democracy, was a twisted and distorted form of democratization that, paradoxically, embraced authoritarian means. My broader aim in this book is, accordingly, to propose a rethinking of the impact of civil society development on regime forms and a rethinking of the nature of interwar European fascism.

The remainder of this introduction accomplishes three main tasks that lay the analytic foundations for the rest of the book. I first develop a definition of fascism as an "authoritarian democracy." I then present the Tocquevillian approach to interwar fascism and develop some key theoretical and empirical criticisms of it. The chapter then turns to a discussion of Gramsci, explaining how his concepts of civil society and hegemony (and particularly the connection between them) provide a useful corrective and extension of more conventional Tocquevillian approaches to civil society. Finally, I close with a brief consideration of my analytic and case selection strategy and adumbrate the argument to come.

Fascism as Authoritarian Democracy

What is a fascist regime? Unfortunately there is very little consensus about this question. Some scholars favor a highly restricted definition that refers at most only to Italy and Germany, classifying other regimes as "authoritarian" or "traditional authoritarian."[6] Others argue for a much broader approach, emphasizing the similarities among all capitalist authoritarian states.[7] A third group of scholars seeks to establish detailed typologies of various kinds of authoritarian regimes.[8] Although all of these conceptual strategies shed light on different aspects of interwar authoritarianism, none of them are perfect. The first risks circularity by defining fascism in a way that makes it equivalent to the interwar authoritarianisms produced by Italy and Germany. The second strategy risks obscuring crucial differences among authoritarian regimes by calling them all fascist, while the third risks burying its object under a bewildering variety of labels. The approach I take tries to strike a reasonable compromise among these positions. I believe that a rather broad swath of authoritarian regimes in interwar Europe are usefully understood as fascist, not least because their political elites often consciously modeled themselves on the "classic" fascist regimes of Italy and Germany. I also hold that there were enormous variations in the types of fascism produced in different national contexts. My concept of fascism, I hope, is general enough to allow for conceptual analysis but sensitive enough to capture these important variations. Let me, then, define this regime type.

Fascist regimes, in my view, are best understood as authoritarian democracies.[9] By this seemingly paradoxical formulation, I mean that fascist political elites claimed a form of democratic legitimacy even as they ruled through authoritarian means.[10] Fascists dismantled parliaments, elections, and civil rights but embraced fully the modern state's claim to represent the people or nation.[11]

Defining fascism as an authoritarian democracy is bound to raise two sorts of objections. The first and most obvious one is that fascist regimes are generally understood as antidemocratic dictatorships. Indeed, much of the literature on fascism concentrates on the "breakdown of democracy."[12] This framing relies either explicitly or implicitly on a very specific definition of democracy as a procedure for selecting political elites through universal suffrage.[13] There are many very good reasons for adopting a proceduralist definition of democracy, but for my purposes in seeking to understand why civil society development seems to have led to fascism, such a definition is not helpful. By *democracy*, I mean a principle of legitimacy or sovereignty.[14] From this perspective democracy is not so much a regime as, in Mosca's phrase, a "political formula" that can be combined with a variety of institutional forms.[15]

Liberalism and authoritarianism, in contrast, are sets of institutional arrangements that can claim democratic legitimacy, but need not.[16] Fascists tended to reject liberalism but embrace democracy as a political formula. They argued that membership in regime-sanctioned parties and corporate groups were a more adequate method of establishing popular rule than the "outdated" techniques of parliament and elections.[17] As James Gregor writes, in his acute summary of the doctrinal basis of Italian fascism: "Individuals in liberal societies, lumped together geographically for the purposes of exercising suffrage, shared little in common. As a consequence, there was little unanimity in terms of interests, projects, or intentions that might constitute the 'general consensus' that, in turn, could provide the 'democratic' support for elite rule."[18] The fundamental problem with liberalism, from the fascist perspective, was not that it was democratic, but precisely the opposite. Elections and parliaments, from the fascist perspective, were intrinsically incapable of representing the interests of the nation. Because of this, the nation must be represented through some other mechanism. The rule of the people, from the fascist perspective, had become, at least in modern conditions, incompatible with parliamentary government. It is in this sense that one might say that fascists were authoritarian democrats and that fascist regimes were authoritarian democracies.

The second sort of objection one might make to defining fascism as an authoritarian democracy concerns the issue of "totalitarianism." Many scholars suggest that fascist regimes, unlike other forms of authoritarianism, were totalitarian, and therefore are most similar to the soviet political system.[19] In contemporary comparative and political sociology, the distinction between authoritarian and totalitarian regimes continues to be very important.[20] In my view the essence of totalitarianism lies in the existence of a monopolistic single-party organization.[21] Although I believe that such organizations characterized some fascist regimes, particularly the Italian and German ones, I also think it is unhelpful to equate fascist regimes as such with single-party dominance. In other words, some fascist regimes were totalitarian, others not. Authoritarian democracies (fascist regimes) could be established using institutions other than, or alongside, a mass mobilizing party. For example, traditionalist institutions such as the church could form a functional substitute for a mass party. This occurred to some degree in Spain. Alternatively, fascism might do away with party organizations altogether in favor of state-organized corporate groups. This was the predominant solution in Romania and was widely discussed in Italy. I return to this issue below in my discussion of the three forms of authoritarian democracy that emerged in Italy, Spain, and Romania in the interwar period.

At this point the reader might object that all modern political regimes claim some form of popular mandate and that therefore the existence of such a claim is not a useful criterion for distinguishing among regime types. However, fascist regimes were quite unusual because they conceived their form of authoritarianism specifically as an alternative to electoral democracy. Fascists did not justify their regimes as exceptional or "parenthetical" dictatorships, nor as a form of transition from a class society to a nonclass society. Rather, the fundamental basis of the fascist claim to legitimacy lay in the belief that fascism offered a superior way of connecting the population to the state in modern economic and social conditions. In short, fascist regimes not only claimed popular legitimacy, they constructed institutions conceived specifically as alternatives to electoral democracy.[22]

Fascism as a form of rule was thus an unusual combination of democratic legitimacy and authoritarian means. Fascists combined the claim to represent the people with a rejection of politics as the institutionalized struggle of groups over control of the state. Fascists held that elections, parliaments, and discussion about public affairs—in short, the stuff of politics—were incapable of constituting and representing a "general will." They therefore attempted to replace political struggle, and representative institutions, with a form of nonpolitical interest representation. In this sense fascist regimes were never exactly rightist or leftist; they represented instead a distinctive rejection of politics as such. What might the connection be between this type of regime and the development of voluntary associations? To begin to answer this question, it is necessary to address the Tocquevillian tradition.

The Tocqueville Thesis

A broad tradition of scholarship links regime forms to the development of civil society. More specifically, scholars have argued that the development of a vibrant civil society is associated with liberal democracy. Conversely, the absence or weakness of civil society is often argued to be a facilitating condition for authoritarianism. For the purposes of this discussion, it is useful to call this the Tocqueville thesis. Let me briefly explore its logic.

Civil society is a deeply contested term. Over the last twenty years an enormous amount of theoretical energy has been spent attempting to define it.[23] At the most general level it can be understood as a specific type of intermediate structure, a concept William Kornhauser defines as follows: "We can conceive of all but the simplest societies as comprising three levels of social relations. The first level consists of highly personal or primary relations, notably the family. The third contains relations inclusive of the whole population, notably the state. The second level comprises all intermediate relations, notably the local community, voluntary association and occupational group."[24] When scholars speak of civil society as being dense or strong, they mean that this set of organizations existing between individuals and the state is developed.[25] Yet this definition does not capture fully the concept of civil society, because it includes compulsory organizations and corporate groups of the type common to old regimes across Europe. Most theorists of civil society see such organizations as incompatible with the degree of individualism characteristic of modern society.[26] Civil society, in the modern sense, refers to an intermediate structure with many voluntary organizations, which by allowing individuals to enter and exit, combine individual rights with communal solidarity.

One of the central positive benefits of voluntary organizations, according to the Tocquevillian thesis, is that they promote cooperation. By drawing men and women outside of the restricted sphere of the family and the economy, associationism leads people to look beyond their restricted self-interest, providing a sense of community that combats the individualizing tendencies of modernity.

As Tocqueville writes, "Local liberties ... which induce a great number of citizens to value the affection of their kindred and neighbors, bring men constantly into contact ... and force them to help one another."[27] Civic associations are thus supposed to counteract individualism and the threat of administrative tyranny that this implies.[28] But associations are held to have a moderating as well as a mobilizing influence, because they link men and women to local forms of politics. As John Hall correctly points out, Tocqueville sees the constraints that American civil society places on popular participation as one of its major virtues.[29] "Civil associations," in Tocqueville's words, "far from directing public attention to public affairs, serve to turn men's minds away therefrom, and getting them more and more occupied with projects for which public tranquility is essential, discourage thoughts of revolution."[30] Tocquevillians, then, tend to emphasize the integrating as well as the mobilizing function of voluntary associations.

The mass society theorists (particularly Arendt, Lederer, and Kornhauser) have done the most to extend the Tocquevillian argument into an account of "totalitarianism"—of which fascism is a subtype. Their claims invert Tocqueville's original account of democracy. While Tocqueville insists that civil society guarantees liberty by balancing the state, the mass society theorists argue that totalitarianism derives from the absence or weakness of civic associationism that unleashes the state.[31]

Following Lederer and Arendt's groundbreaking early work, William Kornhauser presents the most systematic exposition of this view.[32] The intermediate structure for Kornhauser plays three basic roles: it siphons off political demand, acts as a moderating influence on demands from below, and restrains popular participation. So in a situation where the intermediate structure is strong, diffuse authority exists, both encouraging a certain degree of popular participation and insulating the political center.

A "strong" intermediate structure, for Kornhauser, leads to crosscutting affiliations, in which individuals belong to more than one association and the associations have only partially overlapping interests: "Extensive cross-cutting solidarities favor a high level of freedom and consensus: these solidarities help prevent one line of social cleavage from becoming dominant, and they constrain associations to respect the various affiliations of their members lest they alienate them."[33] The development of associations thus allows for the emergence of multiple affiliations, which means that majorities are contingent, issue specific, and changeable.[34] In contrast, where the intermediate structure is weak, mass movements can emerge. These movements, under some conditions, can develop into "totalitarian movements," which then became the basis of "totalitarian regimes" characterized by a "state of total mobilization."[35] For the mass society school, then, authoritarianism is based on social atomization: the absence of a "strong" intermediate structure.[36] Some aspects of the mass society argument, especially its claims about "mass psychology" and its equation of fascist and communist movements, are rather quaint sounding. Still, the basic claim of this school, that a weak intermediate structure, or "civil society," is a major cause of authoritarianism, continues to be widely held.[37]

The mass society argument, and its various contemporary versions, adheres closely to Tocqueville's original analysis of modernity. Where Tocqueville sees associations tending to produce civic engagement and therefore to protect liberty, the mass society theories argue that an absence of associations produces political apathy, a condition that they see as conducive to fascism. The central proposition of Tocquevillians is that interwar fascist regimes were the result of a transitional crisis in which the old corporate intermediate structure was rapidly destroyed without allowing for the development of a new one.

The Problems of the Tocqueville Thesis

The Tocquevillian thesis provides a compelling, logical, and elegant account of regime variation. It also has considerable empirical support. And yet, when it comes to explaining fascism, the thesis suffers from a paradox clearest in the work of Hannah Arendt. For Arendt, and neo-Tocquevillian arguments following hers, fascism is the result of *both* mass political apathy and fanaticism, and both of these outcomes derive from the collapse of civil society. Arendt stresses that one of the preconditions of modern authoritarianism was a withdrawal from engagement with public affairs in the nineteenth century.[38] But more acutely than the other mass society theorists, she sees a contradiction between outcome and explanation in this argument. She holds that this lack of interest in public affairs, which latter neo-Tocquevillian arguments would call an absence of civic engagement, is of limited usefulness to "totalitarian" regimes such as fascist ones. Such dispositions, she writes, "are a positive hindrance to totalitarian movements which can tolerate bourgeois individualism no more than any other kind of individualism."[39]

The reason is that totalitarianism demands an attitude of selfless activism. Thus, she argues, it is not the selfless and egotistical *mob* but the selfless and other-regarding *mass* that forms the basis of totalitarian regimes, but she provides no explanation for the transition from *mob* to *mass*. Instead, the breakdown of associationism produces both. It is responsible, then, for both a "disengaged" and a "hyperengaged" population. This, however, is having it both ways. It makes a single variable (civil society) responsible for two opposite outcomes: apathy and fanaticism. What produces this tension in Arendt's account?

One obvious explanation is that the historical experience of fascism cannot remotely be ascribed to the phenomenon of political apathy or disengagement, which may be a problem for advanced democracies [40] but was not a serious problem in interwar Europe. As all historical accounts of fascism emphasize, fascist regimes came to power "amidst popular enthusiasm."[41] Further, in virtually every case where a fascist regime came to power, fascist parties were among the largest political organizations in the country. In Italy the Partito Nazionale Fascista (PNF) was the third most important mass party organization—after the Partito Socialista Italiano (PSI) and the Catholic Partito Popolare Italiano (PPI)—by the time it came to power in 1922. In Spain, the coalition that Franco led during the Civil War had the backing of the massive Confederación Española de Derechas Autónomas (CEDA) and the Communión Tradicionalista organizations as well as the smaller but rapidly growing Falange. In Romania, Corneliu Codreanu's Totul pentru Tara (TPȚ), together with other groups of the radical right, took over a quarter of the vote in the elections of 1937. These were big, powerful political movements supported by large sectors of the population who were deeply committed to them.

Fascist mass followings presented fascist political elites and their allies with a set of opportunities and constraints that profoundly shaped the character of the emerging regimes. Fascist leaders could claim a popular legitimacy and mobilize this hard core of support against enemies. At the same time they had to satisfy their followings materially, at least to some extent. There was constant pressure from below to create new institutions that could provide jobs and spoils to the followers. These two factors, the opportunity to appear as a popular leader and the pressure from below exercised by followers, are crucial to understanding the dynamics of fascist rule. It strains credibility to suggest that such movements could have emerged in societies suffering from widespread political apathy, as Tocquevillian arguments might lead us to expect. There is also a simple empirical problem with the Tocquevillian claim that there was a widespread collapse of voluntary organizations due to economic modernization in late nineteenth-century Europe. This does not seem to have been true. Fascism followed a period of very rapid associational development, especially in the form of rural cooperative organizations. Robert Putnam, writing about Italy, well explains the significance of this rural cooperative movement for the study of civil society: "These voluntary associations signified less an idealistic altruism than a pragmatic readiness to cooperate with others similarly placed in order to surmount the risks of a rapidly changing society."[42] Cooperatives arose in many countries in the late nineteenth century as a way of aiding agrarian producers who were put under severe pressure by falling grain prices. They provided credit, jobs, and leisure and were often vehicles for political mobilization. Theoretically (although not always in practice) they embodied the principle of self-help. Further, much evidence suggests that the first two decades of the twentieth century were a period of rapid development in the agrarian cooperative movement.[43]

Indeed, the basic point that fascist regimes emerged where civil societies were highly developed is becoming rather widely accepted. For example, Ariel Armony, Sheri Berman, Bernt Hagtvet, and Rudy Koshar have pointed out that Weimar Germany possessed a highly developed civil society that appears to have aided the Nazi seizure of power.[44] These considerations focusing on interwar Europe are generally in line with a growing body of work that casts a skeptical eye on associationism. Jason Kaufman argues that fraternalism in the United States promoted racism and nativism and undermined the growth of a powerful trade union movement.[45] Armony holds "that organizations that might seem compatible with democratic dispositions and orientations can multiply undemocratic beliefs."[46] Robert Putnam himself, often considered the main exponent of the neo-Tocquevillian position, acknowledges the theoretical possibility of a "Dark side of Social Capital."[47]

What is the theoretical upshot of these serious empirical problems? A body of work broadly within the Tocquevillian tradition has sought to account for them by revising the Tocquevillian argument in key respects. The problem with the Tocquevillian argument, from this perspective, is that it assumes that all voluntary associations are good for democracy. A critical literature has emerged suggesting the need to distinguish between good "democratic" associations and bad "antidemocratic," "extremist," or "parochial" ones.[48]

This distinction between good and bad voluntary organizations, in my view, is scientifically dubious. As Armony has correctly noted, "the presence or absence of 'democracy' features in groups cannot be used as a decision rule for determining what civil society is and what it is not."[49] Indeed, this distinction has many of the characteristics of what the great Hungarian philosopher of science, Imre Lakatos, terms a degenerating problem shift.[50] The distinction between types of association is extraneous to the basic logic of the Tocque-villian argument, which in its pure form is rigorously structural, for the classic Tocquevillian position is that voluntary associations, *whatever their explicit purposes,* socialize men and women into politics and thereby undermine the threat of bureaucratic despotism. Skocpol's work on American civil society is commendably rigorous in this respect, since she includes the Ku Klux Klan in her count of civic associations.[51] To argue that some voluntary associations have democratic effects while others do not is empirically dubious and begs the question why this might be the case.

In this book I pursue a different strategy: one that attempts, by using elements from the work of Antonio Gramsci, to reconstruct the Tocquevillian approach as a progressive problem shift [52] that can incorporate and explain anomalous evidence. This reconstructed theory of civil society is distinct from other critical work on civil society because it rejects the notion that fascism arose out of a pathological form of civil society. Such an analysis fails both to do justice to the real nature of civil society development in interwar Europe and to appreciate the paradoxical nature of fascist movements and the regimes that arose from them. Although fascism as a political project was radically hostile to liberalism, it contained some straightforwardly democratic aims, as I suggested above. Most centrally the fascist project was concerned with making the modern state more representative of the nation than was possible with liberal parliamentary institutions. The contemporary critical literature on civil society has failed to appreciate this point, because it has consistently confused liberalism with democracy and authoritarianism with antidemocracy. Accordingly, much of this critical literature defines fascist movements, incorrectly, as antidemocratic.[53] This confusion is a serious obstacle to understanding fascism, and just as importantly, leads scholars to misspecify the implications of fascism for civil society theory. Fascist movements are much less anti-Tocquevillian, and in fact much less antidemocratic, than they might initially seem. The rise of fascism was not the result of a particularly fragmented, apolitical, or hierarchical civil society; rather, it was the consequence of a particularly vibrant form of civil society development that occurred in a specific political context. The key to explaining fascism lies in the connection between this political context and associational development.

From Tocqueville to Gramsci: Reconstructing Civil Society Theory

One of the central characteristics of the Tocquevillian thesis as classically formulated is that it says surprisingly little about political organizations. Political parties and organized currents of opinion are assumed, in this literature, to be products of associational development or to be so profoundly shaped by associational development that they are not independent factors in explaining political development. Indeed, for many scholars there seems to be no clear conceptual difference between political activity and more broadly associational activity, since both are treated as instances of "civic engagement."[54] The most obvious way this occurs is the use of evidence on engagement, such as political participation, and evidence on associations, such as censuses of voluntary organizations, as alternative specifications of the same underlying concept.[55] The problem with this approach is that it fails to recognize the relative independence of political organizations in relation to voluntary associations. Gramsci is useful primarily because he focuses on the interaction of civil society and politics, rather than reading one off the other.

Civil Society

Gramsci, a founding father of Italian communism and a revolutionary Marxist, could be called the Tocqueville of the left, for, like the French aristocrat, the Sardinian Marxist was centrally concerned with the political consequences of associationism. Civil society in Gramsci, as in Tocqueville, is best understood as a third sector or intermediate structure between the state and the economy.[56] As Gramsci writes in his note on the intellectuals: "What we can do, for the moment, is to fix two major superstructural 'levels': the one that can be called 'civil society,' that is the ensemble of organisms commonly called private, and that of 'political society' or 'the State.'"[57] By emphasizing that civil society is a "superstructural" level, Gramsci implicitly replaces the classic Marxian model of economic base and political superstructure with a three-sector one including economy, state, and civil society.[58] He uses this model to contrast Eastern Europe, with its "primordial and gelatinous" civil societies, to Western Europe, where "there was a proper relation between state and civil society."[59]

Gramsci argues, again like Tocqueville, that the development of civil society is important because it tends to promote democracy. Thick civil societies undermine the effectiveness of direct repression, corruption, and the appeal to narrow economic interests as strategies of rule.[60] As associationism develops, then, states must increasingly claim a popular mandate if they are to govern effectively. Although this is by no means incompatible with class rule, it means that effective class rule will require some popular legitimation.[61] This is very close to the Tocquevillian analyses presented above, but there is a fundamental difference between Gramsci and the Tocquevillians. While Tocquevillians tend to suggest that the development of civil society has direct political effects, Gramsci argues that these effects depend heavily on the establishment of hegemony: a process that requires attention to the specifically political relationships within and among decisive social classes.

Hegemony

Hegemony emphasizes the relative autonomy of the political and cultural dimension of social life from its economic determinants. However, the concept is difficult to define and has been used in myriad ways. I use the term, as Gramsci did, to refer to a specifically political dimension of class formation. Arguing against economistic Marxism, Gramsci identifies three aspects of class formation: occupational group solidarity, the solidarity of social classes "in the purely economic field," and intellectual and moral solidarity across classes.[62] Importantly, the third and last form of class formation does not occur and cannot occur on the basis of common economic interests alone. Instead, "it is the most purely political phase, and marks the decisive passage from the structure to the sphere of the complex superstructures."[63] Gramsci insists on the difference between the "relation of social forces ... closely linked to the structure" and "the relation of political forces ... an evaluation of the degree of homogeneity, self-awareness and organization attained by the various social classes."[64] Hegemony, in general, refers to this last, political and cultural, dimension of class formation.[65]

More specifically, hegemony refers to a type of political relationship among fractions of social classes and across classes. A hegemonic relationship exists when a particular group within a class or a particular class within a society exercises intellectual and moral leadership rather than simply naked coercive power over a set of other intraclass groupings or classes.[66] Hegemony implies that conflict among and within groups takes the form of "cooperative antagonism" rather than "zero-sum conflict."[67] A group or class is hegemonic to the extent that it successfully *articulates* its particular interests in terms of a broader interest that can stretch from the interest of a class to that of the nation as a whole. To the extent that a "hegemonic" class or class fraction identifies and pursues this broader interest, it increases its political capacity by improving the material, moral, and political circumstances of the groups over which it exercises hegemony. Gramsci's central model for this type of political relationship is French Jacobinism. The Jacobins were hegemonic, because they converted the demands of the "Third Estate," which were initially the demands of a limited corporate group, into a set of demands involving the whole people. Thus, the French Revolution, which began with a set of complaints on the part of groups within the old regime, became the demand for a national assembly.[68] In other words the interests of an economic corporate group, the Third Estate, came to be articulated as a set of national claims. This transition from corporate group to hegemonic class allowed the French bourgeoisie to form an alliance with the peasantry limited only by the outer bounds of its class interests; the merit of the Jacobins is that they pushed the French bourgeoisie to the very limits of its hegemonic capacity.[69]

The transition from economic corporate group to hegemonic class is a political process relatively independent from class formation at the economic level. Economic corporate groups may possess a high degree of occupational and interest group solidarity without linking their economic interests to broader national goals.[70] The classic example of an economic corporate group is the Italian bourgeoisie. According to Gramsci, "They aimed at stimulating the formation of an extensive and energetic ruling class, and they did not succeed: at integrating the people into the framework of the new state, and they did not succeed."[71] In short, for Gramsci the basic difference between the Italian and French bourgeoisie lies at the level of their political development, their hegemonic capacity.[72]

Hegemony requires the development of political organizations, usually political parties, that are relatively autonomous from narrowly based "economic-corporate" interests. In this sense the concept is quite similar to Samuel P. Huntington's notion of political institutionalization, that is, "the development of political organizations and procedures that are not simply the expressions of the interests of particular social groups."[73] It is in these organizations that the work of articulation, the linking of immediate to broader national goals, occurs.

How does hegemony form? For Gramsci this is mostly a "top-down" process. Hegemonic relationships first develop among particular fractions of the social elite or dominant classes and then spread outward and downward. It is useful, I think, to schematize these developments in terms of three interrelated stages of hegemonic development: intraclass hegemony, interclass hegemony, and counterhegemony.[74] *Intraclass hegemony* refers to the process by which a particular class coalesces politically around a project of social transformation usually associated with a particular class fraction. *Interclass hegemony* refers to the process by which this project expands to include groups outside the class core of the initial hegemonic project. *Counterhegemony* refers to the process by which groups outside the hegemonic alliance attempt to develop an alternative hegemonic project. Each stage of hegemonic development shapes subsequent stages.

According to Gramsci the establishment of an effective political alliance within a social class (intraclass hegemony) increases the chances of an effective political alliance across classes (interclass hegemony). In contrast, economic corporate politics not only fragments classes and class fractions internally, it also undermines their ability to pursue cross-class alliances. So, according to Gramsci's argument, one should expect the formation of intraclass hegemony among fractions of dominant classes to be strongly associated with their ability subsequently to establish interclass hegemony.

Interclass hegemony is also linked to the formation of counterhegemony. To the extent that a class is hegemonic, it does not rule directly as a class. Instead, the class rules in the name of a broader national interest, which more or less corresponds to its particular corporate interests. Since there is always a gap between the particular interests of the dominant class and the broader interest through which it establishes its claim to rule, this interest can become a point of reference for nonelites who can articulate their interests as better corresponding to it. The gap between class interest and national interest is therefore crucial for the development of counterhegemony. In its absence politics remains an economic corporate struggle. Because there is no gap between the interest of the group and the interest of the nation that can be exploited by a counterhegemonic movement, nonelites tend to articulate their claims in the same economic-corporate terms as the dominant class. Economic-corporate politics, therefore, cascades down the social structure from the dominant classes to nondominant classes in a self-reinforcing cycle of political decay or organic crisis.[75] Conversely, there is a direct relationship between the hegemony of the social elite and the counterhegemony of nonelites. To the extent that dominant classes successfully establish political organizations that are not directly subordinated to particular economic interests, both interclass hegemony and counterhegemony are facilitated.[76]

Hegemony, to summarize the discussion so far, refers to a specifically political dimension of class formation. A dominant class's hegemonic capacity is therefore relatively independent of its degree of economic development. A "strong" bourgeoisie is by no means ipso facto a "hegemonic bourgeoisie," nor is a hegemonic bourgeoisie an economically dominant one. Gramsci's argument implies that an economically strong class can be politically and culturally weak, while a hegemonic class can be economically undeveloped.[77] The construction of hegemony is a specifically political and cultural process that cannot be read off class formation as an economic process. Hegemony, or more precisely, hegemonic politics, develops through a sequence of related historical phases: first as intraclass hegemony, then as interclass hegemony, and finally as counterhegemony. The stronger intraclass hegemony is, the more likely it is that a dominant class will exercise interclass hegemony as well. A hegemonic dominant class also tends to produce counterhegemony. The development of hegemony, therefore, cannot be understood in zero-sum terms. It is not the case that a strong dominant class implies a weak subordinate class. On the contrary, the formation of a hegemonic dominant class provides a framework for the formation of oppositional classes.

As will become clear in the course of this analysis, I find this theoretical perspective extremely useful for understanding fascism. For what is most obviously similar about the dominant classes (or social elites) of Italy, Spain, and Romania in the interwar period is their hegemonic weakness: their inability to articulate a national task capable of establishing a cross-class alliance and their inability to construct solid political organizations within which to pursue their class interests. I believe that this failure had far-reaching negative consequences not only for elites but also for the organization of nondominant classes. Fascism, I would suggest, can be explained only if this specifically political weakness, one that first affected elites and then spilled over into nonelites, is kept firmly in mind.

The Contingent Connection between
Civil Society and Hegemony

Finally, to flesh out more fully the approach established in this book, it is necessary to sketch the connection between civil society and hegemony. Although hegemony and civil society may develop together, there is nothing in Gramsci's theory to suggest that they must. In my view this is a great strength of Gramsci's argument. Hegemony is established through a political process taking place within dominant classes and then spreading across classes. Civil society development, in contrast, is caused mostly by economic factors, although the concept does not refer to strictly economic organizations. Since hegemony and civil society derive from different processes, it is quite possible that civil societies might develop in the absence of hegemony.[78] This is what distinguishes Gramsci's theory of civil society most clearly from the Tocquevillian accounts discussed above. Whereas Tocquevillians tend to argue that there is a direct link between the development of voluntary associations or civil society, and the kind of political organizational development that the term *hegemony* captures, Gramsci sees the relationship between them as fundamentally contingent. Hegemony and civil society may develop together, but there is no theoretical reason to suggest that they must do so.

For the purposes of understanding fascism, the possibility that civil society might develop in the absence of a hegemonic politics is very important. Gramsci calls these situations "Organic Crises," which he defines as decisive turning points in which the democratic demands produced by civil society cannot adequately be expressed through existing political institutions. This leads to a crisis of representation in which "the traditional parties, in that particular organizational form, with the particular men who constitute, represent, and lead them, are no longer recognized by their class (or fractions of a class) as its expression."[79] Fascist regimes were the consequences of just such a crisis in which the "traditional parties" and the forces of opposition were outstripped by a rapidly developing civil society.[80] In this context the democratic demands of civil society tend to develop against the regime of political parties and are often expressed as skepticism about all forms of political representation. Fascism, then, develops out of this general crisis *of* politics. Fascist movements are well adapted to such situations because they claim to transcend the political. These movements are therefore perfectly positioned to exploit the crisis of political representation caused by a situation of civil society overdevelopment in relationship to hegemony. Fascism, a political project aiming to establish a new relationship between the nation and the state, can be expected to emerge where social elites fail to develop hegemonic political organizations in the context of rapid civil society development. The fascist political project arises as an attempt to redress this problem of hegemonic weakness by creating an authoritarian democracy: a regime that claims to represent the people or nation but rejects parliamentary institutional forms. Rather than being connected to a specific stage of economic development, or a specific state form, fascism must be understood as the result of a *political* crisis rooted in the combined and uneven development of civil society and hegemony.[81]

Methodological Approach

The analytic approach of this book combines two types of comparative strategy: negative case analysis that structures the narrative of each individual case, and a more conventional method of difference that links the cases. Negative case analysis works by contrasting evidence with prior theoretical convictions.[82] It is appropriately used when a large gap exists between predictions derived from theory and observed outcomes. The gap between theory and observation is not used in negative case methodology to falsify theory but to stimulate its development.[83] Theory, in negative case methodology, acts as a method for identifying anomalies, instances that appear to contradict a key theory, or a better set of theories, and are in need of intensive study. As such it is a very efficient way of using sociological theory to stimulate the formulation of empirical problems and the further extension of theory.[84] I focus on three cases (Italy, Spain, and Romania) that pose some serious challenges to the Tocquevillian account of the connection between civil society and regime variation and are consequently all negative cases. Their political development stands sharply at odds with the Tocquevillian argument linking civil society development to liberal democracy and the absence of civil society development to totalitarianism. But it is not my position that these cases falsify the Tocquevillian argument; they are rather inconsistent with it and point to the need for theoretical reconstruction.[85] I use these instances to show how the Tocquevillian theory of civil society development is best understood as a special case of the broader Gramsci-inspired formulation of civil society theory.

From this perspective, the three cases, Italy, Spain, and Romania, are mutually reinforcing anomalous instances. But I have chosen them also because they are crucially different, each exemplifying a distinct form of fascist regime. The discussion so far has focused on the problem of fascism generally. But fascism assumed very different forms. I believe that it is possible to distinguish among three varieties of fascism. In the first type, party fascism, the nation was understood as a *political project*. The nation does not yet exist, or exists only *in statu nascendi*. The party fascist regime is representative of this *future nation*. In traditionalist fascism, the nation exists but has been corrupted.[86] The fascist regime therefore represents this true nation corrupted by liberal institutional forms. The fascist project consists in returning to this form. In statist fascism the state *constitutes* the nation not by educating the population, as in party fascism, but by organizing the population into interdependent corporate groups. Strictly speaking, in this last form of fascism there is no relationship of representation, because the state and the nation are the same thing. These three varieties of fascism map closely onto the three regimes that this book discusses. While I develop these types in greater detail in later chapters, it is worth briefly adumbrating them here.

Party Fascism: Italy

Italy is the classic party fascist regime.[87] Italian fascist political elites conceived the party as a pedagogical institution. As Sergio Panunzio, one of the more gifted fascist political theorists, puts the point, the Fascist Party is "a great national school of political education."[88] Many scholars agree with Panunzio's formulation. For example, Ernst Nolte , Renzo De Felice, and George Mosse in their classic works all emphasize the fascist attempt to nationalize the masses.[89] Emilio Gentile has recently followed their lead, emphasizing the importance of the Fascist Party for the regime.[90] Historians in the Marxist tradition have also contributed to this literature. Victoria De Grazia, following the lead of Palmiro Togliatti,[91] emphasizes the importance of mass organizations for the fascist regime.[92]

Traditionalist Fascism: Spain

Spanish fascism differed profoundly from its Italian counterpart, because it was dominated by a traditionalist conception of the nation. Spanish traditionalists attempted to reactivate already existing forms of representation and tended to reject the political party as an appropriate pedagogical instrument.[93] Instead, in traditionalist fascism the nation was to be represented through the family, the monarchy, and the church.[94] As Victor Pradera writes, "Without tradition there is no nation."[95] An authoritarian political party emerged in Francoist Spain, but it was constrained by powerful nonparty institutions and contained within itself traditionalist elements.[96] This was a fascist project turned firmly toward the past.

Statist Fascism: Romania

Statist fascism, in contrast to party fascism, was not a pedagogical project, nor was it a return to tradition such as Victor Pradera advocated. Instead, statist fascism sought to constitute the nation through *organization*. The Romanian economist Mihaïl Manoïlescu developed the most consistent expression of this view: "In the corporative system, the individual is no longer a simple unity equal to himself, whatever might be his economic and social importance; he receives on the contrary a political importance, proportioned to his social, cultural or economic function, that we can also call his national function."[97] This form of fascism was neither based on the political party nor on preexisting institutions supposed to embody the nation. Instead, the legitimacy of this political order was based on its claim to constitute Romania as a national society in the state. This form of fascist regime was briefly dominant in Romania in the period from 1938 to 1940.

These three forms of fascism arose out of three specific paths of civil society development that I term "autonomous," "elite dominated," and "state led." In the Italian case civil society developed "from below." Rural direct producers themselves established voluntary organizations and cooperatives. This was associated with party fascism. In Spain the landed elite, in alliance with the church, was the driving force behind associational development. This produced traditionalist fascism. In Romania the highly statist Liberal Party was the driving force behind associational development. This produced statist fascism.

Conclusion

The following three chapters present empirical analyses of Italy (chapter 2), Spain (chapter 3), and Romania (chapter 4). Chapter 5 evaluates the evidence for non-Tocquevillian accounts of fascism, while chapter 6 draws a series of broader conclusions. Drawing on the Gramscian perspective, my narrative of these cases comprises five comparable stages: the initial establishment of oligarchic liberalism, the development of civil society, the failure of hegemony, the period of organic crisis, and the rise of fascism. I show how, through a specific sequence of historical events, Italy, Spain, and Romania experienced civil society development without a corresponding development of hegemonic politics. Because of this, the democratic pressures associated with civil society development from the late nineteenth century emerged in antiliberal forms. Fascism emerged out of this coincidence of hegemonic weakness and strong civil society. However, the fascist project took a different form in Italy, Spain, and Romania primarily because of differences in the development of civil society. In Italy, where this development was autonomous, party fascism emerged. In Spain, where civil society development occurred under the aegis of the social elite, traditionalist fascism was the outcome. Finally, in Romania, where the state was the main actor in sponsoring civil society development, statist fascism consolidated.

These case studies, then, can be read in two somewhat different ways. In one sense they sketch three similar routes to fascism. In another sense my book is a study in contrasts focusing on the connection between types of fascism and different forms of civil society development. The analysis attempts to balance these two projects while also emphasizing the importance of the events through which these patterns of political development unfolded.

Before diving into the historical material, it might be useful to ask why all of this matters. The first reason concerns civil society. The experience of authoritarianism in interwar Europe suggests some caution about civil society. The development of civil society within certain well-defined political contexts may have very positive effects. But the construction of a political context within which civil society can function to "make [liberal] democracy work" is not a consequence of the development of civil society itself. Rather, the political context has to be established *first*. This critical and historical perspective on civil society resonates with a growing body of research that casts a skeptical eye on Tocquevillian arguments.[98]

This leads to a second set of considerations about democracy. A large body of literature has argued that liberal democracy was produced by pressure from below. While this book does not directly engage such arguments, its analysis of fascism suggests a note of caution. As my analysis will make clear, in certain respects the reason that Italy, Spain, and Romania became fascist regimes, rather than mass democracies, was closely connected not with the weakness of popular forces but their strength. Decisive political actors took the project of democracy extraordinarily seriously in all three countries. The problem was the strength of this democratizing thrust—for popular forces took democracy so seriously that they threatened the pillars of elite domination. The elite's inability to blunt the democratic thrust, within a liberal framework, was the underlying cause of fascism in these cases. If this argument is correct, it implies perhaps a slightly different theory of democratic consolidation in other parts of Europe than those that prevail in contemporary social science. Perhaps it was not the strength of the humble but the relative ease with which their demands could be incorporated, given the hegemonic capacity of the social elite, that explains the smooth transitions to mass democracy in France and Britain. This at least is one possible implication of the analysis developed here.

2

Party Fascism

Italy, 1870–1938

Why did Italy, instead of making a smooth transition from constitutional liberalism to mass democracy, produce the world's first fascist regime, and why did this regime take the form of "party fascism"? The main argument of this chapter is that fascism was the consequence of rapid civil society development in a political context defined by three historically linked failures of hegemony: first a failure of intraclass hegemony, then a failure of interclass hegemony, and finally a failure of counterhegemony. The development of civil society in this political context, far from strengthening liberal institutions, undermined them. Fascism arose from this crisis as a movement proposing to establish a representative state without politics: an authoritarian democracy.

This chapter is an analytic narrative comprised of five roughly chronological stages: it begins by investigating intraclass hegemony in the period of national unification. I argue that intraclass hegemony in Italy was weakly developed. Instead of a solid alliance forming between landed and moneyed interests, the Italian social elite remained fragmented into territorially defined interest groups. Organizationally and ideologically it was never a national ruling class. The chapter then moves to an analysis of the development of civil society in the late nineteenth century. Here

I show that liberal rights were established enough to allow for the development of voluntary associations. Associationism was particularly pronounced in the countryside, occurring first under the protection and sponsorship of the social elite and then developing autonomously from the 1890s forward. Under the pressure generated by these developments, Italian social elites attempted to establish interclass hegemony from the turn of the century. But since this attempt occurred on the basis of a weak form of intraclass hegemony, it succeeded only partially, and by 1911 it had failed. Finally, in the post–World War I period, the Italian Socialist Party (PSI) and its allies attempted to institute counterhegemony to establish a mass democratic state. But this project also failed, paradoxically because of the previous failure of intra- and interclass hegemony. Since these earlier forms of hegemony had not succeeded in adequately nationalizing Italian politics, counterhegemony also could not be articulated in national terms. These three historically interlinked failures of hegemony, in the context of rapid civil society development, produced a crisis of politics, out of which the fascist movement, and eventually the fascist regime, emerged.

Intraclass Hegemony in Post-Risorgimento Italy

Italy's dominant classes in the period after national unification failed to establish intraclass hegemony. This was partially a consequence of the history of Italian state formation and partially a consequence of restricted suffrage. After the defeat of Napoleon in 1815, Italy was divided into seven main states. Piedmont, in the northwest corner of the peninsula, was an autonomous principality ruled by the Savoyard monarchy. To the east, Lombardy-Venetia was an Austrian province. Tuscany and Modena were Austrian archduchies, and Parma was given to Napoleon's second wife, Marie-Louise. The church directly ruled the Papal States in the center of the country. South of Rome the largest political unit on the peninsula was the Kingdom of the Two Sicilies, which united Sicily with most of the southern peninsula. The native population controlled none of these political units, except for Piedmont. Broadly speaking, Austrians controlled the north and the Spanish Bourbons the south. Nineteenth-century Italy was a geographical zone in which political divisions followed dynastic lines.[1]

The presence of multiple foreign powers on Italian soil meant that diplomatic and military factors shaped unification. The process began from Piedmont. Given its small size, the Piedmontese could unify the peninsula only by maintaining good relations with the French and discouraging Austrian intervention: two diplomatic priorities incompatible with radical social transformation. The conflict between them became clear with the Italian nationalist Giuseppe Garibaldi's (1807–1882) expedition to the south in 1860. Garibaldi threatened both to arouse the rural masses and to unseat the papacy—outcomes unacceptable both to the French and the Austrians. In part to avoid foreign intervention, the main conservative architect of unification, Count Camillo Benso di Cavour (1810–1861), acted to check Garibaldi by marching Piedmontese troops to the northern border of the Kingdom of the Two Sicilies, thereby blocking his advance to the north. Cavour subsequently attached southern Italy to the new kingdom through a series of plebiscites. The last act of unification was a bloody civil war (1861–1865) fought against an alliance of ex-Bourbon retainers and the southern peasantry. A military and diplomatic process in which one small state rapidly extended its institutions to the peninsula as a whole substituted for either popular or elite mobilization from below. Italian unification, and the corresponding establishment of a liberal regime, was thus experienced not as liberation but rather as occupation by a large sector of the population, especially in the south.[2]

After unification, royally appointed prefects who were mostly Piedmontese dominated the institutions of local government. They provided for public health, distributed public works, were in charge of the schools, and deployed the police. They also controlled the right of assembly and kept a sharp eye on associations. Sitting atop these myriad local despots, parliament functioned as a deal-making forum for elite interests. No political parties existed to aggregate interests at a national level, and only a narrow stratum could vote until 1912, when suffrage increased from about 7 percent of the population to about 20 percent.[3]

Even within this restricted electorate, Italian governments were not voted into office. Rather, they formed in parliament through a process known as *trasformismo* (transformism). Prime ministers and cabinet positions were determined by postelectoral deals rather than through competition among competing programs in the country. This had a corrosive impact on the formation of parties, because it undermined the context of institutionalized struggle within which political organizations form. Agostino Depretis (1813–1887) established the basic model of transformism in the aftermath of the elections of 1882 (the first on the basis of expanded suffrage), when he invited deputies of the parliamentary group known as the Destra Storica (Historical Right) to "transform themselves" by joining his government. The deputies responded to two basic pressures: those of their local electoral clique and those of the amorphous majority.[4]

This method of constituting governments worked best when deputies were relatively independent of party organizations so that they could be available for deal making. The powerful prime ministers who dominated Italian liberalism therefore worked to disorganize coherent political groups that might subsequently form the basis of true party organizations.[5] As Federico Chabod put it, liberal Italian political technique "aimed at the formation of a parliamentary majority of the center that would allow one to govern by 'dissolving' ... the theoretical differences of programs in parliamentary practice."[6] Thus Italian governments tended to become big tent governments of the center that could shift slightly to the right or to the left depending upon circumstances. Transformism, then, undermined the development of political parties not only in the population at large but, more importantly, among the restricted elites, whose interests were reflected in the political institutions of the newly unified state.[7]

The Italian social elite, to summarize, lacked intraclass hegemony. From the very beginnings of the unified state, liberal institutions were imposed from above, not only on the population broadly, but also on local elites themselves. Further, Italian parliamentary practice tended to discourage the formation of parties after unification. The consequences of this initial absence of intraclass hegemony became evident at the beginning of the twentieth century. But before exploring this side of the story, it is necessary to take a step back to investigate the development of Italian civil society.

Civil Society in Italy

The lack of intraclass hegemony among the Italian social elite did not undermine the development of voluntary organizations. On the contrary, Italy had one of the oldest and most developed civil societies in Europe. Its origins lie in the period of the self-governing communes of the twelfth and thirteenth centuries. Already by the seventh century towns had begun to recover on the peninsula, offering a unique space for political freedom within the feudal order. Within these towns numerous confraternities and guilds arose, acting as surrogate families, providing insurance, pensions, and political clout to less privileged groups.[8]

Civil Society Development in the Pre-Giolittian
Period, 1870–1900

With unification civil society strengthened, as mutual aid societies, confraternities, and guild organizations proliferated. These were highly local and dominated by preindustrial urban professions, such as artisans and shopkeepers. They provided insurance, pensions, funeral services, and Sunday and weekend schooling and were often religious.[9]

This expansion was connected to the project of national unification, because the leaders of unification tended to view associations as an effective and inexpensive method for strengthening political order. To some extent the liberal elite promoted associational development as an alternative to more conventional state-centered forms of rule. By encouraging thrift, political moderation, and cooperation, associations could be useful in developing a docile and productive population.[10]

This general liberal program had two main strands: a democratic one associated with Giuseppe Mazzini (1805–1872) and a moderate one associated with Luigi Luzzatti (1841–1927). Mazzini emphasized that voluntary associations could both promote cooperation across class lines and discipline their members.[11] He was particularly drawn to the model of English and Belgian producers' cooperatives, which for him would eliminate class differences. As cooperatives developed, the distinction between capital and labor would disappear. Salaries would be distributed according to "the necessities of life," and profits would be distributed according to the quantity of labor that each member contributed.[12] Mazzini also stressed the role of the state in promoting popular associations, and particularly cooperative societies.[13] Given widespread rural poverty he insisted that the new democratic state would have to make funds available for the promotion of "voluntary workers' associations."[14] All of this was in the service of creating a popular nationalism that could stabilize the post-Risorgimento political order.

Mazzini also emphasized the disciplining role of popular associationism, basing his critique of industrial capitalism on the idea that wage work, because of its length and irregularity, undermined the process of working-class self-education: "You work ten or twelve hours a day: how can you find time to educate yourselves? The greater part among you earns barely enough to sustain yourself and your family: how can you find the means to educate yourself? The precariousness and the interruptions of your work make you pass from excessive activity to habits of dissolution: how can you acquire the tendency to order, regularity, and assiduity?."[15] One of the main purposes of the association for Mazzini was thus to provide the means of civic education to workers.

Because of its focus on the order-producing consequences of associations, Mazzini's democratic conception could blend rather easily with the more conservative ideas of the moderates grouped around Luzzatti. The moderate model tended to focus on the provision of credit, rather than production. Luzzatti suggested organizing small savings banks that would both provide workers some protection against unemployment, old age, and sickness and link their interests to owners.[16] For both groups, however, one of the primary purposes of associationism was to establish social order.[17] The nineteenth-century liberal elite was thus united in the view that popular associations could aid in the construction of a unified Italian state.[18]

During the 1880s this liberal model was put to a severe test. In 1878 parliament established a protective tariff on industry that drew investment to the cities and away from agriculture. Instead of producing an industrial takeoff, much of this investment was channeled into a speculative real estate boom and therefore did not create a stable basis for urban employment. During roughly the same period grain imports from Russia and the United States threatened Italian agriculture. Both of these processes tended to produce rural un- and underemployment, sparking protests among peasants and agricultural day laborers. The crisis also generated an unprecedented wave of associational development among agrarian direct producers.[19]

Elites continued to be heavily involved in the development of associations in these decades. For example, a masons' cooperative founded in 1887 in Milan was subsidized partly by the king.[20] Degl'Innocenti points out that many of the first day laborer cooperatives were "encouraged precisely by large proprietors and aristocratic circles."[21] In Umbria, in the center of Italy, upper-class Freemasons (including barons and counts of the old local aristocracy) were the driving force behind the mutual aid movement.[22] The first society of day laborers in Ravenna (discussed in more detail below) was founded with the help of a local bank and the king.[23]

Besides these local initiatives, the conservative moderates and the Mazzinian democrats responded to the agrarian crisis by founding a national organization of cooperative societies: the Federazione Nazionale delle Cooperative (National Federation of Cooperatives).[24] It aimed at promoting the development of cooperatives by pressuring the state to pass favorable legislation, such as tax breaks and public works contracts.[25]

Nowhere was the strategy of associationism as a means for guaranteeing social order more in evidence than in the Po Valley, the heart of agrarian unrest in this period. Preunification Emilia-Romagna formed part of the Papal States and possessed an extremely rich heritage of religious and lay associationism. Most of these institutions provided some kind of social assistance to specific categories of the population. As Ridolfi writes, "In particular in the provinces of Ravenna and Forlì there existed a spider-web of 'pious works' capable of ensuring some type of social protection to almost the entirety of the population."[26] These institutions were revived and transformed in the face of the crisis of the 1880s.[27]

The surge of cooperative activity in this important region needs to be understood in the context of a series of economic transformations in the 1870s and 1880s. In Emilia-Romagna during these decades agrarian entrepreneurs undertook big land reclamation projects called *bonifica* (improvement), which involved converting swampland to arable pasture. *Bonifica* destroyed the livelihood of small fishermen and fowl hunters from the coastal regions around the seaside town of Ravenna on the Adriatic coast, and these people were often then employed in further land reclamation. Once land was reclaimed, however, this labor was redundant.[28] A casual and shifting unskilled agricultural labor force emerged whose numbers were accentuated by the collapse of agricultural prices that was a general feature of Italian, and indeed European, agriculture in the 1880s. This situation produced massive strikes in the late nineteenth century.[29] As a contemporary observer, Maria Pasolini, writes, "The increase, in both number and strength of the *braccianti* is accentuated every year and is very worrying to the proprietors."[30] Conservative involvement in establishing agrarian cooperatives was at least partly a response to this situation.

As a result of these shifts *braccianti* (day laborer) cooperatives flowered.[31] Far from being the expression of a spontaneous disposition to associate, these organizations expanded in response to specific policies. State and local authorities began in the mid-1880s to sponsor public works projects to soak up excess labor in the hopes of alleviating class conflict in the region. Cooperatives, in which the members pooled their labor and shared salaries, formed to compete for these.[32] The Associazione Generale degli Operai Braccianti (General Association of Laborers) established in Ravenna in 1888 typified these organizations and indeed formed a model for other day laborer cooperatives. It is therefore worth discussing in some detail.

The purpose of this cooperative was "the constitution of a fund that would permit the assumption on its own account of the greater part of public and private works that today are deferred to the most unbridled, and often dishonest speculation."[33] By contracting jobs "the workers ... reduced to miserable conditions by the greed of private contractors, aim to take the first steps on the road to their emancipation, since once their conditions of work have been improved and once they have been removed from any dependence the association will offer them a way of educating themselves and of removing themselves from the state of subjection in which they find themselves today."[34] In short this was conceived as an organization of workers that would remove the unemployment problem by forming an enterprise.

Only workers could be members of the Ravenna organization. For each contracted job, they were divided into squads of ten men and paid according to piecework rates determined by a technical committee comprised of four "experts," a lawyer, and an engineer. For jobs outside the province of Ravenna, the organization provided for lodging and a cook. Given the poverty of the agrarian day laborers, the organization required sponsorship. It received initial support from the monarchy and a local bank.[35] By most accounts the Ravenna cooperative was a success, winning a number of local jobs. But its major economic achievement was draining the swamps at Ostia around Rome.[36] This job required workers to construct canals from which standing water was drained into basins that then pumped into the sea.

The Ravenna cooperative received state support throughout the 1880s. According to Zangheri, "It was natural ... that the prefect and the government tended to turn to their own advantage the extraordinary novelty of a restless, undisciplined and aggressive mass, that was giving itself an order, a discipline and that brought its combativeness to the level of initiatives and legal competition."[37] Internally the association was organized along highly democratic lines. It had a general assembly, a technical committee, and an accounting committee. The minutes record "frank, open and at times bitter discussions,"[38] suggesting a lively internal political life. It also successfully completed an impressive array of jobs. The commune and a local agrarian consortium financed the first jobs of the Ravenna cooperative.[39] Other day laborer cooperatives emerged during this period as well. Some were pure workers' societies, while others admitted shareholders.[40]

The Ravenna cooperative nicely illustrates the close relationship between popular associationism and the developmental project of the post-Risorgimento social elite. This was a voluntary organization, the primary purpose of which was to compete for public works contracts with the national state. These projects aimed at laying the foundations for a more advanced economy. The prefect saw the association as a means of strengthening the state, since the cooperative imposed discipline and organization on its members.

Day laborer cooperatives were restricted mostly to the Valley of the Po, but other forms of cooperation spread more widely.[41] Credit cooperatives were particularly important to smallholders because they were a way to escape usury and pawning.[42] These institutions generally began with very little capital, relying instead on their members' willingness to deposit money. Further, instead of providing collateral against the loan, the debtor was advanced a small sum on the basis of "honor." This required considerable faith, for the bank had to trust that its debtors would repay their loans, while the depositors had to trust that the bank would make good lending decisions.[43]

During the 1880s, to summarize, a dense web of agrarian associations emerged in Italy, especially in the north. These organizations, however, were closely connected to the social elite. Their development was part of the Risorgimento nation-building project. It is correct to speak of an organized civil society that lasted up until the 1880s, but not an autonomous one. This would begin to change in the 1890s.

From Patronage to Independence

The agrarian crisis of the 1880s had shaken the landed elite in the north. But conservative control over rural popular associationism remained largely intact until the 1890s.[44] It was only with the beginning of increasing class differentiation and autonomous political movements that the patronage model of associations finally broke down.[45] Politically, socialism and Catholicism embodied this threat, raising the specter of a countryside mobilized against the liberal state.

Agrarian socialism was the most dramatic of these movements. Founded in 1892 in Genoa, the epicenter of the PSI shifted quickly to the Valley of the Po. At first a movement of isolated leaders, it began to penetrate the Italian countryside in the 1880s, facilitated in part by the predominance of Mazzinian organizations. The most distinctive feature of Italian socialism was its rural base. According to official party statistics from 1897, about 73 percent of party members lived in non-urban centers in that year.[46]

The growing strength of socialism had very important consequences for the organization of popular associationism. Socialists took a lively interest in coop-eration from their political beginnings. The cooperatives were, in the words of Giovanni Rossi (a doctor influenced by Fourier and anarchism), "sort of socialist colonies, where production and consumption would be carried out in common."[47] By the 1890s cooperatives were being established under socialist leadership.[48]

The importance of Catholicism also increased in the cooperative movement in the 1890s. The Catholics broke away from the socialists in 1894, forming their own organization. Yet Catholicism in Italy was by no means an exclusively reac-tionary force. In the Italian context Catholicism could not form a close alliance with the monarchy. Since the house of Savoy (that is the Piedmontese monar-chy) unified the peninsula against the temporal power of the pope, the Catholic Church tended to be hostile to the new state and adopted many popular demands.[49]

The Catholics organized under the aegis of the Opera dei Congressi, an umbrella institution including cooperatives, rural banks, and insurance schemes.[50] Like their socialist counterparts they expanded under the pressure of the agrarian crisis, but with the aim of stabilizing small property holders rather than establishing collective farms.[51] Yet, as with the socialists, Catholic control over the coopera-tive movement increased at the expense of the liberals associated with national unification. As Ciuffoletti writes: "Up until 1892 Masonic and liberal-democratic 'benefactors' organized rural funds, but from then on it was the Catholics who took the initiative, founding in just five years almost five hundred rural funds in Veneto and Friuli."[52] The 1890s was a decade of transformation as direct elite con-trol over popular associationism weakened. It was from this period that the Italian cooperative movement assumed a distinctively political character, with its close links to the PSI and the Catholic Church.[53]

The shift was palpable in the leadership of the cooperative movement. At the 1894 conference of the Lega Nazionale delle Cooperative (National League of Cooperative Societies), the successor organization to the National Federation of Cooperatives described above, the socialists for the first time took over control from the conservative moderates seeking to link the cooperative movement to explicitly political aims: the establishment of socialism and the democratization of Italian government, especially at the local level. From 1899 onward cooperatives became active in local government, pressuring authorities for subsidies to working-class organizations and seeking to influence elections. An alliance formed within the league between the democratic and socialist forces that linked associationism to a broader program of political transformation.[54]

It may be useful at this point to summarize the developments discussed above with some basic quantitative evidence on producers' cooperatives, which developed out of land reclamation projects, and credit cooperatives, which provided loans to smallholders.[55] Table 1 summarizes the growth of the cooperative movement

Table 1   The Growth of Cooperative Societies in Prefascist Italy
(in number per million inhabitants)

Region	1888	1902	1910	1915
Piedmont	38	74	137	179
Liguria	19	94	203	313
Lombardy	15	96	213	300
Veneto	11	102	93	183
Emilia-Romagna	19	138	360	570
Tuscany	32	93	195	279
Marche	12	100	164	201
Umbria	7	54	102	148
Lazio	3	48	183	328
Abruzzo and Molise	7	21	38	47
Campania	4	27	54	68
Apulia	6	31	78	119
Basilicata	4	41	45	75
Calabria	2	26	41	81
Sicily	8	42	67	100
Sardinia	1	15	39	74

Sources: MAIC 1890; Degl'Innocenti 1977.

Note: The 1902 figures for Basilicata and Calabria were calculated from a total figure from 1902 that did not differentiate between the regions. I split the figure according to the ratio of the population for each region from the 1901 census figures. All the figures have been adjusted according to the census nearest the date they were published. For 1888 and 1902 this was the 1901 census, for the 1910 figures this was the census of 1911, and for the 1915 figures this was the 1915 census.

from 1888 to 1915. The data show a dramatic increase in the number of cooperative societies during the late nineteenth and early twentieth centuries in every region of Italy. Across the peninsula as a whole, the number of cooperatives per million inhabitants increased by 26 times. In some regions this figure was much higher. In Lazio, for example, there were 109 times as many cooperatives in 1915 as in 1888, in Emilia-Romagna 30 times as many, and in Sardinia 74 times as many. This evidence suggests that Italian civil society was strengthening dramatically in the early years of the twentieth century.

Associationism was an elite-driven process pursued as a means of strengthening a weak nation-state until the mid-1890s. Notables sponsored various types of voluntary organizations: social dairies, consumer cooperatives, producer cooperatives, and credit societies. By the 1890s, however, this program was becoming more difficult to sustain, as autonomous political movements led by socialists and Catholics began to emerge in the countryside. What then set in was a period of transition, the result of which was the emergence of an autonomous civil society.

Interclass Hegemony

The development of civil society had important political consequences. From the late nineteenth century, Italian political elites had to take greater account of popular forces. Two models for dealing with the newly mobilized countryside emerged: a repressive model associated with the name of Francesco Crispi (1819–1901) and a neotransformistic model associated with Giovanni Giolitti (1842–1928).

During the late nineteenth century, under Crispi's leadership, conservative forces began to push for a more openly authoritarian state. In 1885, in large part as a response to the agricultural depression described above, landowners in both northern and southern Italy formed the League for Agrarian Defense, an organization that pushed for lower land taxes, increased tariffs on imported grain, and a new land register. The group managed to establish an alliance with cotton manufacturers and industrialists. In 1887 this coalition successfully pushed through a tariff and attempted to pursue a policy of imperialist expansion abroad and repression at home. By the 1890s it came close to establishing an authoritarian regime. But military defeat in Africa in 1896 ended the Crispi government. Although repression continued intermittently until 1901, no solid authoritarian coalition would reemerge until the rise of fascism in the twenties.[56]

Instead, by resorting to a filibuster during a debate over the imposition of martial law, liberals in parliament stood up to the attempt to rule by decree. Although the reasons for the survival of liberalism in Italy in the 1890s deserve their own study, one factor was probably the continuing strength of progressive landholders within the ruling elite.[57]

Giovanni Giolitti's rise to political dominance in 1901 is a fundamental turning point in Italian history, for Giolitti greatly relaxed political repression. This led to an explosion of associational development among both elites and nonelites.[58] These developments were the result of a new and pragmatic approach that gave wide latitude to reformist socialism and Catholicism. Giolitti allowed the autonomous political mobilization of the countryside and refused to deploy the police in labor disputes. The basis of this turn was a very specific theory of the role of civil society in a political democracy. Giolitti held that the development of voluntary organizations themselves would create a stable mass democracy in Italy. There was little need, consequently, to sponsor or control associations.[59]

As a project of civil society development, the Giolittian turn was a major success. The period associated with his control of Italian parliament witnessed an associational revolution no longer constrained by the paternalistic vertical patterns that characterized the late nineteenth century. Among peasants and workers this manifested itself in an explosion of voluntary associations. Such organizations also developed among the landed and industrial bourgeoisies of the north. Seton-Watson summarizes the results of the Giolittian period in the following terms: "Throughout the north trade unions, peasant leagues and chambers of labour multiplied in their hundreds. In one branch of industry after another, disciplined workers' organizations were established, and with the spread of the movement to the agricultural laborers, the whole northern countryside seemed suddenly to come to life."[60] Plus, the patronage links that had characterized agrarian associationism up until the 1890s were definitively broken by the turn of the century. By 1914 a developed and autonomous civil society had emerged in Italy.

These developments were not confined to organizations among nonelites. After the turn of the century industrialists and agrarians organized many economic associations. Prior to 1901 Italian property owners could count on the *carabinieri* (the state police) to directly intervene in cases of labor unrest. But

Giolitti's reaction to a general strike in 1904 indicated a departure from this practice. Instead of deploying the police, as had occurred six years before during the 1898 crisis, the government ignored the strike but called elections, in the hopes of penalizing radicalism at the polls. This new strategy forced social elites to organize, since they could no longer rely solely on repression.[61]

It is not surprising, therefore, that the decade and a half prior to World War I was a golden age of elite associationism. The Federazioni Italiani dei Consorzi Agrari (Italian Confederation of Agrarian Consortia) organized at Piacenza in 1892 to provide its members with technical help, credit, and seeds. In 1899 the organization had 50,000 members, but this figure had grown to 125,000 by 1910. In addition a number of agrarian "unions" formed to combat increasing worker militancy in the countryside. In 1909 a group of agrarian associations purchased the Bolognese newspaper *Il Resto del Carlino*. Industrialists also became more organized in this period, and the industrial bourgeoisie as a class grew substantially under Giolitti. Associational development began with the Lega Industriale di Torino (Industrial League of Turin) founded in 1906. This quickly spread to an alliance between Turinese industry and Lombard finance, and by 1910 the Confederazione Generale d'Industria (General Confederation of Industry, or Confindustria), the first national organization of Italian industry, developed. But this organizational development did not lead to the formation of a party of industrialists.[62]

There were some attempts to establish such a political organization, for example, the Associazione Nazionalista Italiana (Italian Nationalist Association, or ANI) formed in Florence in 1910.[63] But it remained restricted to industrial interests linked to the arms industry and was not widely popular among the class as a whole. Similar attempts to establish an agrarian party also failed to bear fruit. Thus, the hegemonic weakness of the Italian social elite was not the immediate result of a "relation of social forces" in Gramsci's terminology.[64] In fact, the Italian social elite, in both its industrial and agrarian wing, was highly organized. The weakness of the social elite was instead a matter of the "relation of political forces."[65]

The continuing political weakness of the Italian social elite, despite its increasing organizational capacity, was a consequence of the preservation of the main pillars of transformism during the Giolittian period.[66] From the turn of the century to roughly 1914, a single majority, with various prime ministers, held together by a personal loyalty to Giolitti (who generally controlled the political system regardless of the prime minister) dominated parliament. Its cohesion was based in part on the strategic use of state largess. In the 1890s Giolitti's first period in power ended because of a scandal involving payments from the Bank of Rome to parliamentary deputies. Around the turn of the century more than half of the parliamentary deputies were in the pay of the government. This systematic corruption of the political class had a corrosive effect on the formation of parties.[67]

Restricted suffrage worked in the same direction. In the three "classic" Giolittian elections (1900, 1905, and 1909), although the electorate grew, it remained well under 10 percent of the population. The electoral impotence of socialism and Catholicism allowed Giolitti to be lenient toward them. This strategy had a strong regional component as well. Parliamentary majorities were generally anchored in a group of deputies from southern Italy. The seats of these deputies were safe, providing a solid bulwark for governments that could lean left or right depending on circumstances in the north, where electoral competition was more open. This set of arrangements meant that the partial opening of the political system did not lead to the development of political parties among the Italian dominant class.[68]

The contrast with political organizations of nonelites was total. Although Italy lacked bourgeois and landholder parties, it developed very large and well-organized socialist and Catholic parties, although as will become evident, these never became truly national in scope. The PSI first began to achieve serious political success in municipal elections that gave it control over several important Italian communes by the 1890s. In some communes in most regions, the party had several representatives in the municipality. Socialist governments provided new opportunities for political participation. One of the preferred means was the use of referenda to solve local problems. For example, at Milan the socialist-controlled council held a referendum on funding for the opera house. At Oneglia the entire population voted on municipal taxes, even those who, according to the national electoral rules, were prohibited from voting.[69]

The PSI also developed a significant organizational presence during the Giolittian period. Cooperatives, mutual aid societies, and people's houses often grew out of "circles": groups of friends and sometimes groups of families, who gathered to drink wine. Socialist organizations blended political, economic, and recreational activities. For example, socialist theater performances sometimes took place within mutual aid and cooperative societies. Cooperatives were often also lending libraries and were sometimes associated with a people's school.[70]

Chambers of labor were also important. They combined territorial and class-based principles of membership. Their main purpose was to find work for their members, although they also sometimes included mutual aid and leisure activities. Each had a number of affiliated "leagues," often organized on an extremely restricted professional basis. These developed in the 1890s as hiring halls but quickly expanded to provide cooperative services and leisure-time activities.[71]

The socialists promoted associationism in part to break the influence of bourgeois culture. As the famous orator Camillo Prampolini (1859–1930) put the point: "Our congresses are our parliament; and the deliberations that are carried out there are our laws. Our sections are, in a certain sense, our communes. Our leadership is our government."[72] Indeed, possession of the party card became a form of alternative citizenship, carrying its own set of rights and duties for militants. By purchasing the party card the militant had the right to vote in referenda and to select the party's leadership but also the duty to be a good citizen. This included avoiding duels, paying dues on time, attending meetings, and being "politically coherent."[73] Party leaders also aimed to separate party members from the broader community. In the 1890s socialists began to develop an alternative calendar of festivals, including the anniversary of Marx's death and the collapse of the Paris Commune, aimed at separating party members from nationalist and patriotic festivals that were nothing but "the festivals of the bourgeoisie and its conquests."[74] This tactic influenced even the most fundamental rights of passage: birth and death. Benito Mussolini (1883–1945), particularly in his capacity as head of the socialist section of Forlì, emphasized the importance of establishing a profound separation between party members and circumambient Catholicism. A statement issued by the party's April 1910 congress reads as follows: "The collegial congress holds the Catholic faith to be incompatible with socialist coherence and stipulates expulsion from the party of members who follow religious practices or tolerate such practices in their children. It establishes a specific obligation for socialists to avoid religious marriages, the baptism of children and all other cult ceremonies."[75] Italian socialism thus developed an intense and oppositional form of political participation.

Despite this impressive organizational growth, the PSI was never able to break fully with the Giolittian system. Most strikingly it remained financially dependent on the Italian state. Between 1889 and 1901 more than 5 million lire worth of contracts were ceded to the cooperatives under a law that allowed them to compete for public works contracts up to 100,000 lire. Indeed, this sponsorship was part of what drove the expansion of these organizations during the early twentieth century. The PSI became, paradoxically, a privileged interest group within the liberal state.[76]

Socialism was not the only political force to fully develop in the Giolittian period. Political Catholicism also developed rapidly in the years after the liberal turn. An especially important part of Catholic activities was the provision of microcredit through the *casse cattoliche* (or small Catholic banks). Large proprietors were involved in funding these organizations, whose purpose was at least in part to undermine political radicalism in the countryside.[77] But the evidence seems to suggest that internally they were quite democratic. The banks had a general assembly that elected their board of directors and relied heavily on horizontal relations of trust. According to Fabbri, "They were numerous above all in the low plain of the Po where they multiplied rapidly in the small communes, in the fractions, and in the small rural towns, even without their own capital, basing themselves on the mutual and unlimited responsibility of the members, who knowing and frequenting one another daily furnished an effective guarantee of mutual control."[78] Thus, although many of their major theorists espoused a vertical model of class collaboration, the organizational practice of the movement tended to contradict such doctrine. The Catholic peasant leagues were actually very close to the model of reformist socialism, a tendency that became more pronounced after the war, with the rise of Don Luigi Sturzo (1871–1959), who cut the movement's official ties to the church and espoused an openly democratic program.[79]

As both the socialist and Catholic political movements strengthened, they threatened the delicate balance of the Giolittian system, which was also being undermined by a slowing of the Italian economy between 1910 and 1913. The concession of universal suffrage in 1912 was an attempt to respond to these problems. Giolitti's aim in expanding suffrage was to increase the strength of the moderates within the PSI. Instead, it led to the rise of the radical wing, led in this period by the revolutionary firebrand Benito Mussolini. The Mussolinian revolt within the PSI was directed against collaboration with Giolitti. The intransigent left under his leadership demanded at the 1912 Congress of Reggio Emilia, the expulsion of the right wing and the prohibition of any alliances with nonsocialist groups either within or outside of parliament, thereby undermining the political autonomy of deputies in parliament. These policies were aimed clearly against the tactical compromises that formed the basis of Giolitti's politics. After the ascendancy of the left under Mussolini's leadership, the PSI shifted from being a support of the Giolittian system to one of its main political enemies.[80] The socialist radicals found support in revolutionary syndicalism, a radical but not socialist movement. The syndicalists successfully split the Confederazione Generale del Lavoro (General Labor Confederation, or CGL), forming the Unione Sindacale Italiana (Italian Syndical Union, or USI) in 1912.[81]

These two movements joined forces, most notably during the Settimana Rossa (Red Week): an antimilitarist demonstration that ended in violence, provoking a massive and unplanned general strike linking socialists, anarchists, and republicans. Immediately prior to the war, then, the crucial supports of the Giolittian system seemed to be collapsing.[82]

As the popular forces became an increasingly unreliable ally, liberal political elites looked to nationalism and imperialism as alternatives. This process began with Giolitti's involvement in Libya. But it was Antonio Salandra (1853–1931), Giolitti's main political rival, who would carry it to the point of intervening in World War I: a political and social disaster inextricably linked to the emergence of fascism in Italy. Intervention in this bloody—and from the Italian perspective, strategically pointless—conflict was an attempt to establish a popular basis of support in the context of an increasingly organized population, increasingly unavailable to the political establishment.[83]

Giolitti's partial opening of the political system, then, had paradoxical consequences. While the Piedmontese statesman encouraged associational development among nonelites, he worked hard to maintain elite control over the main levers of political power. Instead of strengthening the political organizations of the Italian social elite, this exacerbated their weakness. It also encouraged the development of nonelite political organizations that were either indifferent or hostile to the liberal system: socialism and Catholicism. One might have expected that, with the rise of these two mass oppositional movements each linked to a party, the liberal center would begin to organize more formally. And there were many prominent political figures pushing in this direction.[84] But this did not occur, in part because liberal elites had no incentive to risk open elections. The very measures that Giolitti used to protect the political privileges of the social elite guaranteed that they would be unable to penetrate a rapidly developing civil society. As Giolitti's rough working alliance with reformist socialism collapsed, some liberals began to search for an alternative basis of popular support in nationalism and imperialism. This need for a new form of popular legitimacy was directly linked to Italy's involvement in World War I— laying the groundwork for the social and political crisis out of which fascism would emerge.

The Giolittian period is best understood as a failed attempt to establish inter-class hegemony. Why did the attempt fail? The main reason is that Giolitti lacked a substantial party organization. Because of this he never really incorporated popular forces into his governing coalition. They formed instead an external support for ideologically incoherent coalitions. This outcome resulted from his simple extension of the logic of transformism that his predecessors had initially applied to regionally fragmented elites, to a major class divide.

Counterhegemony

As the troops returned from the killing fields of World War I, a new period opened in Italian politics: a phase of counterhegemony, in which a variety of popular movements attempted after the war to pursue a new democratic project. Given the weakness of the Italian dominant class, and the discredit into which it had fallen as a result of Italy's reckless intervention, one might have expected this moment to produce a breakthrough to stable mass democracy. But this did not occur. Instead, the counterhegemonic forces fragmented into competing groups in much the same way as the Italian dominant class had earlier. The result of this frag-mentation was a widespread crisis of politics out of which fascism would emerge.

The Postwar Moment and the Failure of Counterhegemony

Mass-mobilizing wars, as Theda Skocpol has rightly argued, are good for civil soci-ety.[85] Italy in the post–World War I period was certainly no exception. Groups across the political spectrum mobilized in response to the war and its immediate aftermath. The desire for a new, more representative state was widespread among them. The post–World War I period seemed to promise a fundamental transfor-mation of the Italian political system. A broad, leftist, democratic, nationalist movement that aimed to lead an interclass coalition to modernize Italian soci-ety and political institutions swept up many of the returning veterans.[86] Yet none of the existing political forces proved able to lead these various currents. Neither organized socialism nor the Italian liberals championed the democratic demands of the left nationalists. Fascism stepped into this vacuum, constituting itself as an antisocialist and antiliberal civil society movement. It was the failure of this counterhegemonic movement that would lead to the fascist seizure of power.

Veterans' organizations are the clearest manifestation of civic mobilization in postwar Italy. The largest, with 550,000 members, was linked to the Catholic Popular Party (PPI). The war also produced a number of civilian defense organizations, especially after the defeat of the Italian army at Caporetto, which led to Austrian occupation in parts of northern Italy. These tended to be middle class and on the political right; but many of these associations' members also demanded a new, more responsive political order outside the framework of the corrupt Giolittian system.[87]

The movement that would come to be called fascism, more specifically the *fascio di combattimento* (combat league), developed out of this milieu. Founded on March 23, 1919, it was initially conceived as a loose umbrella organization that would provide a framework for common action for organizations of veterans. In the words of an official fascist chronicler, its purpose was "to unite in a single *fascio* with a single will all the interventionists and the combatants, to direct them toward a precise aim, and to valorize the victory."[88] As it expanded, the movement often simply annexed preexisting organizations.[89]

One might think that the close connection between the veterans' organizations, war, and nationalism would make them authoritarian, narrow-minded, and exclusivist. The reality is much more nuanced; Italian nationalism was politically ambiguous. The struggle over whether or not Italy should intervene in World War I tended to push Italian nationalists to the left. Initially, they tended to support the Central Powers: Germany and the Austro-Hungarian empire. Part of this support derived from a genuine admiration for German authoritarianism as a political and social model. But Italy's participation in World War I weakened the pro-Austrian and pro-German tendency within nationalism, because the government entered the war on the side of France, England, and Russia.[90] Interventionism, a policy that all nationalists supported, thus became linked to the support of the democratic countries: France and England.

Interventionism also attracted significant support from the left. The first significant leftist forces to shift to support for intervention were the revolutionary syndicalists, a section of whom organized the Fascio Rivoluzionario d'Azione Internazionalista (Internationalist Revolutionary Action League). These groups had been involved in revolutionary politics for years but sought a new strategy in the aftermath of the failure of Red Week, discussed above.[91] Under their influence Mussolini now began to embrace war, publishing on the 18th of October "From Absolute Neutrality to Active and Operative Neutrality." This piece was the beginning of the former socialist leader's separation from his party and was enthusiastically glossed by the young Antonio Gramsci—who would later be one of the founding members of the Partito Comunista Italiano (PCI)—in *Il grido del popolo* (The Cry of the People) at the end of October.[92]

From November of 1914, with the founding of Mussolini's newspaper *Il popolo d'Italia* (The People of Italy), to May of 1915, when Italy intervened in the war, numerous intermediate cadres from the PSI joined the left interventionist groups. Membership in the party dropped steadily throughout the years of the war. In the aftermath of the war, these ex-socialists formed a definite leftist current within the broader Italian nationalist movement and tried to establish themselves as the leaders of a democratic front. Their central goal in the immediate postwar period was the establishment of a constitutional assembly that would broaden suffrage and undertake social reforms. Mussolini himself supported this program.[93]

The end of the war thus saw the consolidation of a distinct nationalist left, which tended to support popular democratic claims. For example, Mussolini's *Il popolo d'Italia* constantly reproached the reformist socialists for their political timidity in this period.[94] The paper's editorial board also supported one of the first factory occupations, which I discuss in more detail below, at the Franchi-Gregorini firm in Bergamo.[95] At Fiume, a border town between Italy and Yugoslavia, the poet Gabriele D'Annunzio (1863–1938) established a "republic" in September of 1919.[96] One of D'Annunzio's top advisers was the revolutionary syndicalist Alceste De Ambris (1874–1934), who convinced D'Annunzio to adopt a corporatist constitution called the Carta del Quarnaro (Carnaro Charter), calling for a system of political representation in which labor unions would take the place of political parties. D'Annunzio and his followers also attempted to make contacts with the PSI to lay the foundations for a March on Rome that had definite leftist connotations.[97] Early fascism was part of this nationalist left, as is clear from its first political program, adopted in June of 1919, calling for expanded suffrage, a steep tax on war profits, workers' participation in management decisions, and direct election to the senate.[98] The Italian fascist movement thus emerged out of the process of left-wing mobilization that swept Italy in the immediate postwar period.

Why, given fascism's initially democratic character, did the movement develop into a form of violent paramilitarism associated with vested interests? To answer this question it is essential to examine the left. Italy's participation in the war created an economic and political crisis that spurred a period of unprecedented leftist insurgency in the years 1919 and 1920. The safety valve of immigration was closed off after 1913, as the United States and other countries placed new restrictions on migrants, while at the same time the war led to serious price inflation.[99] Steep rises in the cost of living formed the basic economic context of social unrest during the period known as the Biennio Rosso (Red Biennium). Adding to the atmosphere of political excitement was the introduction of proportional representation. Single-member constituencies had tended to favor the conservative liberal center. The new voting system, in contrast, favored mass parties with a national reach, thus favoring the PSI and the PPI.[100]

Strikes broke out in 1919 and 1920 among telegraph and railroad workers, metallurgy workers, and automobile workers in the city of Turin and among day laborers in areas of north-central Italy. Many, especially in industry, were conducted without the sponsorship of the reformist union organizations. In 1919 the CGL reached an agreement with the employers' organization, Confindustria, covering hours, wages, and rights of representation within the factory. This accord quickly unraveled in a series of wildcat strikes throughout the summer and fall of that year.[101]

The high point of the Red Biennium occurred in the winter and early spring of 1920, during the occupation of the factories and the general strike of April. The occupations began as a technique of labor protest that would avoid the negative consequences of a strike but still squeeze industrialists sufficiently to force them to bargain. Instead of workers walking off the job, they would continue to produce, thus forcing owners to continue paying overhead.[102] These strikes were planned in part to demonstrate that the working class could organize production by itself and that, as a result, private ownership had become technically superfluous. Further, they were often accompanied by the demand that the company in question "be entrusted to the management of the collectivity of workers belonging to the company."[103] The technique seems to have begun among metallurgy workers in Genoa, Piedmont, and Milan and some factories in smaller towns in north-central Italy, the most highly industrialized areas of the country.[104]

The most dramatic instances of mobilization, however, occurred in the countryside. Proprietors suffered from unfavorable prices (industrial inputs were relatively much more expensive than agricultural outputs); increased taxes; and excess labor costs imposed by the success with which socialist leagues, often in alliance with socialist municipal governments, forced owners both to pay workers more and to hire unemployed day laborers and smallholders. These economic issues linked directly to political struggles. Mass strikes and demonstrations in the summer of 1919 due to the rising cost of living allowed the chambers of labor to achieve an unprecedented control over the labor supply. No one could hire outside the socialist organizations.[105]

During February and March of 1920, in the countryside around Turin peasants undertook a "systematic invasion of the lands of the large proprietors,"[106] formed a red-guard organization, and began to set houses on fire. Indeed, agrarian socialism in Italy promised a thorough alteration of rural class relations, either through the redistribution of land, or the establishment of collectively run farms.

To make matters worse—from the perspective of the Italian political elite—the PSI emerged in the postwar period as a major electoral force. Already in the 1913 elections, the first on the basis of universal male suffrage, the PSI showed itself to be a national political power without parallel on the peninsula. The party was the first organization to use a modern political campaign, including systematic research on the electoral districts, printed propaganda materials, public meetings, critiques of political adversaries, and advertising. All of these techniques were redeployed to great effect in the elections of the postwar period. In the national elections of 1919, the party won 156 seats. Together with the 100 seats of the PPI, this formed a major challenge to the traditions of parliamentary practice on the peninsula. The socialists tripled the number of their deputies compared with 1913, and they won roughly a third of the popular vote. The other votes went to local slates, weakly linked to national politics.[107]

The administrative elections of 1920 consolidated these already impressive gains. The PSI won every major northern urban center: Turin, Milan, Genoa, Venice, Florence, and Bologna. In Piedmont, Lombardy, Emilia-Romagna, the Veneto, and Tuscany, the party made massive gains in the number of communes under its control. In 1914 it controlled a total of 451 communes, about 5 percent of all communal governments in the country. By 1920 the party controlled 2,115 communes, or over a quarter of all municipal governments.[108]

Perhaps just as important was the emergence of the PPI. Although Giolitti had been able pragmatically to ally with this party, some sectors of the prewar Catholic current were quite radical. The Catholics, like the socialists, had benefited enormously from the expanded suffrage and proportional representation of the postwar period and, like the socialists, they controlled a solid bulwark of associations in the northeast of the country, as I have shown above. All of this mobilization took place in the context of continuing political weakness among the social elite. As the head of Confindustria put the point, "Our political parties are vile in their infamy."[109] This inability to win mass electoral support for a conservative political project was a fundamental reason that sectors of the social elite would come to support fascism in the twenties.

What was the connection between socialism and the nationalist left described earlier? It is obvious enough that the two were in competition for much of the same constituency. Yet one of the central political facts of the postwar period was the continuing electoral strength of the PSI despite the defection of many of the party's major leaders. This blocked any attempt to peel off the working-class organizations and attach them to a nationalist political project. Thus socialist organizations acted to insulate the organized working class from the left nationalists.[110]

This gave the PSI an enormous historical responsibility: the promotion of the many legitimate democratic demands that had arisen in the crisis of the postwar period. The party, however, proved unprepared to act as the champion of a democratic state.[111] It did not embrace the demand for a constituent assembly, and it quickly came under the spell of the soviet model. Despite clear signs of a highly mobilized civil society, the PSI proved unable to act as a political channel for this movement. This inability was partly the result of highly contingent strategic blunders, but it was also closely connected to the political development of Italian socialism during the Giolittian period. The concrete achievements of the Socialist Party were usually focused at the municipal level, while the ultimate goal of socialist transformation was projected into a nebulous future. This combination reflected the constraints that the party had faced in the period of restricted suffrage under Giolitti but also the privileges that it enjoyed. As a result of its historical entanglement with transformism, the party had been "municipalized." As Angelo Tasca vividly puts the point: "The socialist activity of the post war period had created in Italy—at the beginning of the epoch of the telephone and the railroad—hundreds of small 'republics,' of socialist 'oases,' without any communication among one another, like in the middle ages, but without the bastions that at that time defended the cities. Socialism resulted from the sum of thousands of local 'socialisms.' The lack of a national conscience, municipal 'campanilismo' [attachment to the local bell tower] constituted a serious handicap for Italian socialism."[112]

As a result of this localism, the 156 deputies of the party elected to parliament in 1919 were simply an inert blocking force, capable of irritating and frightening the right but incapable of carrying forward a positive policy at the national level, because such a policy did not really exist. The PSI had failed to become the champion of the interests of the society "as a whole." This led to a strange combination of reformist political practice and rhetorical radicalism. For example, in 1920 the CGL signed a pact in Moscow pledging its support to the universal Soviet Republic. During exactly the same period it urged its members to participate in a moderate insurance scheme in which workers would buy into a fund together with employers and the state. This contradictory amalgam of reformism and radicalism came to a head with the factory occupations discussed above. At a meeting held in Milan in September of 1920, the leadership of the CGL and the PSI both attempted to distance themselves from the strike, dealing an enormous political blow to the party membership. By late 1920 the two red years had fizzled without producing any concrete results. The PSI was thus strong enough to block a nationalist revolution from the left, but as a result of its previous incorporation into the Giolittian system, was too strategically bound to local politics to carry out its own democratic revolutionary project. It was the failure of socialist leadership in the crucial years after the war to embrace a broad democratic agenda that would open the way to fascism.[113]

The failure of Italian socialism to put itself at the head of a broad democratic coalition was a consequence of its historical entanglement with the transformist system of political rule. As a result of the many privileges the party won at the local level, it remained without a proper strategic perspective at the national level, even in its most revolutionary periods. This would prove disastrous in the postwar years because, although the party was quite capable of antagonizing the middle classes, it was structurally incapable of carrying out an actual social revolution.

National Syndicalism: An Ideology of Antipolitics

The failure of a broadly based democratic revolution at this moment produced a crisis of politics out of which fascism emerged. Distinctively, the fascist movement did not propose a new political solution to Italy's problems; instead, it identified politics as the problem. In this, the movement drew on a series of critiques of the liberal state going back to the Giolittian period. These ideas formed an antipolitical ideology of civil society, or associationism, which was a central part of fascist doctrine both during the movement's rise and during the regime itself.[114]

The dominant ideology of the fascist movement came from two main sources: nationalists and syndicalists. Together they formed the doctrine of "national syndicalism." Although these doctrines had very different lineages, they shared one important similarity: both insisted on the artificiality of politics and the need for direct nonelectoral forms of political participation.[115]

Syndicalism began as a heterodox current within the Socialist Party in 1902, as a result of the reformist leadership's decision to support the government and establish tactical alliances with the liberals. The reformists, the syndicalists suggested, were being co-opted by transformism; what was needed instead was a new political order based on self-governing occupational groups that would break the dominance of the PSI.[116]

The most important syndicalist figure for the subsequent development of fascism was Sergio Panunzio (1886–1944). Panunzio began his political career in 1902, when he became the political secretary of the local socialist group of Molfetta in southern Italy—precisely during the crisis within the PSI pitting the revolutionary syndicalists against the reformists. He understood socialism more as a postliberal political system than a postcapitalist economic order. Working-class organizations, he argued, had created a new form of law outside the liberal state. This, Panunzio hoped, would constitute the foundation of a new political order comprised of concentrically organized syndical republics linked together in trade union federations that mixed economic and political functions.[117] Like many intellectuals in Giolittian Italy, Panunzio emphasized the importance of nonstate forms of organization—civil society.[118] As he writes, "The disorganization of the state and the organization of society are objectively the central and essential 'facts' of the current period."[119] Syndicalists should work to establish a new political order congruent with these conditions.

A strikingly parallel set of ideas developed among Italian nationalists. Nationalism was initially antithetical to syndicalism, because most syndicalists were strongly antimilitarist, at least until 1911. The nationalists formulated their ideology by drawing a contrast between two Italies: a "real" Italy comprised of "producers" and a "political Italy" dominated by Giolittian politics.[120] Perhaps the clearest expression of this position can be found in the writings of Alfredo Rocco (1875–1935).[121] The modern state, argued Rocco, achieved its highest expression at the beginning of the eighteenth century in absolutist France. This state was based on corporations that transcended individual interests and linked the political order organically to the population. He believed that the relationship between state and society had changed for the worse following the dissolution of the French corporations in 1789. The French Revolution resulted in an "agnostic state" that treated all individuals as abstract citizens but was not connected to them.[122]

For Rocco the modern organization of production tended toward the organization of bosses' and workers' syndicates and therefore undermined the individualism upon which liberal political thought rested.[123] The twentieth-century tendency to organization thus reversed the nineteenth-century trend toward atomization. The central problem was that the new organizations pursued the interests of their members to the detriment of society as a whole. Rocco summarized the situation this way: "Now we have arrived at this situation: that in the presence of the weak and absent state, a war of all against all, a war fought with all material and moral means emerges ... The Middle Ages with its miseries and horrors returns."[124] How could this situation of internal civil war be overcome? The key to the problem was to "empower" the state. This was not to occur at the expense of civil society. Instead, associations were "to be transformed from instruments of struggle for the defense of particularistic interests, into organs of collaboration for the achievement of common ends."[125] In part this would involve a "statization" of the syndicates, but it also implied a transfer of certain functions, such as professional instruction and economic policy, to them. The ambition was not to destroy civil society but to colonize it. "The state," writes Rocco, "is not something different and above society; it is society itself insofar as it organizes itself, that is inasmuch as it exists and lives, because organization is life."[126] The main task of contemporary politics, according to Rocco, was to reincorporate interest organizations into the state.[127] Rocco's political project, then, could be understood as an attempt to align the modern state with an increasingly organized civil society, in a way reminiscent of syndicalism.

These two ideological currents (revolutionary syndicalism and nationalism) were very different, but they shared a common disdain for liberalism, which they saw as fundamentally unrepresentative. Both the syndicalists and the nationalists praised the virtues of social self-organization and direct action. It was this that made it possible for them to fuse into national syndicalism in the postwar period. The two strains of thought, and particularly their critique of the limitations of parliamentary government, were very influential on many prominent fascist leaders.

Many of the leaders of the Italian fascist movement had personally participated in the syndicalist revolt against reformist socialism. Michele Bianchi (1883–1930), who played a critical role in the fascist seizure of power, began his political career as the editor of the Roman edition of the socialist newspaper *Avanti!* In 1904 he was elected as a delegate to the Socialist Party congress in Bologna, where he supported the syndicalist left around Enrico Ferri (1856–1929) and Arturo Labriola (1873–1959). In subsequent years he worked for the Genoa chamber of labor, where he edited a newspaper called *Lotta socialista* (Socialist Struggle). In this period as well he supported the revolutionary syndicalist line of the party. In the period between 1907 and 1912, he moved between Ferrara, Naples, and Parma working for the local chambers of labor, and socialist leagues. Bianchi was responsible for developing a strategy of controlling labor supply by organizing hiring halls under the control of the chamber of labor. In the agitation over the war, he was very active in the interventionist left and espoused an alliance between nationalism and syndicalism. Bianchi was also at the forefront of fascist paramilitary violence in the twenties.[128]

Umberto Pasella, together with his brother Guido, was responsible for organizing violent strikes in the area around Ferrara in an effort to proletarianize the sharecroppers.[129] Pasella was also one of the first general secretaries of the fascist movement and ably kept the organization going in the difficult period from 1919 to 1920.[130] He later played an important role in the March on Rome (October 28, 1922). Angelo Olivetti (1874–1931), Sergio Panunzio (1886–1944), Edmondo Rossoni (1884–1965), all figures who played some role in early fascism or had important influence on early fascist leaders, had contact with the Ferrara chamber of labor, a center of revolutionary syndicalism.

Agostino Lanzillo (1886–1952), who was an important early collaborator of *Il popolo d'Italia* but left the movement over political differences with the fascist right in 1921, also had extensive experience in revolutionary syndicalist circles. Lanzillo wrote a doctoral thesis on Proudhon and corresponded personally with Sorel.[131] Like Michele Bianchi he was a revolutionary syndicalist and was part of the Ferrara chamber of labor in 1908.[132] Giovanni Marinelli (1879–1944), the administrative secretary of the PNF for most of the fascist regime, was also an ex-revolutionary syndicalist.[133] Thus the influence of national syndicalism was broad and deep.

National syndicalist ideas were also evident during the regime. The fascist minister of corporations, Giuseppe Bottai (1895–1959), espoused syndicalist ideas in a 1935 speech, stating: "There are two fundamental aspects of modern life: the division of labor, that is to say the specification of functions, and the grouping together of homogenous entities, that is to say, the coalition of those who undertake a similar function ... That which is, however, specific to modern society is the following fact: one may say that associated groups, or as we would say in Italian [rather than French] 'associative groups,' encompass the entire social organism."[134] This statement drew on the basic idea that the modern state should be based on a completely organized population no longer in need of specifically political representation.

National syndicalism, the main doctrinal current in Italian fascism, was an ideology of civil society. Its analysis of the contemporary period claimed that associational development had undermined the viability of the liberal state form requiring not a political solution but a technocratic solution. This was not, however, an antidemocratic ideology. The fascist movement emerged out of a diffuse set of demands for making the Italian state more representative of Italian society, not less so. In this, the fascist ideologues and their followers discussed above were in agreement with a broad critique of Italian liberalism that had developed in the decades before World War I.[135]

The Development of Fascism: From Movement to Party

Early fascism was not a political party; it was instead a "league," a group of men loosely linked by their shared nationalism and contempt for the Giolittian system. In the two years after its founding, fascism experienced two major transformations. The first was a "turn to the right," in which the movement formed an alliance with the social elite. The second was its transformation from a league into a "party-militia." The fascist movement's turn to the right was a consequence of the specific, unevenly developed political terrain that I have described above. While the party was blocked in its attempted alliance to the left, on the right of the political spectrum the organizational weakness of the social elite, developed during the Giolittian period but rendered critical by the Red Biennium, opened a vacuum that inexorably drew fascism toward it. A movement that began as an amorphous left democratic movement thus *became* a rightist movement. Yet, while the social content of fascism changed, its political project remained fundamentally similar to what it had always been. This was a revolt against the Giolittian liberal system in the name of an organic direct representation of the nation. This project was twisted and altered in many ways, especially through the fascist movement's perpetration of systematic terrorism against socialist organizations in the countryside. Seen in proper perspective, these were tactical shifts; they did not touch the movement's central element: to build an organic national democracy. But since this project could not be realized with the cooperation of the socialists, and since the Socialist Party was large and powerful, the fascist project would necessarily take an authoritarian form.

The turn to the right occurred in the wake of two major political defeats: the national elections of November 1919 and the local elections of November 1920. These failures proved that the movement was unable to penetrate the socialist electorate, the natural constituency for its initial leftist program.[136] As a consequence fascism underwent major internal changes. It lost some of its previously leftist membership at the local level and began to form an alliance with conservatives and property owners. These groups had been organizing to break the power of socialism independently of fascism; but now the two allied. There was also a transformation in the Milanese central committee, which increased its conservative elements and reduced, but did not eliminate, the ex-socialist and syndicalist element. This turn to the right was further confirmed when the futurists abandoned fascism after the November 1921 Rome congress. In late 1920 and early 1921, a new phenomenon thus emerged: an alliance between the Fascist Party and the social elite, particularly the agrarians in northern Italy. This alliance formed the social basis of squadrism: the dissemination of terror among the agrarian population, especially those associated with the PSI.[137]

Squadrist violence first emerged in the Venezia Giulia in northeastern Italy and then spread to the Emilia-Romagna in the Valley of the Po after November of 1920, as a direct result of the socialist victories in the administrative elections of November of that year.[138] By the winter of 1921, the fascists were established in the Bologna-Ferrara-Piacenza triangle and thus controlled the entire Valley of the Po. By the spring of 1921, squadrism moved into Umbria and Tuscany. Before the crisis of fascism in the summer of 1921, discussed below, the fascist occupation (squadrism) extended to all of Venezia Giulia, a part of the Veneto in the northeast, the entire Valley of the Po (except for Cremona, Parma, and the Romagna),

Alessandria, and the rice-growing regions around Novara, Tuscany, Umbria, and Apulia. Most of Lombardy and also Piedmont and Liguria was outside of the fascist ambit. The last wave of squadrist violence before the March on Rome began in late July of 1921 in response to the socialist "legalitarian strike." In this last period the squadrists occupied Genoa, Ancona, Milan, and Livorno.[139]

Although the fascists removed and often killed the socialist leadership of the peasant leagues and other associations of agrarian direct producers, the members of these organizations were not simply scattered. Rather, they were forced to adhere, more or less involuntarily, to new fascist organizations.[140] Local fascist leaders were not above using this mass base to pressure both Mussolini and later the Italian state itself. The regional distribution of squadrism suggests that the fascist movement was connected to the civic mobilization that had grown up during the war. The movement also seems to have had an ambiguous relationship to socialism, attacking it politically while seeking to occupy its organizational structure.[141] Where these organizational materials were missing, above all in the Italian south, squadrism did not take hold. Table 2 presents the relevant evidence. As Robert Putnam and many others have pointed out, there have been sharp regional differences in the incidence of voluntary associations in Italy.[142] How did these relate to fascist mobilization? Emilia-Romagna, Tuscany, and Lombardy were the three regions that consistently produced the highest numbers of fascist fighters (so-called *squadristi*) the largest number of fascist cell organizations, and the largest number of fascist leaders. Table 2 compares this regional concentration of fascist cells and fascist martyrs with the number of cooperative organizations per 100,000 persons in 1915. It shows that fascist cell organizations and fascist martyrs were most common in the regions where rural cooperative organizations and agrarian leagues were most developed: Lombardy, Emilia-Romagna, and Tuscany. At the very least the evidence suggests that civil society was not an obstacle to the development of fascism here.

What kind of movement was fascism during the period of squadrism? One might think that the turn to the right and the emergence of political violence would be associated with an abandonment of the national syndicalist ideas of national renewal and class collaboration that characterized the movement's early phase. But there is no evidence of this. Instead, many of the men within the movement most committed to the original doctrines of early fascism were also deeply involved in squadrism. Especially important among these men were the so-called intransigents.

Table 2   Cooperatives, Leagues, Fascist Cells, and Martyrs (in number per 100,000)

Region	Cooperatives in 1915	Leagues in 1912	Cell organizations in May 1922	Martyrs in 1921
Basilicata	36	0	1	1
Abruzzo and Molise	68	0	3	1
Sardinia	64	1	1	1
Calabria	117	1	2	1
Campania	231	4	1	1
Sicily	374	6	1	1
Marche	225	5	4	2
Apulia	263	5	2	2
Umbria	104	5	9	3
Veneto	669	5	7	1
Piedmont	620	8	4	2
Lazio	447	9	4	2
Tuscany	770	12	15	4
Lombardy	1,477	15	9	3
Emilia-Romagna	1,575	100	13	6
Liguria	389	16	4	1

Sources: Gentile 2000; Degl'Innocenti 1977.

The rapid growth of the fascist movement, its participation in an electoral alliance with the Giolittian liberals (the national bloc), and Mussolini's attempt to reach a truce with the PSI created serious unrest within the fascist movement, leading to a full-scale revolt against Mussolini from within.[143] Fascism's emergence as a party in December of 1921 was the result of a bargain between the "intransigent" wing, which opposed these various political maneuvers, and the Milanese leadership, which desperately wanted to reassert some control over the base.[144] The most important figures among the intransigents were Roberto Farinacci (1892–1945), Dino Grandi (1895–1988), Italo Balbo (1896–1940), and Pietro Marsich. All to varying degrees were linked to agrarian interests.[145] But they were also all major exponents of national syndicalism and thus cannot be interpreted as a distinct "rightist" faction within fascism. Balbo and Grandi were both students of Sergio Panunzio at the law faculty in Ferrara. Marsich was a young Venetian lawyer who came from the Partito Radicale (Radical Party). The elections of 1919 convinced him that political renewal could come only from outside the parliamentary system, and as a result he adhered to early fascism. He had a vision of the new fascist state that was close to that of the revolutionary syndicalists. The violent squadrist wing of the Fascist Party was thus intimately connected to the left nationalist side of the movement.[146]

Fascism arose out of the failure of the counterhegemonic movement in the immediate post–World War I period. The PSI, the PPI, and the left nationalists were unable to come to an agreement on how to establish a functioning mass democracy in Italy. This produced a crisis of politics. Fascism was never a political ideology, nor did it propose a political solution to Italy's postwar problems. Instead, fascism emerged as an antipolitical movement promising to build a state on the basis of expertise, technique, and apolitical occupational groups. The movement drew on the existence of a strong civil society, both ideologically and organizationally. Ideologically fascism presented itself as the representative of civil society, understood as "real Italy" and opposed to the corrupt political class. Organizationally fascism used the materials of civil society to build its own movement.

Party Fascism: The Italian Regime, 1922–1938

What kind of regime did the fascist movement establish? Italian fascism is best understood as an authoritarian democracy. The regime sought to encourage participation without politics. It did this in two somewhat different ways. First, through its corporative structures, the regime attempted to fragment the Italian population into numerous interest groups or categories, seeking to replace citizenship as an abstract political category applying to all people within a territorial unit with the "citizen producer," whose rights and duties were linked to occupation.[147] But the regime also pursued a second project, in some tension with this first one, for, together with the fragmentation of the population, it also sought to foster a national consensus through the party. Both of these projects were fundamentally antipolitical. The theory behind the first was that the corporatist fragmentation of the population could allow for a spontaneous consensus, while the theory behind the second project was that indoctrination and propaganda could take the place of politics. To understand this specific amalgam of corporatist and party-state, it is important to consider events immediately after the fascist seizure of power.

A fascist government came to power as a consequence of the March on Rome, an ambiguous insurrectionary movement that created a crisis of the weak government of Luigi Facta (1861–1930) and led to Mussolini's installation as prime minister. The March on Rome was a watershed in Italian history because the fascist movement had imposed itself on the king through extraparliamentary means. But it was not yet a transformation of the Italian state. Mussolini acceded to power through formally constitutional channels: the monarch called him to form a coalition government. Furthermore, although he had come to power on the basis of a process of violent paramilitary mobilization, his relationship to the fascists was quite ambiguous. As *duce* (leader) of the fascist movement, he was indispensable, but he never held the position of general secretary and often strove to present himself as a political figure above "his" party. There is even evidence that Mussolini would have preferred a regime based on a deal between chastened working-class organizations and leading industrial and agrarian interests rather than the party-state that eventually emerged.

A key question then is: how did the Mussolini government become a party-state, how did "party-fascism" emerge? Party fascism was the result of a ferocious factional struggle within the fascist movement, pitting those who wished to establish a nonparty regime against the intransigents, who had their power base in the squads and the syndicates. To grasp why Italy under Mussolini became a party-state, it is thus essential to understand why the nonparty option lost out.[148]

It is useful to begin this discussion by noting certain important parallels between Mussolini's political maneuvers in the early twenties and Giolitti's failed project in the earlier part of the century. After the destruction of many of the political organizations of Italian socialism, Mussolini, like Giolitti before him, sought to establish an alliance with the remnants of the Italian labor movement. However, a return to this model of political rule was impossible under the conditions that prevailed in the early twenties. Let us briefly examine why.

Many in Mussolini's entourage were eager to rid themselves of the troublesome fascist intransigents, whose political usefulness plummeted after the seizure of power. Proponents of this position suggested that the population should be organized into apolitical occupational groups whose interests would be mediated in local corporatist chambers. A central element of this strategy was an alliance with the CGL, bringing decisive mass support to a Mussolini government while eliminating or sharply reducing the role of the Fascist Party and unions.[149] The CGL was still the most powerful workers' organization in Italy, especially in the industrial triangle of Milan, Genoa, and Turin immediately following the March on Rome, and there is considerable evidence that Mussolini preferred this solution.[150]

Many reformist socialists seem to have been supportive of this attempt, and numerous contacts took place between them and figures in the fascist regime in the period from January to July 1923. One of the first steps on this path was the Pact of Palazzo Chigi, signed on December 21, 1923, between the major figures of Italian industry and the fascist syndicates. The pact recognized Confindustria as the legitimate representative of the employers, while affirming the principle of "syndical freedom," meaning that the fascist syndicates would have to compete alongside the others for members.[151] Palazzo Chigi was a crushing defeat for the fascist syndicates. The leadership knew that it could not compete with the CGL in open elections. Edmondo Rossoni, the fascist union leader, knew that, because of the weak fascist base among workers and peasants, even an implicit alliance between Mussolini and the reformist socialists, such as Palazzo Chigi represented, would threaten their position. The agricultural workers that they had "organized," with the help of squadrist violence, would flow back to the CGL and government positions would go to CGL leaders rather than fascist syndicalists. Thus late 1923 and early 1924 were very difficult for the fascist syndicates. They faced the hostility of the conservatives and the socialists and the unreliability of Mussolini. If successful, an alliance with the CGL would mean either a dramatic drop in the membership of the fascist syndicates or a fusion between the fascists and the CGL, which could only weaken the power of the fascists. By February of 1924 the leadership of the CGL declared that the membership was free to vote in the upcoming (partially rigged) elections according to its conscience. This was a major step toward a formal separation from the PSI and a more open alliance with the Mussolini government. By early summer 1924 it seemed that collaboration was imminent.[152]

Certainly such an agreement would have followed established patterns of Italian political deal making, as well as having considerable support among the industrialists.[153] The emerging alliance between the Mussolini government and the CGL was basically a reedition of the Giolittian coalition between the industrial working class and major capitalists, on a new, authoritarian basis. In sum this was a return to transformism. To understand the emergence of a party regime in Italy, it is therefore crucial to grasp why this new version of an established political style failed to consolidate.

There were two very different types of opposition to the Pact of Palazzo Chigi and the broader political project of which it was an expression: the fascist intransigents and the noncollaborationist wing of the Socialist Party. The intransigents were made up mostly of ex-squadrists and fascist union leaders, led respectively by Roberto Farinacci and Edmondo Rossoni. Farinacci, the notorious Cremonese squadrist, saw any agreement with the socialist organizations as a direct threat to fascist claims on political power and the spoils it brought, but his resistance to the Palazzo Chigi accord was quite ineffectual.[154] Squadrism was weakening in the period immediately after the March on Rome, as Mussolini's policy moved toward normalization. The fascist union movement led by Rossoni was in an analogous position. Its program in the summer and the winter of 1923 was to establish a monopoly over labor representation, thus pitting the fascist unions against both their socialist enemies in the CGL and the industrialists and agriculturists. Throughout November of 1923 Rossoni's syndicates went on the attack against the industrialists.[155]

Opposition to the solution embodied in the Pact of Palazzo Chigi also came from an entirely different direction: the noncollaborationist wing of the PSI. The most important representative of this position was Giacomo Matteotti (1885–1924), a reformist socialist deputy killed, probably accidentally, by a fascist squad in the summer of 1924. His assassination was closely related to Mussolini's attempt to establish an alliance with the CGL. Matteotti's last speech to the chamber of deputies on the 30th of May 1924 was aimed precisely against this attempt, insisting instead on an intransigent antifascist line.[156] The assassination was aimed partially at removing what was seen as an intransigent obstacle to an alliance with the remnants of the socialist unions.[157]

A strongly anticollaborationist line persisted within the CGL as well. Considering the general political situation in Italy in 1924 and 1925, an atmosphere of squadrist criminality openly protected by judges and police, the socialist union organization successfully completed an amazing number of collective bargaining agreements: ninety-one agreements that encompassed 295,000 workers. These successes were compounded by a number of symbolic acts, such as a referendum for the socialist Federazione Italiana Operai Metallurgici (FIOM) and a plan to stop work early in October of 1924. All of this underlined the impossibility of Mussolini's attempt to reestablish transformism along authoritarian lines.[158]

The Matteotti crisis had immediate and severe political consequences that came very close to bringing down the fascist government. On the 12th of June, six days after the socialist deputy's disappearance, the opposition withdrew from parliament to form the Aventine Secession. Following the crisis there was a resurgence of fascist activity that dissolved Mussolini's support on the traditionalist right. The leaders of Confindustria (the main industrialist association) sent Mussolini a note demanding normalization and control of the squads. Then the liberals around Giolitti began to go into opposition. As Mussolini's support dissolved, the weight of the intransigents within fascism, particularly the syndicalists and the squadrists, increased. In order to win back some of the ground lost, the fascist syndicates undertook a series of strikes, beginning in July of 1924, precisely as the Matteotti crisis was reaching its peak. In the fall of 1924 and winter of 1925, the fascist squads reinforced this wave of mobilization, spreading violence and terror in the countryside. By December of 1924 this wing of the party was in open revolt. Mussolini's speech of the January 3, 1925, which politically was the turning point toward a full fascist regime, was made under the pressure of a squadrist ultimatum—either radicalize the regime or cease to lead fascism. It was fascist mobilization from below, therefore, that pushed Mussolini to radicalize.[159]

Mussolini now moved to establish a new, much more authoritarian state while not fully adopting the intransigent fascist line. The instrument of this transformation was the police structure: the prefects of the old liberal state. Immediately after Mussolini's speech of January 1925, Luigi Federzoni (1878–1967), the conservative nationalist minister of the interior, who, within the fascist coalition, was on the opposite end of the political spectrum from the intransigents, sent notes to the prefects, demanding the immediate closure of all opposition party organizations. At the same time, in early January Federzoni put pressure on the prefects to bring the intransigents into line. But repression against the PNF worked only partially, for the party was too deeply entrenched in civil society to be repressed through police mechanisms. In February and March of 1925, the fascist syndicalists led major strikes in Brescia, Milan, and Trieste culminating in the massive "fascist strike" of March 1925. There were two primary issues involved in these strikes: the relationship between the fascist unions and the CGL and the nature of the emerging fascist regime. The stronghold of the fascist unions was Brescia, located at the foot of the Alps near Lago di Gada, and the heart of the Italian metallurgy industry. The fascists had employed their technique of "occupying" socialist organizations to great effect here. The fascist strike began over the issue of salary increases at the Togni firm. Augusto Turati (1888–1955), who had been at the head of anti-socialist violence, issued an appeal to Bruno Buozzi, to ally with him in calling a general strike for all of Lombardy. The FIOM supported the fascist strike, and by March 13 there were 150,000 workers on strike in Lombardy. Thus the fascist syndicates and the FIOM struggled together against the employers' organization in a strike involving hundreds of industries and tens of thousands of workers.[160]

The fascist-CGL strike thus brought together political currents attacking the Palazzo Chigi accord from two entirely different perspectives. While the socialists sought to defend, and if possible extend, the remnants of Italian democracy, the fascists wanted a transition to a new, more authoritarian state. This mobilization from below was as decisive for the final shape of the fascist regime as the squadrist offensive of the summer of 1924 had been.

The political foundations of the fascist regime were constructed, accordingly, in a context of massive fascist insurgency. The critical year was 1925. It began with Mussolini's attack on the Aventine opposition and his ban on opposition parties. Under pressure from the Fascist Party organization, it went much further. The two key legislative acts were the Pact of Palazzo Vidoni, signed in October of 1925, and the syndical decree of April 3, 1926, giving a fascist monopoly to the representation of all economic interest groups. Palazzo Vidoni replaced Palazzo Chigi and established a new relationship between Confindustria and the fascist unions. The confederation of industry agreed to recognize the confederation of fascist corporations as the exclusive representative of labor, thus eliminating the bargaining power of any nonfascist organization. In addition the confederation of industry agreed to fascisticize—changing its name to the Fascist General Confederation of Italian Industry. In exchange for these concessions, the confederation of fascist corporations agreed to recognize the confederation of industry. This agreement was the basis for the law of April 3, 1926, requiring regime organizations for all the professions. The basic concept here was that a single fascist syndicate would be established for all economic activities. By the spring of 1926 the legislative basis for a fundamentally new type of state was in place.[161]

The emergence of a party fascist regime was premised, then, on pressure from below. The prefects and the interior ministry were quite hostile to the squads and the syndicates, as was Mussolini himself after he came to power. The fascist monopoly over interest representation was established, in part, against the national state, not with its aid. In the absence either of an alliance with vital economic interests or full possession of the state, what was the basis of fascist power? The answer, as I have already hinted above, is that the fascists had entrenched themselves in civil society. They had occupied, in the most literal sense, the preexisting structure of voluntary associations, which they could now exploit to bring pressure to bear for a further expansion of their power. Without this organizational material it is inconceivable that the Fascist Party could have resisted pressure from the conservatives in the Italian state.

The Structure of the Party Fascist Regime

A fascist regime, characterized by a symbiosis of party and state (party fascism), emerged in Italy only after 1925. The most obvious indicator of this new state form was the growth of a massive parallel administration separate from the ministerial bureaucracy. This took three main forms: the party, the syndicates, and other parastate organizations. During the early period of fascist rule, Mussolini's government attacked the ministerial bureaucracy, seeking to reduce its numbers, and from 1926 to 1932 the government imposed a hiring freeze. The real administrative transformations occurred outside the ministries in the so-called parastate, the key organization of which was the *ente pubblico* (public entity): publicly recognized juridical persons constituted to undertake specific tasks. During the years from 1922 to 1943, 352 such public entities were established, including two types of institutions: the "mass organizations" of the fascist regime, such as the party, the syndicates, and the corporations, and public-private partnerships that made infrastructural investments. This proliferation of organizations outside the ministerial bureaucracy is somewhat paradoxical because the parastate was often connected to specific organized interests. To understand better what was typically fascist about it, it is useful to examine more closely the key political *enti pubblici*: the party and the syndicates.[162]

It is well to begin with the party, since this was the most important fascist institution. By the midtwenties, this initially anarchic organization showed definite signs of bureaucratic sclerosis. The transition from Farinacci, whose term as general secretary ended in 1926, to Augusto Turati is often argued to mark the total subordination of the party to the state. Yet the PNF maintained a degree of institutional autonomy from the Italian state and formed a decisive base of support for Mussolini, the full importance of which would emerge only when the conservatives began to abandon the regime in the midforties. To understand the fascist regime, it is therefore essential to understand the Fascist Party.[163]

The PNF under the regime had three levels of organization. The most local was the *fascio* (literally "bundle," but more meaningfully "league"). These formed part of a provincial "federation of *fasci*" headed by a federal secretary. Finally, there was the national organization headed by the party secretary.[164]

During most of the regime the PNF was materially autonomous from the Italian state. Until 1940 fascist federations were self-financing. The official acts of the party, political and administrative dispositions issued by the national directorate, make this clear. The 1935 disposition on the "carding and financing" of the party identifies four sources of funding: the sale of cards, the sale of badges, ordinary contributions, and extraordinary contributions. The central party headquarters sold cards and badges to the provincial federations, which resold them to members at a fixed price. The federation kept the difference between the price at which they purchased the card from the national directorate and the price at which they sold it to the membership. Ordinary and extraordinary contributions were also collected at the provincial level. Unlike the profit on the cards, the provincial federations kept all of these funds, as the acts specify.[165] The regulations for party financing do not specify any procedures for transferring funds from either the national directorate or the state. According to the acts, the PNF lived, rather, on profits from the sale of cards, badges, and contributions.[166]

The rules governing the collection of resources were vague, leaving federal secretaries considerable discretion. For example, there was no national price for a party card. Rather federations established various rates depending on local conditions. The budget for the Milanese federation for the year "XIII" had four card prices, from 12 to 5 lire, priced presumably according to the members' income.[167]

Despite their varying prices, party cards were the most formalized type of all fascist resource collection. Only members paid dues, and this limited to some extent the resources that could be collected. Another kind of limit operated as well, for there is evidence that it was often difficult to get members to reenroll. A document from Imperia, a city in the region of Liguria, from February of 1933 illustrates this. The report says, "It is common opinion that a good part of the fascists will decide not to renew the card because they do not trust the use to which the funds are put."[168]

Contributions, both extraordinary and ordinary, were more vaguely defined. They were supposed to be levied on people enrolled in the party, not on the territorial jurisdiction. All official documents insist that the federation avoid coercion and that contributions be levied in relation to the "economic possibilities of those enrolled."[169] But these provisions seem to have been ignored in some cases and a regime of quasi taxation established. For example, an inspector's report from Rome states, "In the regional peripheral groups it is habitual to have recourse to concrete threats against those who do not adhere with the desired solicitude to monetary requests for assistance."[170] A report from 1935 suggests a similar conclusion. Here the inspector writes: "It is said that in the months of September and October all the sections of the *fascio* of the various regions of the capital will organize a lottery for assistance work and general expenses, through objects more or less voluntarily offered by the shop owners of each region. Until now these have shown themselves to be little favorable to such frequent contributions, often solicited in an 'extractive' and intimidating form."[171] In the same report, one reads, "At the *Gruppo Trevi* a tax is imposed on store owners."[172]

These practices were not limited to Rome. An inspector's report from Turin in 1940 suggests that a similar situation existed there: "The groups, while not having regional autonomy for accounting purposes, procured funds to provide directly for the distribution of 'subsidies' and various assistance activities, putting aside any surplus for the construction of a local 'seat'."[173] The Genoese federation had the same organization. As the inspector writes, "In almost all cases the *fasci* and the regional groups live on their own [*vivono di vita propria*], but in the cases in which the balance closes in a deficit the federation turns over as a subvention the sum necessary to balance the budget."[174] The Mantuan federation was organized this way as well: "The financial means for *fasci* and regional groups are furnished by the Federation out of assistance funds to combatants, but these advances are also supplemented by spontaneous offerings that the *fasci* receive."[175] An inspector's report of the federation of Pola in 1942 indicates the same thing. Admittedly the situation here was extraordinary, as fascism itself was beginning to collapse under the pressure of the war, but the inspector notes that there were no records of any budgetary control over the provincial *fasci*.[176]

More-sophisticated methods existed as well. For example, the Genoese federation established a *conto terzi*, or "account on behalf of third persons." The local employers' syndicate started the *conto terzi* in 1927–1928 as a committee for financing the *Journal of Genoa* and various activities of the PNF. After the sale of the journal in 1931, the account survived as a financial collaboration between the federal secretary and presidents of the employers' syndicates. At the beginning of every year, the federal secretary would propose a series of activities for the party, including clothes for the youth, the construction of summer colonies, youth houses, and so on. Then, in agreement with the presidents of the employers' syndicates, a contribution would be established for each of the syndicates for these activities. Apparently this collaboration was highly successful. The *conto terzi*, according to an administrative report, allowed the construction of thirty-eight buildings associated with the party in the province of Genoa. The inspector remarked on the success of the collaboration between the party and local capitalists. He wrote that with "the income given by these big capitalists and the colossal banking, commercial and industrial organization of Genoa ... the federation has been able to accumulate an imposing stock of real-estate ... of over thirty five million lire in value."[177]

Fascist organizations funded their welfare program, the Ente Opera Assistenziali (EOA), in a similar way. After 1930 this constituted a major part of all federation budgets. Like the other services of the party, it was funded by contributions. An inquiry of the *fascio* of Lodi in 1932 indicates that "Signora Gelurin looks after the collection of rates for children to be sent to the sea and mountain colonies and she deposits the money, it seems without any documentation, in a lump sum with the *Fascio*."[178] Indeed, the local party organizations seem to have provided services for the members that did not differ too much from those that had been common among the prefascist socialist and Catholic associations. For example, the Lodi federation aided many of its party members by paying their health insurance to a local mutual fund.[179]

The evidence above suggests that the PNF remained a partially autonomous organization within the authoritarian regime that consolidated in Italy after 1925. The party was a parallel channel of resource collection. Further, party organizations carried out a number of projects at the local level, such as building summer camps for young people and providing rudimentary welfare services that had been the province of voluntary organizations prior to the regime.

The Syndicates

A partially separate structure of organizations developed around trade unions and employers' organizations, grouped together in fascist terminology as "syndicates." In Italy after 1926, workers' and industrialists' organizations were kept separate. Edmondo Rossoni, the leader of the fascist trade unions, struggled to incorporate industrialists and workers into the same organization between 1926 and 1928. But after internecine party struggles Mussolini decided to break Rossoni's organization into autonomous national confederations. The result of this struggle was a structure of national syndical confederations, six employers' organizations and six workers' organizations for industry, agriculture, commerce, credit, and insurance, along with the syndical confederation of land transport, sea and air transport, artisans and professionals, and artists. In addition to these organizations there were hundreds of local ones, some of which operated on a territorial basis, some of which operated on a professional basis. In legal terms the syndicates were "autarchic entities," that is, organizations that carry out a public function outside the state hierarchy.[180]

As in the case of the Fascist Party, this bureaucracy was paid for by a system of fees. All workers in a given category of production were required to pay fees to their syndicate, regardless of whether they were enrolled or not, and the members who were enrolled were required to pay other unspecified expenses. This money was then recycled into the fascist mass institutions paying for salaries, social work, insurance, and the construction of an entire government ministry: corporations.[181]

The period from 1928 to 1936 was the low point of the Italian fascist working-class syndicates. The Pact of Palazzo Vidoni had eliminated factory representatives, and the breaking apart of the industry-wide union structure in 1928 weakened the unions further. Yet by 1936, in the wake of the declaration of the empire after the invasion of Ethiopia, and at the height of Mussolini's personal popularity, the syndicates retook the initiative. The after-work organizations (*dopolavoro*) were removed from the party and given to the syndicates, and factory representatives were reestablished.[182]

The Italian fascist regime thus emerged as party fascism: a fascist state supported by a fascist movement that put the regime under continuous, if sporadic, pressure. Surrounding the ministerial bureaucracy of the old prefascist state, a group of parallel organizations emerged by the late twenties. This outcome was not the result of a predetermined drive toward totalitarianism pushed forward by Mussolini. On the contrary, the *duce* had initially tried to block the growth of fascism. The attempt to rule solely on the basis of the prefascist bureaucracy failed because certain segments of the fascist movement had entrenched themselves in civil society. Parts of the party and union apparatus had become the channel through which demands were placed on the state. In appeasing these sectors, Mussolini granted them a monopoly on interest representation. The fascist regime emerged out of a process of bargaining between the central bureaucracy and intransigent fascists.

Conclusion

Why did Italy consolidate in the interwar period as a party fascist regime? The main argument of this chapter has been that fascism was the consequence of rapid civil society development in the context of nonhegemonic politics. The initial hegemonic weakness within the Italian social elite undermined the development of interclass hegemony during the Giolittian period and the development of counterhegemony after World War I. The development of civil society, given this political context, led to a crisis of politics from which fascism emerged. It is worth briefly reprising the stages of this story here.

After unification, Italian social elites failed to develop strong political organizations. Instead, they remained a collection of locally rooted clienteles. This was partially the result of the specific way that Italy formed as a nation and partially the result of the workings of Italian liberal institutions. Unification was the result of diplomatic maneuvering and military imposition. In the south of the country, local elites experienced unification as occupation. The formal and informal restriction of political rights to the very privileged also paradoxically weakened the political organizations of the Italian dominant class. Because relations of patronage continued at the local level, parliament was filled with men tied to these groups. Transformism in parliament exacerbated this weakness, tending to dissolve strong political organizations among the social elite. The Italian social elite, consequently, lacked adequate organizations for articulating its own general interests, that is, intraclass hegemony.

The absence of intradominant class hegemony did not undermine the development of civil society. After the unification of Italy in 1871, despite restricted suffrage and the regionally based corruption of the electoral process, the Italian regime respected enough basic civil rights to allow for the rapid expansion of civil society, especially in the north of the country. These developments took place in two waves. First, up until the 1890s associational development was mostly under the control of the liberal elite. Large landholders, and even the monarchy, were instrumental in establishing the first day laborer cooperatives in the Valley of the Po. But liberal sponsorship had broken down by the 1890s, as the new organized mass movements of socialism and Catholicism took control of the associational movement. By the 1890s, then, an autonomous civil society had begun to emerge in Italy.

Associational development in Italy had important political consequences. By the turn of the century, the political class shifted from a concern with intraclass hegemony to focusing on the problem of interclass hegemony: a project most consistently championed by the Piedmontese prime minister Giovanni Giolitti. Giolitti was acutely aware of the political isolation of the liberal state, and his reformism aimed at redressing this problem. At the center of his efforts was a more liberal framework for civil society development. He refused to use the state police to put down strikes and actively sponsored agrarian socialism. Associational development was therefore very rapid during the period associated with his political dominance. The same cannot be said of the political organizations of the social elite. Despite his reformist policy, the Giolittian system maintained severe suffrage restrictions and regionally based electoral corruption. As a result the Giolittian period was characterized by a sharp contrast between the continuing political fragmentation of the social elite and the development of large organized currents of opinion aimed against this elite. The first mass party organizations in Italy were either hostile or indifferent to the liberal state. The fateful turn to imperialism after 1911 was connected with these developments, for the liberal political elite began to search for an alternative basis of popular legitimation in the absence of a strong party organization. This policy culminated in the disastrous decision to intervene in World War I, bringing inflation, debt, and a mass of returning veterans who were difficult to reintegrate into Italian society.

During the postwar period a new phase opened up, as a series of counterhegemonic movements emerged. Following the war, wide strata of the population supported the establishment of a democratic state, but no political force was able to articulate these basic aspirations. The new environment of mass politics disoriented the liberals. The socialists underwent a process of radicalization precisely during this period, while the PPI remained too isolated from the other democratic forces to lead them. I have emphasized that the fascist movement had an ambiguous relationship to this democratic wave. Its origins lay precisely in the mobilization following World War I as a movement of the left. Many of its principal figures also espoused ideas that were close to radical democratic critiques of the Giolittian system developed in the prewar years. National syndicalism was an ideology of civil society. Further, fascism was strongest organizationally in precisely those zones of Italy with the most-developed civil societies. The movement shifted to authoritarianism, and to the right, because of its inability to penetrate the socialist electorate and because of the pressing need among conservatives for an adequate political organization. Thus, as a consequence the specific path of political development in Italy, one characterized by a pervasive absence of hegemony, civil society development did not lead to a transition to mass democracy, but rather to fascism.

The presence of a mass Fascist Party had decisive consequences for the regime that emerged in the midtwenties. Mussolini in power proved to be a highly pragmatic figure. Much like Giolitti before him, he was willing to strike bargains with any organized group that would give him support. Much of his tactical maneuvering in the period immediately after the March on Rome was aimed at reestablishing the old Giolittian coalition of reformist socialism and the industrialists on a new authoritarian basis. This project proved impossible for two reasons: the continuing resistance of organized socialism and pressure from the Fascist Party and union organizations. Both socialist resistance and fascist mass pressure (with the two forming a paradoxical alliance in March of 1925) were made possible by a developed civil society not fully under the control of the social elite or the state. Mussolini ceded a political monopoly to the PNF because he could not co-opt the socialists and he could not simply eliminate his own political basis of support using the police. Had Italian civil society been less autonomous from elite and state control, a different outcome in Italy, even after the March on Rome, would have been certainly conceivable.

What are the broader lessons of this Italian story? There are two main ones worth pondering. The first concerns civil society, and the second hegemony. Civil society development in Italy was a key reason for the development of Italian fascism. Associations provided organizational resources to the fascists. Where civil society was underdeveloped, especially in the Italian south, fascism was generally slow to take hold. Furthermore, civil society development, in the Italian context, promoted an antipolitical ideology that was a central doctrinal element in mature fascism. Italian fascism attacked liberal political institutions, such as parties and parliaments, as artificial obstacles to a spontaneous national consensus produced by the disposition to associate. Fascist corporatism embodied this view by attempting to eliminate political representation in favor of functional representation.

The connection between associationism and fascism in Italy, however, raises an important question. Was there something specific about Italian civil society that predisposed it to providing support for fascism? The evidence I have presented suggests not. The Italian cooperative movement in particular was highly democratic and embodied a degree of local control that fits perfectly with the Tocquevillian model. Further, there is little evidence to suggest that Italian civil society suffered from unusually high levels of fragmentation, hierarchy, or exclusiveness. Fascism did not draw on "bonding" versus "bridging" social capital. Rather, it capitalized on precisely those democratic impulses that Tocquevillians praise. Indeed, national syndicalism was an ideology of civil society. The paradoxical consequences of Italian civil society development are therefore not best understood in terms of civil society itself. The problem was instead political. More specifically, Italy had never developed hegemonic politics: social struggle remained largely a set of conflicts among restricted interest groups, and not properly political conflict at all.

This suggests a more general set of conclusions about how political power should be understood. Italy's path to fascism shows that the balance of power among social groups and classes is not a simple zero-sum game. The political and ideological weakness of dominant classes does not translate into the strength of direct producers. Instead, the more dominant social groups make claims to rule in terms of a broader national interest transcending the particular interests of their group, the greater the likelihood that nondominant groups can articulate their counterclaims in national terms. Conversely the absence of hegemony among social elites can become a political handicap for precisely those forces struggling against them. Since the Italian dominant classes had never been able to establish their rule in terms of a national interest, the very idea of a national interest was unavailable as a tool for constructing a counterhegemonic bloc. The democratic opportunity of the postwar period was thus lost in a welter of incompatible projects. As it turned out, then, the absence of hegemony among the social elite led to an absence of counterhegemony among nonelites. The development of civil society, in a context that lacks a hegemonic politics is a fundamental danger for all social groups because it will tend to a general crisis of politics. This is the central lesson of Italian fascism.

Readers may find the argument development above overly deterministic. It may be worth emphasizing, then, two major historical turning points in the Italian story: the Giolittian period and the period immediately after World War I. The attentive reader will have noticed the centrality of the Giolittian experiment to this account of fascism. Fascism, I have argued, was a consequence of the process of rapid civil society development set off by the Giolittian turn. Can one imagine a different type of historical trajectory? Aside from the Giolittian path, which combined a more or less liberal attitude to popular movements in the north, while maintaining a regime of restricted suffrage and relying on southern deputies, two clear courses of action were open in 1900. One was a transition to a full democratic regime, the course proposed by the alliance of socialists, radicals, and republicans that had been instrumental in the liberal opening at the turn of the century. Universal suffrage granted at this point probably would have arrested the process of political fragmentation that occurred during the Giolittian period and may have strengthened the political organizations of the social elites sufficiently to have allowed them to face organized socialism and Catholicism. Alternatively, a more openly authoritarian strategy could have been pursued. This would have involved a strengthening of the monarchy and greater repression. This option probably would have eliminated both a fascist and a liberal democratic outcome in the interwar period, and for basically similar reasons. By imposing a full-scale police regime at this early date, the rapid growth of an oppositional civil society could have been avoided.

Instead, Giolitti combined these strategies by granting considerable civil and political rights for the north while continuing to rely on southern deputies to bolster his parliamentary majority. Although such a strategy could work in the short term, it undermined the development of a mass party organization guided by the social elite, while at the same time it unleashed civil society development. Giolitti's attempt to extend liberal hegemony, therefore, exacerbated the structural problems that he inherited. This particular combination of a liberal opening in the absence of a corresponding political opening is of great significance for the subsequent emergence of a party fascist regime in Italy. The Giolittian experience eliminated the possibility that liberals might be the beneficiaries of associational development.

The implication of the Giolittian experience is clear enough. Civil society development in the absence of adequate political reform is unlikely to produce a stable liberal democratic outcome. On the contrary, civil society development under these conditions is likely to promote antiliberal political movements. It is at least arguable that restricting associational development may be preferable to promoting it where appropriate political reform is impossible. This is simply another way of saying that the development of civil society and the development of hegemony are independent processes that have to be analyzed separately. Civil society development certainly promoted democracy in Italy, but it did not promote liberalism.

The historical options in Italy following the war were fundamentally open, although the options themselves were different from what they had been a decade and a half earlier. In the absence of a hegemony guided by the social elite, the socialists might have been able to establish a mass democracy in Italy, had they pursued a different alliance strategy. As Tasca has pointed out, however, the party abandoned its democratic program in favor of a revolutionary one precisely at the moment that the achievement of mass democracy was within its grasp. Instead of forming alliances with the broad spectrum of forces interested in establishing a functioning democracy, the PSI alienated these allies, particularly the returning veterans. This political misstep was not, of course, a purely "subjective" failure but had deep roots in the Giolittian period. The party's leadership had little national political perspective in the postwar period, in part because of the long experience of restricted suffrage. The extremely limited role the party played on the national stage encouraged both an unhealthy localism, described by Tasca as *campanilismo*, and a dangerous revolutionary adventurism. Both were to work to the detriment of Italian democracy in the postwar period.

The most general message, then, might be that politics matters. Italian civil society, especially by the post–World War I period, was not in any sense backward, at least not in those areas that were the decisive recruiting grounds for the Fascist Party. Actually the fascist project of authoritarian incorporation is inconceivable without a highly developed civil society. In Italy liberal institutions were associated with the rule of a narrow oligarchy, and the movements that grew out of the development of Italian civil society were, quite logically, antiliberal. The central question of the postwar period was, of course, whether this democratic but antiliberal thrust would take a rightist or a leftist form. The historical entanglement of socialism with the Giolittian system provides the answer, for the democratic demands of civil society in the postwar period could not be implemented through an alliance with a Socialist Party that had abandoned that movement at precisely the moment it had become a historical possibility.

3

Traditionalist Fascism

Spain, 1876–1945

Why did Spanish liberalism succumb to fascism, as opposed to developing as a mass democracy, and why did fascism in Spain assume a traditionalist form? The collapse of Spain's democracy in the thirties derived from causes analogous to those in Italy: namely, the failure to develop a hegemonic politics in the face of an associational boom. As in Italy weak intraclass hegemony among the dominant classes produced a weak interclass hegemony and finally a failure of counterhegemony. In the early thirties this generated a political crisis out of which a fascist response emerged, but the specific historical path that Spain followed to this similar outcome differed from Italy's. Although the early twentieth century was a period of rapid associational development in Spain, these associations remained under the control of landlords and capitalists. This gave Spanish social elites an organizational basis for maintaining mass support, despite the collapse of their explicitly political organizations in the early thirties. The fascist project in Spain thus relied on these organizations, not a newly minted mass party, as in Italy.

As in the Italian narrative, the analysis here traces the development of Spanish fascism through five stages. It begins by investigating intraclass hegemony in the period of the Restoration monarchy. Spanish liberal institutions consolidated during this regime, which arose in the aftermath of the radical First Republic. During the Restoration, narrow suffrage combined with regional differences to produce a dominant class split into local patron-client networks, as in Italy. This did not, however, undermine the development of civil society. Especially after 1885, the Spanish political order was open enough to allow for the development of associationism, particularly in the countryside. Yet this phenomenon remained under the control of social elites through the twin organizations of regional nationalism and Catholicism. Despite remaining under the control of the social elite, the development of civil society had important political consequences. It undermined the clientalistic politics of the Restoration and led to the search for interclass hegemony. The most consistent attempt to extend hegemony to non-elites took place during the Primo de Rivera regime. This military dictatorship only further weakened the Spanish social elite and laid the political foundations for the rise of Franco.

Intraclass Hegemony in Liberal Spain

The Spanish liberal regime emerged in 1876 out of the destruction of the revolutionary thrust of 1868. Its liberal institutions formed on the basis of restricted suffrage and rampant electoral corruption, while the clientalism of the Spanish political system fragmented the social elite, undermining intraclass hegemony. This would become a fateful weakness during the first decades of the twentieth century.

The two basic political groups or parties (the moderates and the progressives) that would contend for power throughout the nineteenth century emerged during the Carlist Wars. These groups represented "the two principle sections of the landed oligarchy, the wine and olive growers of the south and the wheat growers of the center."[1] Antonio Cánovas del Castillo (1828–1897), the conservative architect of the Restoration monarchy (1876–1923), stabilized the political system by establishing a mechanism through which the dynastic parties (the conservatives and the liberals, heirs of the progressives and the moderates) would regularly alternate in power without the intervention of the army, and also with limited input from the population. What historians have subsequently termed the Canovite system had two principle features: *caciquismo*, which might loosely be described as clientalism, and *el turno pacifico*, a system of party alternation. The parties operated as political machines, distributing benefits to *caciques* (local bigwigs),[2] who could then deliver votes. They alternated in power by striking bargains in Madrid, not through winning elections. Voting was managed by state employees and generally so corrupt that it played little role in determining who governed.[3]

During the late nineteenth century this system extended out from its original southern and agrarian basis in Andalusia to the smallholding areas of the north and the Basque Country.[4] Until the turn of the century the Liberal and Conservative parties formed relatively coherent blocks; and because of this the Canovite system worked.[5] Three factors undermined its coherence during the twentieth century: the emergence of an activist monarch who wanted to play a greater role in choosing his ministers, a generational change within the parties, and the decline of *caciquismo* in some urban areas.[6] But even after the collapse of *el turno*, political corruption—*caciquismo*—remained widespread in most of Spain. Tusell suggests that vote buying actually increased as the *el turno* broke down in Andalusia.[7] Thus a proliferation of personal patronage networks began to replace the unified parties that were the key to the Canovite system.[8] The only way out of this impasse was a full-scale attack on the *caciques*. As I show below, this required a degree of intradominant class cohesion that proved elusive.

The Spanish social elite, to conclude, was fragmented into rigid patron-client networks. It was therefore divided by bitter political infighting, but this political weakness did not undermine the development of associationism.

Civil Society and the Social Elite in Spain

Some regions of Spain, particularly Catalonia and Valencia, were part of the same Renaissance city-state culture that produced the dense civil society of north-central Italy. Catalonia had a surprisingly highly developed parliament (the Cortes) by the thirteenth century, and self-governing towns and communes were also common.[9] It is perhaps unsurprising that these Mediterranean regions, together with the smallholding districts in the north of the country were the places with the most-developed civil societies in the liberal period.

Spain in the 1880s suffered from increased competition for its agricultural products, and this tended to radicalize the rural population, as various agricultural interests tried to offload the costs of market integration. Intersecting with, and exacerbating, this economic crisis was a geopolitical catastrophe: the crushing defeat of the Spanish in the war of 1898. A wave of bread riots, tax protests, and strikes followed the defeat. In response to commercial crisis, class struggle, and military defeat, prominent leaders of the liberal state began to insist on the need to establish a wider popular base for the Restoration regime.[10]

These events, combined with the establishment of universal suffrage in 1890, promoted three main forms of associationism: socialist and republican associationism, regional nationalist associationism, and Catholic associationism. After 1885, during the first liberal turn, a rich texture of working-class and artisans' associations developed in many Spanish towns, including reading circles, recreational associations, electoral groups, unions, and hiring halls. Politically they were mercurial, blending republican, anarchist, federalist, and socialist ideas. The Partido Socialista Obrero Español (the Spanish Socialist Workers Party, or PSOE), established in 1879, was among the earliest socialist parties in Europe. Its membership increased from 6,000 in 1896 to 57,000 in 1904, and during the period from 1910 to 1912 the socialist union organization grew from 40,000 to 120,000 members. But these developments were restricted to urban areas, a fundamental limitation in a society where 51 percent of the population was still employed in agriculture in the twenties. Thirty-one percent of the socialist union organization's (the Unión General de Trabajadores, or UGT) affiliates were located in Madrid in 1902, and this had risen to 58 percent by 1908. Thus Spanish socialism remained confined to a few urban centers. Even in the cities the movement's strength was uneven. One of the most striking features of Spanish socialism is its failure to organize in Barcelona, by most accounts the most industrialized city in late nineteenth-century Spain. Republicanism also remained a marginal movement, confined to some southern cities and to Catalonia.[11]

Civil society development also took the form of regional nationalist movements. The Catalan Party, the Lliga Regionalista (Regionalist League), and its industrialist backers, sought to create a mass basis for the regionalist movement, largely by sponsoring associations. Catalonia had a long associational tradition. At the elite level there were societies for agricultural improvement promoting the use of fertilizers and organizations of large proprietors, such as the Federació Agrícola Catalana Balear (Agrarian Federation of Catalonia and the Balearics) and the Instituto Agrícola Catalán de San Isidro (Catalan Agrarian Institute of Saint Isidore). In addition there existed industrialists' organizations, such as the Foment del Treball Nacional (The Organization for the Promotion of National Work). At the nonelite level there were highly local organizations, many of which were converted confraternities, tax-paying organizations, or organizations for managing collective resources like water. As part of the broader regional nationalist mobilization discussed above, the elite organizations began to sponsor associations of small property owners in order to support regional nationalism. They also sponsored an organization called the Liga Agraria (Agrarian League), which established a network of agrarian chambers lobbying the state to reduce railway fees and impose tariffs in the name of "agrarian" interests. Unlike socialism or democratic Catholicism in Italy, these Catalan nationalist organizations espoused conservative doctrines of class collaboration.[12]

The most distinctive feature of civil society development in late nineteenth-century Spain was social Catholicism. Spanish Catholicism was at the service of political and social power. Even during the turbulent years of the nineteenth century, Spain was always an officially Catholic country. The constitution of 1876 reinforced this relationship, declaring Catholicism the state religion and guaranteeing episcopal representation in the senate. The state paid for the upkeep of church buildings and the clergy, and all education had to accord with Catholic doctrine.[13] The church was also responsible for virtually all of the meager welfare provisions and schools of late nineteenth-century Spain.[14] This may explain the major boom in the religious orders during the late nineteenth century. According to the census the number of people involved in male religious orders grew from 683 in 1860 to 10,745 by 1901. The total number of religious houses grew from 1,188 in 1888 to 4,470 by 1923.[15]

The Spanish church of the nineteenth century was also closely connected to the social elite. Church organizations, stripped of resources of their own during the process of land privatization in the nineteenth century, allied closely with the wealthy and turned toward charity and social assistance.[16] With the arrival of universal suffrage in 1890, this alliance solidified further. Socialists and republicans were beginning politically to penetrate the countryside and threaten the agrarian oligarchs. In response landowners began to promote Catholic associations.[17]

The main protagonist of this movement initially was the Castilian Jesuit Antonio Vincent (1837–1912). In the 1890s Vincent established a series of Catholic workers' circles in Valencia. Headed by an unelected central council, each circle had a patron saint whose leadership organized spiritual exercises and communions and struggled against blasphemy. Economically these organizations restricted themselves to mutual aid provided in money and in kind and abstained from bargaining or strike activities.[18] In an attempt to spread the model of the workers' circles, Vincent held regional and "diocesan" assemblies in the early years of the twentieth century. Garrido Herrero describes them this way: "They all must have been very similar. The bishop convoked the rectors and some of the 'principle' agriculturalists to a cycle of lectures given—almost always—by father Vincent. The Jesuit explained to them what agrarian syndicates were and proposed a model statute to them. During the following months the foundations would proliferate through the dioceses."[19] Unlike craft or trade unions, the primary purpose of father Vincent's circles was to "remediate the apostasy of the masses."[20] The model of interclassist and religious associationism seems to have done well in the countryside, where it led to the emergence of a vast network of Catholic rural organizations. These developed in two waves during the first two decades of the twentieth century. First, there was the emergence of the *cajas rurales* (rural banks). Then, beginning around 1904, the *sindicatos agrícolas* (agrarian unions) movement developed.[21]

A central purpose of both these organizations was to provide credit to renters and day laborers. These would then form a stratum of conservative small proprietors. The *cajas* drew on their members' small contributions to finance their activities.[22] But local elites were often behind their development as well. In Zamora the landowner Luis Chaves Arias was important. In Murcia an official from the Ministry of Finance, Francisco Rivas Morean was key. In Navarre the parish priest Victoriano Flamarique was the primary organizer. In Plasencia a sociologist, Polo Benito, established the first institution.[23]

The *sindicatos agrícolas*, which developed out of the *cajas*, were cooperative organizations that helped with marketing agricultural products and allowed their members to buy food and equipment at low cost. They sought to preserve an agrarian "community" against the threat of market penetration and urbanization. Their members were owners, small proprietors, and workers who came together under the aegis of a priest.[24] Often they were highly moralistic, refusing loans to members who had been seen drinking, and were supposed to embody Catholic doctrines of class collaboration and morality.[25]

Given the characteristics of Catholic associationism, it is not surprising that conservatives such as Eduardo Dato Iradier (1856–1921) and Antonio Maura (1853–1925) were eager to promote it. In 1904 Maura proposed a law, subsequently passed in 1909, exempting agrarian associations from paying taxes if they regis-tered as an agrarian syndicate with the civil governor. Progressive governments (i.e., the left wing of the *el turno*) routinely rejected their approval on the grounds that the organizations were too Catholic, and insisted on strict legislation to ensure that the associations were not overtly religious. The *sindicatos agrícolas*, then, were not really autonomous voluntary organizations; instead, they devel-oped as part of a specific political strategy promoted especially by the landed elite for dealing with rural unrest.[26] The state, in contrast to the landowners, was mostly absent from this process. In Spain in 1918 the national bank provided loans to only 197 syndicates—under 6 percent of all cooperatives.[27] In short, civil society development in Spain was driven directly by social elites, and par-ticularly by the agrarians.

The agrarian syndicates were the organizational backbone of political Cathol-icism as well. Although prior to the Second Republic there was no Catholic political party, the syndicates acted as a pressure group on the conservatives. In 1917 the Confederación Nacional Católico Agraria (National Catholic Agrarian Con-federation, or CNCA), including eighteen regional federations, formed in Madrid. The organization had two main leaders, a large Castilian proprietor named Anto-nio Monedero Martín, and a Jesuit priest, Sisinio Nevares. The local leadership positions were also always reserved for the large proprietors.[28]

These organizations tended to solidify the political control of the southern agrarian elite over northern smallholders. The minutes of meetings studied by Samuel Garrido Herrero contain notations describing the "expulsion of those members who fought in the last election the candidate supported by this syndi-cate."[29] Father Vincent himself emphasized the "obligation that everyone has to take part in the elections, giving our vote to the Catholic candidates."[30] In some cases syndicates expelled members for expressing views contrary to religion, or their loans were revoked.[31]

Catholic associationism expanded in two periods in the early twentieth cen-tury: from 1906 to 1910 and from 1916 to 1922.[32] The late twenties generally seem to have been a period of stagnation for the agrarian cooperative movement. How-ever, by 1933 according to official statistics there were 4,266 agrarian syndicates in Spain.[33]

How can the development of civil society in late nineteenth-century Spain be summarized? The expansion of political rights, the agrarian crisis, and military defeat combined to produce the beginnings of a civil society in rural Spain. Voluntary associations increased during the first two decades of the twentieth century because of the agrarian depression, which encouraged organization and the initial spread of republican and socialist political organizations to the countryside. But Spain's social elite remained mostly in control of this process through two important organizational frameworks: the Catholic Church and regional nationalism. The *sindicatos agrícolas* in northern Spain provided credit as well as market and consumer services, while at the same time reenforcing the political dominance of the landed elite. Within Catalonia, nationalist organizations closely linked to industrialists and agrarians predominated. Thus an elite-dominated form of civil society emerged here. As I argue below, this specific path of civil society development provided fundamental organizational resources to the social elite and had important consequences for Spain's subsequent political development.

Interclass Hegemony

As associationism developed in Spain, the fragility of the Canovite political system became more evident. Spanish politicians were deeply aware of their growing political isolation. In response, top political leaders attempted to reform the Canovite system from within to provide it with greater popular support. There were three main attempts: one under Antonio Maura (1853–1925), one under José Canalejas (1854–1912), and one under Francesc Cambó (1876–1947).[34] The failure of these men to break the back of the *cacique* system, in the context of the increasingly organized civil society described above, laid the ground for the rise of Spain's first twentieth-century dictator, Miguel Primo de Rivera (1870–1930).

Antonio Maura attempted to reform the political system between 1907 and 1909 by imposing obligatory voting, reforming the electoral lists, and decentralizing government. Maura's project might have succeeded had it not been for Spain's military involvement in Morocco. A call-up of reservists in July of 1909 from Catalonia to fight in the North African colony sparked a mixed anticlerical and regional revolt that the Madrid government bloodily suppressed. The event, Semaña Tragica (Tragic Week), had major political consequences. In response to the bloodshed, the liberals in parliament demanded Maura's resignation.

Segismundo Moret (1838–1913), their leader, now formed a block of the left. These events broke the already strained alliance at the national level between the Catalan regionalists and the conservatives, and undermined relations between the liberals and the conservatives themselves. The monarchy was forced to take a more active role in forming governments, since worsening relations among deputies made the agreements on which *el turno* was based impossible.[35] This ended the conservative attempt at reform.

José Canalejas pursued the second attempt to reform the Canovite system from within in the period from 1909 to 1912. Reversing the Maura policy of repression that had developed after Tragic Week, Canalejas pursued anticlericalism and reestablished relations with the Catalan bourgeoisie; this was a more progressive version of Maura's revolution from above. But if Maura's attempt lacked a solid connection with the Catalanists because of his links to Castilian centralism and big landholders, Canalejas's project was undermined in the opposite direction: it lacked the vital social support of aristocrats in Madrid. As was true of Maura, then, Canalejas proved unable to solidify an alliance between the main landholding and capitalist groups to pursue a project of modernization from above.[36]

The third reform attempt was the most ambitious, and probably had the best chance of succeeding. During World War I (1914–1918) both republicans and socialists mobilized for intervention, and after the bolshevik seizure of power the mass base of both the socialists and the anarchists began to expand and radicalize.[37] The Catalan regionalist leader Francesc Cambó attempted to exploit these variegated currents of unrest to force the convention of a constituent assembly that would establish a more advanced democratic state. Catalan regionalists dominated the assembly movement, but it also included political representatives of Asturian and Basque heavy industry, the PSOE, and elements of the army.[38] As Boyd remarks, this was an "attempt at bourgeois revolution."[39] Cambó's goal was to remove, or at least weaken, the landed oligarchy in Madrid.[40] The assembly movement, however, suffered from the same intrinsic weakness as the conservative and liberal attempts at reform described above. It was unable to bridge the political gap separating the Catalan and Castilian social elite. Perhaps the most crucial weakness was the absence of any alliance with the Maurist conservatives who formally shared many of the movement's aims. Only by forming an alliance with this group could Cambó plausibly present himself as leading a national, rather than regional, movement. But there were other weaknesses as well. The military *juntas* were important but unreliable allies because their demands had to do with pay, and they could easily be peeled off from a coalition that appeared both too regionalist and too socialist for many military men. Finally, the Regionalist League that Cambó headed was itself committed to expanding democracy only to the extent that this was compatible with the economic interests of the textile producers.

Thus, it is not surprising that, at the first sign of a threat from below, the assembly movement collapsed. The precipitating event was a socialist-led general strike supported by the anarchist Confederación National del Trabajo (CNT), which broke out in response to the refusal of a railway firm to rehire a hundred striking workers in August 1917.[41] In response to this movement, the monarchy came to terms with the army,[42] met the demands of the military reformers, and then crushed the socialist-anarchist alliance.[43] The Regionalist League also beat a hasty retreat, as its members now realigned with the oligarchy, joining the very conservative Maura government.[44] These men sought once again to establish some regional autonomy for Catalonia. Their project, however, was undermined by the increasingly powerful anarchist CNT, which claimed to have a national membership of 714,028 at the end of 1919.

The Maura, Canalejas, and Cambó episodes can each be understood as attempts to construct interclass hegemony for the Spanish social elite. These were all attempts to articulate a national project capable of establishing some mass support for the liberal state. For specific historical reasons each of these attempts failed. But there was a broader structural issue as well. In each case the fragmentation of the social elite undermined the reformist project. Thus, both the Regionalist League's regional nationalism, and liberal anticlericalism antagonized the conservatives. Similarly, the mixture of political Catholicism and centralism, which allowed Maura to win some support, tended to alienate the Catalans and the liberals. These episodes show how the failure of intradominant class hegemony undermined the project of interclass hegemony as well, for the ideological and organizational forms in which interclass hegemony was most possible tended to exacerbate intradominant class conflict. With the failure of these attempts, a new model of political incorporation emerged, which would only further fragment and weaken the social elite.

The Military in Morocco

As the civilian politicians lost credibility through failed reform attempts, the army gained wider autonomy to conduct foreign policy and was increasingly seen as a potential vehicle for reform. The final crisis of the Canovite system was set off by an unsuccessful offensive in the Moroccan interior pushed for by the army itself. In 1920 an ambitious general named Manuel Fernández Silvestre (1871–1921) drove deep into the interior, where his overextended supply lines and unreliable troops were easy prey for the forces of Muhammed Abd al-Karim (1882–1963), the Spanish-educated leader of the Moroccan resistance.[45] Abd al-Karim smashed the Spanish in a counteroffensive that lasted through much of July 1921 and painfully underlined the weakness of the military.[46]

The struggle over "responsibilities" (i.e., to determine who was at fault in the disaster) quickly became a crisis from which the Canovite regime could not recover. The conservatives attempted to bury the issue, prohibiting its debate in the Cortes, while the liberals concentrated their fire on the generals, thereby alienating the army from the parliamentary regime and further consolidating its corporate identity. The crisis also left the monarchy deeply exposed, for it was heavily implicated in the military disaster. The king responded by establishing a government of "national concentration," including heads of all the main liberal and conservative factions. He also insisted on placing two top Africanista generals in the chamber (González-Tablas and Millán-Astray). This failed to produce a reasonably strong civil government. Indeed, the last Maura government disintegrated because of its inability to agree on a Moroccan policy.[47]

The Rise of Praetorianism in Barcelona

After the failure of the Moroccan policy, and in the face of the growing strength of anarchism in Barcelona, the Canovite regime was effectively dead. In Catalonia a new political order began to emerge from 1920 to 1923 under the rule of the civil governor Severiano Martínez Anido (1862–1938), which would extend to the whole of the peninsula after 1923. Not content to rely entirely on the army, Martínez Anido formed relations with a right-wing paramilitary organization called the Somatén, committed to the defense of social order and led mostly by very wealthy men. He also formed close relations with an ultra-right-wing union organization called the Sindicatos Libres (Free Trade Unions), which bore some resemblance to Italian fascist unions.[48] The Somatén were initially popular militia organizations that grew out of *hermandades* (brotherhoods): organizations of neighbors that had developed in the Middle Ages to protect life and property from the predations of brigands and feudal lords. In the aftermath of the collapse of the assembly movement, many Catalan property owners and their allies thought of reorganizing the militia as a civilian police force and strike-breaking squad.[49] This transformation, from popular militia to armed guard closely connected to the Catalan business community, was completed in 1919. In that year the militia achieved the status of a *guardia civil* during a general strike related to a dispute at an electrical company called La Canadiense (the Canadian).[50]

The newly organized Somatén had three levels: districts, neighborhoods, and blocks. At each, a boss was responsible for transmitting orders from the army to the membership. There were three classes of members: those who were charged with defending the street from their houses, those charged with defending vital strategic points in the neighborhood, and finally the flying squads, who could be used for attack or to reinforce key areas.[51]

The militias did not engage only in police operations. They delivered mail, cleared tram car tracks, supplied stores and supermarkets with goods, and generally tried to keep urban life going during any possible general strike.[52] It is unsurprising, then, that many descriptions of the Somatén emphasize their selfless civic activism. For example, one of the founding members of the Madrid organization, which emerged as a copy of its Catalan counterpart, argued that "just as, as citizens it is incumbent on us to serve the military to defend the fatherland from external enemies, so as members of civil society, the condition 'sin qua non' for individual and collective well-being, all of us have the obligation ... for civil service to maintain peace, prosperity, and life, and in sum, all of the foundations of the social order and economic equilibrium against internal enemies."[53] The Somatén, however, was not a political organization, in the sense that it did not engage in electoral politics. Although closely linked to the Catalan Regionalist League, it included men from most of the conservative political parties in Catalonia.[54]

The main purpose of the organization, aside from providing an auxiliary force for maintaining order during a general strike, was the inculcation of Catholic values. Members of the Somatén dedicated themselves to the Virgin of Montserrat, "traditional patron of the armed Somatén of Catalonia, and one of their public acts was ... open-air mass."[55] Félix Sánchez, a member of the organization, wrote a brief "catechism of the Somatén," summarizing its aims: "In the religious order we must be the example of morality in our words and our acts; in the political order we must be the defenders of the civil rights of good citizens, and in the social order, we must be the mirrors of goodness, being faithful advisors of those who ... claim to seize rights that do not belong to them."[56] The Somatén was a traditionalist organization. Its members did not aim at a political order beyond liberal democracy, but rather a return to regional autonomy, corporatist representation, and Catholicism.

During the late teens and early twenties, local Somatén sprang up across Spain. The large landholders' association called the Asociación de Agricultores de España (the Association of Spanish Agriculturalists), and particularly one of its leading members the Vizconde Val de Erro, who was both a major landowner and a military figure, actively promoted this nationalization. Val de Erro encouraged the extension of the Somatén into the countryside. The agrarian association agreed to adopt the statute of the Catalan organization as a model and was thus a major force in extending this organizational form. Although the project of establishing a national organization failed, in part because of the reluctance of the civilian government to strengthen the military, the association was able to promote the development of Somatén in Madrid, Valencia, Alicante, Mallorca, Jaén, Málaga, Granada, and Zaragoza.[57]

The difficulties that the Somatén faced are instructive. Reports to the Ministry of the Interior indicate that "apathy, dispersion, and *caciquismo* were the main impediments to the development of the Somatén in *Santa Cruz de Tenerife*."[58] In areas of strong *cacique* domination such as Guadalajara and Gallegos the Somatén was weak as well. And, "in Andalusia, *caciquismo*—above all in the small villages—was a fundamental permanent obstacle to the development of the Somatén, which never reached 16,000 members in the entire second military region."[59] Clientalism and corruption appears to have been the main obstacle to the expansion of the Somatén, which was most well established in Catalonia, Old Castile, and the Basque Country, and weakest in Andalusia and Extremedura.[60]

This distribution maps closely onto civil society development in liberal Spain. Associational development was concentrated in certain regions: primarily in northern and eastern Spain. Table 3 draws on three associational censuses to demonstrate this regional variation: one on workers' associations conducted

Table 3 Regional Variation in Civil Society in Spain (in number per 100,000)

Region	Associations in 1928	Workers' associations in 1904	Workers' associations in 1913	Bosses' associations in 1913	Mixed associations in 1913	Nonprofessional associations in 1913
Galicia	8	4	34	17	1	5
León	9	6	18	25	1	21
Aragon	10	4	15	46	2	18
Andalusia	10	8	26	13	1	5
Asturias	10	7	41	34	2	3
Murcia	11	4	29	21	1	11
Extremadura	12	8	11	19	1	10
New Castile	16	11	28	22	2	13
Catalonia	25	23	49	45	3	96
Valencia	26	13	44	40	5	21
Basque Country	28	20	82	47	4	33
Old Castile	29	10	30	52	4	13
Navarre	44	7	16	64	4	9

Sources: Instituto de Reformas Sociales 1915, 1907; Ministerio de Trabajo y Previsión 1930.

in 1904 and two later general associational censuses (one from 1913 and one from 1928). The first column presents evidence for all associations from the 1928 census. The table can be summarized by counting the number of times that any particular region falls within the top five regions in terms of the indicators provided. Catalonia and the Basque Country were both in the top five provinces on all six indicators of civil society. Valencia was among the top five provinces in terms of five of the six indicators, and in terms of the number of bosses' associations per 100,000 persons in 1913, this province ranked sixth. Old Castile was in the top five regions on four of the six indicators, Navarre was in the top five on three of the six indicators. According to this criterion Catalonia, Valencia, the Basque Country, Old Castile, and Navarre were the regions with the strongest civil societies in early twentieth-century Spain. The stronghold of the Somatén was in Catalonia, as I argued above. The organization failed to take hold of the latifundia zones of the south. These paramilitary organizations, therefore, did best where civil society was the most developed and did worst where associationism was least in evidence.

The second form of organized support for the new praetorian order that developed in Barcelona in the twenties was among the working class. On the fringes of social Catholicism, a group of ex-Carlist traditionalists founded a movement in October of 1919 called the Sindicatos Libres, or "free syndicates." The first meeting of the organization was in the Ateneo Obrero Legitimista, a Carlist workers' association. Unlike the older Catholic unions that were common in Catalonia prior to World War I, the Sindicatos Libres were heavily "workerist," having no formal relationship to the church hierarchy and espousing a sometimes quite radical social doctrine.[61] Initially, these organizations found willing sponsors among Barcelona's industrial elite because they were able to confront the anarchist action squads.[62] Their relationship with the employers, however, began to shift during Martínez Anido's tenure as civil governor, as they became more directly linked to the state. The civil governor used the Libres as a parapolice force.[63] Further, the blanket repression of the CNT gave the Libres a political opening because they were the only functioning working-class organization. Thus, precisely as a consequence of Martínez Anido's repressive regime, the numbers of the Libres expanded to around 175,000 members.[64]

The Martínez Anido regime was clearly connected to a failed democratic breakthrough. The inability of the civilian political parties to incorporate newly mobilized popular forces led the Catalan elite to support a military solution, a model that was then generalized to the peninsula as a whole after the coup of Miguel Primo de Rivera.

The Primo de Rivera Period (1923–1931):
The Destruction of the Dynastic Parties

Unrest in Barcelona quickly resumed after Martínez Anido's departure in 1922. Already by February of 1923 the CNT was beginning to reorganize, a process that would culminate in a major transport strike in May. This coincided with a period of complete breakdown in civilian government at the local level. Miguel Primo de Rivera emerged as a major political figure in this vacuum of authority, becoming the local military commander of Barcelona in March of 1923. He established himself as a compromise figure, receiving delegations of workers and bosses and seeking to arbitrate the transport strike.[65] The political and social unrest of Barcelona in the early twenties had an enormous impact on him. During 1920 he had moved close to Martínez Anido's position that anarchism must be confronted militarily. His arrival in Barcelona only confirmed this view. But he was not closely linked to either the paramilitary Somatén or the Libres, the organizations that formed Martínez Anido's main bases of support. In fact, the general's seizure of power, which occurred in September of 1923, did not depend on the mobilization of civilian support at all.[66] To rule, Primo de Rivera sought to establish a broad social coalition aimed against the established party system.[67]

Primo de Rivera's dictatorship divides into two main periods. From September 1923 to December 1925, the dictator ruled through a military directorate that attempted to use the army to destroy *caciquismo*. From December of 1925 to September of 1930, a new, civilian directorate emerged and the dictator made a number of efforts to expand the popular basis of the regime. These two policies shattered the preexisting organizations of the social elite, while at the same time strengthening socialism and republicanism. In a sense, Primo de Rivera succeeded where Maura, Canalejas, and Cambó had failed, unintentionally laying the political foundations of the Second Republic.[68]

The directorate's first significant act was a purge of the civil governors: local civilian authorities who had been appointed by royal decree under the Canovite system. Written in the manifesto accompanying Primo de Rivera's coup was a statement dismissing all incumbent civil governors and replacing them with military men.[69] This reform broke the close connection between the civil governor and the dynastic parties, for civil governorships were generally considered patronage posts for the parties. The new men who occupied these positions after Primo de Rivera's seizure of power tended instead to be career military figures from outside the province and without clear political commitments or links to the local power structures over which they now presided.[70]

Reinforcing this transformation at the provincial level was an all-out attack on the municipal governments. In October of 1923 over 9,000 local municipal governments were dissolved and placed under the control of *delegados gubernativos* (governing delegates), military figures who acted as local petty despots charged with rooting out corruption. The basic mechanism on which these men relied was denunciation, anonymous complaints against officials in the local administration. In Málaga, for example, the *delegado gubernativo* established an office of complaints on November 2, 1923, that received 250 written denunciations in a single day.[71]

The *delegados gubernativos* were also entrusted with the moral regeneration of the people. For example, the military directory sent to all the *delegados* a pamphlet directing them to promote the teaching of gymnastics, the cultivation of rabbits, and the encouragement of personal hygiene. One *delegado* forbade cruelty to animals, prohibited littering, and stipulated norms for the correct way for people to greet one another in the street.[72] All of this was part of a broader project to eliminate the basis of the old politics.[73]

Paradoxically for such a conservative figure, Primo de Rivera thus presided over the destruction of the organizational bases of the Canovite system. He concentrated his attacks on the dynastic parties, assaulting their leaders in official notes, prohibiting them from holding positions in public companies, and removing their names from street signs. Many of the most significant party leaders retired to a private existence under these conditions. Their previous clients scattered, joining either the Unión Patriótica (UP), the state party discussed more fully below, or the republicans. The parties that had governed Spain for fifty years collapsed under this pressure.[74]

Regime elites attempted to replace these organizations with nonpolitical interest groups of the most varied kind. There was, consequently, significant associational development in Primo de Rivera's Spain, but it occurred only outside the framework of the discredited, fragmented, and powerless dynastic parties. Middle-class associationism expanded in the late twenties and early thirties.[75] Some of these organizations, like rifle clubs, the boy scouts, and exploring societies, were apolitical. Others were oppositional. According to newspaper accounts, 450 mostly middle-class, republican clubs existed in 1926.[76]

The directorate proved itself utterly incapable of creating an adequate party to channel these organizations in support of the dictatorship. Instead, clientalism reemerged in the regime organizations: the state party Unión Patriótica, the Somatén, the *comités paritarios* (abritration boards), and the corporative parliament. Far from building an adequate political organization for the social elite, the dictatorship tended to fragment and weaken the very interests on which the uprising was initially based.[77]

The leaders of the UP in the northern and eastern provinces were mostly men from Catholic political organizations who had not been part of the political system previously. In the southern provinces presidents or vice presidents of the local branch of the UP were former senators or deputies of the conservative or liberal parties from the *el turno*. In other regions Primo de Rivera relied on "new men," but these simply became new bosses.[78]

The failure of the UP to incorporate Catalan industry was perhaps the most striking political weakness of the regime. Catalan industrialists provided Primo de Rivera's coup with decisive social support, which he handsomely repaid by channeling state funds to shipping, railroads, and hydroelectric power and by granting a state monopoly to airway traffic and the extermination of rats. The famous merchant-adventurer Juan March (1880–1962) was granted a monopoly over selling tobacco products. The crowning achievement of these policies was the nationalization of the petroleum industry. This direct state largess was buttressed by stiff import tariffs on agricultural machinery and sulfates (used for fertilizer) and export tariffs on agricultural products. However, the Catalans were never politically incorporated into the regime, because they resisted joining the UP. They remained instead a powerful corporate pressure group.[79]

Paradoxically, the consequences of the Primoverrista dictatorship for the working class was somewhat more positive. Labor policy was based on a twin strategy of repression and incorporation. The repressive wing, controlled by Martínez Anido in the Ministry of the Interior, was aimed overwhelmingly at anarchist and communist militants. The incorporationist wing of the regime, institutionally based in the ministries of Development, Treasury, and Labor, sought to establish a productivist bloc based on an alliance between industry and the reformist unions. The difference between the two sides of the regime was evident in the response to a wave of strikes that broke out in 1925. Disturbances headed by leaders of the CNT (the anarchist union federation) were the responsibility of Martínez Anido and thus were dealt with as a matter of public order. By contrast, those led by the UGT were resolved through collective bargaining.[80]

The man responsible for orchestrating the incorporationist strategy under Primo de Rivera's regime, Eduardo Aunós (1894–1967), was directly influenced by Italian corporatism. Aunós's policy, however, contained a strongly democratic and pro–working class element, maintained the integrity of working-class voluntary organizations, and preserved the right to strike. A royal decree of November 1926 established twenty-seven corporations: one for each branch of production. Within each, the heart of the system consisted of arbitration boards called *comités paritarios*, including representatives of both workers and owners and headed by a state-appointed president and vice president. The representatives to these boards were elected by voluntary organizations that maintained their autonomy outside the corporative structure. Thus, while membership in the corporatist organizations was obligatory, true voluntary organizations existed within them. Aunós wanted the corporations to develop into classless "producers' syndicates." Yet in practice they favored the socialists. Industrialists sharply criticized this system of labor organization, calling Aunós the "white Lenin."[81]

All of this had the effect of strengthening the UGT. During 1924 a mutual accommodation began to develop between the socialist unions and the regime. Socialists had leading positions in the councils of state, in the national institute of social security, and it was socialists who led the Spanish delegation to the International Labor Organization in Geneva. Socialist organizations were decisively favored by Primo de Rivera's brand of corporatism.[82]

The socialists took advantage of this benevolent environment. From September of 1922 to December of 1930, the number of members organized by the UGT increased from 208,170 to 277,011. This gradual expansion was followed by explosive growth as the regime collapsed between December 1930 and December 1931. The new rural socialist federation, the Federación Nacional de Trabajodores de la Tierra, or FNTT, drove this growth. The rural federation expanded from 147 unions with 27,340 members in April of 1930 to 3,319 sections with 451,337 members in June of 1933, thus becoming the largest federation within the UGT.[83] Over the decade from 1922 to 1932, the total number of UGT locals grew from 1,198 with 208,170 members to 5,107 with 1,041,539 members. As I emphasized above, the PSOE-UGT prior to the midtwenties had little organized presence in the countryside, leaving most agrarian organizing to the anarchist CNT. The restriction to a few skilled trades in urban areas was the sociological basis of moderate socialism. The influx of the rural proletariat into the Socialist Party through the FNTT put sharp pressure on the moderate leadership.[84]

The development of the Catholic and conservative agrarian syndicates was paradoxically much less impressive during the Primo de Rivera period. From 1919 to 1929, according to official statistics, the number of agrarian syndicates fell from 4,451 to 2,276 and the number of members collapsed from half a million to approximately 200,000. But their organizations survived, and many of the leaders of the regime at the local level came from this milieu.[85] One of the striking paradoxes of the dictatorship, then, was its promotion of socialism combined with its failure to establish adequate political organizations for the social elite. This failure becomes clearer when one examines the pattern of interest representation that developed in the late twenties.

The task of converting Primo de Rivera's *pronunciamiento* into a regime fell to an institution called the Asamblea Nacional Consultiva (National Consultative Assembly). This corporative parliament was to propose a new constitution, replacing the 1876 settlement. The king, Alfonso XIII de Borbón (1886–1941), was deeply resistant to it, since he saw any alteration of the Canovite constitution as a threat to his authority. At the dictator's insistence, however, the decree establishing the assembly was issued in September 1927.[86] The assembly embodied a conception of interest representation similar to the arbitration boards described above. As in the case of these organizations, the national consultative assembly combined a commitment to corporatist representation with the preservation of freedom of association.[87]

Representatives to the National Assembly were divided into three groups: the UP delegation, representatives of "activities, classes, and values," and representatives of the state. Under each of these headings, different rules governed their selection. Representatives of local government, in addition to ex officio representatives from the bureaucracy, made up the category of state representatives. The representatives of municipalities were chosen from mayors and provincial councils by the provincial governments, who themselves had been appointed by the dictatorship. Provincial representatives were elected from the provincial deputations. In addition there were ex officio members from the army, the church, and the administration as well as a group of dignitaries appointed by the government. The party delegation was comprised of the provincial party heads of the UP. The government also appointed the representatives of activities from among corporations, cultural institutions, royal academies, and educational institutions.[88]

The Primo de Rivera period, in sum, is best understood as a failed attempt to establish interclass hegemony, one connected to the prior history of the Restoration monarchy, which had failed to produced a cohesive dominant class: intraclass hegemony. Much as Giolitti's policies in Italy depended on a tactical alliance with forces hostile to the liberal state, so Primo de Rivera's dictatorship rested on the external support of the socialist union organizations. In addition, the Primoverrista regime systematically dismantled the existing political organizations of Spain's dominant classes. During the twenties industrialists and landowners reverted to pursuing their interests in a direct "economic-corporate" fashion and abandoned politics altogether. This pattern of organized interests left a heavy negative legacy for the Second Republic.

Counterhegemony in the Second Republic

The collapse of the political organizations of Spain's dominant classes in the late twenties was dramatic. It produced a democratic opening exploited by a coalition of socialists and republicans that culminated in the Second Republic, by far the most politically democratic regime in Spanish history up until that point. Yet the weakness of Spain's social elite turned out to be a serious handicap for the country's prospects for a stable liberal democracy. First, the absence of a consolidated right produced a corresponding fragmentation and inconstancy on the left. At the same time it led to a dangerous withdrawal from politics among the traditionalist sectors of the north and center of the country. These weaknesses would lead to the collapse of the Second Republic.

The Transition to the Republic (1930–1931)

The Primo de Rivera regime collapsed because of a defection of the social elite, not because of a mass movement from below. The poorer regions in the south and the industrial northeast were both relatively immune from unrest. Indeed, the Socialist Party and union organizations were the last major groups to withdraw their support from the regime. It was precisely the interests that had initially backed the coup that brought the regime to an end.[89]

Weighty economic interests moved into opposition by the late twenties. Although many industrialists benefited from expenditures on public works, the dictatorship's protectionist policies were quite unpopular with agrarians. Wheat, olive, and orange producers who benefited from inexpensive imported fertilizers and open foreign markets found the dictatorship excessively oriented to industry. In 1928 the Confederacíon Gremial Española, a small shopkeepers' organization that had initially been attracted to the regime's policy of order and peace, withdrew its support. Even the very industrialists who had initially benefited from public works reinforced this free trade bloc, moving against the regime. By early 1929 the social backbone of the dictatorship, Catalan industrialists, moved into opposition, prompted both by Eduardo Aunós's social policy and the collapsing value of the peseta. This increasing lack of political confidence in the regime's deficit-financed development project was one of the main causes of a damaging flight from the peseta that began in early 1928. In 1929 a special committee of experts assembled to address the problem. It insisted that a reduction of public expenditure was inevitable.[90]

After the collapse of Primo de Rivera's dictatorship, an interim military government under general Dámaso Berenguer (1873–1953) took up the reins of power. The king tasked him with returning the country to the *el turno* system: a difficult proposition, because Primo de Rivera's all-out attack on it, especially on the Liberal Party, had undermined the foundations of Spanish constitutional government. Nevertheless, the general's strategy was to call elections that could be safely managed to produce a conservative government capable of guiding the country back to normality, defined as a return to *el turno.* The various republican groups that had emerged during the dictatorship firmly resisted this move, first through a failed insurrection and then by orchestrating a boycott of the elections. After the abstention campaign a return to the Canovite system was impossible. A colorless coalition government led by Admiral Juan Bautista Aznar (1860–1933) presided over municipal elections on April 12, 1931, the results of which constituted a plebiscite for the republic and forced Alfonso XIII's resignation.[91]

The collapse of the dictatorship, together with the destruction of the Spanish party system, left a fragmented political landscape. The republicans, made up of myriad groups, occupied a broad centrist ground. On the left stood the Republican Action Party and the Radical Socialist Republican Party. These were groups committed to an extensive program of economic and social reform. In the center were the historical republicans gathered around Alejandro Lerroux in the Radical Party. To the right was the Liberal Republican Right, led by Miguel Maura and Niceto Alcalá-Zamora (1877–1949). In addition, the republican coalition included a number of regional parties, most importantly the Catalan Left (Esquerra Catalana). These groups remained politically strong throughout the republic, and republican politicians remained in control of the prime minister's office until 1936. Yet their organizations remained personalistic and fragmented.[92]

To the left of the republican center, the situation differed. As I have shown above, both the PSOE and the UGT were closely linked to the Primo de Rivera dictatorship. Unlike the older dynastic parties, they benefited substantially from cooperation with the regime. This explains why the PSOE went into opposition against it only in July of 1929. Even at that point its opposition was limited to rejecting the dictator's proposed constitution.[93] The UGT refrained from taking part in the various political strikes against the dictatorship in the summer of 1930, leaving these in the hands of communists and anarchists.[94]

The situation on the right at the beginning of the Second Republic differed. The UP had failed to become a viable vehicle for right-wing opinion. Indeed, during the same period that the PSOE was gaining strength under the dictatorship, political organizations of the right were weakening, leaving it disorganized.[95]

At the beginning of the Second Republic, then, a situation of civil society development in the absence of elite or dominant class hegemony had emerged. This led to a set of historical possibilities that pointed beyond liberal democracy: an opportunity for a radical social democracy and the danger of an authoritarian democracy of the fascist type. The failure of the first would lead to the establishment of the second.

The Republic: A New Political Order

The Second Republic breaks into two very clearly demarcated phases: a leftist phase lasting from 1931 to 1933 and a rightist phase from 1933 to 1936. In 1936 the left again assumed power under the aegis of the popular front. A radicalized PSOE under the leadership of Francisco Largo Caballero (1869–1946) unleashed massive land seizures during this period, prompting an unsuccessful military coup that produced the Spanish Civil War, lasting from 1936 to 1939. The turning point in this history was in 1932 and 1933, with the radicalization of Largo Caballero, the leader of the Socialist Party, and the constitution of the mass right-wing party, the Confederación Española de Derechas Autónomas, or CEDA.[96]

The first government of the republic, the Constituent Cortes (1931–1933), was led by a coalition of left republicans and socialists under the premiership of Manuel Azaña (1880–1940). This government had a clear opportunity to establish an advanced social democracy in Spain. Its failure to do so is crucial to understanding the collapse of the Spanish Second Republic. Despite their electoral victory, the republicans remained organizationally weak. They were particularly subject to severe class, regional, and religious cleavages that they could not overcome. The Spanish Second Republic demonstrated that the development of civil society during the Primo de Rivera period in Spain, far from making a liberal democracy easier to implement, had made it more difficult.

These problems showed themselves from the beginning. Azaña's government focused on two basic issues: land reform and passing a constitution. It addressed the first through a series of legislative enactments that constituted a fundamental challenge to both large and small landowners. Among the very first acts of the provisional government in July of 1931, just three months after the April elections and before the enactment of the constitution in December, was a series of decrees that dramatically altered the balance of power in the countryside. There were two main groups of laws: one concerning tenants and the other, farm laborers. Landowners were forbidden to expel tenants except for nonpayment or noncultivation. Further, tenants and sharecroppers were given a number of basic rights. They could appeal for rent reductions if the crop had been poor or if the rent exceeded the taxable income of the property. The new decrees also stipulated that they be paid for the value of the improvements undertaken on the farm at the end of the lease. The reform further obliged landowners to offer leases first to workers' societies. This gave the socialist organizations in the countryside great power and was designed to eliminate speculative tenants from subleasing small plots at very high rents.[97]

The provisional government passed a further set of decrees dealing with farm laborers. The reform stipulated an eight-hour day, as well as the right to strike and collective bargaining institutions. Two other decrees were designed to support the market position of rural workers. The first, the so-called *términos municipales* decree, established borders across which landholders could not hire labor. The second decree, called *laboreo forzoso*, prevented owners from withdrawing land from cultivation.[98]

Understood properly these reforms were preparatory to the actual redistribution of land. An agrarian reform package was passed only in September of 1932, in part as a result of a surge in the power of the left republicans following a failed military coup attempt in 1932. This was an extremely complex, but generally moderate, piece of legislation. The bill established maximum limits for various types of land within given municipalities. Only four categories were subject to outright expropriation. The first of these categories were lands that derived from "feudal" jurisdictional rights that had been converted into property rights after the Cortes of Cádiz. In addition badly cultivated lands, continuously leased lands, and lands in irrigated zones that were not irrigated were all also slated for expropriation. Compensation for the expropriated lands was paid on a sliding scale in which price per hectare decreased as the size of the holding increased. Thus the reform was more confiscatory for larger landholders than smaller ones. This legislation remained mostly a dead letter, because the tiny agrarian minority in the Cortes and on the Council of the Instituto de Reforma Agraria (Institute for Agrarian Reform, or IRA) effectively blocked it with a flurry of technical objections.[99]

Nevertheless, the first republican-socialist government had succeeded in fundamentally shifting the balance of power on the land. The republic broke the close alliance between the *guardia civil*, the local landholders, and the municipal governments that had characterized Spanish rural life during the Restoration. Open repression against socialist organizations was no longer an option. Furthermore, the landholders' basic economic weapon, hiring cheap immigrant labor from outside the municipality, had been legislatively weakened, greatly strengthening the power of rural direct producers. Yet this political opportunity was mostly squandered, because the republican-socialist coalition failed to actually carry out significant land reform and as a result did not address the underlying causes of the most severe class conflict of the republic. In part because of Azaña's failure to properly fund the IRA, in part because of determined opposition from the handful of rightist deputies who had been elected to the Cortes in 1931, and in part because of procedural difficulties and administrative incompetence, very little land had been redistributed by the end of the republican-socialist government.[100]

Despite this failure, the various republican reforms had seriously threatened both large and small property holders. The cumulative effect of the eight-hour day, the *términos municipales* decree, and the *laboreo forzoso* increased labor costs and encouraged small and medium-sized owners to rely more on family than hired labor. The *términos municipales* also disrupted very old migration patterns between mountainous villages and the grain-growing regions of the south, which probably created serious hardships.[101] By failing to redistribute land, and thus alter the agrarian social structure, while at the same time severely threatening agrarian profit margins and generally disrupting rural economic life, the republican-socialist coalition virtually guaranteed a reaction from the right.[102]

Such a reaction was further provoked by the constitution. This document, passed in December of 1931, contained two extremely controversial items that became a rallying point for rightist resistance: articles 26 and 44. Article 26 removed state support from the church, dissolved religious orders that swore allegiance to a foreign power, and placed limits on church wealth. The basic aim was to establish a separation of church and state. Article 44 stated that property could be seized by the state for national utility. In a country where the church employed 1 of every 493 persons and maintained considerable moral authority at the local level, such a reform was bound to be extremely provocative. The republican-socialist coalition antagonized the right without touching the structural bases of its social power. It failed to carry out the promised reforms and in so doing opened the door to a rightist backlash.[103]

Overlaying these conflicts of class and religion was the problem of regionalism. Regional disaffection with Castilian centralism was one of the major issues that brought down the Primo de Rivera regime. The first republican government sought to address this issue by allowing limited regional autonomies. In doing so, however, it opened the door to the emergence of what the socialist leader Indalecio Prieto (1883–1962) called a "Vaticanist Gibraltar" in Navarre and the Basque Country. These were the only zones that had returned conservative candidates in the elections of April 1931; and they were clearly strongholds of the right. The Azaña government therefore resisted their claims to autonomy.[104]

Many scholars have correctly emphasized the pressure for radical reforms that the PSOE faced after the entry of the rural proletariat into the party's ranks in the late twenties and early thirties. But the problem of the large landed estate in the south was relatively contained. It was certainly possible to meet the most pressing needs of the agrarian proletariat without antagonizing the smallholders. Perhaps the fundamental error of the Azaña government was that it alienated northern smallholders unnecessarily through its anticlerical legislation.[105]

The Azaña government was weakened not only by these threats from the right but also by discord within its own coalition. The shadow of the Primo de Rivera regime lay heavily on this early republican government. The PSOE was by far the most important political organization supporting the republic. Yet the party had been late in supporting the idea of democracy, in part because it had gained considerably from the dictatorship. In addition, partly in reaction to the experience of the assembly movement described above, the PSOE's leadership was skeptical of collaboration with "bourgeois" parties, such as the republicans. Further, the republican regime itself had by no means broken completely with the repressive tendencies of the Spanish state. Azaña pushed through a law for the defense of the republic, authorizing the establishment of assault guards and instituting a strict censorship regime.[106] The failure of this first republican government to carry through a consistent program of democratic reform opened the door to mass mobilization from the right.

The Rise of the Right

There were three main currents of the right in Spain: political Catholicism, monarchism, and fascism. The first two were much more powerful than the third and effectively eliminated the political space for an Italian-style party fascist regime. This was to be very important for the particular type of fascism that emerged in Spain.

The push to construct a mass party of the right began following the electoral victory of the left in April of 1931. The first organized resistance came from Acción Nacional, whose affiliated organizations rose from twenty-six in late 1931 to thirty-six a year later. Two other groups joined Acción Nacional: the organization of Catholic intellectuals called the Asociación Católica Nacional de Propagandistas (ACNP), and the confederation of smallholders' unions, the CNCA, described earlier in this chapter. These organizations joined with other locally based agrarian groups, especially those in Valencia, to form the Confederación Española de Derechas Autónomas (CEDA) in February of 1933. This was a very large party. Its leadership claimed over 700,000 members. For the first time in Spanish history, Catholicism became politicized. Previously, the church pursued its aims through the Conservative Party of the *el turno* system. This new political party used the organizational power of the church to reestablish a rightist coalition between large southern landholders and northern smallholders.[107]

The CEDA was the most important force on the right, but it was not the only one. Monarchism could become a political movement, because the declaration of the republic both gave monarchist mass mobilization a reason for existence and reduced the salience of one of the enduring lines of political division within the movement: that between supporters of the Alfonsine monarchy and those who backed the Carlist "pretender." The Alfonsine monarchists had organized into the Unión Monárquica Nacional (UMN), the successor to the UP organization, to contest the 1931 elections. With Alfonso's abdication, it was not Alfonsists but Carlists who now assumed a central place among the forces of order.[108] Carlism's initial expansion occurred during the same period as the CEDA. According to its official party newspaper, the movement had 540 circles, 803 youth sections, and a membership of 700,000 in 1934. It also had now established a national presence.[109]

Throughout the republican period the Carlist leadership devoted itself to organizing a paramilitary called the Requeté.[110] This organization was rooted in a dense network of associations. According to the movement's official publication, *Boletín de Orientación Tradicionalista*, the organization had over 700 local councils, or *juntas*, 350 circles, 250 youth sections, 300 women's groups, and 80 Requeté sections. Carlism was more than a political organization. It provided a full range of cultural experiences for its members. There were Carlist libraries, orchestras, choral societies, movie theaters, and drama clubs that performed Carlist plays. The circles provided welfare and recreation, as well as becoming training centers for the Requetés. The Carlist organization in Navarre drew on the Agro-Social, a Catholic syndicalist organization that had thousands of affiliates and controlled a vast network of rural savings banks and cooperatives at the beginning of the republic. With these organizations the Carlists could fight the left with substantial electoral and paramilitary means.[111]

This sudden and unexpected revival was mostly due to the republic's anticlerical policies. But Carlism, even more than the CEDA, was able to draw on a dense network of preexisting civic associations. The movement was especially strong in Navarre, Castile, Valencia, and Catalonia, although under the able leadership of the Andalusian Carlist Fal Conde, who became secretary general of the communion in May of 1934, it spread more widely, both regionally and socially.[112]

The rapid reemergence of the right at the beginning of the Second Republic was made possible by the control that the social elites, and especially the agrarians, held over civil society through the church.[113] The collapse of the dynastic party system was thus much less devastating than it might initially have seemed. These formidable organizations of the right in 1933 delivered a crushing defeat to the republican-socialist coalition that had governed Spain since 1931. Azaña's left republicans were reduced to 36 seats and the socialists to 58, while the CEDA entered parliament with 115 seats, making it the largest party in the Spanish parliament. But it was not strong enough to form a government of its own and thus formed an alliance with Lerroux's Radicals, who had won 104 seats. Thus, from 1933 to 1936 Spain was governed by a right-leaning coalition under the ex-republican firebrand Lerroux.[114]

The emergence of the CEDA as a mass electoral force constituted a radical challenge to the republic. This party seemed clearly committed to a strategy of fundamental constitutional reform, and the political model of its leadership was the authoritarian corporatist regime in Austria. Although its leader, José María Gil Robles (1898–1980), denounced fascist violence, he rejected a parliamentary regime based on universal suffrage in favor of a Catholic corporatist reorganization of the state.[115]

The electoral defeat of the left exacerbated a process that had already begun in 1932 and was fateful for the survival of the republic: the profound radicalization of the PSOE. Part of this radicalization was connected with the political transformation of the party's leader, Largo Caballero, who had initially been a strong proponent of reformism but who was increasingly coming to see CEDA as a fascist organization. Much more important was the fact that the failure of the land reform, and employers' obstruction of the decrees that had been designed to improve workers' bargaining power, created seething discontent within the FNTT by 1932.[116]

With the new majority in the Cortes, it was obvious that none of the already considerable problems the land reform faced would be immediately resolved.[117] Further, unemployment in agriculture reached its peak precisely in the period between winter of 1933 and spring of 1934, as the new government came to power. The repression, however, had temporarily destroyed the socialists. The CEDA rapidly aimed to move the regime further to the right. From 1935 the agrarian reform was rendered a dead letter because of a clause that repealed the provisions that "prevented direct cultivators from altering the status of their farms in order to bring them below the size limits at which they could be seized."[118] The turn to the right, however, was limited by the coalition government within which CEDA operated. The radicals became involved in a series of financial scandals that eventually forced Lerroux to resign. Left with the choice of calling elections or appointing Gil Robles as prime minister, Alcalá Zamora chose the former. This meant that the CEDA would have to face the electorate again.

The electoral campaign of 1936 was a contest between a rightist national front, in which CEDA was the primary player, and the popular front of the left. The institutional advantages of the right were considerable. It had huge financial resources and could use the government machinery to guarantee some outcomes, especially in the south. The right appears to have used a great deal of violence as well, although there is no systematic evidence. Preston describes widespread vote buying, the illegal arrest of supporters of the popular front, closures of the socialist Casas del Pueblo, and proscriptions of left-wing "scrutineers" (i.e., ballot counters). It was also during this campaign that CEDA came most closely to resemble a fascist party. This was especially true of the youth wing of the party, the Juventud de Acción Popular (Youth Popular Action, or JAP). A JAP manifesto from the 1936 campaign demanded a reform of the constitution, the elimination of the Socialist Party, and press controls.[119]

One of the central causes of the collapse of the Third Republic was the construction of an alliance between the large landholders and smallholders in the CEDA. In many respects the CEDA laid the foundations of the Francoist state, but these developments, paradoxically, preempted a fascist outcome of the Italian or German type. The Spanish social elite had no need to support a pseudorevolutionary mass party, given its substantial organizational resources, and particularly its close alliance with the Catholic Church. This explains the fundamental weakness of party fascism in Spain.

The first truly fascist political figure was Ernesto Giménez Caballero (1899–1988), a man whom Hugh Thomas describes as an "excitable would be D'Annunzio."[120] Giménez Caballero founded in 1930 a small Spanish nationalist party attached to a newspaper called *La Gaceta Literaria*.[121] Two more fascist groups emerged in 1930. The first was called the Juntas de Ofensiva Nacional Sindicalista (JONS), established by Ramiro Ledesma Ramos (1905–1936), an ex-unionist who was attracted to fascist syndicalist ideas.[122] During roughly the same period, Onesimo Redondo Ortega (1905–1936) founded a group in Valladolid that was slightly more traditionalist than Ledesma Ramos's group. A fourth fascist group, called the Falange (or phalanx), was founded in 1933 under the leadership of Primo de Rivera's son, José Antonio Primo de Rivera (1903–1936). These various groups merged in 1934 to form the first openly fascist party in Spain. But their numbers remained very small. Fascism proper would gain considerable influence after the victory of the popular front in 1936, when "the Falangist line became very attractive."[123] But through the early thirties it was a minor political force. Payne writes that the "strongest nuclei of the Falange were to be found in Madrid and in the Valladolid district of Leon–Old Castile."[124] But the most important point about Spanish fascism is its political impotence. The Falange managed to poll only 46,000 votes in the 1936 general elections, making it the weakest political force in Spain.

The Catalan Exception

In Catalonia the balance of forces was fundamentally different. The history of this region under the Second Republic thus constitutes a useful control for the arguments developed above. The declaration of the republic coincided with the establishment of Catalan regional autonomy. A provisional regional government called the Generalitat was established under an alliance led by the Catalan Republican Left (Esquerra Republicana de Catalunya, or ERC).[125] After difficult negotiations with Madrid, Catalonia won an autonomy statute giving the region control over direct taxes and internal administration.[126] The region was governed by a local parliament that closely resembled the mixed parliamentary-presidential system that controlled Spain as a whole.

Many of the conflicts that undermined the republic in other parts of Spain existed in Catalonia as well. The depression probably affected this region more than other parts of Spain, because it was more closely linked to international trade. Led by militant anarchist organizations, labor disputes increased by five times between 1931 and 1933.[127] In addition, there was a serious agrarian conflict that came to a head in 1934. The issue here was a law on agrarian contracts that allowed sharecroppers to purchase land if they had cultivated it for fifteen years.[128] The legislation raised a constitutional issue, because it was not clear that the Catalan parliament had jurisdiction over social policy. An alliance of the Lliga and the Institut Agrícola Català de Sant Isidre successfully brought the case to the Court of Constitutional Guarantees, which overturned it.[129]

Yet the polarization between CEDA and the socialists that occurred in the rest of Spain, did not fully develop here. Even before the 1934 uprising, the Catalan Left and right came close to reaching a deal on the lease law. By 1936 the two main Catalan parties were able to reach a compromise over this issue.[130] Aside from this specific agreement, Catalonia seems to have been relatively immune from political violence and the destruction of churches common in other parts of Spain. This was so, despite extremely combative labor relations in the region. What explains this exceptionalism?

Here the social elite was relatively unified, and it had a long tradition of political organization in the Lliga. This party, as I argued above, achieved considerable mass support in certain periods of its history. Although it had been weakened and discredited by collaboration with the Primo de Rivera regime, the Lliga was not destroyed like the main dynastic parties of *el turno*.[131] The social elite in Catalonia was therefore not in the position of seeking an entirely new political organization to confront the electorate. As a result, the right in Catalonia could reconstitute itself as a loyal opposition to the ERC at the regional level.[132]

The situation on the left was also entirely different. Socialism was extremely weak in Catalonia despite the fact that this was the most industrialized region of Spain. In its place the anarchist CNT dominated the trade unions, and the ERC occupied the left wing of the political spectrum. The latter political party had emerged out of internal political struggles within the Catalan nationalist movement and thus shared many of the same regionalist aims as the Lliga.[133] Political demands from below in Catalonia were therefore channeled through a regional nationalist party framework that did not lead to the dramatic polarization characteristic of Spain as a whole.

From the perspective developed here, it is extremely suggestive that Catalonia did not suffer from significant political violence during the Second Republic. Instead, the Lliga and the Catalan Left were able to work together on a new agrarian contract law.[134] Certainly one aspect of the difference between Catalonia and the rest of Spain was the early construction of an effective elite political party. This seems to have put Catalonia on a fundamentally different historical path from the rest of the country.

The Civil War and the Rise of Traditionalist Fascism in Spain

The 1936 elections showed that the Spanish population was highly organized and mobilized. Furthermore, despite the considerable degree of mass right-wing mobilization during the Second Republic, and especially after the Asturias uprising of 1934, the right could not achieve power in Spain through electoral means. This left the army as the only plausible bearer of a conservative project. It was thus natural that, after the February defeat of CEDA and its allies, the right would begin to turn toward supporting a military coup. The model for those who supported this option was the Primo de Rivera regime. Yet as events were to show, it was impossible to reimpose an apolitical military dictatorship on the model of the

Primoverrista regime in the changed circumstances of the thirties. The attempt to do so failed, leading to the rise of Francisco Franco and traditionalist fascism.[135]

The garrison at Melilla in Morocco "pronounced" on July 18, 1936. But the coup was supported by only about half the military. Only four major-generals on active service joined the rebel side. The navy remained loyal to the republic, leaving the crucial African colonial troops stranded in Morocco. Indeed, many scholars have suggested that, without Axis military support at this crucial juncture, the republic might easily have been able to regain control.[136]

Instead of issuing in a quick transition to a military directorate, the uprising thus split the country along its fundamental political lines of division. In areas of traditional leftist strength, the *pronunciamiento* set off a series of local uprisings in which socialists and anarchists seized municipal governments. This action secured Madrid, Barcelona, Valencia, and Bilbao, cities containing most of the population and industrial might of Spain, for the republic. But in the north and center of the country, areas of CEDA strength, the military rebels were victorious. The nationalists were particularly successful in Carlist Navarre, where thousands of volunteers stepped forward to aid the nationalist cause. The battle lines of the civil war thus formed as a consequence of a failed military coup.[137]

Information on the regional distribution of the nationalist militias shows their areas of strength. They prevailed in the smallholding regions of the north and center of Spain, as shown in table 4. The table suggests that the Spanish provinces with the highest number of militiamen per population were Navarre, Álava, and Logroño, followed by Valladolid and Palencia. The first of these provinces was a Carlist stronghold, while in the others the militias were probably divided between Carlists and the Spanish fascist Falangists. Most historical accounts also argue that fascist mobilization in the thirties was concentrated in Old Castile. This pattern is quite suggestive. Again, as was true of the twenties, the regions dominated by latifundist agriculture were mostly excluded from the authoritarian coalition. Instead, right-wing mobilization was strongest in the densely organized civil societies of north-central Spain.

The transformation of the political conflict of the Second Republic into a military conflict after the failure of the 1936 *pronunciamiento* had very important consequences for the internal organization of the Spanish right. The nationalist uprising initially was politically ambiguous. Some of its leading figures wished to establish a brief caretaker government that would quickly return the country

Table 4 The Regional Concentration of Falangist Militias in the Civil War

Province	Possible volunteers (in thousands)	Actual volunteers	% of possible volunteers who enrolled
Galicia	371	2,400	0.6
Salamanca	56	652	1.0
Granada	53	600	1.1
Huelva	59	700	1.2
Cordova	55	1,000	1.8
Badajoz	58	1,210	2.0
Cádiz	84	2,000	2.3
León	73	1,700	2.3
Sevilla	134	3,500	2.6
Zamora	47	1,232	2.6
Guipúzcoa	50	683	2.7
Ávila	37	1,062	2.8
Segovia	28	787	2.8
Cáceres	74	2,668	3.5
Burgos	59	2,413	4.0
Valladolid	50	2,934	5.8
Palencia	34	2,369	6.9
Álava	17	2,446	14.4
Logroño	34	7,619	22.3
Navarre	58	17,016	29.1
Málaga	—	300	—

Source: Casas de la Vega 1974, 64, 93, 120.

to a more conservative form of civilian rule than the leftist Second Republic.[138] Others were more radical, proposing either a return of the monarchy or some version of fascism. In addition there was little agreement about who would lead the nationalist side. At the beginning of the rebellion, a Junta de Defensa (Defense Council) coordinated the uprising from its headquarters at Burgos. Initially, Francisco Franco, who would later rise to the position of *generalissimo*, was not part of this organization.[139]

The shift to full-scale war played into Franco's hands. As general of the Army of Africa in Morocco, he commanded the only battle-hardened troops available in Spain. Control of this major military force, therefore, increased his political authority as the country slid toward civil war. And of all the leading generals involved in the uprising, Franco had the closest relationship to the fascist governments in Germany and Italy, establishing himself as the main conduit of crucial

Axis military aid. Franco's rise within the Burgos *junta*, to the position of *caudillo*, or supreme leader, corresponded to a shift toward a more explicitly fascist model within nationalist Spain: consolidated in April of 1937 with the establishment of the FET-JONS single party. Franco himself had few political ideas. But he was acutely aware of the need for some civilian organization to provide a degree of pacification behind the battle lines and sustain morale. It was natural that he would gravitate to fascism, under the circumstances. The international prestige of the Axis countries was at its zenith in 1936; and Franco's brother-in-law, Ramón Serrano Súñer (1901–2003), had studied in Rome and was a great admirer of Italian fascism. The *caudillo* was determined to avoid what he saw as the error of the previous military regime in Spain, the Primo de Rivera dictatorship, which, as I have shown above, lacked a strong single-party organization. Franco thus rejected a purely personalistic dictatorship and adopted the fascist model of rule.[140]

Using the enormous personal power that he had rapidly accumulated within the nationalist zone, Franco forced a unification of all the political currents within it. This led to a merger in April of 1937 of the Carlist traditionalists and the Falangists into the cumbersomely named hybrid organization, the Falange Española Tradicionalista y de las Juntas de Ofensiva Nacional-Sindicalista (FET-JONS). In the aftermath of the unification, hundreds old Falangists (the so-called *camisas viejas*, or "old shirts") were imprisoned, including Federico Manuela Hedilla (1902–1970), the party's leader. A group of neo-Falangists around Serrano Suñer dominated the new FET-JONS. In the five years following the unification decree (1937–1942), the FET-JONS attempted to build up the power of this party. As head of the political council of the Falange, Serrano Suñer attempted to turn the party in a decidedly fascist direction by placing his followers in important positions within it, making it the foremost political organization of Francoist Spain.[141]

The FET-JONS's attempt to establish a party fascist regime, however, was unsuccessful. The party occupied a subordinate position within the regime. The *caudillo* established a regular government by decree on January 30, 1938, reserving full powers while establishing eleven ministries (foreign affairs, justice, defense, finance, public works, public order, industry, education, agriculture, and organization and syndical action) each given wide autonomy within its area of competence.[142] The FET-JONS was in control only of two of these: agriculture and syndical action and organization. The repressive and administrative core of the state remained firmly in conservative and military hands, while welfare and "mass" organizations were turned over to the FET-JONS.[143] The FET-JONS implemented these provisions by making the syndical organization into a branch of the party. In the early forties the party was organized into three branches and four vice secretariats. The syndicates were placed under the vice secretariat of social works. The whole sphere of economic interest associations then became a fief of the party.[144]

For some years after final victory in the civil war in 1939, the FET-JONS pushed for greater power within the regime. A leading figure in this push for strengthening the party was the radical Falangist Gerardo Salvador Merino. This man sought to establish functioning vertical syndicates incorporating workers and employers as part of a broader plan aimed at radicalizing the Francoist state. But Salvador Merino was forced out under pressure from the regime's conservative forces without being able to achieve much.[145] The party fascist project continued until the reversal of the fortunes of the Axis powers in 1944. The Falangists were able to establish a mass party organization and a large social work and propaganda apparatus and to fuse the positions of the provincial governor and leader of the FET. Yet they remained hampered by their inability effectively to pressure the regime from below.[146]

The FET-JONS was not, however, the only mass organization available to the Francoist regime. The social Catholic organizations that had developed vigorously during the Second Republic, as I showed above, were much more important. With the outbreak of the Civil War, the Spanish clergy overwhelmingly supported the nationalist cause. One reason for this support was the rash of church burnings and killings of priests that followed the July 18 pronouncement. But the support of the Catholic leadership for the uprising was not merely a reaction to these provocations. Much of the Catholic leadership saw the war as an opportunity to re-Christianize Spain. Indeed, Catholicism provided the main ideological justification for the conflict as a clash of civilizations: a Catholic Spain and a Marxist anti-Spain.[147]

Social Catholicism also provided critical organizational resources. In 1942 the CNCA was transformed into the *Unión Nacional de Cooperativas del Campo* (UNCC). Ninety-eight percent of the cooperatives associated with this organization were *sindicatos agrícolas*. Plus, the UNCC was led by men who were previously prominent in the *sindicatos* movement. The organization was partially under church control, since the bishop had the right to nominate the chancellor of local organizations. The UNCC became one of the largest mass organizations in

Franco's Spain. In 1940 it was comprised of 2,726 syndicates with 275,000 members. In 1949 this had increased to 4,334 syndicates with 843,000 members.[148]

Given how extraordinarily reactionary and repressive the Franco regime was, it may seem perverse to classify it as an "authoritarian democracy." Yet many of the men who fought and died on the nationalist side during the civil war desired political institutions that were more representative of Spanish society than those of the Second Republic or the corrupt liberal regime of the nineteenth century.[149] Without their decisive support at the beginning of the civil war, it is possible that the uprising would never have been able to defeat the republic on the battlefield. Further, the social Catholic organizations that were such an important part of Spanish agrarian history formed the infrastructure for one of the prominent mass organizations of the Franco regime. The Francoist state certainly had civic foundations, in fact, much broader civic foundations than its predecessor and model, the Primo de Rivera dictatorship.

Conclusion

Why did Spain consolidate as a traditionalist fascist regime in the interwar period? The key to Spanish fascism lies in the development of a vigorous civil society in a context of nonhegemonic politics. As in Italy, an absence of intraclass hegemony in the late nineteenth century undermined the formation of interclass hegemony that in turn made the construction of counterhegemony difficult. None of this, however, undermined the development of civil society. The outcome of the development of civil society in this political context was traditionalist fascism. It may be worthwhile here to recapitulate the various phases of this story.

The Canovite system under which Spain was governed from the late nineteenth century did little to encourage the formation of intradominant class hegemony. The system excluded the majority of the population from political participation and consolidated the power of the landholding oligarchy. But it also split the social elite into competing patronage networks, thereby undermining its ability to pursue a coherent modernization program. Spain thus lacked organizations that could establish solid intradominant class alliances (intraclass hegemony).

Despite this, civil society developed under the Restoration monarchy in part because some basic civil rights were legally guaranteed after 1887. During the agrarian crisis of the late nineteenth century, small landholders took advantage of this liberal environment to establish credit and consumer and producers' cooperatives. Initially it seemed that socialist, republican, and anarchist forces might gain a foothold in this developing rural associational texture. But a determined campaign headed by large landholders to establish Catholic associations linked to the church hierarchy prevented this development and secured an alliance between small and large proprietors. This pattern of civil society development under the direct control of the landed elite was vital to subsequent political developments in Spain.

The development of civil society, even in the elite-dominated form described above, had important political consequences. By the end of the first decade of the twentieth century, the Spanish liberal elite began to search for ways to expand support for the Restoration monarchy. Important political figures, such as Maura, Canalejas, and Cambó, sought to overcome the isolation of the constitutional monarchy by pursuing a reform program aimed at the power of the political bosses operating at the local level. The failure of these attempts at reform increased the power of the army, paving the way for the rise of Primo de Rivera. The Primoverrista dictatorship is well understood as an attempt to extend the hegemony of the social elite by establishing an alliance with parts of the industrial working class. This project was a political failure. The support gained from alliance with the socialists depended on the dictatorship's ability to provide concrete material advantages to the working class. As this became more difficult in the late twenties, socialists abandoned the regime, becoming crucial partners in the coalition of forces that would establish the Second Republic. Furthermore, military rule demolished the dynastic party system by depriving its leaders of the patronage that had been the lifeblood of these organizations under the Restoration monarchy. The dictatorship's apolitical corporatism also further fragmented already highly divided elite interests. At the same time the Primoverrista regime stimulated the development of civil society, especially on the left.

The consequences of the connected failure of intraclass hegemony and interclass hegemony undermined the development of counterhegemony in Spain. The republicans were too fragmented and too committed to a program of rigid anticlericalism to carry through a democratic program. The socialists were relatively indifferent to the question of regime form, viewing the republic as a bourgeois institution. The forces of the right were openly hostile to the republic for much of the thirties, although some sectors of the right, especially the Carlists, expressed a desire for fundamental political reform. An intense process of civic mobilization thus occurred in a political context in which this mobilization could not be channeled to support a liberal democratic outcome. The result was a wave of anti-liberal civil society mobilization that polarized the population.

This process was particularly pronounced on the right. The historically dense civil societies of north-central Spain now supported a mass political movement that was democratic, in the sense of demanding a representative state, but deeply hostile to parties, elections, and civil rights. The decisive political defeat of these forces in the 1936 elections touched off a military uprising whose political project was initially ambiguous. Many of the leading figures involved in it sought to establish a parenthetical dictatorship that would quickly return Spain to a civilian government. Yet the opportunities and constraints created by the development of civil society, both during the Primo de Rivera period and during the Second Republic, made such a project unworkable and pushed the generals toward a fascist model.

But Spanish fascism differed sharply from its Italian counterpart for reasons that were closely linked to its pattern of civil society development. For, while it is clear that voluntary organizations expanded, especially among the rural population, during the first part of the twentieth century, the social elite maintained its dominance over these developments in north-central Spain. With the destruction of the dynastic party organizations during the Primo de Rivera period, this position of strength in civil society became decisive. The church-linked organizations of social Catholicism were the only ones available for garnering mass support for conservative interests.

The considerable organizational power of Catholicism across the Spanish right explains the striking weakness of party fascism in Spain; for the Spanish social elite had no need to flirt with an exotic new organization and ideology. Rather, the political force that would ultimately bring down the Second Republic, and that provided valuable support to the 1936 uprising, was an alliance between small and large landholders cemented by the organization and ideology of social Catholicism. If the CEDA and its allies organized as the national front had won the elections of 1936, the Falange might have remained a totally insignificant force. As it was, the Francoist state relied heavily on Catholicism. Thus, while the fundamental reason for the rise of fascism in Spain was a crisis of politics produced by the development of civil society in the presence of a nonhegemonic social elite, the solution to this crisis was largely determined by Spain's particular form of elite-dominated civil society development.

Spain's political and social structure by no means predestined it to produce the Francoist dictatorship. The example of Catalonia shows that, where the social elite had managed to constitute itself as a hegemonic force, a transition from liberalism to mass democracy was possible. Two important historical turning points punctuated Spain's road to traditionalist fascism. First, the failure of the assembly movement to establish a functioning democratic regime in the postwar period was decisive. Had the Catalans been able to break out of their regional stronghold by forging an alliance with the conservatives around Maura, it is possible that the Primo de Rivera experience, with all the negative consequences that this had for Spain's chances for liberal democracy in the thirties, might have been avoided.

The options at the beginning of the Second Republic were still fundamentally open. Had the first socialist-republican coalition government focused its land reform on those areas with the most severe inequalities, and left aside the clerical issue, it might have been able to win at least grudging support from the smallholders of the north and center. This was a difficult proposition for a number of reasons, and by 1934, in the aftermath of the Asturias uprising, had been effectively eliminated. But this did not detract from the fact that Spain in the early thirties contained a number of historical possibilities. The actions of men and women in concrete historical circumstances mattered greatly to the outcome.

Spain's path of political development demonstrates the close relationship between democracy and fascism. That the Franco regime was the outcome of a failed military uprising, not a successful one, is crucial to understanding its nature and development. Franco's rise to dominance within the nationalist coalition occurred because the *pronunciamiento* model had become impossible. This was largely due to the development of Spanish civil society. The supporters of the republic, rather than accepting a new *caudillo*, as had occurred in the twenties, organized to defend the regime. In addition, the conspirators themselves could now rely on mass organizations comprised of the various rightist political organizations that had not existed prior to the thirties. This meant that if authoritarianism were to come to Spain, it would take the form of fascism.

What are the broader lessons of the Spanish path to fascism? Spain's experience underlines again the fundamental importance of politics in shaping the consequences of civil society development for regime outcomes. Tocquevillians are correct to emphasize that associationism is linked to democracy. But the concrete institutional form that this democratic demand will take depends on the balance of political forces. In Spain, civil society development was unlikely to lead to a smooth transition to liberal democracy, because a nonhegemonic dominant class had corrupted liberal institutions. In the concrete circumstances of the thirties, the question was whether civil society development would lead to a form of radical democracy beyond liberalism, or to fascism. The outcome was by no means predetermined. Yet there were certain historical factors operating to undermine a radical democratic solution. The most important of these was the incorporation of the socialists as junior partners during the Primo de Rivera dictatorship. This strengthened the narrow economism of the PSOE and undermined the development of a truly political perspective. The consequence was that the socialists never fully embraced the republican project and failed to seize the opportunity presented by the democratic opening of the early thirties.

4

Statist Fascism

Romania, 1881–1940

The tension between the fascist movement and the fascist regime that eventually consolidated in Romania was much greater than in either Italy or Spain, for Romania produced a form of "statist fascism" between 1938 and 1940 premised on the violent suppression of its very large, and politically successful, fascist party. This regime, the dictatorship of King Carol II, adopted the language and organization of the Garda de Fier (Iron Guard), Romania's fascist party, while eliminating its leadership. Despite the particularly statist form that fascism assumed in Romania, this chapter argues that the causes of Romanian fascism were similar to those that produced fascist regimes in Italy and Spain. A hegemonically weak social elite turned to fascism in the face of a highly mobilized civil society to construct an authoritarian democracy. But in one crucial respect Romania differed from Italy and Spain. Associationism here developed under the aegis of the state much more obviously than in either of the southern European cases. This both blocked the development of organized social groups with which the Romanian fascist movement could ally and left state elites with a much freer hand to use violence against the movement than was the case farther to the west.

This chapter follows the narrative framework established for Italy and Spain in chapters 2 and 3. Beginning with a discussion of the failure of intraclass hegemony during the liberal period, the chapter then discusses the development of a state-sponsored agrarian civil society within this framework. The third and fourth stages of the analysis focus on the attempt to establish interclass hegemony in the dramatic period after World War I, and the failure of counterhegemony in the late twenties. Finally, the chapter discusses the rise of Romanian fascism.

Intraclass Hegemony in Liberal Romania

The Romanian social elite, like its Italian and Spanish counterparts, was divided politically during the liberal period. In the late nineteenth and early twentieth centuries liberal and conservative parties alternated in power through a system that closely resembled the *el turno* mechanism in Spain. Yet restricted suffrage and the highly state-dependent nature of Romanian elites produced an extremely conflictual intra-elite politics.

Romania began to emerge as an independent state in the 1850s, as the result of the Paris Peace Conference, which brought the Crimean War to a close in 1856. During this period the country adopted some of the trappings of a liberal regime. However, as soon as the boyars gained control of their internal affairs, they passed legislation weakening peasant claims to land while maintaining their control over labor. Prince Alexander Cuza (1820–1873), the regent of the new state, reacted to this parliamentary landlord reaction by dissolving the assembly and launching land reform through the use of a decree law. Isolated from the landed elite, Cuza's attempt to establish a peasant-based populist dictatorship failed, and he was driven from the country in 1866.[1]

The 1866 constitution, the document that would govern Romanian political life until 1917, was the expression of this landlord reaction. It established firmer property rights in part so that the boyars could take advantage of expanding demand for grain. Liberal institutions also served as a protection against Russian influence, allowing Romania to solidify its alliances with the powers to the west. The constitution established universal suffrage but weighted it according to a collegial system that gave overwhelming influence to large landholders and the urban ruling strata.[2]

Two dynastic parties dominated this system: the conservatives and the liberals.[3] Both remained personalistic and split by factional struggle, leaving a large space for monarchical interference.[4] When a party in power began to fragment under the pressure of cliques, the monarch would step in to appoint a new prime minister, who would subsequently organize elections to give the new party a majority in the chamber. Thus, much as was the case in Spain, changes in the government preceded elections, rather than developing out of them.[5] Ministers could easily pressure centrally appointed prefects, who could in turn be counted on to manipulate the electorate.[6]

Within the limited circle of people who possessed political rights, there were ferocious factional struggles. Two were particularly important: that between the emerging bureaucracy and the large landholders and the ethnic struggle between Romanian elites and what was largely a non-Romanian commercial middle class. In the late nineteenth century, with the growth of the Romanian state, a conflict developed between the bureaucracy and the big landholders. State employment had historically played a central role in sustaining the Romanian social elite, since boyar families were unable to transmit their political privileges through heredity. If their sons did not obtain state employment, they could easily swell the ranks of the large petty nobility, which had few privileges apart from being exempt from forced labor. The Romanian landed elite was thus historically not a landed aristocracy but a service class.[7]

The 1864 land reform instituted under Cuza, despite creating clear property rights, did not change this feature of the boyar class. Rather, these people continued to live in the cities and to be oriented to state employment, leaving the management of their estates to large tenants, who were usually ethnic minorities. The growing Romanian state drew the less affluent members of the boyar aristocrats into the bureaucracy especially. This was the basis of the "statist middle class," a group of decisive importance for Romania's interwar history.[8]

The liberal leader Ion Brătianu (1821–1891) supported this group's interests in the late nineteenth century. In 1876 he attacked the political predominance of the large, more politically independent, boyars by merging their electoral college with the less independent small landholders, who were more closely tied to the state.[9] Arrayed against this "statist middle class" stood a group of conservative reformers who gathered around the journal *Junimea* (Youth). They sought to break with the oligarchic system in the 1880s, elaborating a traditionalist nationalism aiming to diminish the influence of French cultural and political models.[10] But, although they briefly assumed power in 1888, their movement had no popular following.[11]

Longstanding linguistic and national divisions also undermined the unity of the social elite. The "bourgeoisie" was a foreign element. From the late eighteenth century the rulers of the principalities pursued a policy of attracting Jews from Russia. A distinct Jewish minority was also added to the ethnic mix after the annexation of Transylvania, where the Jewish population spoke German, was relatively wealthy, and assimilated. In the Regat and Bessarabia, Jews spoke Yiddish and lived in self-contained ghettos, forming an ethnically distinct ersatz bourgeoisie. They tended to be local moneylenders, publicans, and foremen for large landholders. Specific legal measures reinforced their separation from the peasant population, for until 1918 they could not live in the countryside.[12]

There was, to summarize, little political cohesion within the social elite, despite its exclusive control over the state. Instead, Romanian politics in the nineteenth century was characterized by sharp struggles between the statist middle class, the old boyar aristocracy, and the Jewish bourgeoisie. Intraclass hegemony was not much in evidence.

Rural Associationism in Romania

Given its extreme economic backwardness, and the highly repressive political order described above, associationism in Romania was surprisingly well developed, even prior to World War I. Credit cooperatives and land-leasing societies began to emerge in the late nineteenth century. In 1903, however, these organizations were subordinated to the Romanian state. Thereafter, they were inextricably bound up with the development project of the Partidul Naţional Liberal (Romanian Liberal Party, or PNL).

The basic issue around which associationism developed in Romania was access to credit. Because Romania's banking system was heavily biased toward industry, many rural producers were forced to turn to local usurers for credit to buy seeds and equipment and purchase land. In some cases usurers were local political authorities, such as the mayor. Indebtedness was not only a problem in itself but was also a path toward the loss of freedom, for creditors could demand labor services from their debtors.[13] Romania's early liberal governments, partially under the pressure of peasant unrest, attempted to redress this problem by establishing an Agricultural Credit Society in 1881. Initially this organization was supposed to be funded by a mix of private and state funds, but reluctance to back rural loans meant that it effectively became a state institution in 1892.[14]

For a series of reasons the Credit Society proved inadequate to its self-imposed task of breaking the bonds of rural usury. The bank branches were located in the district capital, some distance from the villages in which rural borrowers lived. Also, the borrower had to obtain a guarantee from the mayor and the local tax collector, which cost a commission fee. Finally, there was no upper limit to the loan, so that wealthy landholders could consume all the available credit. A series of credit cooperatives called people's banks emerged in part to redress the inadequacies of this centralized way of distributing credit.[15] Concentrated in the mountainous parts of Oltenia, where local trade was most developed and where the peasantry was less subjugated to landlord control than in the grain-growing plains, they were true rural voluntary associations run by villagers and local teachers better able to assess credit risks than the distant Credit Society.[16]

Connected to the people's banks, were two other types of rural association: cultural circles and cooperative societies for leasing. The cultural circles were leagues of village schools that tried to "sponsor community projects of a general cultural or economic nature."[17] During the public meetings cultural circles instilled "religious and patriotic sentiments" and promoted discussion of "hygiene, dress, nutrition, animal husbandry, and more rational cultivation of gardens and fields."[18] The discussions of the cultural circles also often encouraged the establishment of popular banks and cooperatives. But they also seem to have pursued political aims, especially combating the spread of socialism.[19] Cooperative leasing societies formed to lease land directly from landowners, thereby eliminating the large leaseholder. After the land was leased, individual members of the cooperative would then cultivate their land separately.[20]

These early autonomous efforts, however, were quickly subordinated to state control. Leaders of the PNL saw cooperation as a way of combating agrarian socialism and began to promote it between 1900 and 1902, and the rapid growth of the popular banks prompted greater legal regulation of them. This led to the 1903 popular bank law, which established the Agricultural Credit Society, creating the cumbersomely named Agricultural Credit Society and Central Bank of the Popular Banks (hereafter referred to as the Central). In some respects state intervention strengthened the banks, for they now had access to reliable funds and could sue their debtors who, after the reorganization, owed money to the Romanian state. Yet these benefits came at a price: the Romanian state exercised strict control over the Central.[21]

The Ministry of Finance appointed six of the seven people who sat on the bank's administrative council, leaving one appointment to the Ministry of Education. A 20,000,000 *lei* government grant financed the Central's activities. With this financial support came state supervision. The local banks were required to submit a yearly budget to the Central, and the state-appointed board could change the management of the banks. The Central also acted as a deposit bank for the local banks and thus held all the financial resources.[22] An intermediate level of organization developed in 1905 with the constitution of federals of popular banks. These organizations gathered funds from a number of popular banks and had direct relations with the Central.[23]

After 1903, when the cooperative movement had been linked to the state, it also became part of the PNL's strategy of industrial development. The liberals wished to encourage the emergence of a rich peasantry and create a landless proletariat available as a labor force for urban industry while also preempting rural unrest. The popular banks and the cooperatives were appropriate instruments for this project, because they tended to favor enterprising, relatively well-off peasants.[24]

This was particularly true of the leasing cooperatives, which promoted the interests of the relatively affluent in the village at the expense of the estate owner, the large leaseholder, and the rural poor. The conservative parliamentary representative Ion Lahovari (1844–1915) made this point explicit in his objections to popular banks: "But supposing you are dealing with an association of 500 peasants who are not paying you under the pretext of a bad harvest, hail or animal pest, what will you do to get your property back? You would need a regiment. And what government would put it at your disposal? ... Leasing to ... associations, after a short time, amounts to expropriation without indemnity."[25] Rural associationism was linked to the liberal development strategy aimed at supporting rich peasants against both landholders and the rural poor.

This attempt to incorporate part of the peasantry into a project of national development failed, laying the foundations for a radicalization of the rural population in the years from 1904 to 1907. Rent levels were the main issue. The leaders of the cooperative movement were reluctant to push for sharp reductions in rent, because they feared this would encourage large landholders to sell their estates in small parcels, thus fragmenting landed property and undermining the purpose of the leasing cooperatives. Resistance to the cooperatives and popular banks, however, pushed peasants to radicalize their claims. Out of the failure of the cooperative movement emerged a populist program, led by Vasile Kogălniceanu (1863–1941), the son of one of the major figures of Romanian independence. Kogălniceanu argued that the real enemies of the Romanian peasants were the leaseholders, particularly those who were foreigners or Jews. He argued for a sharp reduction in rents that would lead to the breakup of the very large estates.[26]

A tax collected to insure peasants against drought touched off a massive revolt in early 1907. This uprising began as a protest against Jewish leaseholders in Moldavia. It then spread to Wallachia in the south, and transformed into a full-fledged peasant uprising focusing on land redistribution. The revolt of 1907 and its aftermath underlined the repressive and oligarchic nature of Romanian liberal institutions. The incumbent liberal government ferociously repressed this movement, killing 11,000 peasants in the process.[27] After this uprising, there were no more attempts at a liberal opening toward the peasantry until 1917.

Agrarian associationism, to summarize, was state sponsored in Romania. The movement of popular banks, which had developed autonomously in the 1880s, was rapidly co-opted by the Central, which managed both deposits and loans.[28] The turn toward a democratic state in the post–World War I period did not transform these relations of dependency. The cooperative movement was so entangled with the Romanian state that by the twenties cooperatives were collecting taxes, in the form of grain deposits, from the peasantry.[29]

Although the Romanian bureaucracy played a central role in sponsoring rural associationism, large landholders were also mostly resistant to this phenomenon. Their opposition appeared early. In 1889 the Conservative Party (the political expression of the big landlords) abolished the liberal government's law on cooperatives.[30] They were also fundamentally hostile to the 1904 cooperative law, because they rightly saw it as a method of expropriating the large landed estate.[31] The promotion of cooperation in Romania was closely linked to the policy of state-led industrialization promoted by the PNL. While rural associationism thus lacked autonomy in Romania, neither was it a transmission belt for binding rural smallholders into a conservative alliance, as in Spain. These institutions increased in the first two decades of the twentieth century. In 1900 there were only 88 popular banks, but by 1928, when Romania's first democratically elected government came to power, there were 4,810 popular banks with almost a million members.[32]

Romanian civil society developed rapidly in the late nineteenth and early twentieth centuries. But it did so under the impetus of the state. In the 1880s rural direct producers began to self-organize as a way of escaping usury, but from 1903, these associations were subordinated to a central organization that exercised political control over them. State control actually expanded after 1918. Although it is not the case that agrarian associationism was absent in Romania, it developed in a specific way. In Romania civil society was neither autonomous, as in Italy, nor subordinated directly to the social elite, as in Spain. Instead, it was a bureaucratic project.

Interclass Hegemony

A number of fundamental changes occurred in Romania in the decade after World War I. Indeed, the country came tantalizingly close in this period to establishing a workable democracy based on the alternation between the PNL and the National Peasant Party (Partidul Național-Țărănesc, or PNȚ). Yet these organizations ultimately proved incapable of establishing interclass hegemony. This failure was the consequence of the absence of a well-structured opposition between the left and the right following the destruction of Romania's Conservative Party. To place the attempt to construct interclass hegemony in proper historical context, it is important to begin the discussion by emphasizing the extraordinarily repressive nature of the Romanian social elite prior to World War I.

Before the war, outside of the narrow elite, most Romanians' contact with the state was through the local mayor: a plenipotentiary holding both police and judicial powers and ruling over a commune consisting of a number of villages. Formally, the mayor was elected by universal suffrage, unlike the parliamentary representatives, but the wide administrative powers he possessed allowed him to influence the vote. The mayors responded to the prefects above them and the local landlords in their commune.[33]

During the period from 1866 to 1917, they played a crucial role in enforcing agrarian relations. This is clear from the prime position reserved to them in the Law on Agricultural Contracts: a piece of legislation that allowed tenants and landowners to convert debt obligations into labor services—and which effectively reestablished coerced labor in the Romanian countryside. Since villagers had a constant need for cash, and little access to it, they easily fell into debt. The Law on Agricultural Contracts allowed creditors to redeem these debts by demanding work from their debtors, and occasionally landlords imposed collective liability if one person from the village defaulted. One of the primary tasks of the local administration was to enforce these obligations, if necessary with the use of the army. This meant that prior to World War I, for the vast majority of the Romanian population, the state was a purely repressive force.[34]

A huge cultural divide separated the Romanian social elite from the peasantry. During the period of Ottoman domination, Romanian became the language of the peasants, while Greek was the language of the professions and was spoken in the towns, thus stunting the development of a national aristocracy. After independence (1878) the cultural influence of France increased, displacing Greek influence. Boyars and the educated middle classes wrote and spoke in French. Their consumer goods and clothing also came from the West. The three-quarters of the population who lived on the land were thus culturally foreign to the ruling elite.[35]

Prior to World War I, Romanian political institutions were completely subordinated to the interests of a nonhegemonic social elite; the institution of constitutional government went hand in hand with the social subordination of the peasantry. As a result, parliamentary leaders were not adequately backed up by autonomous extraparliamentary political organizations. This set of institutions was deeply shaken by Romania's involvement in World War I.

Romania's international situation at the outbreak of World War I in August of 1914 was similar to Italy's. The country formed part of the Triple Alliance, but, as has already been suggested above, it was culturally closer to France, and therefore the Entente, than to Germany and Austria. Furthermore, the territorial gains that the Central Powers could offer (Bessarabia at the expense of Russia) were considerably less than the Entente (Bucovina and Transylvania at the expense of Austria-Hungary). The country's political elite hoped to enter the war on the Entente's side at the decisive moment and make major territorial gains. The Italian offensive on the Isonzo seemed the perfect opportunity, and the Romanians invaded Transylvania on August 25, 1916. While the offensive was an initial success, discipline soon broke down. Romania then suffered a crushing counterattack from both the west and the south, and by winter of 1916 only Moldavia remained under its control. It was in this desperate situation that the idea of both land redistribution and effective universal suffrage was born, in an attempt to stiffen the fighting capacity of the peasant army.[36]

These measures were insufficient to stave off military collapse. King Ferdinand (1865–1927) installed a pro-German Conservative cabinet under the leadership of Alexander Marghiloman (1854–1925) to sue for a separate peace in the spring of 1918. The result was a reactionary puppet regime heavily reliant on German troops that attempted to subvert the implementation of land reform and universal suffrage that the monarch had promised in 1917. In October of 1918 the situation changed again as Romania reentered the war against the Central Powers. The Romanian offensive against Hungary, which lasted into the summer of 1919, toppled that country's prosoviet government and led to the annexation of Transylvania to Romania, thus establishing Greater Romania. The Conservative Party's humiliating collaboration with the Germans accelerated its collapse. Land reform finally eliminated it as a political force, thus undermining one of the main bulwarks of Romania's political system. The elimination of a clearly defined right would have important consequences for subsequent political developments.[37]

No country in Europe gained more from World War I than Romania. The old state had more than doubled its territory, from 137,000 square kilometers to 294,000. It had gained Transylvania from Hungary, Bessarabia from the Soviet Union, and Bucovina from Austria. And although there was considerable unrest in the immediate postwar period, the Romanian social elite seemed willing to make the concessions necessary to secure a functioning democratic state. Greater Romania was also blessed with considerable natural resources. This is not to say that the war did not disturb Romanian politics. Living standards had fallen throughout the country as a result of the war, producing working-class and peasant unrest. Further, Greater Romania included a number of national minorities whose loyalty to the new regime was questionable. This was particularly true of the Hungarians in Transylvania, but the Romanian social elite initially responded to these threats in a very flexible and effective way.[38]

The Rise of the Liberal Party (1923–1928)

Romania's political landscape in the immediate postwar period was confused. A popular wartime general, Alexander Averescu (1859–1938), swept to power, supported by an amorphous Liga Poporŭlui (People's League) following the elections of 1919. He undertook three crucial tasks: repressing the general strike of 1920; arresting the delegates of the Partidul Socialdemocrat (Social Democratic Party, or PSD) who voted for affiliation to the Third International; and initiating land reform. This unsettled period lasted for only a few years, leading to a new phase of liberal dominance that began with the passage of a constitution in 1923 and lasted until the 1928 elections. Although the liberal governments of this period demonstrated many authoritarian traits, they also achieved a number of fundamental reforms that laid the foundations for a new two-party system to replace the alternation between the prewar liberals and conservatives.[39]

The 1923 constitution established a form of guided democracy. It conceded universal male suffrage (women were not given the right to vote until 1946) and minority rights, yet it also established firm administrative control over elections. Local governments could be packed with central state appointees, the upper house of the parliament contained members by right, rights of association were severely restricted, and the declaration of martial law eased. In 1926 Romania adopted a so-called regime bonus, copied from the Italian fascist electoral law of 1924, that automatically gave any party winning 40 percent of the vote half of the parliamentary seats and distributed the remaining seats according to the proportion of the vote that the parties had won, while excluding any party that won less than 2 percent of the seats. These measures were extremely controversial, for they were passed by a parliament packed with PNL deputies and were thus made without consulting any of the other political forces, particularly the Partidul Național Român (Romanian National Party, or PNR) and the Partidul Țărănesc (Peasant Party, or PȚ), discussed in more detail below. Yet the measures that the PNL deployed to win elections, especially the establishment of the regime bonus, forced a consolidation of the party system, a promising development for Romania's democracy. Twelve parties presented candidates in the period between 1922 and 1926. This number had been reduced to seven in the years between 1926 and 1928, and of these only three made it over the 2 percent threshold for national representation. A two-party system appeared to be consolidating by the late twenties, and this was largely due to the constitution of 1923.[40]

These administrative changes of course also reflected the interests of the PNL in controlling the new democracy. The national liberals, who had emerged as the party representing the remnants of large landed property, banks, and industry made full use of the tools the constitution provided.[41] As Heinen writes: "Such a political organization could hardly count on the support of a wide share of the population. Its position of power was the result not of a generalized popularity, but rather of its organizational power and, what was even more important, of the influence it exercised over King Ferdinand."[42] Only with the aid of these administrative tools was the party able firmly to control Romanian elections until the late twenties.[43]

The PNL's policies were not narrowly repressive. Instead, the national liberal leadership instituted economic policies designed to win support from the peasantry, and encouraged the development of agrarian voluntary associations. This was a project of interclass hegemony, broadly similar to the Giolittian experiment in Italy and the Primo de Rivera regime in Spain. The center of the national liberal project was land reform. When the liberals returned to power in 1923, they distributed 40 percent of all arable land. With this reform the party aimed to create a stratum of improving farmers who would form the basis of an internal market for industrial goods. Unfortunately, land redistribution was an economic disaster. Part of the reason for this was that the PNL's policies of industrial development conflicted with the needs of agriculture. Through a series of four "nationalization" laws passed in 1924, the government placed restrictions on the share of foreign ownership in industry in raw materials and energy, and funneled credit to industry and manufacturing, but did little to provide resources to the agrarian population. Thus, while the peasants now had land, they had no access to capital to invest. Further, the PNL established a tariff regime that worsened the terms of trade between agriculture and industry. High export tariffs on agricultural goods lowered agricultural prices in Romania, while high import tariffs on industrial products increased the costs of agricultural inputs. The per-capita value of exports collapsed between 1913 and 1925, as peasants increased their consumption rather than output.[44]

One of the most striking developments during the twenties was the explosion of rural associationism. This was very much a project of the PNL elites as well. After the land reform of the postwar period, a series of new institutions developed: consumer cooperative societies, production cooperative societies, cooperative societies for purchasing or renting land, cooperatives for distributing land, and other types, such as cooperatives for exploiting the forests or fishing. All of these institutions expanded rapidly, especially in the twenties, as table 5 shows. One of the main reasons for this expansion was that the new owners needed access to funds, and with the disappearance of landlords, who had provided some credit, even if at usurious rates, the banks were their only

Table 5 The Development of Romanian Cooperative Societies in the Twenties

Type of society	1921	1922	1923	1924	1925	1926	1927	1928
Credit cooperatives (popular banks)	3,211	3,213	3,747	3,956	4,207	4,413	4,766	4,810
Societies of supply and sale	1,959	2,248	2,912	3,252	3,339	3,339	2,886	2,623
Societies of production	—	—	—	242	257	321	405	344
Landholding societies	—	—	102	125	123	119	100	104
Land-purchasing societies	—	—	104	177	220	297	343	402
Societies for the exploitation of forests	730	823	830	843	889	918	862	819

Source: Mitrany 1930.

source. Further, the cooperative became the main institution for distributing land.[45] The land reform distributed pieces of land to associations of resettlement, organizations that often then transformed into cooperative farms. The number of consumer and marketing cooperatives also exploded during this period, reaching 7,500 in 1928.[46]

The Romanian state also established agrarian chambers and a Union of Chambers of Agriculture. These organizations were supposed to provide political representation to agricultural interests as well as advice and training to agrarians. Each was comprised of seventeen elected and eleven appointed members. Only farmers who possessed a minimum of 3 hectares, or renters who rented more than 10 hectares, were allowed to elect members, thus excluding the poor peasants from representation.[47]

This explosion in the development of Romania's agrarian civil society, like the earlier developments, was driven by the Romanian state, and more particularly by the PNL. During the postwar period the powers of the Central further expanded. Its name was changed to the Central Office of Agrarian Reform and Agricultural Co-operation, and the organization was divided into sections: banks, buying and selling societies, cooperative farming societies, and rural mortgage and land registry. The first three of these sections had an autonomous administrative board comprised half of state employees and half of elected representatives of the banks. All of these organizations continued to be heavily dependent on state funding, and state appointees continued to comprise their leadership. One of the main projects of the Romanian political elite during the twenties, then, was the promotion of rural voluntary associations. The evidence suggests that, at least in quantitative terms, this project was a major success.[48]

The results of the PNL's period in power were strikingly contradictory. Seen from one perspective the period of liberal control during the twenties was one of radical reform: universal suffrage, land reform, and associational development were all vital parts of this program. Yet the PNL also became ever more associated with authoritarian methods of government during precisely this period of opening. The party guaranteed its political control by repressing and falsifying electoral results. Further, its economic program, after the midtwenties, was radically incompatible with the interests of the vast majority of the population. The various attempts to create a prosperous class of well-organized small farmers who might support the Romanian state proved ill conceived. The partial opening of the national liberals combined with their continuing reliance on corruption and repression, but the party had forced a consolidation of Romania's political spectrum and carried out some basic reforms, particularly land reform.

The Peasant Party

The one political organization that should have been able to establish a democratic regime in Romania was the National Peasant Party (PNȚ). This organization was founded in October of 1926 as the merger of the Nationalist Party that advocated for the rights of the Romanian population in Transylvania from the late nineteenth century, and the Peasant Party, which had developed in prewar Romania. These groups represented quite different interests. The Nationalist Party represented the interests of Transylvanian intellectuals and small merchants. The Peasant Party, in contrast, was rooted in the intellectual strata of the villages of the Regat (Moldavia and Wallachia). The program of the newly unified party advocated legality, a reduction of tariffs, and effective universal suffrage.[49]

The PNȚ's ideology was thus eclectic; but one powerful strand was Constantin Stere's agrarian populism. Stere (1865–1936) came from a boyar family and had initially been close to the social democrats. In a series of articles written after the 1907 peasant uprising, he sketched out an alternative course of development for Romania, arguing that industrialization would inevitably fail because the country lacked access to foreign markets for industrial goods. As a result, the economy should be developed on "peasantist" foundations. Smallholding would form the basis of the economy, supplemented by a handicraft industry for internal consumption and a nationalized extractive sector.[50] The decisive political consequence of this idea was that many of the leaders of the peasant party rejected industrialization as a development strategy. This of course implied that the strategy of state-led industrialization pursued by the PNL should be abandoned in favor of a path more compatible with peasant interests.[51]

The PNȚ's opportunity to exercise power came in 1928 as the result of a financial crisis. The national liberal attempt at forced industrialization destabilized the *leu* because it led to a balance-of-payments deficit. To shore up the currency the regime attempted to take out a foreign loan. This search for international financial backing provided an opening for the democratic opposition in the form of the PNȚ. The party's leader, Iuliu Maniu (1873–1953), organized a mass protest in May of 1928 designed to embarrass the government while it was searching for international support. In response to this pressure, the national liberals called for elections in November of 1928. In these elections, probably the cleanest in Romanian history up to that point, the PNȚ won a crushing victory, garnering 78 percent of the vote and 316 seats in the chamber. Its allies (the social democrats, Germans, Magyar peasants, Zionists, Bulgarians, and Ukrainians) added another 33, while the PNL won only 13 seats. The liberals would not return to power until 1933. The PNȚ's victory was therefore a historic opportunity.[52]

The national peasant government broke sharply with the policies of forced industrialization and domestic repression that had prevailed under the liberals. The government lifted martial law, which had been in place continuously from 1918 to 1928, and relaxed the xenophobic restrictions on foreign investment. The PNȚ, however, did not follow a consistently propeasant policy. The unified platform agreed upon in 1926 represented a sharp turn away from the pure peasantism of men like Stere. The leadership of the party, especially its Transylvanian nationalist wing, emphasized the need to increase productivity rather than protecting family farms. Indeed, in some respects the PNȚ government showed itself to be more committed to the development of agrarian capitalism than the PNL. In 1929 it reversed a 1925 law from the previous national liberal period prohibiting the sale of redistributed land. Thus, instead of protecting smaller holdings, the party made more land alienable. Accompanying this policy was new legislation on the cooperative movement designed to benefit wealthy peasants. By funneling credit to these organizations, the PNȚ leadership did little to help the majority of the rural poor who had supported the party. Rather, the main outcome was to increase differences between relatively wealthy peasants, who could use the credit, and the poor, who could not. However reasonable in purely economic terms, such a policy was politically disastrous.[53]

Partly because of the worsening international economic climate, but partly also because its agrarian policy alienated the rural poor, the PNȚ failed to carry through its reform program. Although the party remained an important political force until the midthirties, there are indications that it could not overcome the authoritarianism of the Romanian state. In February of 1929 the government suppressed a miners' strike in the Jiu Valley. Later that year a scandal broke over the torture of a man wrongly suspected of attempting to kill a high government minister. In an attempt to reign in a hostile press campaign, the PNȚ seized newspapers in early 1930.[54]

Elections in 1930 and 1931 showed a dramatic decline in support for the party. The PNL regained its strength, and for the first time candidates of the extreme right and left gained representation. The failure of the PNŢ to lead a full break-through to democracy is one of the great tragedies of Romanian contemporary history, and it opened the path to the rise of Romanian fascism.[55] Since this is a major turning point in the story, it is worth exploring further here. There are three main reasons for this failure: the economic circumstances of the late twenties and early thirties, the heterogeneous interests that the party represented, and the organizational weakness of the party itself. It is important to recognize that the PNŢ came to power during a very difficult economic period precisely as collapsing wheat prices devastated agriculture and created a serious problem of rural indebtedness. Any government in these circumstances would have had difficulty in pursuing peasant interests. Yet factors specific to the PNŢ as a political organization also played a role. The PNŢ represented very heterogeneous interests. The party's unification was generally favorable to its Transylvanian nationalist wing. In contrast, the more purely peasantist wing occupied a relatively subordinate position. This meant that the PNŢ government tended to pursue the political aims of universal suffrage and good government first, leaving crucial economic issues unaddressed, and thus putting the party at odds with the vital interests of much of the country.[56] Finally, and perhaps most importantly from the perspective of this analysis, is that the PNŢ remained—like the PNL, which was its main adversary—a patronage organization divided into numerous patron-client networks linked to specific political families. This organizational factor became crucial after the return of the monarchy to Romania in June of 1930.[57]

How should the twenties be evaluated? Despite the continuing authoritarianism within both the PNL and the PNŢ, Romania made significant progress toward the establishment of a functioning liberal democracy in this period. Its political elites had carried through an impressive land reform, established universal suffrage, and erected a political system based on party alternation. Of course there were significant problems. The economic reforms of both parties had failed, corruption continued to shape elections, and the rapid expansion of the Romanian state meant that it had to deal with both restive national minorities and hostile powers along its borders. Still, the country's prospects for democracy seemed at least as good as those of any of the other cases discussed in this book. The return of an activist monarch in Carol II would dramatically change the political situation.

Counterhegemony

The late twenties presented a crucial democratic opening, which could lead to a democratic outcome only if a strong, counterhegemonic movement emerged. But hegemonic politics had not developed in Romania. The PNȚ therefore suffered from the same tendency as the more established political forces to split into narrowly based interest groups. The party's weakness was revealed by the return of the Romanian monarch.

The collapse of Romania's interwar democracy cannot be understood without appreciating the massive impact of Carol II's resumption of the Romanian throne in June of 1930. This event was important because it reversed the gradual consolidation of a two-party system that had begun in the twenties. Historically Romania had a strong monarchy, but by the late twenties this institution had weakened. By the time of King Ferdinand's death in 1927, Carol II, his son, was living in France with his mistress Elena Lupescu (1885–1977), having abandoned his wife and son in Romania. From January of 1926 George Buzdugan, a regent who was to hold power until prince Michael, Carol's son, came of age, was the formal sovereign of the country. The developments toward democracy in the late twenties occurred in this vacuum of royal authority, which allowed for the consolidation of both the PNL and the PNȚ. Given this situation Carol's restoration became a major political issue and a fundamental watershed in Romania's political history.[58]

King Carol returned to Romania in June of 1930, just as support for the PNȚ was waning. He claimed the throne and ended the regency by demoting his son Michael to the post of Grand Voevod of Alba Iulia. Scandalized by the fact that Carol brought his Jewish mistress back to the country, Maniu, the leader of the PNȚ, resigned in October of 1930.[59]

Carol's return coincided with the rise of an authoritarian court camarilla that formed an alternative center of power within the Romanian state. The Italian fascist model of rule fascinated the new monarch.[60] He wished to establish himself as a new type of plebiscitary king.[61] This involved two related policies, the destruction of Romania's political parties and the establishment of a mass fascist movement that might provide the monarch with civilian support. The camarilla that surrounded and supported this project was comprised of three slightly different groups. The first were personal followers of Carol, such as his private secretary, and particularly his mistress Elena Lupescu. The second were political figures who saw in the new monarch a vehicle for their own projects for reconstructing the Romanian state, such as Nae Ionescu (1888–1940), Mihaïl Manoïlescu (1891–1950), and Costantin Argetoianu (1871–1952). Industrialists made up the third group.[62]

The most consistent theoretician of the Carolist political project was the Romanian economist Mihaïl Manoïlescu (1891–1950). Manoïlescu had begun his career as an opponent of the peasantist development project. According to him the peasantist claim of a nonindustrial path to the modern world was a chimera. Industrialization had to take place. This required state support for industries whose productivity was higher than the average productivity of the country. In practice such a policy could be carried out only at the expense of the peasantry, since it would exacerbate the price difference between industrial and agricultural products, thereby transferring resources from agriculture to industry. In a society where peasants constituted the vast majority of the population, such a program was incompatible with representative democracy, and thus Manoïlescu quite naturally shifted his position from a rather conservative liberalism to authoritarianism during the thirties.[63]

Manoïlescu's vision of the new Romanian state was heavily indebted to Italian fascism. Against the nineteenth-century liberal state, he argued for a state that would be the "bearer of an idea." But in seeking to develop a workable authoritarian project for Romania, he argued that the monarchy, rather than a political party, should be the key instrument. As Heinen argues this represented Manoïlescu's position in Romanian politics. Without a significant organization of his own, his project necessarily relied on an alliance with the monarchy. Manoïlescu was a top member of the camarilla. He was in contact with Carol, even prior to the latter's return to Romania. In an audience with the king in September of 1930, he expounded a plan for a monarchical dictatorship. A constituency for something like his program started to coalesce after the depression of the thirties began to bite.[64]

The relationship between the Carolist camarilla and the Romanian political establishment was extremely complex. It is possible to distinguish between three periods. During the early thirties (1930–1933) Carol attempted to rule with the aid of individual personalities against the national liberal establishment. In the midthirties (1934–1937) the camarilla and the PNL reached an uneasy accommodation under the government of Gheorge Tătărescu (1886–1957). The relationship between Carol and the PNL remained tense, however. As I show in the following section, the rise of a mass fascist party in the late thirties presented the monarchy with an opportunity for establishing a more openly authoritarian regime than was possible before.

The immediate effect of the camarilla was to weaken the PNȚ. One of Carol's very first acts was to attempt to establish a government of broad national unity to replace the PNȚ government led by Maniu. Both the PNȚ and the PNL resisted this move, because they saw in it an attempt to replace the role of elected parliamentary majorities with the will of the monarch. Having failed to establish a promonarchist government of national unity, Carol changed his strategy to promoting monarchist factions within the major parties. This proved much more successful, especially within the PNȚ, where a split developed between Iuliu Maniu, who was generally hostile to Carol, and Alexander Vaida-Voevod (1872–1950), who was supportive of the monarch. This fragmentation, actively encouraged by the camarilla, tended to further reinforce Carol's position by creating political instability. In the period from 1930 to 1940, Romania was governed by 25 cabinets and 18 different premiers. Carol achieved this aim by arbitrarily dismissing prime ministers and fostering splits between "court" and "excluded" groups within each party, thereby dissolving their political coherence and making royal intervention appear necessary. These maneuvers reversed the process of political consolidation that had begun in the twenties. In 1931, 37 political groups existed. In 1932 there were 61, and in 1933 this had exploded to 102. This manner of forming governments widened the chasm between parliament and the real political situation in the country and was fertile ground for fascist mobilization.[65]

The PNȚ suffered most from Carol's machinations. Initially it seemed the party had weathered the storm, winning over 40 percent of the vote in the elections of July 1932, giving it a substantial majority in the chamber. However, Carol's appointment of Alexander Vaida-Voevod, leader of the extreme right of the PNȚ, as prime minister did the party serious harm. He would later (in 1935) be expelled from the PNȚ and found his own semifascist group: the Frontul Românesc (Romanian Front, or FR). Prior to World War I, he had been on the extreme right of the Transylvanian National Party and was politically close to the populist mayor of Vienna, Karl Lueger (1844–1910), who influenced Adolf Hitler's early ideas. His period of rule deeply damaged the democratic credentials of the PNȚ and did much to open the way to mass fascism in Romania. There were three main reasons for this. First, Vaida-Voevod pursued an ambiguous policy toward the extreme right, and particularly its foremost organization the Iron Guard. During the peasant government of 1928 to 1930, Vaida-Voevod met with the leader of this movement, Corneliu Codreanu, and expressed sympathy for his views. In power he showed little inclination to take a hard line against the right. Second, the Vaida-Voevod government also brutally repressed an oil workers' strike in early 1933, using the military and passing legislation easing the declaration of martial law. This terribly damaged the PNȚ's claim to represent a broad popular coalition. Finally, a major scandal broke out in the wake of the discovery of secret Romanian military documents at the Bucharest office of the Czech arms maker Skoda. Surrounded by corruption and having shown itself willing to wield the army against the population, the PNȚ saw its popularity collapse.[66]

Paradoxically, given the fact that there were many points of agreement between the PNL and the camarilla, the liberals proved in some respects more resistant to Carol's blandishments. In fact, the PNL maintained its organizational cohesion and remained the dominant political force up until 1937. To understand why, it is important to examine developments within this party.[67]

Carol's return provoked a split among three wings of the liberals: the PNL Gheorge Brătianu, an antimonarchist splinter party; the "old liberals," linked to the main branch of the Brătianu family; and the "young liberals" around Ion Duca (1879–1933). These internal tensions were the result of broader changes within the social elite, particularly the increasing importance of large industry, a group more closely linked to the young liberals than the Brătianu family. Up until the end of the twenties, producers of consumer goods and the banks occupied a dominant position within the ruling social coalition.[68] These men made money primarily by funneling foreign credit to local landholders. They were also the most important figures in the PNL and distributed credit through the "liberal banks." The depression worsened their position, because it affected agriculture more than industry. Price levels indicate the difference. Taking 1929 as the base year, the prices of agriculture fell almost 56 points from 1929 to 1934. Industry was also affected, but much less so. Its prices dropped only 18 points over the same period. This further exacerbated the "price scissors," making industrial products relatively more expensive for agricultural producers and leading to rural indebtedness and a severe banking crisis. In addition, since the banks attached to the liberals were heavily dependent on foreign finance, they were highly exposed to the worldwide banking crisis as well. These developments, consequently, increased the relative power of heavy industry, as opposed to bankers, within the ruling coalition.[69]

This "new industry" was closely linked to the state, primarily because of the latter's decisive role as a consumer of industrial goods. The Romanian state in 1937 and 1938 consumed 70 percent of industrial output. The state railway company alone consumed 80 percent of domestic coal production. Continuing this state largess, in the context of Romania's restricted domestic market, was therefore a matter of economic survival for Romanian industry. But since this policy of state-led industrialization implied a reduction in rural incomes through heavy taxation, it was naturally an authoritarian project. King Carol's corporatist project of state-led development based on squeezing agriculture could find decisive social support among this group.[70]

However, none of the various wings of the PNL provided unqualified support to Carol. The PNL–Gh. Brătianu was openly antimonarchist, and the remaining Brătianu old liberals were also quite hostile to Carol. More surprisingly, perhaps, the young liberals themselves were also critical of Carol. The issue that irritated this wing of the party was the monarch's ambiguous attitude to organizations of the extreme right. Ion Duca brought relentless pressure to bear on Carol during the Vaida-Voevod government. The latter, as I suggested above, was Carol's favorite.[71] As head of the PNL Duca organized mass demonstrations against his regime and even called for a mass march on Bucharest in November of 1933 that the PNȚ was forced to outlaw. The party's program called for a strengthening of the parliamentary system, a policy of intransigence against the extreme right, and punishing corruption. In many respects the young liberals around Duca had now assumed the reformist mantle of the PNȚ.[72]

Carol's return to the political scene had thus led to the collapse of the PNȚ, but its effects on the PNL were more ambiguous. By the time Duca had come to power, the PNL and the camarilla had established a working relationship, but there was considerable mutual hostility between the camps. Over the next five years Carol would attempt to establish relations with the extreme right, using it to pursue his own statist fascist project.

The above paragraphs have described the rise of the court camarilla, its role in the weakening of the PNȚ, and the alliance that emerged between the young liberal wing of the PNL and Carol in the midthirties. In the absence of these developments, it is not possible to grasp the significance of the rise of a mass fascist party in Romania. Party fascism in Romania gained national importance by placing itself consistently on the side of nonelites. The Romanian fascist movement was thus not so much an antidemocratic movement as an antiliberal movement responding to the failure of parliamentary institutions to address adequately the problems of the majority of the Romanian population. This was particularly true of the period between 1935 and 1938, when it became a mass party.

To understand these developments and their connection to the broader political context of interwar Romania, it is necessary to return briefly to the period immediately after the war. The first radical right organizations were anticommunist student groups that gained some notoriety in the agitation following World War I. One of these was called the Guard of National Consciousness, a union-busting organization in which the future leader of Romanian fascism, Corneliu Zelea Codreanu (1899–1938), began his political career.[73] As the leftist high tide receded, in part as a consequence of land reform combined with Averescu's policy of repression, the radical right shifted its focus from antibolshevism to anti-Semitism in its search for political space.[74] In 1922 Codreanu, together with Alexander Cuza (1857–1947) and others founded the National Christian Union.[75] This organization later developed into Romania's first radical right-wing party, the anti-Semitic Liga Apărării Național-Creștine (League of National Christian Defense, or LANC), founded in 1923. The anti-Semitic extreme right, however, remained a marginal political force throughout the twenties. In its most successful election of the twenties, that of 1926, the party won under 5 percent of the popular vote.[76]

The LANC was a somewhat heterogeneous organization divided between those who wished to pursue anti-Semitic policies within the framework of the liberal state, like Cuza, and those, like Codreanu, who held that a radical transformation of the political system was necessary. These tactical differences ultimately led Codreanu, now a law student, to break with his former mentor Cuza and in June of 1927 to found his own organization called the Legiunea Arhanghelul Mihail (Legion of the Archangel Michael, or LAM). Membership in the LAM required a period of apprenticeship in the local cell and "brotherhood" organizations. In 1930 Codreanu established a second organization: the Garda de Fier (Iron Guard). Although initially conceived as an umbrella group including members of all political parties, it seems to have remained virtually indistinguishable from the LAM. Finally, after a period of severe repression in the midthirties (described below), the Iron Guard reemerged as the Totul pentru Țară (All for the Country Party, or TPȚ) and won significant electoral support in the 1937 elections.[77]

Codreanu saw himself as divinely ordained to lead the Romanian people. He drew on rituals from Romanian popular religion, spoke with dead people, and believed in miracles. Precisely because he avoided programs and themes, it is difficult to place the movement politically. The legionaries were anti-Semites, but this did not distinguish them from any other political force, apart from the social democrats. The movement had no discernible political program but was heavily inflected by religion. Codreanu wanted to form "new men" through rituals of suffering and sacrifice. It is not even clear that Codreanu conceived of his organization as an instrument for the seizure of political power in the conventional sense. The LAM and Iron Guard had little initial success. Codreanu had hoped to attract support away from the LANC, but his movement was too strange, and its goals were too close to the more established anti-Semitic right to have much impact.[78]

Organizationally the LAM combined a party and paramilitary organization, although the latter never developed. It sought to grab headlines through acts of spectacular violence. Initially, its main targets were Jews, but as a paramilitary anti-Semitic movement Codreanu's group remained of limited significance. During the late twenties and early thirties, it never approached the percentage of votes that the LANC won. More importantly, radical anti-Semitism never attracted wide support in the Romanian electorate. At its highpoint the LANC was able to win only a little more than 5 percent of the vote.[79]

It is crucial to distinguish between two main phases of development in the Iron Guard: a period up until 1932 in which the movement remained an insignificant political sect dominated by students and a period from 1932 to 1938 in which it became one of the most important currents in Romanian political life.[80] The date is significant because it coincides with the sharp turn to the right within the PNȚ described above. Indeed, Codreanu's legion moved into the vacuum created by these developments.[81] The party had its first significant political successes as it shifted from a narrowly anti-Semitic program and toward espousing more populist demands. This change in program went together with a redefinition of the organization's main enemies from Jews to the political authorities. Codreanu expressed this shift in tactics in his memoirs. There he writes: "The Romanian people will not be able to solve the Jewish problem unless it first solves *the problem of its political parties.* The first aim to be reached by the Romanian people on its way to topple the Judaic power that oppresses and strangles it, will have to be *the toppling of this political system.*"[82] Although shrouded in anti-Semitism, this passage emphasizes the primacy of the struggle against political parties.

The Iron Guard's turn toward populism began with Codreanu's public support for the railway and oil workers' strike discussed earlier and his denunciation of its bloody suppression. He declared in parliament that, far from being a Moscow-backed plot, the oil and rail workers' demands were an understandable response to deprivation.[83] It was in response to this populist stance, rather than anti-Semitic hooliganism, that the government banned the wearing of uniforms by political organizations and increased its repressive activities against the guard. The repression continued under the new PNL Duca premiership, leading to the arrest of 18,000 members of the guard and the deaths of three of them.[84] Codreanu's group resisted this repression forcefully, by assassinating the prime minister. The legion, then, posed a real physical threat to the Romanian authorities. They vigorously responded. Over 500 of Codreanu's followers were killed during the thirties, and the LAM was outlawed in 1934.[85]

After the repression of 1934 following Duca's assassination, the legionary movement entered a period of crisis. Codreanu faced a serious challenge from the leader of the legionary youth movement, Mihail Stelescu (1907–1936), who criticized the personalistic leadership of the guard and its uncritical attitude toward Germany. In part as an attempt to reestablish some control over his organization, he founded the TPȚ in December of 1935 under the formal leadership of the ex-general Gheorge Cantacuzino-Granicerul (1869–1937). With the founding of this organization, the legionary movement shifted decisively away from paramilitary tactics.[86] Politically it positioned itself as a determined opponent of the camarilla. In late 1935 the legion took part in demonstrations in support of the republican Dimitrie Gerota (1867–1939), who had been jailed for speaking out publicly against the monarchy. The end point of this development was the electoral pact that the TPȚ established with the PNȚ and the anti-Carolist liberals in 1937. By 1937 Codreanu's movement was at the forefront of a coalition of forces struggling against Romania's corrupt political system.[87]

What were the main political aims of the legionary movement in the period from 1935 to 1938? This question is difficult to answer. All of the evidence suggests that Codreanu was an enthusiastic admirer of Mussolini and Hitler, but the domestic political meaning of this attitude is difficult to specify. In an interview with a Romanian newspaper in 1937, Codreanu explained his position, in contrast to Iuliu Maniu, the leader of the PNȚ, this way: "Mr. Maniu is for democracy. I am of an entirely different opinion, as well as being against dictatorship. A new epoch is beginning, in which a new system is emerging until now unknown to us. I am for that."[88] The legionary movement thus aimed at a new, as yet undefined political system that would be neither a dictatorship nor a democracy.

More concretely, the legionary movement of the thirties focused on practical schemes of social reform and personal development. These projects were focused above all on transforming "men." The creation of new forms of solidarity and discipline was a central element in its program. The movement was organized into a series of local cells, called "nests," made up of three to thirteen members, the leaders of which were supposed to emerge from below.[89] Recruitment to the legion relied heavily on face-to-face relations. Each new member was supposed to recruit five further members, thus creating socially homogenous nests. The idea behind this strategy was to minimize social conflict within the movement and increase the effectiveness of propaganda. Peasant nests would discuss issues related to farming, the intellectual nests would devote their time to clarifying doctrinal differences between the legion and the other groups of the far right. In Weber's view the "capacity of leaders had to be proved by every chief—who was not appointed from the center but forced to establish himself, showing by achievement and activity that he could build his own following."[90] Followers subscribed to a set of basic rules: discipline, work, silence, self-education, aid, and honor. The nests did not restrict themselves to spreading propaganda but also helped the population with practical problems. In the bi-elections at Neamț in 1931 the legion covered the districts with activists who went from family to family, helping with the harvest and organizing evening meetings. Legionnaires repaired roads, bridges, and churches and built wells and dams. During the thirties, as the legion's importance increased, the movement established a proletarian group, organized labor camps, and set up a chain of restaurants and department stores, as well as a hospital and welfare organization. According to Codreanu there were 4,200 nests in 1935, 12,000 in January 1937, and by the end of the year, 34,000.[91]

What were the social groups to which the movement appealed? There are four main sources for answering this question: a study of local groups in the county of Radauti in 1936, a study of the Carmen-Sylva work camp, a list of members accused in the trial of Prime Minister Duca, and a list of members killed in prison in 1939. Students constitute the highest percentage of members in all of the last three sources, while peasants make up a surprisingly small percentage of the membership. The 1936 study, in contrast, shows students making up 5 percent of the members of local groups, and farmers 69 percent.[92]

This evidence, however, is difficult to interpret, for two reasons. First, many students probably came from wealthy peasant households. Very elite groups, industrialists and big landholders, sent their children to study abroad in France or Germany, and these people would thus not have been included. Poor peasants, in contrast, lacked the means to educate their children. The second difficulty derives from the "samples." People who participated in the work camps and stood trial were probably full-time activists. It is thus hardly surprising that students constituted the highest percentage of members of these organizations. Therefore, the 1936 study of local groups probably gives the fullest picture of who was involved. Taken as a whole the evidence suggests that the legion had serious support in the universities and among some parts of the peasantry.[93]

My analysis of the legionary movement argues that its popularity derived from its determined opposition to the authoritarian forces that controlled the Romanian state. I have left out of the account one crucial alternative explanation that needs to be addressed, for Codreanu's various political organizations were all virulently and notoriously anti-Semitic. How did this contribute to the legionary movement's popularity? There is a lot of evidence to suggest that anti-Semitism in Romania was not a specifically fascist ideology and as such cannot account for the party's success. As I hinted above, the legionary movement developed as a splinter organization from the LANC. This older organization was a much a more established and exclusively anti-Semitic party than the legionary movement. It had already occupied the radical anti-Semitic position within the Romanian political life prior the emergence of the Iron Guard. The electoral evidence shows that the Iron Guard was unable to attract significant support in areas where the LANC was established. As a consequence of this basic structural factor, the movement was forced to broaden its message in order to win greater support. The legionary movement's political success tracks precisely its turn away from an exclusively anti-Semitic program. Nor was anti-Semitism the exclusive province of the radical right. Tătărescu paid for the train tickets of anti-Semitic students, and the police provided them with weapons to attack Jews in Iași in August of 1925. In fact, one might argue that anti-Semitism was so pervasive in Romanian life in the thirties that it was hard to mobilize around the issue politically.[94]

The political crisis that led to the rise of Romania's fascist movement follows a pattern evident from both the Italian and Spanish cases. A democratic opening produced by rapid civil society development remained unexploited by existing political organizations. A mass fascist movement, championing a set of basic democratic demands but radically hostile to liberalism, arose in the vacuum thus created. The populism of the Romanian fascist movement and its organizational weakness were both linked to the particular statist pattern of civil society development that characterized Romania. The movement attacked the political class as an unrepresentative clique, often linking it rhetorically to the Jews.

The Rise of Statist Fascism (1937–1940)

The above section has shown how a mass fascist movement in Romania emerged out of the failure of counterhegemony. Codreanu's party became a significant political force by championing the interests of peasants and workers and demanding an end to corruption. This placed Romania's fascist movement at loggerheads with the Romanian state. Yet the existence of a mass fascist movement presented the monarch in particular with an opportunity for creating a new mass regime, one that he tried to exploit with some success in the late thirties. However, international events conspired to undermine this project, leading to the ambiguous dictatorship of Ion Antonescu (1882–1946).

Carol's attempt to establish a dictatorship, as I argued above, faced resistance from the forces who were most closely allied to the monarch—particularly the young liberals around Tătărescu. The 1937 elections removed these constraints because of their devastating consequences for the PNL. Despite the fact that the liberal list won a plurality of the vote (36%), in the conditions of interwar Romania this indicated a massive failure, for the cabinet had been unable to engineer an electoral margin that would trip the "government bonus" mechanism established by the 1926 electoral law.[95] In contrast, the PNȚ and the TPȚ between them had won over 35 percent of the vote and together had a right to the same number of seats in the chamber as the PNL. Enmity between the PNȚ and the national liberals precluded a government of national concentration based on an alliance between the main "democratic" forces. A legionary-peasant government was a theoretical possibility, but Carol had already decided prior to the voting to appoint the anti-Semitic Octavian Goga (1881–1938) as premier in the event of a liberal defeat.[96]

Codreanu's TPȚ had, in contrast to the national liberals, achieved a major victory. This organization in 1937 had 272,000 members, comprising 1.5 percent of the population.[97] It won about 16 percent of the vote, just 4 points behind the PNȚ. As I have shown there were serious tensions between the monarchy and the legion. Codreanu fiercely resisted all overtures to link himself to the monarchy. The most spectacular manifestation of the legion's resistance to Carol was the establishment of an electoral pact with the PNŢ in November of 1937. Codreanu's group thus entered the elections as a prominent member of a coalition of political forces dedicated to limiting the arbitrary power of the king.

The relationship between Carol and the legion was more ambiguous than these facts suggest. Up until 1933 Codreanu's movement was generally monarchist. Carol hoped to come to terms with the organization as late as 1937. It is important to stress that the antiguardist repression of the thirties was virtually all initiated by powerful figures among the national liberals, and not by the monarch himself.[98] On the contrary important players within the royal camarilla provided substantial financial support to Codreanu's movement.[99] Despite considerable repression, the courts and the police were relatively lenient concerning legionary crimes, and Carol appears to have entertained the hope of using the movement as a support for his own ambitions. The major obstacle to a fusion of the two movements was Codreanu himself.[100]

The electoral outcome of 1937, then, presented both opportunities and dangers to the monarch. Although it demonstrated a deep antipathy toward the entire political class, it also allowed Carol to eliminate the last obstacles to his longstanding personal ambition of instituting a fascist regime. He responded to the victory by installing a nonguardist government of the extreme right, completely unjustified by the electoral returns, headed by Goga, but including Alexander Cuza as a minister without portfolio. The Goga-Cuza government, in power from December 1937 to February of 1938, was supposed to win mass support away from the legion by adopting much of its anti-Semitic program. Left-wing, Jewish-owned newspapers were outlawed, only Christian journalists were allowed free passage on trains, and Jewish pub owners were deprived of their licenses. In addition, quotas were decreed limiting Jewish numbers in state employment, the professions, and education. At the end of January 1938 all Jews were required to prove their citizenship in court.[101]

These measures were a political failure. The legion continued to criticize the Goga government and engage in violent struggle against it.[102] The Romanian anti-Semitic extreme right, far from incorporating Codreanu's movement, was locked in a life-and-death struggle with it. On February 8 the situation abruptly changed, when the Cuzists and the guard signed an electoral pact. A royal seizure of power followed almost immediately from these developments. On February 10, after a final effort to invite Codreanu into a government of national concentration, Carol cashiered the Goga government and established a royal dictatorship under the cover of Miron Cristea (1868–1939), the patriarch of the Orthodox Church, and Armand Călinescu (1893–1939), an efficient and ruthless bureaucrat.[103]

The royalist dictatorship that issued from these events constituted itself partially as an emergency regime against Codreanu's movement. The king reimposed martial law, placed local government under the control of the military, and established a new constitution, much of which was directly aimed at the legion. Priests were prohibited from using their spiritual authority for political purposes. Article 8 forbade political associations with a religious basis. Article 15 prescribed the death penalty for political murders, a favorite tactic of the legion, and jury deliberations were declared open to make prosecution easier. Article 67 stated that only residents who had been Romanians for three generations could be prime minister: a provision explicitly designed to bar Codreanu from the premiership.[104]

Carol's regime, however antiguardist, was not a prophylactic dictatorship designed to save Romania from the threat of fascism.[105] On the contrary it was a clear attempt to impose a fascist regime "from above." In June of 1940 Carol established the Frontul Renaşterii Naţionale (Front of National Renaissance, or FNR) as a single-party organization and initiated discussions with the Germans over how to "nazify" his regime.[106] It was the mass electoral success of the TPŢ that had made this move possible by fatally weakening the national liberals. Carol could then present himself, both to his country and to history, as a figure above the political fray. Paradoxically his establishment of statist fascism was enabled by the emergence of a mass fascist movement, which was increasingly anti-Carolist.

The decisive move against the legion, however, came after the German annexation of Austria. Codreanu responded to this event by sending Hitler a telegram to which it was rumored a reply had been received. The interior minister, Calinescu, intercepted the message and used it as a pretext to act decisively against the legion. During the spring of 1938 most of the legion's senior leadership was arrested, together with thousands of rank-and-file members. Codreanu himself was imprisoned as part of this repression and was strangled in prison in November. In reaction the remnants of the organization, under the leadership of the Transylvanian philosophy teacher Horia Sima (1907–1993), assassinated Calinescu, setting off another wave of bloodletting. This repression ended the history of the

Iron Guard as an autonomous social movement. From 1938 onward it became a terrorist organization closely tied to German interests.[107]

Carol's attempt to establish a statist fascist regime was short-lived. With the rise of a powerful national socialist Germany, the fundamental determinants of Romanian politics shifted across its borders. The collapse of the regime came when Carol was forced to abdicate because of the humiliating terms imposed on Romania by the German Vienna Award of 1940, which demanded large territorial concessions from Romania in favor of both Hungary and Bulgaria. Romania's capitulation in the face of German pressure was especially humiliating, given the costly rearmament program that the monarchy had backed from the early thirties, and the close, almost subservient relationship Carol had sought to establish with Germany. As a direct result of this foreign policy fiasco, the monarch was forced to abdicate on September 5, 1940.[108]

Paradoxically the collapse of Carol's regime as a result of the German-imposed Vienna Award arrested the country's evolution toward statist fascism. Carol had appointed General Ion Antonescu, who now established a regency with Carol's son Michael as the monarch. Antonescu initially tried to come to terms with the Iron Guard to provide his military dictatorship with some civilian support. The resulting "National Legionary State" proved unstable, as Horia Sima's guard unleashed a reign of chaos and terror that disgusted and horrified the general. In January of 1941 the guardists attempted to seize power, but Antonescu with the tacit support of Hitler, crushed this uprising.[109]

Antonescu's dictatorship was strongly directed against the men who had supported the Carolist project. He attacked the court camarilla, forcing anyone who occupied one of a number of high-level positions to declare the sources of their wealth. His basic political project was to enforce legality at every level of the administration. Further, Antonescu guaranteed a level of personal and political freedom greater than that which obtained under the Carolist dictatorship.[110]

The political history of interwar Romania contains a number of parallels with that of Italy and Spain. As in the southern European cases, in Romania the social elite was too politically weak to tolerate a functioning democratic regime. In the one fully democratic election of the period (that of 1928), the PNȚ soundly defeated the national liberals, thus threatening the program of state-led industrialization that was the central plank in the liberal program. The PNȚ, however, proved to be a fragile political force, in part because it continued to split into two fundamentally different wings. Support for the party faded during the thirties, partly to the benefit of Codreanu's legion. But the legion proved incapable of seriously challenging the dominant class coalition that was gathered around Carol and intent on industrialization from above.

Conclusions

Why did statist fascism come to dominate Romania in the late thirties? This chapter has argued that Romanian fascism, like its Italian and Spanish counterparts, was the result of associational development in the context of a failed hegemonic politics. Civic associationism supported democracy in this context, but not liberal democracy. However, Romania's specific form of associational development, state led rather than autonomous or elite led, had important consequences for the form of fascist regime that the country produced in the late thirties. Romania's fascist movement could not exploit a strong network of peasant self-organization, nor could it present itself as the white guard of threatened but highly organized landholders. As a result the movement was quickly subordinated to a project of statist fascism centered on the monarchy. It is worthwhile here to recapitulate the five stages of Romania's path to fascism.

Romania's social elite, despite enjoying considerable social power, failed to develop intradominant class hegemony. The constitution of 1866, which established the modern Romanian regime, was imposed at the expense of the mass of the population. The prefect at the local level was virtually omnipotent and played a major role in keeping the peasantry subordinated to the large estate owners. The political emancipation of the serfs thus went hand in hand with their social subordination. Paradoxically, this corrupt liberal system, which guaranteed elite control over the levers of political power, also weakened its ability to face universal suffrage. Despite strict restrictions on suffrage, fierce infighting broke out between the conservatives and the liberals, who vied for control over the all-important state budget. The Romanian social elite thus lacked both intraclass hegemony and interclass hegemony. These two weaknesses were connected. It was precisely the fragmentation of the social elite that prevented it from pursuing a coherent project of interclass hegemony.

Many members of the Romanian social elite were aware of the problem that the Romanian state lacked any significant popular support. They sought to overcome this weakness by organizing the countryside: attempting to establish a rural civil society. This was not a completely top-down affair. Autonomous cooperatives had emerged in Romania from the late nineteenth century. Yet they lacked the necessary legal guarantees to operate freely, and they were often too poor to survive. Liberal elites attempted to co-opt this movement and to spur its development by channeling state funds to establish popular banks after 1903. While this led to associational development, it also subordinated civil society development to the state to an extraordinary degree. The cooperative movement was virtually an arm of the ministerial bureaucracy. The 1907 peasant uprising showed that associationism had failed to incorporate the peasantry. No further attempts at reform occurred until after World War I. But Romania's pattern of associational development had important consequences for the country's subsequent political evolution.

The post–World War I period saw Romania enter a third stage of development, an attempt to establish interclass hegemony by pursuing dramatic political and economic reforms. Romania's politicians achieved a considerable amount in this period. They established a radical land reform that fatally weakened the Conservative Party, thus laying the foundations for a more unified and modern social elite than had existed hitherto. They also granted universal suffrage, but despite this progress, the Romanian social elite remained without an organization that could win elections. The PNL governments of the twenties relied on electoral manipulation and martial law: a legal device that was continuously in use from 1918 to 1928. The postwar attempt to establish mass support for the liberal state thus remained fundamentally incoherent. The political system opened enough to allow for the formation of mass parties organized against the liberal state but not sufficiently to allow the PNL to benefit politically from this opening.

The decline of the national liberals in the late twenties created a democratic opening that the PNȚ attempted to exploit. This party's political vision was ambiguous but clearly pointed to a fundamentally different model of society from that of the liberals. In its most consistent version it proposed a peasant democracy based on widespread landownership and handicraft industry. The PNȚ, however, did not break sufficiently with Romanian parliamentary practice to institute this project. It remained overly oriented to the crown and was quickly drawn into the practices of electoral corruption and court politics that had previously weakened the Liberal and Conservative parties. By the early thirties, then, both the liberals and the PNȚ had failed to exploit the opportunity to develop a truly democratic regime that the development of civil society, both before and especially after World War I, had presented.

A mass fascist movement in Romania began to develop only after the failure of the liberals and the PNȚ to establish a working democracy. Indeed, Codreanu's

Iron Guard was able effectively to position itself as a protest movement against the increasingly authoritarian neoliberal regime that consolidated between 1934 and 1937. The key to Codreanu's success was his rejection of parliament as an appropriate forum for the representation of Romania's national interests. Like his fascist counterparts in other countries, Codreanu rejected the political class as a corrupt and false representation of the Romanian people. His authoritarianism was paradoxically based on the democratic claim that only extraordinary individuals could represent the Romanian people. The violent anti-Semitism of the guard was also a consequence of its authoritarian democratic character. Codreanu linked Jews and politicians together as figures who undermined the national self-determination of the Romanian people.

Codreanu's party fascism, however, was not strong enough to impose itself on the Romanian state. It faced two basic problems, both deriving from the lack of autonomous civil society development in Romania. First, the Iron Guard lacked a strong organizational basis. It did not control a viable union movement or structure of rural cooperatives. Second, the overweening power of the political elite in Romania undermined the development of a political contest between left and right in which a strong fascist movement could emerge. The tactics of Codreanu's movement were closely connected with these conditions, for its most important political achievements were acts of isolated terror against important political figures in the Romanian state. The legion's disintegration in the face of the crackdown by King Carol after the elections of 1937 is particularly revealing. Instead of resisting state repression and pushing for a radicalization from below, Codreanu's movement collapsed.

It would, however, be a mistake to equate the failure of party fascism in Romania with the failure of the fascist political project as such, for this would ignore the equally important statist fascist project centered on the monarchy. The Carolist dictatorship that emerged after the 1937 elections represented the victory of this current. This regime reflected a fundamental departure in Romanian politics. It attempted to create mass popular support for an authoritarian monarchy. It is hard to evaluate the real viability of this project, because international events moved swiftly to undermine it.

Was some kind of fascist outcome in the interwar period an inevitability for Romania, given its geopolitical position and fundamental poverty? It seems rather difficult to argue this position. Romania had achieved the goal of national unification during the war, and its landholding class had been severely weakened by land reform. Further, an agrarian civil society was rapidly developing from the late nineteenth century. The key turning point in Romanian history was the collapse of the PNȚ and the return of Carol in 1930. But, as I have argued, the PNȚ's failure to grasp this opportunity cannot be understood in purely subjective terms. It was connected with the absence of a hegemonic dominant class in Romania. The habits of clientalism and factionalism that split the social elite infected the PNȚ as well.

What are the broader implications of Romania's path to fascism? In some respects the Romanian case shows more clearly than any analyzed so far the decisive importance of politics in explaining the fascist outcome. Romanian politicians confronted the basic social structural problems of their country directly by instituting land reform and granting universal suffrage. These reforms were not enough, however, to create hegemony. Liberalism in Romania remained without a viable national project capable of winning mass support, and the clientalistic style of politics that had developed in the nineteenth century continued into the postwar period, weakening any party's ability to link democratic claims to liberal institutional forms. Codreanu's fascist movement developed in the political vacuum left by the failure of Romania's parties to carry out a democratic project. He replaced the project of liberal democracy with a project of fascist authoritarian democracy.

Romania's path to fascism also demonstrates the importance of the particular form of associational development for the fascist outcome. Indeed, viewed from this perspective Romanian political development is quite paradoxical. Arguably, one of the reasons that Romania failed to consolidate as a democratic state in the interwar period was its lack of an autonomous civil society. This led to an organizationally weak peasantry that was unable to insulate the leadership of the PNȚ from the clientalistic pressures of Romanian political life, but these conditions also made a party fascist regime impossible to establish. Romania's state-dependent form of civil society development undermined the organizational conditions in which a fascist party could gain enough strength to seize power. The Iron Guard remained without developed mass organizations that could be used to mobilize support. The royalist clique around Carol thus instituted the fascist regime in Romania. This was not simply a preventative or parenthetical dictatorship designed to protect Romania from the threat of fascism. The Carolist dictatorship represented the decisive victory of the statist fascist forces that had gathered around the crown from the early thirties.

Why did this happen? Part of the answer lies in the specific nature of Romanian civil society. Agrarian associationism in Romania remained strikingly state dependent. The popular banks and chambers of agriculture were state-run affairs with no close links to the party system. King Carol's machinations further exacerbated this situation by fragmenting the already weak party system. It was this very amorphousness that allowed the legion to emerge as an inchoate protest movement against the Carolist project, but it is also what explains the guard's weakness in the face of state repression. The legion had no ability to use the basic tools of a political party. No general strike, mass protest, or paramilitary insurrection broke out in response to Carol's repression, because the organizational bases for these activities did not exist. Isolated "nests" linked only by their common devotion to the person of Codreanu proved powerless once the leader himself had been eliminated.

5

Considering Alternatives

The analyses in chapters 2 through 4 have argued that the development of voluntary associations was a major factor in the emergence of fascism in Italy, Spain, and Romania. However, readers familiar with comparative analyses of fascism may rightly wonder how these cases fit with explanations that are not centered on civil society.[1] It is the central task of this chapter to consider this issue. Among the variety of theories that attempt to explain the rise of fascism, two broad streams of scholarship are evident. The first, exemplified by Barrington Moore Jr.'s *Social Origins of Dictatorship and Democracy: Lord and Peasant in the Making of the Modern World*, is broadly Marxian. Moore's central argument holds that fascist regimes are connected to late and uneven capitalist development, producing a medium-strength bourgeoisie allied with labor-repressive agrarians. The second is Weberian, and in contrast to the Marxian focus on class relations, concentrates on states. For scholars in this tradition, fascism was closely connected to the survival of old regimes that could form a rallying point for conservatives into the modern period. To what extent do these approaches form compelling alternatives to the Gramscian account that I have developed so far? This chapter briefly summarizes the Moorian and Weberian arguments and then examines the evidence for them in Italy, Spain, and Romania. I then consider two cases, Hungary and Germany, that would seem initially to confirm the Moorian and Weberian arguments and suggest how these cases might be better understood in terms of the Gramscian framework developed in earlier chapters.

The Moore Thesis: Authoritarianism and Labor Repression

Perhaps the most influential explanation of interwar fascism is that associated with the name of Barrington Moore Jr. The Moore thesis is a broadly Marxian argument that explains fascism as a regime form appropriate to semi-peripheral capitalist societies. For thinkers in this tradition interwar fascism was the result of an alliance among the state, a medium-strength bourgeoisie, and labor-repressive agrarians to confront the twin challenges of geopolitical and geoeconomic competition and peasant and worker insurgency. This set of conditions, for Moore and his followers, is the historical legacy of a missing bourgeois revolution.[2]

Moore's argument depends centrally on the notion of labor-repressive agriculture, a concept that requires some explanation. Moore, following a common Marxist argument, distinguishes two forms of agrarian landed class: those that attempt to increase their rate of return through innovation and labor-saving investment (agrarian capitalists) and those who achieved the same end through labor squeezing and coercion (labor-repressive agrarians).[3] According to Moore, because of their reliance on political mechanisms to extract surplus, labor-repressive agrarians have a strong tendency to support repressive states: "While a system of labor-repressive agriculture may be started in opposition to the central authority, it is likely to fuse with the monarchy at a later point in search of political support."[4] This alliance between the government and big landed proprietors attempting to increase their rate of return through political mechanisms is a key historical precondition for fascism in Moore's scheme.

A further component, however, is needed to produce fascism: the emergence of a "medium-strength" industrial bourgeoisie. For Moore, the attitudes of industrialists, in an economic context dominated by labor-repressive agriculture, are likely to be authoritarian. This is because the home market for manufactured goods under these circumstances is weak, since a large part of the agrarian population persists on very low wages or is removed from the money economy entirely.

Industrialists in this situation are likely to ally closely with the state, seeking protective tariffs and state contracts, especially for arms production, and they are likely to support the imperialist search for overseas markets.[5] An alliance of mutual interest thus develops among segments of agrarians and industrialists, as both seek to use state power to support their interests. Each of these actors plays a specific role in the Moore story. The agrarians are the dominant partners, while the commercial and industrial bourgeoisie are a crucial, but subordinate, ally. The main point for Moore is that the vital economic interests of these dominant classes become directly linked to the possession of political power.

This coalition can become the basis of a fascist regime as a result of mass political insurgency among workers and peasants. Where ruling classes who are dependent on the control of political mechanisms to guarantee their social position face a sudden wave of mobilization from below, particularly one such as the leftist high tide after World War I, they are likely to support a transition to a more openly authoritarian system. Further, the maintenance of a large peasantry available for mobilization constitutes a fundamental condition for fascist mass mobilization.[6]

Recent extensions of the Moore argument have modified it in two ways. First, they have relaxed the focus on strictly labor-repressive agriculture, replacing it with a broader argument about large landholding. Second, they have abandoned the assumption that the bourgeoisie is an intrinsically prodemocratic force.[7] Nevertheless, scholars working in the Moore tradition have tended to retain his central argument that the emergence of a rough working coalition, or alliance, among large landholders, medium-strength industrialists, and the state is one of the main factors tending to lead to fascism in the interwar period.

The Moore argument is ultimately based on the idea that fascism is the outcome of the emergence of a dominant class coalition in which the foremost member, the landed elite, extracts social surplus through repression. The presence of this kind of dominant class, then, tends to shape the political attitudes of industrialists as well, making them disposed toward authoritarianism. Neither agrarians nor big capitalists can afford to grant the political and civil rights necessary to a fully functioning liberal democracy, because such rights are incompatible with their methods of labor control. Although these classes may support a liberal political system in which a restricted electorate supports party alternation in a parliament, as soon as democracy threatens, they fall back on fascism.

The Weberian Approach:
The Legacies of the Old Regime

Hintze, Tilly, Skocpol, Ertman, Downing, and Mann have all emphasized the importance of state structures as institutions.[8] These scholars tend to argue that state structures have influenced regime outcomes independently of the level of economic development or the structure of class relations. They stress that bureaucratic absolutist regimes developed in the absence of modernized social structures in many places in continental Europe. This had two consequences. First, highly developed old regime bureaucracies formed an instrument that social groups could "use" to pursue their interests. Thus, where old regimes were strong, the landed elite had greater repressive capacity than where they were weak. The behavior of key social elites, accordingly, cannot be understood solely with respect to their position in production but also is also the result of the political institutions available for realizing their interests. Further, bureaucrats within old regimes could act autonomously from all social classes. In a situation of intense international competition, such agents might be expected to espouse extreme nationalism, militarism, and state-led development strategies.[9]

Michael Mann has done the most to link the Weberian argument to interwar European fascism, arguing that state structures were decisive in explaining its rise. Mann distinguishes between "dual states," in which a monarchy and court closely linked to the bureaucracy shared power with a relatively weak parliament, and liberal regimes where parliamentary sovereignty was fully established. In dual states conservatives were tempted to fall back on the executive. In contrast, in liberal regimes, party competition could deal with most political crises.[10] In southern and Eastern Europe, the combination of military and political crisis with universal suffrage had ideological consequences for conservatives, who saw political mass mobilization as a threat to the traditional neutral and transcendent function of the state.[11] Economic and military crises combined with political mass mobilization and preexisting political structures to generate a division between a democratic northern and Western Europe and an authoritarian south and east. As Mann summarizes his own argument, "Fascism reflected a crisis of the dual state, the 'semi-authoritarian, semi-liberal' state found across one-half of Europe, faced with simultaneous transitions to liberal democracy and the nation-state just as these countries were beset by economic and military crises."[12] Thus, for Mann the democratic north and west of the continent remained immune to fascism, primarily because it possessed established liberal parliamentary institutions, while the south and east of the continent was susceptible to this form of rule because of strong old regimes and weak parliaments. Within this zone fascism became a mass movement only when it was anchored in a "constituency that enjoyed particularly close relations to the … nation-state."[13] Mann's argument is that fascism resonated with the values and interests of this "nation-statist" core.

Gregory Luebbert's comprehensive account of regime variation in the interwar period also rests partially on a Weberian argument, for Luebbert holds that fascist regimes arose only in countries suffering from "liberal weakness." This weakness was the result of territorial fragmentation that divided the middle class.[14] Although Luebbert's argument is more focused on parties than Mann's account, like Mann, he holds that, where parliament had established itself as the main forum for political conflict, liberalism survived. Weberians, in contrast to the Moorian Marxians, tend to emphasize the persistence of an authoritarian bureaucratic state in an advanced industrial society rather than the existence of a "premodern" elite to explain fascism.[15] The key empirical implication of this position is that interwar fascism should be understood as the consequence of a backward, or "petrified," political structure in the context of a rapidly modernizing society.

Italy, Spain, and Romania from the Marxian and Weberian Perspectives

The Marxian and Weberian accounts are by no means incompatible with one another. They could easily be combined into a powerful theory suggesting that fascist regimes should emerge in countries with (1) powerful agrarian elites and medium-strength industrial bourgeoisies who (2) supported strong old regimes. Does this accurately describe the prefascist history of Italy, Spain, and Romania? In this section I provide a brief empirical test of each of these arguments.

Italy

Let me begin by examining the Italian case. The modern Italian state formed late. As Metternich said at the Congress of Vienna, Italy in the nineteenth century (until 1861, and then definitively 1871) was a "geographical designation," not a political unit. Prior to unification Italy lacked a national monarchy. Part of the reason for this is that classic feudalism existed virtually nowhere on the peninsula outside of Piedmont.[16] Instead, two quite different political structures developed in the north and the south. From the eleventh century politically autonomous towns whose ruling strata were merchants and landowners dominated northern Italy. In contrast, in the south towns were relatively rare and were subordinate to monarchical authority. From about 1220 to 1240 Frederick II abolished internal tolls, established a foreign customs office, minted money, built a fleet, created a professional army of Islamic mercenaries, and established the beginnings of a bureaucracy. He then attempted to extend his rule north. But, with most of the population and a much more advanced economy, an alliance of city-states under the leadership of the papacy called the Northern League was able to defeat these repeated incursions. The legacy of these conflicts (the Guelf-Ghibelline wars) was a politically and socially divided peninsula that would thereafter become prey to foreign incursions, especially from the Austrians, the Spanish, and the French. Thus, precisely during the period of classic absolutism, the Italian state remained fragmented and occupied by foreign powers.[17]

Since Italy failed to establish a national monarchy in the early modern period, its only experience as a unified state was under the aegis of liberal institutions. The Savoyard monarchy had adopted a liberal constitution in 1848 that transmitted two important features to the political order that emerged from the Risorgimento. First, the Italian state had a strong executive who exercised substantial control at the local level through appointed prefects. Second, this executive was constituted in parliament. The monarchy was a surprisingly marginal part of the domestic political order of unified Italy.[18] The Albertine statute (1848) formally granted the monarchy the right to name ministers without regard to parliamentary majorities. But in practice this rarely occurred. Even prior to unification in the Piedmontese parliaments, governments formed out of majorities in parliament. The prime minister in Italy was therefore a very powerful figure, and the focus of Italian political life was parliament, not the Savoyard court.[19]

The centrality of the parliamentary executive in Italy meant that groups whom one might have expected to constitute a basis of support for the monarchy instead focused on parliament. There was no significant counterrevolutionary current in Italian politics pining for an old regime. Indeed, among the most reliable supporters of the liberal regime at the national level were the "backward" southern landholders and their allies. The southern delegates were always the backbone of all prefascist Italian governments, and all of the major Italian liberal thinkers (Croce, Spaventa, and Vico) were southerners.[20] Parliament, to conclude, was the central political institution of unified Italy. Further, the ideology of liberalism thoroughly permeated the Italian social elite. There simply was no old regime to fall back upon.

The regional composition of the Italian bureaucracy further demonstrates how thoroughly the liberal state integrated southern elites. Initially, northerners dominated the Italian administration.[21] However, during the 1880s and 1890s the regional composition of the ministerial bureaucracy changed, as the ministries filled with southerners. By the early twentieth century northerners were largely excluded from bureaucratic careers.[22]

Table 6 presents evidence from the Ministry of Finance, showing the overrepresentation of southern and central areas in the Italian ministerial bureaucracy. As the table shows, the center and south of the peninsula were overrepresented in the ministry. While the south (Campania, Basilicata, Apulia, and Calabria) had 20 percent of the population in 1931, 25 percent of the employees of the Ministry of Finance were from regions in this area in 1932. Similarly the center of the peninsula (Tuscany, Umbria, Marche, Lazio, Rome, Abruzzo, and Molise) contained 21 percent of the population, but 36 percent of employees in the ministry were from this region. Finally, the north (Valle d'Aosta, Piedmont, Lombardy, Liguria, Trentino–Alto Adige, Veneto, Venezia Giulia, and Emilia-Romagna) contained 47 percent of the population in 1932, but only 19 percent of the employees of the ministry were northern. The liberal state, to summarize, rather successfully integrated southern Italian elites. There was virtually no social support for the reestablishment of an old regime in Italy.

Table 6 Employees in the Ministry of Finance by Region of Birth

Region	1932		% of the population in 1931
	No.	%	
North	846	19	47
Center	1,561	36	21
South	1,094	25	20
Islands	730	17	12

Source: Salvati 1992.

It is worthwhile, at this point, to consider more closely the social character of the Italian dominant class.[23] There were four types of Italian agriculture in the late nineteenth century: small owner-operated farms in the northwest; capitalist agriculture with improving middle tenants on long-term leases in the Valley of the Po, the triangle of land wedged between the Italian Alps, the Apennines, and the Adriatic coast; sharecropping in the center; and latifundia agriculture in the south.[24] The areas most important for the discussion of the Moore thesis are the Valley of the Po and the south.

The agrarian political economies of these two zones differed. In the Po Valley, serfdom had ceased to exist for centuries by the nineteenth century. Entrepreneurs on long-term leases made significant improvements to the productivity of their farms by investing in canals and drainage projects and converting fallow land to pastures to allow for continuous cultivation.[25] The basic unit of production was the *cascina*, a consolidated farm with a complex system of crop rotation sometimes lasting over ten years.[26] Many farmers in the Po Valley were also engineers, because the management of water required technical competence. This was capitalist agriculture, not labor-repressive market-oriented agriculture, because the owners who produced for the market sought to increase the productivity of their land through systematic investment rather than through labor squeezing. Indeed, the basic social problem that market integration caused in this zone was unemployment and underemployment: an indication of systematic labor-saving investment.[27]

Southern agriculture differed. It was certainly commercial but much less clearly capitalist. Commercialization developed rapidly in the south during the Napoleonic period, as the emperor's brother-in-law, Joachim Murat (1767–1815), abolished feudal rights and laid the foundations for a free market in land. These reforms created speculative activity, as "Neapolitan financiers and courtiers" purchased estates.[28] But land purchases had little impact on the organization of farms. The estates were generally rented out piecemeal to a land-starved and indebted peasantry and were not "seen as a source of production."[29] A similar wave of privatizations occurred in the late 1860s, as the new Italian state sold off public lands, mostly in the south (2.5 million hectares out of a total of 3 million hectares privatized)—an operation that further augmented the stratum of absentee landlords.[30] Within the south landlords tried to increase rates of return by paying low wages and charging high rents. In Apulia a chronically underemployed and therefore politically weak casual day labor force concentrated in agro-towns worked large latifundia.[31] In Sicily the new owners, who were often old tax collectors, squeezed peasants for rent.[32] Within agriculture, then, the two key sectors of the Italian peninsula were split between capitalist agrarians, who dominated the Valley of the Po, and market-oriented agrarians, who relied on squeezing and who prevailed in the south.

Italian industry, concentrated in Liguria, Piedmont, and Lombardy, was equally diverse. Much of it was highly competitive and supported free trade, while other sectors (railroads, steel, shipbuilding, cotton cloth manufacturing, and sugar refining) demanded and received substantial state support.[33] Italian dominant class interests were thus diverse. In the north something very close to an "English model" of agrarian capitalism and industry had emerged. In the south a pattern much closer to Moore's labor-repressive commercial agriculture prevailed.

Having sketched the diverse interests of the main social elites, I now turn to examining their relative political weight. The southern landed aristocracy had a distinctly subordinate political role. It played little role in national unification: a process, as I have stated above, led in the 1850s and 1860s by the Savoyards—the ruling house of the smallholding Piedmontese region in northwestern Italy. The Savoyards allied with a broader stratum of progressive landholders in the north, who were interested in low taxes, low tariffs, security of property, and access to markets. This group of capitalist agrarians from Piedmont, Lombardy, and Tuscany was the leading force on the peninsula. Large southern landholders were part of this coalition but only as junior partners.[34]

Did labor-repressive agrarians play a direct role in the rise of Italian fascism? To answer this question it is useful to examine the regional distribution of Fascist Party membership and cell organizations. Table 7 presents this evidence. The data demonstrate that fascist membership and organization was concentrated in the north and center of the country: Veneto, Lombardy, Tuscany, Emilia-Romagna, and Umbria. These regions had both the highest concentrations of members and the highest concentrations of cell organizations in May of 1922, five months prior to the fascist seizure of power in October.

What does this evidence say about the Moore thesis? The first crucial observation is that fascism was remarkably weak in southern Italy—outside of Apulia. The lowest levels of organization and membership were in southern regions or the islands such as Basilicata, Sicily, Sardinia, Campania, and Calabria. Since these were also the areas of large latifundia agriculture, the evidence does not seem to support the Moore thesis. In contrast the area where fascism was strongest, northern Italy, was precisely the zone of agrarian capitalism discussed above.

Table 7 The Regional Distribution of Fascism Prior to the March on Rome

| Region | On May 31, 1922 Fascist cell organizations | | Fascist members per 1,000 inhabitants | Members of Fascist Party in May 1922 | Population in 1921 |
	Total no.	No. per 100,000 inhabitants			
Basilicata	4	1	1	565	492,132
Sicily	53	1	2	9,546	4,223,160
Sardinia	9	1	2	2,057	885,467
Campania	32	1	4	13,944	3,343,293
Calabria	26	2	1	2,066	1,627,117
Apulia	52	2	9	20,118	2,365,169
Abruzzo and Molise	48	3	3	4,763	1,513,740
Lazio	54	3	5	9,747	1,997,045
Marche	43	4	2	2,311	1,200,586
Piedmont	134	4	4	14,526	3,439,050
Liguria	47	4	7	8,841	1,337,979
Veneto	245	7	10	34,396	3,318,532
Lombardy	454	9	15	79,329	5,186,288
Umbria	64	10	8	5,410	657,952
Emilia-Romagna	379	12	17	51,637	3,077,080
Tuscany	411	15	18	51,372	2,809,584

Source: Gentile 2000: 462.

This area had undergone important changes during the ten years prior to the fascist seizure of power, for a new stratum of rural proprietors had appeared in these zones. According to Gentile, from "1911 to 1921, the percentage of worker-owners, in Lombardy, grew from 18.29% to 26.54%; in Emilia this percentage grew from 13.33% to 20.26% ... and in the Veneto from 22.59% to 64.30%."[35] Many of these people were probably active in the fascist movement during the early twenties. But they can in no sense be understood as labor-repressive agriculturalists. Rather, they were the latest in a long line of agrarian entrepreneurs. This evidence constitutes a serious problem for the Moore thesis, because it shows that fascism was strongest where productive modern capitalist agriculture prevailed. In the south, where more backward agriculture predominated, fascism was instead very weak.

The discussion so far suggests problems with both the Moorian and Weberian argument. From the perspective of the Moore thesis, the political weakness of the southern agrarians, in comparison to their northern counterparts, is surprising. From the perspective of the Weberians, the precocious liberalism of the Italian state is equally striking. Italy's fascist outcome, in short, is quite puzzling, given the character of the country's political institutions and its dominant social class.

Spain

Spain at first glance seems to pose less of a challenge to the Moorian and Weberian theories than Italy. Unlike Italy this country had one of the oldest national states in Europe and a powerful labor-repressive landed elite. Yet there are two important facts about Spain that sit oddly with the Marxian and Weberian accounts of interwar fascism. First, liberal institutions in Spain were well entrenched by the nineteenth century and the Spanish landed elite strongly supported them. Second, the Spanish ruling elite was deeply fragmented. It did not form a unified reactionary coalition, as the Moore argument would lead one to think.

The beginnings of a unified Spanish state are usually dated from the marriage of Ferdinand of Aragón to Isabella of Castile in 1469. Territorial unification was completed in three further acts: the conquest of Granada in the south in 1492, the incorporation of Navarre into Castile in 1515, and the union of Portugal with the rest of the peninsula in 1580. Yet, despite this early unification, the administrative structures under the rule of Ferdinand and Isabella remained very different. In Castile a process of administrative centralization began in the later part of the fourteenth century. The autonomy of the towns was eliminated, the church domesticated, and the Cortes emasculated by exempting nobles and clergy from taxes. But in Aragón none of this occurred. Instead, Ferdinand reconfirmed local liberties. As a result the new realm united two entirely different administrative systems without any common legal, fiscal, or monetary system. Thereafter, the Spanish monarchy never successfully integrated its territory, leaving Catalonia, the Basque Country, Galicia, and Valencia with strong regional identities into the twentieth century.[36]

Spain's modern political history begins with the Cortes of Cádiz (1810–1813), a rump government established in southern Spain after the invasion of the French in 1808. The constitution that the Cortes passed, which would become the basic document for subsequent Spanish liberalism, established freedom of industry, revoked the legal status of the historic regions, and firmed up property rights. The document both suppressed the corporate organizations of the old regime and replaced the regions with French-style provinces headed by a powerful prefectural authority called the civil governor. A right-wing minority, called the *serviles*, that rejected all written constitutions in favor of a return to the *fueros*, or customary regional laws, opposed this program. The liberal thrust of the early nineteenth century was cut short by the defeat of Napoleon in 1814. The *serviles*, who had struggled against the French, initially supported Ferdinand VII when he returned to the throne as part of the broader Restoration settlement. But Ferdinand was not a great supporter of the traditionalist attempt to reinstitute regional autonomy, and he did not reinstitute the inquisition, seeking rather to rule by the methods of enlightened despotism common in the eighteenth century.[37]

Ferdinand VII's betrayal of the *serviles* laid the foundations for the emergence of Carlism, a phenomenon of great importance to subsequent Spanish history, as chapter 3 makes clear. By the 1820s the disgruntled *serviles* were beginning to seek a new royal candidate. They rallied to Don Carlos, Ferdinand VII's younger brother, who promised to act as a true traditionalist. To the extent that there was a group supporting the "old regime" in Spain, it was these men. The Carlist political program was comprised of two main demands: a reimposition of the inquisition and defense of the *fueros*. Ferdinand VII's death in 1833 gave them an opportunity to mobilize militarily against Isabel, the liberal candidate, and a seven-year war (1833–1840) broke out between Carlist militias and the Bourbon monarchy, followed by two smaller revolts: one from 1847 to 1849 and the second from 1872 to 1877.[38]

The commercially oriented latifundia owner was to a large extent a creation of these conflicts, for the struggle against the Carlists coincided with a period of massive land privatization and the destruction of many of the institutions of the old regime. From 1839 guilds could exist only as "mutual aid societies." In the 1830s and 1840s guilds, brotherhoods, religious banks, and the sheep-herders' corporation called the Mesta were all eliminated or placed under strict new regulation. A central part of this process, especially in southern Spain, was the disentailment of church lands, creating a group of larger tenants concentrated in the latifundia areas (Extremadura and Andalusia) who seized local municipal commons and church lands.[39]

This process changed patterns of landownership. As Lannon writes, "Between 1836 and 1845, 83% of the property belonging to the religious orders was seized and sold."[40] Many of these disentailed estates formed the basis for a new group of agrarian landowners who used their political connections to consolidate their holdings.[41] Riquer i Permanyer suggests that Spanish liberalism was based on a pact in which "the landed nobility renounced its old privileges … and obtained its land in exchange, now fully established as private property."[42] The sale of church lands, according to most accounts, exacerbated the unequal distribution of property.[43] The establishment of extensive rural estates as absolute private property thus was part of the same historical process by which the liberal state in Spain developed: namely, war against the Carlists.

Thus the Spanish liberal state was deeply connected with large southern landholders, an agrarian bourgeoisie that had emerged out of the conversion of feudal powers into private property in the mid-nineteenth century. As Daniele Conversi puts it in a striking phrase, the Spanish state was ruled "by a centralizing landowning oligarchy permeated by Jacobin ideals."[44] This phrase captures well the paradox of the political attitudes of the large Spanish landholders. They were the main social supports of liberalism against a group of smallholders supportive of the old regime.

Liberalism also permeated the army. During the Carlist uprising some generals established private satrapies over their areas of command and also sought to establish political connections in Madrid in order to guarantee support for their particular military strategies and supplies for their troops. Alliances thus formed between particular generals and the dynastic party organizations,[45] and the generals became leaders of different political parties. In Payne's words, "There was no such thing as an 'Army' position in politics, nor an 'Army government.'"[46] *Pronunciamientos* remained largely within the terms of Spanish liberalism.[47] They were divided between progressives, like Baldomero Espartero (1793–1879), and moderates, such as Ramón María Narváez (1799–1868). The army thus internalized the divisions of nineteenth-century liberalism.

Big landlords and the army, then, supported the establishment of a liberal state in Spain. Social support for an old regime came from smallholders in the north and center of the country organized as the Carlists. But these forces were marginalized after 1877. Spain's emergence as a modern political unit under the Restoration monarchy was thus coterminous with the establishment of a liberal parliamentary system.

One might then question whether Spain can meaningfully be understood as an old regime state. But what of the ruling class coalition of the Restoration monarchy? In Spain large landholders who relied on labor repression were a politically decisive element of the ruling coalition. But these social forces never formed an effective alliance with the industrialists.

Spanish agriculture was diverse, as I have already indicated. In the extreme northwest of the country, in Galicia, very small, barely viable holdings were common. In the area stretching from Asturias to Catalonia along the northern rim of the Iberian peninsula, and in Valencia, medium-sized holdings and long-term leases predominated. This area, by most accounts, had the most productive agriculture in Spain in the late nineteenth century.[48] A vast zone of small property on short-term leases dominated the north, east, and southeast of the country. In the south and west, in Extremadura, La Mancha, and western Andalusia, large latifundia employing day laborers dominated.[49] Land privatization in mid-nineteenth-century Spain (affecting 10 million hectares) probably exacerbated the concentration of landownership in the south.[50] To simplify matters it is useful to distinguish between a northern and eastern Spain of smallholders and a southern and western Spain of large estates.[51]

Market penetration in southern Spain altered practices of cultivation relatively little, for market-oriented owners used methods of labor squeezing rather than investment in labor-saving technology in their search for profit. The owner was generally an absentee landlord who rented to a "middle tenant" who then either worked the land directly or subleased it. In western Andalusia and the interior, absentee landlords entered short-term lease-agreements with middlemen who worked the land with powerless day laborers. Instead of reinvesting and increasing output per worker, southern agrarians made profits by charging the highest possible rent and paying the lowest possible wages while squeezing as much produce out of the dependent population as possible.[52]

Although feudalism was abolished in the mid-nineteenth century, many subtler means of political control were widespread. For example, getting a job could depend on political docility.[53] Large landholders had little incentive to pay workers decent wages or replace them with machinery, because labor was cheap and abundant.[54] In sum, southern Spain corresponds very well to Moore's description of labor-repressive agriculture reinforced by market penetration.

The two main industrial pockets were in the Basque Country (mining and then steel making) and in Catalonia (textiles). Catalonia was the most industrialized region in Spain in the nineteenth century. Trade with the Americas, a relatively productive local agriculture, and protectionism combined to favor capital accumulation. Mechanization of textiles proceeded rapidly in the period from 1830 to 1855. The Basque Country, richly endowed with coal and iron ore, increased its iron production by five times between 1865 and 1871. In the late nineteenth century the region also benefited from considerable British investment.[55] The Moore account, then, seems to be confirmed by the main dominant classes in Spain. Market penetration had strengthened labor-repressive landholders in the south, and something approaching a medium-strength bourgeoisie had emerged in the two peripheral regions of the Iberian peninsula. The problem with the Moore argument is that these groups in Spain did *not* form an effective coalition. Instead, regional conflicts posed serious obstacles to the coordination of these interests.

Castilian wheat growers and Catalan and Basque industrialists were certainly capable of striking agreements. After 1886 Catalonia's textile industry experienced a crisis in response to which the major industrialists' organizations began to mobilize for tariff protection, which they won in alliance with Castilian wheat growers and Basque mining interests in 1891. Yet this alliance proved remarkably short-lived. Indeed, protectionism tended to drive the Catalan bourgeoisie toward "micronationalism" rather than Spanish nationalism, and this became a major problem for the consolidation of a Moore coalition.[56]

The critical turning point in Catalan politics, and the first sign of a fundamental break with the Castilian oligarchy, was the 1898 defeat of the Spanish army in Cuba, which had an immediate effect on Catalonia because of the dependence of the textile producers on Cuban cotton and markets. Initially,

Catalan textile producers sought to pursue their interests within the framework of the Conservative Party, and thus were little interested in supporting the various artistic and literary expressions of regional nationalism, rallying instead behind a former captain general of the Philippines, García de Polavieja (1838–1914), who promised administrative reforms to his Catalan supporters. Polavieja attempted to push a proposal to decentralize tax collection to the Catalan regional government, but the central government blocked the move, provoking a deep split between the Catalans and the Conservative Party. In the aftermath of the 1898 defeat, the government increased taxes in order to pay for the failed war effort, but the Catalans balked, calling a taxpayers' strike that was put down by martial law. The conflict resulted in the election of four Catalanist candidates in 1901, and the formation of the Regionalist League, or Lliga, the major Catalan party.[57]

The disaster of 1898 quickly transformed a relatively highly organized bourgeoisie into the main regional nationalist force in the country.[58] Despite Catalan industry's local strength its political marginality in Madrid is striking. According to Balcells: "Of the over nine hundred ministers who served in different Spanish governments between 1833 and 1901, only 25, or 2.7 per cent, were Catalans, a figure far lower than the corresponding percentage of Catalans within the population of Spain (10 per cent)."[59] After its establishment in 1901 the Lliga fought central governments in Madrid over a number of issues. The party was hostile to centralism, liberal trade policy, and, somewhat surprisingly, universal suffrage. Its leaders pushed for corporate representation, protection, and administrative decentralization. Thus, instead of a coalition of agriculture and industry, an increasingly sharp conflict between the two developed after 1898. This conflict characterized much of the politics of the Restoration monarchy and goes some way to explaining the increasing importance of the army after the turn of the century.[60]

Spain is thus rather puzzling with respect to the Moore theory of fascism. Although there was considerable labor-repressive agriculture in the south of the country, and although there was a medium-strength industrial bourgeoisie, a coalition between these forces failed to emerge. As I have argued in more detail above, one of the major reasons for the collapse of Spanish liberalism was the failure of such a coalition, not its success. To conclude, then, Spain had a functioning, if antidemocratic, parliamentary government and a highly fragmented dominant class.

Romania

Romania did not form a territorial unit until the nineteenth century, for the Ottomans successfully played the boyars against the centralizing princes. From "the mid-sixteenth century ... the central power of the state was broken by the Ottomans in favor of the *boieri*."[61] After 1550 this group was "in almost permanent revolt against the state and with local power bases in the villages they controlled."[62] Under the leadership of Michael the Brave in the period form 1593 to 1601, the beginnings of a unified Romanian state emerged. Using Wallachia as a base Michael was able to raise an army strong enough to defeat the Turks and united "all three Romanian principalities for the first and last time until 1918."[63] His assassination and the reassertion of Ottoman domination undermined this process. In the seventeenth, eighteenth, and early nineteenth centuries the Romanian principalities were fragmented. This position of colonial dependency was removed only in 1859 in the aftermath of Russian defeat in the Crimean War, but full independence from Turkey was not achieved until 1878.

The boyar aristocracy adopted the language of Western liberalism in its struggle against Turkish domination. While the high aristocracy wished to restrict the exercise of political and civil rights to itself, the less privileged boyars wanted to extend these more broadly. The Romanian constitution is a typical imitation of more advanced Western models. It provided for freedom of the press, freedom of association, and the separation of powers. The legislative branch was divided into two houses, the monarchy was the executive, and an independent judiciary was established. The prime minister was appointed by the monarch but responsible to parliament, and as a result, executive power tended to be exercised by a cabinet around this figure.[64] These political institutions were closely linked to the interests of the landed elite in Romania, because the liberal constitution of 1866 clarified property rights, allowing them to reap the benefits of rising wheat prices in the late nineteenth century.[65] Romania thus emerged as a national state under liberal political institutions. As a result the boyar aristocracy supported liberalism, in much the same way as its Italian and Spanish counterparts. There was little support for a return to an old regime that had never existed in Romania.

It is worthwhile to examine a bit more closely the structure of the Romanian dominant class. To what extent was Romania dominated by a coalition of labor-repressive agrarians, industrialists, and the state?[66] In the fourteenth and fifteenth centuries pastoralism rather than settled agriculture was the dominant economic activity in the region. Princes who taxed trade ruled over a population of free direct producers.[67] This changed in the sixteenth century with the arrival of the Ottomans. Ruling through Greek princes (the Phanoriots) who politically dominated the boyar aristocracy, the Ottomans imposed heavy taxation on Romania.[68] The Phanoriots subleased tax collection to the boyars, who in turn leased their rights of resource collection to lesser boyars at the village level.[69]

This system of tribute collection required control of the population. The establishment of serfdom was thus closely connected to exaction of tribute. As Chirot and Ragin write: "The states needed huge new revenues to pay the Turkish tribute and they had to tax the villages to get them. Flight from the villages became endemic to avoid taxes, and to stop it, serfdom was decreed."[70] But eighteenth-century serfdom in Romania was not particularly harsh. Peasants were required to provide only six days of labor service a year, against their Russian counterparts, who provided two to three days a week.[71]

Heavier control, as a result of two changes in the international economic context, began in the 1830s. First, the Treaty of Adrianople ended the Turkish monopoly on the grain trade and increased the price of wheat. The large landholders now replaced traditional crops with wheat and corn and began to develop a taste for imported luxury goods from the West. Second, under Russian occupation, a quasi-constitutional document called the Organic Statutes was approved in 1831. The statutes established a legal state, replaced arbitrary rule, and introduced both representative government and the separation of powers. But they also greatly strengthened the power of the landed elite.[72] The Organic Statutes thus "codified the existing privileges of the boyars, legalized the legal restrictions they practiced on the peasantry, and added more burdens to the ones already there."[73] Most importantly, the law strengthened the legal status of landowners. The boyars came into full possession of a third of the land under their control. The main effect of Russian occupation was to increase fees that peasants paid to commute their labor services. The extractive, fiscal character of lord-serf relations in Romania continued throughout the period. The boyars typically rented their land to "farmers" who collected fees and participated little in the management of the estates.[74]

The abolition of serfdom in 1864 increased the role of the Romanian state in supporting the agrarian system. Abolition had two negative consequences for the Romanian peasantry. First, it further firmed up the property rights of the boyars. From 1864 they became outright owners of the land. Following the precedent of the Organic Statutes, they were guaranteed one-third of the village land and all of the forests. Second, the peasantry was expected to compensate owners for the loss of labor services and tithes. Since most peasants could not pay, the Romanian state issued bonds to landholders whose value was repaid by peasant fees paid to the state. One form of repayment was to provide labor services to the estate owners. The government used the army to enforce these obligations. Thus, the abolition of serfdom coincided with the emergence of a state-enforced system of labor coercion.[75]

Land privatization led to speculative subleasing and a sharp increase in rents in the decades after unification. Between 1870 and 1906 rents increased from 100 to 200 percent on most land.[76] Most scholars suggest that this did not reflect increases in productivity but was a product of the weak bargaining position of direct agrarian producers in combination with the power of owners to squeeze. The population of the principalities increased from 4,500,000 to 7,300,000 between 1885 and 1913. Most of these were agrarians living on very small, hardly viable plots of land.[77] Peasants provided tools and draft animals. And thus "landowners' tenants, in responding to commercial incentives, could increase production with little cost to themselves merely by demanding more of him."[78] As property rights consolidated and Romania was increasingly linked to Western wheat markets, owners and tenants responded by increasing pressure on direct producers rather than increasing labor productivity. The situation was worsened by the development of the Romanian state, which levied a crushing burden of taxation on the peasantry as per-capita taxes "more than doubled."[79] These resources paid for urban developments and ports, which benefited the rural population very little. Romania, then, would seem to be a strong case for the Moore thesis: the increasing penetration of the market led large landholders to impose ever-harsher terms on the dependent population.[80]

The subsequent evolution of agrarian class relations in Romania, however, poses challenges to the Moore thesis. Romania experienced massive peasant revolts throughout the nineteenth and early twentieth centuries, culminating in the destruction of the boyar aristocracy in the period between 1917 and 1921.[81] After World War I, as I have shown above, the country underwent the most extensive land reform outside of Russia.[82] Land was redistributed differently in various parts of the country. In the Old Kingdom of Wallachia and Moldavia, this was accomplished through an administrative and bureaucratic process. In Bucovina, Bessarabia, and Transylvania, the peasantry had initiated the process from below.[83] Despite these differences the overall effect of the reforms was dramatic. As Rothschild notes: "Between March 22, 1917, when the first promise of such land reform was given to the faltering peasant troops of the Regat's army, and January 1927, when the expropriations authorized by the legislation of 1917 to 1921 were concluded throughout greater Romania, the government claimed to have expropriated 6,008,098.05 hectares from large holders and to have distributed 3,629,824.75 hectares to small holders."[84] This redistribution is the main factor explaining the surprising political stability of the country in the years immediately following the Russian Revolution.[85]

Although the economic impact of the reform was modest, it had very important political consequences.[86] The reform eliminated the Conservative Party as a political force. No significant political movement in interwar Romania struggled either to protect or reestablish large landed property. This suggests that the labor-repressive landed elite in Romania had been decisively weakened by 1921. Thus, although the Romanian social structure initially seems close to the Moore model, by the interwar period it diverged radically from it.[87]

Romania's agrarian elite conforms closely to the Moore model. Much more clearly than in either Italy or Spain, market penetration was connected to increasing political pressure on direct producers. The army was directly involved in forcing peasants to work. But land reform in the post–World War I period eliminated many of the features of this agrarian political economy. After 1917 a group of state-linked industrialists faced a large peasant class, without any significant agrarian elite. A program of forced industrialization pitted the interests of a tiny urban industrial elite against the mass of the smallholding peasantry, a peasantry that had been widened by land reform. Thus, by the interwar period Romania was not ruled by a Moorian coalition.

What, then, is the upshot of this discussion? There are two important conclusions. First, Italy, Spain, and Romania lacked old regimes. All of these states would be better characterized as "precociously liberal" than "neoabsolutist." The emergence of fascist regimes in them in the interwar period cannot, therefore, be ascribed to backward political institutions. Second, in all three of these countries, the dominant class does not at all well correspond to the Moore thesis. The central empirical problem that Italy, Spain, and Romania pose to this argument is the weakness or absence of an alliance of state-dependent industrialists and labor-repressive agrarians. The reasons for this differed in each case. In Italy there was no social group really comparable to the Junker aristocracy, and even the southern landholders who came closest were a marginal force. In Spain regional conflicts were so serious that they tended to split the key Moorian social elite into a set of competing interest groups. In Romania, a dramatic land reform in the post-war period undermined labor-repressive agriculture prior to the rise of fascism.

From "Negative" to "Positive" Cases: Hungary and Germany

The above paragraphs have established that Italy, Spain, and Romania are not only puzzling from the perspective of Tocquevillian theories of civil society but also pose a challenge to the Marxian and Weberian approach common in much other work on fascism. They are, consequently, strongly "negative" or "anomalous" cases. This raises an obvious question: how does my explanation account for cases that are not so clearly anomalous? I believe that two of these are very instructive: Hungary and Germany. In contrast to Italy, Spain, and Romania, I believe that the Marxian theory of labor-repressive agriculture and the Weberian argument about old regimes accurately describe developments in Hungary and Germany prior to 1918. Yet, where these elements remained in place (Hungary), this seems to have effectively blocked the emergence of fascism. German fascism, in contrast, depended on the destruction of this complex of factors.

Hungary

Hungary possessed most of the structural features that the Marxian and Weberian accounts see as crucial to the development of fascism. Here, the landed aristocracy, together with a broader gentry group, continued to be politically decisive throughout the interwar years. Further, Hungary possessed a powerful and entrenched old regime. And yet this country did not produce a fascist regime, not even statist fascism similar to the Romanian Carolist dictatorship. Alone among the Axis countries, Hungary maintained a functioning parliament until 1944. What explains this? The persistence of Hungarian liberalism was a consequence of the hegemonic capacity of the Hungarian dominant class. Unlike Italy,

Spain, and Romania, Hungary never experienced an organic crisis or self-reinforcing cycle of political decay.

The Hungary of the fourteenth and fifteenth centuries seemed to be on a Western European trajectory. With developed institutions of local government, a parliament, and free towns, a Western-style nation-state was emerging. But in the early sixteenth century the country shifted to a different developmental track. In the period after the death of Matthias Corvinus (1443–1490), the generally favorable position of the peasantry deteriorated, leading in 1514 to a mass uprising after which much of the population lost its previous rights. The "feudal reaction" against Corvinus had disastrous results because it undermined the strength of the peasant army. In 1526 the Turks invaded the country, winning the Battle of Mohács, which eliminated Hungary's political autonomy until 1918. In the late seventeenth century Hungary was again united, under a Habsburg authority that allowed considerable local autonomy through the Pragmatic Sanction of 1722.[88]

During the nineteenth century Hungary entered a classic pattern of semi-peripheral development. In 1910, some two decades after the country's initial industrialization, 62 percent of the population was still employed in agriculture.[89] The Tripartite Code of 1514, the foundation of Hungarian constitutionalism, recognized the rights and privileges of Hungary's nobility: an unusually large group. At the end of the eighteenth century, 1 Hungarian in 20 had a noble title, compared to 1 Frenchman in every 180.[90]

Among those who possessed noble rights, a major division, partly legal and partly economic, separated the magnates or aristocrats from the gentry. The 108 Hungarian, Croatian, and Slovenian aristocratic clans controlled 40 percent of fiefs in Hungary in 1787. Below this group was the "gentry," men who did not possess aristocratic titles but owned substantial land. Below the gentry stood the "common nobility," a group whose economic condition was not very different from the peasantry. They were often local public servants, small freeholders, and tenants and often employees of wealthier nobles.[91]

After 1800 Hungary became an exporter of wheat and wool and a market for industrial goods. These new commercial opportunities combined with the example of Western standards of living, created a modernizing push within the landed elite. But, in classic Moorian fashion, Hungary's integration into world markets reinforced labor-repressive relations and did not produce agrarian capitalism. Instead of leading to investment in farms, equipment, and manufacturing, market integration mostly meant that Hungarian nobles adopted the consumption patterns typical of Western elites. This undermined savings among those who had money, thereby dissipating the potential fund out of which development could be financed.[92]

The dissipation of consumption funds through spending on Western manufactured goods was as much a symptom as a source of backwardness. The general social context of Hungarian agriculture also hindered productive investment. Up until 1848 the landed aristocracy possessed feudal rights, particularly the right to demand labor services. As the large aristocrats increasingly sought to produce for foreign markets, they made liberal use of these rights, as is shown by the expansion in the quantity of land leased to serf tenants in the period between 1787 and 1848. Although serfdom was legally abolished in 1848, this reform was not accompanied by land redistribution. What occurred instead was a turn toward more commercially viable products, reflected in the fall of cattle production and the rise of grain production. Although large landholders had lost their formal right to demand labor services, they still possessed considerable power in the villages. In a context of concentrated landholding and persistently hierarchical relations, magnates tended to pursue a strategy of labor squeezing rather than capital investment to increase output.[93]

There were, of course, important changes in agrarian relations during the nineteenth century. Hungary was swept up in the general European ferment of 1848, and an uprising against feudalism spearheaded by the liberal gentry broke out in March of that year. Although the movement was quickly suppressed, it successfully abolished feudalism and sparked a wave of reformist legislation extending into the 1850s. But these legal reforms did not alter the underlying character of Hungarian agriculture, which remained a combination of small self-sufficient holdings and large units run by magnates who squeezed the labor force. The basic social alliance that was to dominate Hungary until 1944 consolidated in the years after the uprising, especially in the Compromise Period from 1867 to 1914. There were three main partners to it: the high aristocracy, the gentry, and large capitalists.[94]

Hungarian agriculture in the nineteenth century went through two cycles: a boom period lasting from roughly 1850 to 1875, followed by a sharp downturn in the 1880s. The latter was provoked by the collapse of grain prices brought on by lowered transport costs that flooded Europe with cheap American grain. This agrarian depression had important consequences for the relationship between Hungarian landowners and the state.[95]

First, it altered the social character of the gentry. In the years between 1867 and 1895, holdings from 200 to 1,000 acres, those most closely associated with this group, declined from 6,600,000 to 4,260,000 acres. There was also a sharp decline in the number of nobles who were middle-income landowners. In 1809 there were 27,000 people in this category, but by 1890 this figure declined to 9,592. In response to this crisis, Prime Minister Coloman Tisza (1830–1902) made the salvation of the gentry a central goal of his policy. His strategy was to incorporate them into the growing bureaucracy. Thus the number of officials increased steadily in the nineteenth century. Before 1848 there were 16,000 officials, by 1872 there were 32,000, and this figure increased to 119,937 by 1910. This represented a higher percentage of the population than either Germany or Great Britain, despite Hungary's more backward economy. This mass of officials was supported by a very heavy and regressive tax structure. In the late 1860s the government had to organize quasi-military campaigns to collect revenue. Finances were placed on a more solid basis in the 1890s but only by means of a variety of indirect taxes on consumer products. In the period following 1848, then, a significant part of the gentry was converted from an economically independent landed class to a group whose social position depended on the ability of the state to squeeze resources out of the peasantry.[96]

Apart from this mass of impoverished gentry, the interests of the large aristocracy also became more closely linked with the state as this group turned toward the use of political mechanisms to prop up an economic position threatened by cheap grain. In 1878 the Domestic and Farm Servants' Act effectively allowed employers to use corporal punishment against their workers by exempting them from legal liability for "minor acts of violence." The Penal Code passed in the same year outlawed gatherings for the purpose of gaining higher wages. Finally in 1898 the Agricultural Labor Act, also known as the "slave law," made agrarian strikes illegal, criminalized breaches of contract, and committed the police to returning rural workers to their employers. Much of Hungarian agriculture in the late nineteenth century can therefore be described as labor-repressive, in the technical sense that direct producers were deprived of basic civil rights.[97]

The third principal support of the emerging social alliance was industry. The period from 1867 to 1914 saw impressive development in this area. The percentage of the population employed in agriculture dropped from 82 to 62 percent in the period between 1890 and 1910, while the proportion employed in industry increased from 12 to 24 percent.[98] Industry was highly concentrated. The eight largest banks in Budapest controlled 72 percent of all credit and 60 percent of the industries in Hungary. This was a group of "rising industrialists," but peculiarly it was made up of an ethnic minority. Nagy-Talavera writes, with some exaggeration, "In Hungary the Jews constituted the *only* bourgeoisie."[99] This group, too, was closely dependent on the state. Industrialization was largely financed by foreign capital and oriented to foreign markets. Textiles, which are generally considered a consumer good, remained relatively underdeveloped. But the ethnic-minority status of the bourgeoisie also made this group highly dependent on the state. Industrialists represented their interests by forming personal relationships with prominent aristocrats, mainly through marriage. But this involved concessions. Many nobles occupied high positions in banking and industry.[100]

During the late nineteenth century all of the principal partners of the social elite were increasingly dependent upon the state: the gentry as a way to escape its declining economic position; the landed aristocracy to provide coercion and tariffs; and the industrialists, given their minority status, through an alliance with the landed aristocracy. To summarize there is probably no better example of a Moore-type coalition than late nineteenth- and early twentieth-century Hungary. Economic modernization was here led by an alliance of labor-repressive agrarians, big industry, and the state.[101]

Did the agrarian depression of the 1880s stimulate the self-organization of agricultural interests, as occurred farther to the west? A cooperative movement emerged in Hungary in the late nineteenth century. Indeed, the golden age of agrarian associationism in Hungary began in the 1880s, precisely during the period in which the community of interest among the state, the gentry, and the aristocracy was consolidating. In 1879 the Society of Hungarian Agriculturalists formed at a conference in the city of Székesfehérvár in Pest County aimed at addressing the problem of agricultural credit. At the end of 1889 there were sixty agricultural credit societies with 10,000 members, all of which were still concentrated in Pest County.[102]

But these institutions were not the outcome of a strategy autonomously developed by agrarian producers. Instead, they are best understood as state organizations. Around the turn of the century, agrarian cooperatives were placed under a highly centralized Central Mutual-Credit Society for the Kingdom of Hungary that replaced the older Society of Hungarian Agriculturalists as the prime sponsor of agricultural cooperatives. This transition was fundamentally similar to what occurred in Romania after 1903. Although formally independent of the state, the new organization drew significant funds from the treasury, as well as from the country's financial elite. Plus, the director of the new organization was a government minister and the head of the state railroads. The organization appears to have caused a sharp centralization of cooperative activities. After the 1898 reform, the Central Mutual-Credit Society controlled the savings of smallholders, the investments of the villages, and even the property of local orphanages. In 1899 individual cooperatives were reaffiliated with the new organization after a detailed examination.[103]

Cooperation developed rapidly under this new organization, especially in the period from 1899 to 1913. According to Charles Schandl the number of cooperatives increased from 712 to 2,425, while membership expanded from 141,623 to 693,194.[104] The movement also extended its activities beyond the provision of credit to impoverished landowners to establish sellers' and producers' cooperatives. Cooperation also took on a greater political significance as Michael Károlyi (1875–1955) sought to establish an "agrarian consciousness" through "agriculturalist circles" closely linked to the cooperatives.[105]

But this was largely a top-down process. The central organization sponsored the development of a number of agencies overseeing cooperatives in many regions of Hungary. Inspectors were continually sent from the Central Mutual-Credit Society to check on the affiliated cooperatives.[106] In some cases the central organization directly established cooperative societies.[107] Hungary's form of civil society development was therefore fundamentally similar to that in Romania. The agrarian credit cooperative movement was state dependent from the late nineteenth century.

By the postwar period Hungary was dominated by an alliance of industrialists, labor-repressive agrarians, and the state—very similar to that which Moore identified as critical to the emergence of fascism. It also had developed a state-dependent civil society, quite similar to Romania. What were the consequences of this configuration of factors for Hungarian politics in the interwar period?

Hungary was the only state to succumb to a bolshevik seizure of power in the postwar period outside of Russia. The defeat of the Central Powers brought an alliance of members of the Independence Party, the radicals, and the social democrats to power under the premiership of Michael Károlyi. The Károlyi government dissolved the old parliament, established universal suffrage, and removed restrictions on the press. Under the pressure of bolshevik agitation, and more importantly, the crushing humiliation of the Treaty of Trianon, which removed more than half the country's territory and population, Károlyi resigned.[108]

A government of socialists and communists now assumed power. Real control, however, lay in the hands of the bolshevik foreign minister Béla Kun (1886–1938); under his influence the government passed a radical land reform and organized a red army to defend the country's territorial integrity. This government appears to have been relatively popular with the working class of Budapest, but the Kun dictatorship's attempt to institute collectivization alienated the vast majority of the rural population. A flying Squad under Tibor Szamuely (1890–1919) requisitioned grain from the peasants, forced them to accept "revolutionary" currency, and killed several hundred people in the process.[109]

The conservative forces that had fled the Soviet Republic to Vienna and remained under occupied French territory in the east, now counterattacked. The leading figure of the counterrevolutionary forces was Miklós Horthy (1868–1957), an ex-admiral in the Austro-Hungarian navy. Horthy's men, in alliance with roving paramilitary squads and a detachment of Romanian soldiers, now unleashed a "white terror," which was more systematic and bloody than its red counterpart.[110] Horthy was then appointed regent of an absent monarchy, giving him a relatively free hand to run the country. His power at first was constrained by significant constitutional limits. He could not nominate nobles or declare war, and he was subject to impeachment. But during the twenties Horthy expanded his control and by 1933 had achieved the status of a de facto monarch.[111]

Horthy's power was based on balancing the interests of two main conservative constituencies: the aristocratic-industrial bloc and the largely state-dependent gentry "middle class." Over the course of the interwar period, the relative weight of these forces shifted. Up until 1931 the aristocratic-industrial group maintained control. During the thirties the gentry–middle class group contested their power, but this intra-elite struggle never threatened their fundamental alliance. Indeed, the cohesiveness of the Hungarian social elite goes some way to explaining the absence of a fascist regime here.[112]

The man responsible for restoring the old regime in Hungary was István Bethlen (1874–1946), a conservative Transylvanian landowner who wished to reestablish the political and social order of the Compromise Period (1867–1914). To achieve this aim he pursued four basic policies: the subordination of the peasantry, the incorporation of the moderate left, the reinstallation of the aristocracy in its politically dominant position, and, most crucially, the integration of the gentry–middle class in the bureaucracy. Bethlen secured the political subordination of the peasantry through a combination of electoral legislation and party construction. After the elections of 1920, which had returned a number of deputies of the smallhold-ers' party, he reestablished the franchise law of 1913, which restricted the franchise to men over twenty-four who had at least six years of residence and formal edu-cation. These requirements lowered the percentage of the population that could vote from 40 percent to about 30 percent between the elections of 1920 and 1922. The most important feature of the Bethlen government was the reintroduction of open balloting in the 199 mostly rural districts in the countryside.[113] This meant that the government list could guarantee a majority by bringing administrative pressure to bear on the rural electorate.[114] As part of the same overall strategy, Bethlen engineered a merger between his conservative forces and the smallhold-ers' party issuing in the Unity Party in February of 1922.[115] With these political controls in place the prime minister was able to ignore land reform.[116]

Bethlen's attitude to the industrial working class was surprisingly more lenient. He was convinced that workers had to be a major interest group in any modern society and was therefore prepared to grant their political representatives some freedoms. As the result of a pact that the regime struck with the Social Dem-ocratic Party called the Bethlen-Beyer Agreement socialists were allowed to publish newspapers, form associations, and engage in collective bargaining and nonpolitical strikes. In exchange they agreed not to espouse internationalism and to refrain from organizing in the countryside.[117] Electoral competition in the cities, in contrast to the countryside, developed in relative freedom. Janos suggests that this "strange double standard" formed a coherent part of Bethlen's conception of the role of parliament.[118] For Bethlen, as for many continental lib-erals of the period, parliament was a forum not for decision making but debate. This aim could be secured by ensuring pockets of relative freedom within a sea of manipulated districts.

The social democrats thus acted as a domesticated opposition, achieving a token representation in parliament.[119] Cut off from the vast majority of the population, the left was basically politically irrelevant in interwar Hungary. This compromise, according to Nagy-Talavera, played a significant role in the "fascist radicalization of the lower classes in Hungary a decade and a half later, especially that of the workers."[120] One of the most notable features of interwar Hungarian politics is the steady transfer of working-class support to the right from 1922 to 1939. From the perspective of the issues raised in this book, the most important feature of the Bethlen period was that it very effectively reimposed the domination of the same social elite that had risen to power in the late nineteenth century. The magnate-industrialist-gentry alliance was unshaken into the interwar period.[121]

The strength of this coalition had a crucial, and somewhat paradoxical, impact on the development of fascist organizations in Hungary. There is no denying that Hungary in the interwar period produced a plethora of fascist groups. But instead of fusing to form a powerful fascist party capable of seizing power and instituting a fascist regime, they bitterly fought among themselves. As a result Horthy was able to maintain control in Hungary up until the very end of the war, and no fascist regime emerged here. The aristocratic-bourgeois-state coalition could remain in power using the timeworn methods of the police.

The complex situation on the right in interwar Hungary can be simplified by distinguishing between two Hungarian fascisms: gentry and popular fascism. Gentry fascism, as its name implies, had its roots in the petty-aristocracy and free-corps elements that had organized at Szeged after the Romanian invasion of 1920. It had two main leaders: Gyula Gömbös (1886–1936) and Béla Imrédy (1891–1946). Gentry fascism was basically a pressure group within the bureaucracy. Sharply distinct from this movement were the organizations led by Zoltán Böszörmény (1893–?) and Ferenc Szálasi (1897–1946) (the Scythe Cross and the Arrow Cross). Often under severe administrative pressure these movements formed genuine oppositions to the Bethlen system, much like Codreanu's movement in Romania.[122] They were based not on the gentry but on the agrarian population and parts of the industrial working class.

Gentry fascism was the first and most serious challenge to the Bethlen system. In the period immediately following the collapse of the Kun dictatorship, a fascist movement began to organize in the provincial city of Szeged, under French patronage. This movement organized into "social associations," notably the Association of Awakening Hungarians (Ébredö Magyarok Egyesülete, or ÉME) and the Association of Hungarian National Defense (Magyar Országos Véderö Egyesülete, or MOVE). In the twenties these various associations became mutual aid societies for job seekers in the state bureaucracy. There was thus an intimate connection between the politics of the extreme right and the material interests of the place-seeking gentry. Janos argues that their number expanded from 6 in 1919 to 100 in 1920.[123] Hungary's first significant fascist leader, Gömbös, got his start as an activist in MOVE. He was a genuine fascist who had conceived the idea of an alliance between Italy and Germany in the teens. His base of support lay in the numerous "petty" aristocracy, who tended to be virulently anti-Semitic, in part because of their indebtedness and in part because of their dependence on state employment, an area dominated by Jews.[124]

The economic climate of the twenties did not allow this group to make much headway. Bethlen effectively consolidated control over the gentry by expanding state employment. The absolute number of public officials grew from 111,812 in 1910 to 208,946 by 1941. This occurred in the context of a much smaller population in post-Trianon Hungary. Thus the number per resident greatly increased. In 1914, 1 in 377, in 1921, 1 in 134, and by 1942, 1 in 100 persons was in state employment.[125] Remarkably this expansion was associated with a slow improvement in the economic position of state employees during the twenties.[126] Bethlen's attempt to bind the gentry to the ruling coalition was therefore relatively successful. Thus, despite Gömbös's declarations to an Italian newspaper about the vitality of fascism in the region, he was able to mount an effective opposition only in the thirties.

The economic crisis of the thirties had devastating effects in Hungary. By 1930, 20 percent of the Hungarian population was unemployed, with half of these concentrated in Budapest. The crisis had begun with the failure of the Creditanstalt Bank of Vienna, which called in its Hungarian loans and precipitated a flight from the *pengö* (Hungary's currency for most of the interwar period).[127] According to Nagy-Talavera it was the "working and middle classes that suffered the most."[128] In 1932 Horthy appointed Gömbös as prime minister. In doing so he was choosing one faction within the coalition of conservative forces, for Gömbös's base was comprised of secret societies within the bureaucracy and the army.[129] These were gentry strongholds, not redoubts of the high aristocracy.

Gömbös's government differed sharply from Bethlen's in its attitude to political mobilization. The prime minister held mass meetings and rallies, published and distributed a government program consisting of ninety-five theses, and used new media such as radio to promote his views. As part of this program he also reorganized the government party, seeking to minimize the control of the Bethlenites. This party was renamed the Party of National Unity and greatly expanded. In imitation of the fascist example, Gömbös became its "leader" (*pártvezér*) and his associate Béla Marton its general secretary.[130] Under Marton's leadership a party branch was established in each of the 4,000 villages of the country and a fascist militia of 60,000 men was established. The party had a permanent apparatus of functionaries devoted to popular education, social goals, propaganda, and the organization of women. In the second phase of his government, after 1935 Gömbös sought to strengthen the party's position against the state. He entrusted local government to party officials at the same geographical level. In this way these positions, which were crucial sources of patronage, shifted out of the control of the ministerial bureaucracy and under party control. These developments indicate the beginnings of a characteristically fascist dual state, in which single-party organizations jockeyed for power with the central bureaucracy. By January of 1936 Gömbös was even able to spy on officials closely linked to Bethlen.[131]

But Gömbös's gentry fascism was not the only manifestation of fascism in the thirties. The depression unleashed a wave of social unrest that formed the basis for a quite different type of mass right-wing movement. The most significant of these movements was the Scythe Cross, which began to make headway under the leadership of Zoltán Böszörmény in 1932. This man was the son of a bankrupt landowner who had traveled to meet with Hitler in 1931. His mix of peasant radicalism, anticommunism, and anti-Semitism appealed to the agrarian proletariat in the "arid regions beyond the Tisza river, where villages were strangled by large estates."[132] In May of 1936 Böszörmény led an unsuccessful peasant uprising, a March on Budapest. Some evidence on the social basis of this movement comes from the trial of a hundred of the participants. Ninety-eight of these people had no house, land, shirt, or shoes.[133]

One of the principal political conflicts of the Gömbös period pitted these two fascist movements against one another. Böszörmény's newspaper was prohibited, and Gömbös repeatedly harassed him with lawsuits. Nagy-Talavera suggests that "his followers bore the brunt of gendarme brutality."[134] Gömbös's attacks on popular fascism show the limits of his project. The attempt to mobilize the population from above did not give him an autonomous basis of power with which he could confront the establishment.

According to his memoirs Admiral Horthy had decided to remove Gömbös from power in the spring of 1936; but it never came to that, for Horthy's former henchman conveniently died in October.[135] Although it is difficult to exclude the possibility that, had he lived, Gömbös might have been able to carry through his project, the swiftness with which Horthy was able to regain control of this situation suggests the limits of Gömbös's fascism. Horthy's replacement for Gömbös, Coloman Darányi (1886–1939), quickly dismantled the single-party organization that the former leader of the Szeged faction had established. Darányi repressed the erstwhile followers of Gömbös (the so-called orphans) while adopting some of their anti-Semitic program.[136] The single party seems to have been easily cowed. There is no evidence of any resistance to Darányi's moves. The extremely effective social coalition of middle classes in the town and the family peasantry in the countryside, which was the backbone of classic fascism in the German, Italian, and Spanish cases, did not arise here. Instead, it was precisely the conflict between these groups that split the fascist movement apart.[137]

During the late thirties this conflict unfolded again with different characters. Under the leadership of Ferenc Szálasi, a popular fascist mass movement (the Arrow Cross) began to consolidate after Gömbös's death in 1936. It probably combined some veterans of the Scythe Cross and some of Gömbös's disillusioned followers, the Gömbös orphans.[138] Szálasi's movement, however, pursued political objectives that were very different from Gömbös's. Szálasi was not closely tied to the place-seeking petty gentry. His brand of fascism was strikingly populist, rejected political violence, and was not marked by the strident anti-Semitism of most of the Szeged men.[139] Much evidence suggests that the Arrow Cross, by 1939, was the largest political party in Hungary. A secret German report of 1939 stated that there were 500,000 party members, a figure that appears to have declined in the early forties.[140]

The movement also won substantial support among underprivileged groups, particularly the urban and rural working class. The Arrow Cross was regionally strongest in the "Stormy Corner" of southeastern Hungary, where rural unrest was endemic, and also in Budapest.[141] According to Nagy-Talavera, socialist and communist activists recognized the movement's broad popularity by participating in it.[142] In May of 1939 the Arrow Cross won an impressive electoral victory, becoming by far the largest nongovernmental group in parliament, with 49 candidates, against only 5 social democrats and 14 smallholder delegates. Nationally the party won almost half the vote (750,000 out of 2,000,000) and, according to Déak, made serious inroads into the working-class suburbs of Budapest.[143]

The heir to gentry fascism was not Szálasi but Béla Imrédy, a financial expert with international connections whom Horthy appointed as premier in 1937 precisely in order to shift the country to a more conservative and less overtly fascist course than that pursued by Gömbös.[144] Imrédy, to Horthy's surprise, did exactly the opposite, embracing Gömbös's program. He recalled Béla Marton in order to reestablish a new single party called the Movement for Hungarian Life.[145]

Imrédy's tenure ended in 1939 as the result of an investigation, orchestrated by Bethlen, into his supposedly Jewish ancestry. But the broader reason for his fall was his tendency to copy some of the more radical parts of the Arrow Cross program, especially land reform.[146] As with Gömbös before him, Imrédy's project to establish a fascist state in Hungary was undermined by the resistance of the conservative group around Horthy. Conservatives, in Hungary, formed a fundamental barrier against fascism. Hungary was ruled by a classic version of the Moore authoritarian coalition. Szöllösi-Janze argues that the Horthy period was characterized by "strict financial and familial connections between the nobility and high finance/entrepreneurship" under the overall political dominance of the aristocracy.[147] Further, Hungary possessed highly developed, old regime political institutions. It was precisely the persistence of these institutions that explains the absence of a fascist regime in this case.

Germany

Germany is the implicit paradigm case for most sociological theories of interwar fascism, particularly (and unsurprisingly) the Marxian and Weberian approaches. The concepts of revolution from above, authoritarian coalition, and state autonomy are all closely linked to an interpretation of the German empire (1871–1918).[148] I here briefly indicate how Germany might be incorporated into the model sketched in the preceding chapters. To anticipate the discussion, I believe that the Moorian and Weberian arguments are quite convincing as *descriptions* of the social and political structure of prefascist Germany. Yet I am somewhat less convinced of them as explanations of German fascism.

Germany was a collection of principalities prior to the country's unification under the aegis of the Prussian chancellor Otto von Bismarck (1815–1898). Prussia had been one of the strongest absolutist states in the eighteenth century, and its institutions profoundly shaped the new German empire, or Kaiserreich. This state embodied a unique blend of quasi-feudal political institutions, a powerful landed aristocracy, and, by the late nineteenth century, an extraordinarily dynamic industrial capitalism.[149]

The political order of imperial Germany combined elements of federalism, constitutional monarchy, and parliamentary democracy in a tangled institutional framework. It is useful to identify four main centers of power: the Bundesrat, or Federal Council; the monarchy-army-bureaucracy complex; the imperial chancellor; and the Reichstag, or parliament. The German empire was a federal state. The governments of the member states of the empire appointed delegates to the Bundesrat. In the specific conditions of late nineteenth-century Germany, federalism was a recipe for the political supremacy of big landed aristocrats, for Prussia was the classic ground of this social group and also the largest state within federal Germany. Further, since the Prussian Diet, elected through a three-class voting system that guaranteed the dominance of the aristocracy, selected Prussia's delegates to the Bundesrat, federalism became a mechanism for guaranteeing massive landowner influence on political decision making. The King of Prussia, after 1871 Emperor of the Germans, had his power base in the bureaucracy and the army. The civilian bureaucracy was not clearly subordinated to political decision making but often pursued its own policies and had been progressively purged of liberals during the 1880s. Also, the German army was virtually completely autonomous from all other power centers and directly under the control of the emperor. Military budgets were approved for seven-year periods up until 1893, after which date this period was reduced to five years. But civilian oversight of the military was virtually nonexistent until 1918. Alongside the Bundesrat the Reichstag constituted a relatively powerless talking shop elected by universal suffrage. At the center of all these institutions stood the chancellorship held by Bismarck until 1890. These chancellors were analogous to the great parliamentary leaders of liberal Italy, Spain, and Romania. But unlike their counterparts in these more liberal states, these men rose to power not as parliamentary leaders. The members of German governments (the chancellor and his cabinet) were not responsible to parliament and in fact were prohibited from being parliamentary representatives. Their responsibility was toward the emperor.[150]

Much work on imperial Germany emphasizes how the weakness of parliament combined with relatively well-established legal guarantees for the population at large. Most strikingly, imperial Germany achieved early universal suffrage. Adult males over twenty-five had the vote from 1871. In addition, freedom of assembly, the right to strike, and the freedom of association were all relatively secure. Further, the informal mechanisms of notable rule and patronage politics so crucial in Italy, Spain, and Romania were much less in evidence in Germany. This is a key argument amongst those who challenge the notion that Germany's political institutions were distinctively backward or predisposed to authoritarianism.[151] Viewed more closely, Germany's precocious universal suffrage actually underlines the authoritarian character of its state. The German political elite could afford universal suffrage to the Reichstag precisely because this institution was hemmed in on all sides by monarchical and federal institutions immune to the popular will and endowed with much greater power than the elected chamber. In short, it was precisely the weakness of the parliament that explains the granting of universal suffrage and the relative cleanliness of German elections.

What kind of social coalition ruled unified Germany? Big landholding aristocrats were certainly an extremely powerful interest group in the imperial state. Although the serfs were emancipated by 1848, large landholders in eastern Prussia continued to exercise local control over the administration and the police into the late nineteenth century. These men also occupied important positions within the state. Aristocrats dominated the higher levels of the state administration into the 1890s.[152] At the beginning of World War I, "30 percent of all Prussian officers were still noblemen."[153] Further, it seems relatively clear that the nobility constituted a cultural model for the entrepreneurial groups. One indicator of this is the existence of a brisk market in honorific titles and ennoblement.[154] In the decades between 1811 and 1890, large estates expanded by two-thirds in the area east of the Elbe, where commercially oriented aristocrats bent on maximizing profits dominated.[155]

This numerous, rich, and politically entrenched landed aristocracy, however, did not preclude the emergence of an equally rich and assertive class of industrialists.[156] By 1910 Germany had surpassed Great Britain in both iron and steel production, and between 1871 and 1910 the percentage of the population living in large urban areas increased by 24 percent. Limited liability companies were widespread in the 1850s, as the German economy registered impressive growth rates in mining, iron, and steel and was on the cutting edge of second-wave industrialization in chemicals, optics, and electrics. Much of this innovation was independent of the state and indicates an active entrepreneurial class.[157]

More importantly, perhaps, than the purely economic strength of either main segment of the social elite was their close working relationship. There is considerable evidence that the German bourgeoisie fused with aristocratic landholders, although the distinctiveness of this process has been sharply contested.[158] A major stimulus to this accommodation was the long economic downturn after 1873. Landholders wanted tariffs to protect their markets from cheap Russian and American grain.[159] Industrialists, in contrast, wanted cheap grain to keep wages low.[160] However, after the economic downturn of 1873, the industrialists, too, were disposed to protection. The conflict emerged and was resolved with legislation over tariffs and armaments. The first set of tariffs on grain was established in 1879, followed by renewed legislation in 1887 and 1902. In exchange for these controls on grain, the agrarians supported a policy of shipbuilding supported by big industry.[161] By the late nineteenth century, then, big industry, big agriculture, and the imperial state were ever more closely linked.[162]

To summarize then, imperial Germany was characterized by a coalition of rising industrialists and a powerful landed elite. Despite many qualifications, contemporary historical work on Germany seems to confirm the basic thrust of Barrington Moore's analysis.[163] In the period after 1871 there did emerge a coalition of industry, landholding, and the state. The debate is mostly about whether the formation of this coalition indicates a weak, or even medium-strength, bourgeoisie. The paradox of the German case is that its ruling coalition was characterized by both a strong landed aristocracy and a strong bourgeoisie. Thus, given both its state structure and the nature of its ruling-class coalition, Germany's interwar fascist outcome would seem to confirm the Marxian and Weberian approaches.

What about the development of voluntary associations and hegemony? Associational development in Germany from the late nineteenth century was impressive in its extent and followed a pattern familiar from the cases studied above. In the period from roughly 1860 to 1890, voluntary associations were sponsored largely by the social elite. Through the 1880s the Prussian government promoted the formation of "system-supporting" organizations such as veterans' clubs. The Deutscher Kriegerbund (Ex-Servicemen's Associations) grew from 27,550 members in 1873 to 1.7 million members by 1910. Indeed, Hans-Ulrich Wehler suggests that combined membership of all army-related voluntary organizations in imperial Germany was close to 5 million.[164] According to one study of Marburg, there were an average of 2.79 new associations per 1,000 inhabitants for the decade from 1890 to 1899, while in the preceding decade there were only 1.92. World War I gave a further boost to associationism. Charitable organizations for war wounded seem to have been particularly important in Germany.[165]

By the 1890s this early model of patriotic associationism had to compete with system-challenging forms of sociability in the form of Catholic, socialist, and peasant associations. By the early twentieth century important segments of German civil society developed in autonomy from both the social elite and the state. This was particularly true of the associations connected to the socialist and Catholic subcultures.[166]

What was the political context in which these associational developments occurred? There were four main parties in imperial Germany: the liberals; the Zentrum (Center Party), which was the political arm of the Catholic Church; the Conservatives; and the social democrats. Only the last three of these parties were true mass organizations. The Center Party, through church organizations, exercised control over a mass electorate and carved out an authoritarian political subculture. The conservatives were the main political vehicle of the landed elite and the bureaucracy. They also controlled a mass organization, the Agrarian League, which allowed them to win about 14 percent of the popular vote up until 1912. Finally, on the left was the mass Sozialdemokratische Partei Deutschlands (Social Democratic Party, or SPD). From 1890 with the lifting of the antisocialist laws, the SPD consistently won the largest proportion of votes for the Reichstag, and by 1912 had the largest number of representatives in the chamber.[167] The strength of the SPD, and its political isolation from the other parties, made its electorate relatively impervious to attempts at political penetration. Eley has identified this particular pattern of politically uneven development as one of the principal reasons for the authoritarianism of the German bourgeoisie: "The existence of a radical workers' party publicly committed to revolutionary socialism—a factor conspicuously missing in Edwardian Britain—more than anything else forestalled the chances of a 'Gladstonian coalition'."[168] Thus, for Eley, it was not the economic weakness of the German bourgeoisie that was decisive in determining its attitudes but rather a process of uneven development at the level of political organizations.

The relative weakness of elite political parties in imperial Germany led dominant classes to pursue their interests through organized pressure groups outside the party system. Special interest leagues, organizations, unions, and associations proliferated in late nineteenth-century Germany and were the real center of politics. The famed protective tariffs enacted in 1879 grew out of a draft proposal written by the Central Association of German Manufacturers (Centralverband Deutscher Industrieller, or CDI). The building of the German battleships occurred under the pressure of the German Navy League (Deutscher Flottenverein), which was backed by industry and had thousands of members. The SPD itself did not escape this logic of corporatist development. As the trade unions expanded rapidly in the period prior to World War I, political militancy declined.[169]

The similarity between Germany and Italy, to summarize, is not to be found either in the nature of the ruling coalition nor at the level of the state. Both of these, as I have argued above, were very different, but the German pattern of civil society development was strikingly similar to the Italian pattern. In the following section I briefly examine the consequences of this similarity.

Germany's defeat in World War I was a political disaster for conservatives. Many elements of the old regime of course remained. The Junkers were still very powerful, as was the bureaucracy, but the Weimar Republic never successfully integrated the social elite. The constitution of the Weimar Republic was based on two pacts: one between the Social Democratic Party and the army and another between heavy industry and organized labor—the Ebert-Hindenburg Agreement.[170] In the first pact, Friedrich Ebert (1871–1925) agreed to support the Freikorps in its violent elimination of a revolutionary threat from the left, in exchange for acceptance of the republic. The second pact, regulating collective bargaining, was between the unions and heavy industry. This was embodied in the Stinnes-Legien Agreement.[171] The Weimar constitution, written by Hugo Preuss (1860–1925), formalized this agreement. In the new state, "antagonistic interests were to be harmonized by the device of a pluralistic political structure, hidden behind the form of parliamentary democracy."[172] The resulting political order was a pluralist state.

One of the most important features of the Weimar Republic was the absence of an effective mass party of the right and center-right. The liberal center and the right divided between three groups: the German Democratic Party (Deutsch Demokratische Partei, or DDP), the German People's Party (Deutsche Volkspartei, or DVP), and the German National People's Party (Deutschnationale Volkspartei, or DNVP). After the devastating inflation of the 1920s, these began to lose their membership. In contrast, the Catholic Center Party and the SPD remained strong.[173] It was this configuration that created the vacuum that the NSDAP would come to fill. How did this happen?

The political history of the Weimar Republic can be divided into three periods. From 1918 to 1923 there was a period of incipient revolution and counterrevolution; from 1924 to 1929 a period of relative stability; and from 1930 to 1933 a period of authoritarianism leading into the national socialist seizure of power. The history of the NSDAP follows these phases of the republic. From 1919 to 1923 the national socialists emerged as one among a number of extreme nationalist paramilitary leagues characteristic of postwar Germany. These groups grew out of the combination of mass mobilizing citizen warfare, a perceived threat from the left, and the hyperinflation of the early twenties.[174] The leagues were similar to the Italian *squadristi*, except for their extreme anti-Semitism.[175] This first period of NSDAP activity culminated in the failed Hitler, or Beer-Hall, Putsch, planned as an imitation of Mussolini's March on Rome in 1923.[176]

The next subperiod, from 1924 to 1928, was known among the national socialists as the "time of struggles" (Kampfzeit). This corresponded to the period of the greatest stability for the Weimar Republic, one that has no strict parallel in the Italian experience because the Italian fascists seized power so rapidly that they did not have to go through a period of "hibernation."[177] As the republic strengthened, the NSDAP weakened. The main consequence of this period for the organization of the National Socialist Party seems to have been a loose coupling between the paramilitary organization and the political organization. The national socialist paramilitary was called the Storm Detachments (Sturmabteilung, or SA). The SA was formed at the very beginning of the party history in 1920. Unlike the *squadristi*—which emerged in part outside of Mussolini's control, and as I have demonstrated above, as the result of difficult tactical struggle within the Fascist Party—the SA was part of the national socialist organization from the beginning. However, unlike with the the Italian squads, the SA membership did not imply party membership. In the Italian case there was no such distinction between the political and paramilitary organizations. At least in most areas squadrism was fascism in the early twenties.[178] The national socialists seem to have used the SA as a front organization to penetrate sectors of the population, particularly the industrial working class, which was unlikely to join the party organization.

There are two crucial points about this period. First, the weakness of the national socialists was closely related to the relative political strength of the center and center-right organizations: particularly the DNVP. It was only as the Conservative Party declined after 1928 that the NSDAP became significant. Second, the period from 1924 to 1928, that in which the party had the least success, was also its most "leftist" phase. This suggests a parallel with the Italian case, where the party's turn to the right corresponded with political success.

In the second phase, 1928 to 1933, the national socialists began to expand. How did the strength of German civil society affect the mobilization, regime consolidation, and regime development phases of national socialism? Despite the different contexts in which these movements and regimes emerged, the evidence suggests that a strong civil society aided the national socialists, just as it had the

Italian fascists. Berman suggests that many middle-class voters were abandoning the older "notable" parties by the midtwenties.[179] She links this to a withdrawal from engagement with the existing liberal parties and a pursuit of direct action through associations. There is much evidence to suggest that a relatively developed associational sphere was a vital resource for NSDAP organizing.

One way of showing this is to examine the constituencies among which the NSDAP drew the most support: white-collar employees and small peasants. An important question is: were these disorganized? One key piece of evidence concerns the Reichslandbund (RLB), an organization of agrarian interests in the twenties. The NSDAP, through its agrarpolitisch Apparat (aA), systematically penetrated the RLB, first taking over the lower echelons of the organization and then attempting to seize the leadership.[180] As Bernt Hagtvet puts the point: "Instead of proving an obstacle to Nazism in the countryside, the RLB and other agricultural organizations became convenient conveyor belts for Nazi propaganda reaching deep into the rural population. In this way intermediate groups facilitated the rise of Nazism."[181] This is reminiscent of some Italian fascist tactics in the Valley of the Po, although the process was more violent in Italy.

Another important constituency of the NSDAP, white-collar workers, was highly organized as well. There were three main organizations of white-collar workers in the Weimar Republic: the Allgemeine frei Angestelltenubund (AfA), the Gesamtsverband Deutscher Angestelltenwerkshaft (Gedag), and the Gewerkshaftsbund der Angestellten (GdA). The AfA was a left association close to the socialists, the Gedag was a center-right organization, and the GdA was an extreme right antisocialist organization. The total number of white-collar employees organized in these associations was stable throughout the late twenties, but the right-wing organizations, and especially the Gedag, increased their share slightly at the expense of the AfA.[182] Within this constituency there is evidence of a high level of organization, one that increased during the twenties, especially in the right-wing organization most likely to be close to the NSDAP.

More broadly the NSDAP took advantage of precisely the restricted, economic-corporate character of the Weimar parties in the context of a rapidly developing civil society. The party presented itself as, and to a certain extent was, an organization that transcended the class, status, and confessional divisions that had marked German society in the imperial period. It was, in the words of Heinrich Winkler, a "people's party."[183]

While the movement phase in the German case was relatively long, the regime consolidation phase, Gleichshaltung (coordination), was extremely rapid, beginning immediately after the seizure of power in March of 1933 and lasting until 1934. In the space of a few months, independent professional organizations and political parties ceased to exist in Germany. The same process, the reader will recall, took four years in the Italian case and was never entirely completed.

The process of coordination was in broad outline similar to the process of fascisticization. The German Labor Front, the first congress of which was held in May of 1933, was similar to the fascist syndicates. As in the Italian case, and unlike the Spanish case, the labor organization was separated from the party organization.[184] Links between the labor organization and the party organization were established on a personal basis—in the first place because the leader of the Deutsch Arbeitsfront (DAF), Robert Ley, was a major national socialist. But, just as the fascists had, the national socialists depended upon the organizational resources and the lower-level personnel of the non-nazi unions. According to Broszat, the DAF "retained the typical unionist principles of organization with an eye to the union employees taken over in the lower ranks ... who were hardly indispensable for the time being."[185]

The organization of employers in national socialist Germany differed slightly in form from the Italian case but was similar in substance. In November of 1934 trade associations and chambers of commerce were organized under the Reich Group Industry. Like the DAF, this organization had no legal relationship to the National Socialist Party. Still, fascist leaders of industry, like Alfried Krupp (1907–1967), were placed in prominent positions in the associations. But, as Broszat writes, "the old industrial associations were still generally able by skillful adaptations to the new set-up to preserve the influence of the concerns and personalities represented in them."[186]

Did German and Italian fascism generate similar regime types? In one important respect these regimes resembled one another and differed from all the other forms of interwar authoritarianism. They were both dual regimes based on symbiotic party-states. The most obvious similarity between the two regimes lies in the structure of the party organization in the two cases. Neither Mussolini nor Hitler claimed control over his party organization as an official. Neither leader was party secretary, a position generally held by a second-rank figure. This meant that Hitler and Mussolini had a direct and personal relationship to the local leadership that undercut the bureaucratic structure of their party organizations.

The NSDAP was in some ways more centralized than the PNF, and in some ways was less so. The national socialists had a centralized membership roll kept in Munich, while the PNF had no so such record. However, the power and auton- omy of the local (*Gau*) leadership in Germany was probably greater than in Italy, and this was in part the result of the fact that no consultative body existed in this case. In Italy the consultative body of the Grande Consiglio continued to play a coordinating role at the highest level of the party. But, as Broszat points out, the position of the local leadership increased as the regime developed.[187]

What does this brief sketch of Germany's path to fascism suggest? First, the argument that classic fascism corresponds to a specific stage of economic or political development seems very difficult to maintain. The economic and polit- ical structures of Germany were not only different from Italy; they represented in important respects its mirror opposite. To put the point schematically, while Germany was characterized by a "late absolutism," Italy was characterized by a "precocious liberalism." I return to this point in the more general conclusions below, but for now it is sufficient to indicate it. Second, while Germany's political and social structures differed from Italy's, its form of civil society development, and the political crisis that its social elite faced with the emergence of universal suffrage, was very similar.

Conclusions

This chapter has considered the evidence for explanations of fascism that focus on economic and political structures rather than civil society. It has shown that Italy, Spain, and Romania not only pose a challenge to Tocquevillian accounts of fascism but are also counterintuitive cases with respect to the Weberian and Marxist approaches to fascism. I have also argued that the Hungarian and German cases, which initially would seem to confirm these established perspectives, pose problems. It is worth briefly reprising these points here and drawing out their general implications.

Prefascist Italy, Spain, and Romania were not governed by old regimes but rather by constitutional monarchies. Parliament was a central institution in each. Plus, a reactionary alliance among labor-repressive agrarians, bureaucratic states, and rising industrialists either failed to emerge or was decisively broken immediately after World War I. Hungary and Germany, in contrast to these "negative cases," are "positive" with respect to the Moorian and Weberian accounts of fascism. In both countries, a powerful alliance of industrialists and agrarians dominated a strong old regime in the period prior to World War I. And yet, upon closer examination, neither country conforms well to the dominant social structural models of fascism. The evidence from Hungary shows this most clearly. There is no case in interwar Europe that more fully embodies the Moorian authoritarian coalition of labor-repressive agriculture and a medium-strength bourgeoisie. But as the interwar history of Hungary shows, it was the very strength of these social forces that undermined the development of fascism here, for the place-holding petty aristocracy, even when it adopted the elements of fascism, never seriously threatened the Hungarian state. Indeed, they were always on the side of the Horthy regime against the more populist fascism rooted in the countryside and the Budapest proletariat; and it was Horthy's continuing control over the main levers of power that secured the maintenance of some parliamentary forms in Hungary into 1944. To put the point as sharply as possible, although Hungary was never a democracy in the interwar period, the Moorian social coalition that ruled the country prevented it from becoming an openly fascist dictatorship.

Germany is a more complex case, for it appears to confirm the Marxian and Weberian theories of fascism, as well as being generally compatible with the argument in this book. The timing of German fascism is worth underlining, however. Although the country had a strong old regime and possessed some elements of a Moorian coalition, the impact of World War I was unique in Germany. The Weimar Republic, like the period after the war in Italy, the Spanish Second Republic, and the democratic twenties in Romania, lacked an established right-wing party. This fact has created some difficulties for work in the Moore tradition, which has attempted to account for Germany by arguing that the sources of German fascism are to be sought in a conservative tradition that lingered after the destruction of the Junker class. The evidence for this argument is somewhat indirect. Scholars in the Moore tradition emphasize that social support for the NSDAP came from groups that were not integrated into the socialist or Catholic subcultures. The problem with the argument, in my view, is that it says little about the content of nazism. The NSDAP, like the other fascist parties in this book, was not in any sense a simple antidemocratic movement. It was rather an antiliberal movement that aimed to establish an authoritarian democracy. The Gramscian argument that I have developed here makes better sense of the German case because it focuses on events in the Weimar period, particularly the development of German civil society in the absence of a hegemonic organization among the social elite.

The reason for this common weakness is that in different ways the Moorian and Weberian perspectives have tended to conceptualize fascism as a form of "strong state" and thus have focused their explanations on the repressive dimension of state power while neglecting fascist political movements. While it is true that fascist regimes greatly strengthened and used to devastating effect state violence, an exclusive focus on this aspect of them fails to explain their distinctive combination of authoritarian political means and democratic legitimacy. Because of this the classical social structural accounts reviewed above have little to say about the real institutional novelties of this form of rule.

6

Rethinking Civil Society and Fascism

I am now in a position to provide a fuller answer to the central query of this study: Why did civil society development lead to fascism rather than liberal democracy in Italy, Spain, and Romania in the interwar period? My argument is as follows. Civil society mobilization tended to promote democratic demands in interwar Italy, Spain, and Romania, as Tocquevillian analyses predict; but these democratic demands tended to undermine the liberal institutions of these countries due to the interlinked failures of interclass, intraclass, and counterhegemony in them. The development of civil society in this political context increased levels of social conflict, froze parliamentary mechanisms, and delegitimated politics as such. Fascist mass movements arose out of this crisis of politics. These movements attempted to establish new forms of politics that broke radically with liberalism but claimed to be democratic. Of course, the emergence of fascist regimes out of these circumstances was not inevitable. Indeed, various projects of radical democracy such as socialism, social Catholicism, peasantism, and even anarchism were powerful forces at different points in the history of Italy, Spain, and Romania; but the coincidence of a rapidly developing civil society, and the absence of a hegemonic politics, made a fascist outcome more likely in interwar Italy, Spain, and Romania than it would have been had either civil society been less developed or hegemony more developed.

I have made this argument through an analytic narrative of three parallel negative cases. These conclusions briefly summarize the argument of the book by restating the narrative framework used to organize the case studies in more explicitly comparative terms. To facilitate the discussion table 8 summarizes the book's comparative architecture.

Summarizing the Findings

How should interwar fascism and its various forms be explained? The analyses developed so far suggest that fascism was closely connected with the development of civil society in the context of a nonhegemonic pattern of political relationships. Hegemony, to reiterate, is a form of political relationship in which a particular group makes a successful claim to "lead" a set of allied groups. It can take three basic forms: intraclass hegemony, in which structurally similar social classes form an alliance; interclass hegemony, in which structurally opposed social classes form an alliance; and counterhegemony, in which subordinate classes forward themselves as the bearers of a hegemonic project. All of the cases that produced fascism lacked intraclass hegemony prior to the development of civil society and lacked interclass hegemony after the development of civil society. The absence of these two forms of hegemony had the further and paradoxical consequence of undermining the development of counterhegemony as well.

Intraclass Hegemony

In Italy, Spain, and Romania social elites remained organizationally fragmented. They lacked strong political parties that could plausibly function in a context of universal suffrage. Where political parties emerged they did so as groups organized to control the spoils of office, not true political organizations.

There were two main reasons for this. First, the establishment of a national state occurred against the interests of key elite groups in all three cases. In Italy the extension of Piedmontese institutions to the peninsula as a whole

Table 8 Explaining Fascism

	Italy	Spain	Romania	Hungary	Germany
Intraclass hegemony after national unification	weak	weak (except for Catalonia)	weak	strong	weak
Civil society development in the late 19th century	autonomous	elite led	state led	state led	autonomous
Interclass hegemony after civil society development	weak	weak (except for Catalonia)	weak	strong	weak
Counterhegemony	weak	weak	weak	irrelevant	weak
Outcome	party fascism	traditionalist fascism	statist fascism	nonfascist authoritarianism	party fascism

was a source of great bitterness among local elites.[1] In Spain, Catalan elites never formed part of the ruling coalition.[2] In Romania national unification was mostly a project of the lesser boyars, who then became state employees against older more established landowners.[3] In none of these cases was there a unified national elite.

The parliamentary politics of the late nineteenth and early twentieth centuries in all three countries reinforced elite fragmentation. In all three countries the electoral rules restricted suffrage to people with either considerable land or money. In Italy suffrage was very limited until 1912.[4] In Spain the liberals granted formal universal suffrage in 1890, but this was meaningless in the rural areas, where most of the population lived.[5] In Romania suffrage was channeled through a system of electoral colleges that guaranteed control to the very rich.[6] These restrictions on suffrage paradoxically undermined intra-elite cohesion in Italy, Spain, and Romania, for, given the fundamental similarity of the underlying class interests represented in parliament, politics in these countries could only take the form of a struggle over control of the spoils of office. Leon Trotsky in his Balkan war correspondence captures this point most clearly. He writes of Romania that "the more unprincipled the ruling parties and the more elusive the actual differences between their practical programs, the fiercer is the struggle between them, for this is naked struggle for loot, for possession of the public trough."[7] These remarks apply with equal force to Italy and Spain.

Thus, in Italy, Spain, and Romania one of the most remarkable features of their constitutional periods is the bitterness of the political struggle, despite the extremely restricted electorate within which it played out. Backstabbing, schemes between "in" and "out" factions, and friable political parties were characteristic of all three countries. Without an opposition rooted in a distinct social class, political parties remained personalistic. This made the formation of a cohesive intradominant class alliance, intraclass hegemony, difficult.

Oligarchic liberalism, in sum, was not just an antidemocratic set of political arrangements. Even more importantly, it was a political system that tended to weaken the very social elite it served. The system did not allow for the formation of a coherent intradominant class alliance that could articulate a project of national development. This would seriously discredit liberal institutions as civil society became more organized.

The Development of Associationism and the Pressure for Democracy

Despite their many imperfections the parliamentary regimes that dominated Italy, Spain, and Romania were liberal. As such they established legal frameworks that allowed for the development of voluntary associations in the countryside. Under the pressure of cheap grain from the United States and Russia, agrarian producers began to form rural credit organizations and cooperatives in all three countries in the late nineteenth century. Yet there was an important difference in the specific context in which associationism developed in the three cases. In Italy, although the social elite was initially heavily involved in sponsoring these organizations, this relationship had broken down by the 1890s. Here civil society developed autonomously from either the state or the social elite.[8] In Spain, large landholders controlled associationism in the countryside. Here the social elite dominated civil society development.[9] In Romania, the state played a central role in sponsoring associations.[10] Thus, in Italy, Spain, and Romania a similar surge in the incidence of rural voluntary associations led to three different structures of civil society because of the relative power of elites, nonelites, and the central state in each case.

Despite these differences, associational development in all three instances led to demands for an extension of democracy, as the neo-Tocquevillian position would predict. Unrest spread through the Italian and Spanish countryside in the 1890s. The dramatic and brutally repressed peasant revolt of 1907 in Romania was similar. This democratic demand for a state that would represent the population as a whole, could not be expressed within liberal institutions that were clearly antidemocratic. The expansion of rural civil society thus challenged rather than strengthened the fragile liberal systems of these countries.

The Weakness of Interclass Hegemony

The political elites of Italy, Spain, and Romania were deeply aware of their own isolation. They also understood the pressure that the development of civil society placed on the political systems of their countries. In response to associational growth these political elites pushed for reforms designed to broaden support for liberal institutions. In short, they attempted to establish interclass hegemony. But these attempts failed because of the weakness of intraclass hegemony and because they occurred after associational development had already begun.

The attempt to extend interclass hegemony unfolded through very different, concrete historical processes in Italy, Spain, and Romania. In Italy it occurred without a fundamental break in the basic political institutions of the country. Coming to power after the authoritarian turn of the 1890s, Giolitti stopped using police in labor disputes and attempted to establish an alliance with the northern socialists while leaving the south under the control of the landed elite.[11] In Spain the attempt to extend hegemony coincided with the collapse of the previous tradition of oligarchic liberalism. After the failed attempts at reform in the first decade and a half of the twentieth century, Primo de Rivera decisively broke with the Canovite system.[12] Much as Giolitti had done in Italy, the Primoverrista dictatorship sought to establish an alliance with Spain's Socialist Party and pursued a state-led development project. In Romania the attempt to establish interclass hegemony came later than in the two southern European cases but was in some ways much more thorough. In the early twenties the PNL established both universal suffrage and land reform, something that neither Giolitti nor Primo de Rivera had done in their countries.[13]

Despite the many differences among these attempts, they failed for two basically similar reasons: the lack of intraclass hegemony in the period immediately following national unification and the lateness of the attempt to establish interclass hegemony. As a result of the fragmentation of the social elite, reforming political elites lacked an adequate party organization or unifying political project with which to rally mass support. It is important to emphasize that in each case the reformist push came in the context of the disintegration of already weak elite political organizations. In Italy a gradual erosion of the power of the liberal elite unfolded over the first decade and a half of the twentieth century. In Spain the process was much more dramatic, as Primo de Rivera systematically dismantled the Liberal and Conservative parties using the authority of the Spanish state prior to pursuing his reform initiative. In Romania land reform and war discredited the Conservative Party, thus undermining the system of party alternation that had worked, however feebly, since the constitution of 1866.

The reformist political elites of Italy, Spain, and Romania sought to carry out their project of establishing interclass hegemony from a position of political weakness, that is, an absence of intraclass hegemony. Because of this, these elites could afford to open their political systems only partially. Giolitti restricted effective suffrage to the north. Primo de Rivera's reformism extended only to a narrow segment of the working class. The PNL land reform was coupled with a constitution that eased the application of martial law and the manipulation of elections. These partial openings turned out to have negative consequences for the liberal systems of these countries in the long run. Rather than gradually increasing support for parliamentary institutions, they discredited liberalism further. In all three of these countries, the reform efforts were insufficient either to incorporate opposition from below or to force the social elite to organize strong political organizations. The outcome of this process was similar in each case. When effective universal suffrage came (in Italy in 1919, in Spain in 1931, and in Romania in 1928) the elections occurred in the absence of political organizations among the social elite that were capable of winning over substantial popular support. Within this context of intraclass hegemonic weakness, voluntary associations developed rapidly. But they did so in ways that inevitably undermined, rather than sustained, liberalism. Political Catholicism, peasantism, and socialism, rather than liberalism, were the beneficiaries of civil society development.

The political history of these three countries demonstrates the close connection between intraclass and interclass hegemony. In these countries the amorphousness of the dominant class undermined its ability to attract nonelite support. Lacking a political organization, and a political project, the leadership fell back onto an ineffective combination of satisfying concrete material interests and repression.

The Failure of Counterhegemony

The interlinked failures of both intra- and interclass hegemony had a further decisive consequence. They undermined the development of counterhegemony, as well. The absence of effective political organizations among the social elites paradoxically short-circuited the formation of political organizations among nonelites.

The collapse of the project of interclass hegemony following the period of partial opening described above created a democratic opportunity in Italy, Spain, and Romania. Projects of social democracy, Catholic democracy, and peasant democracy welled up during this period. These political movements were organizationally rooted in a developing associational sphere that had emerged outside and against the established parties. Tragically, however, this democratic potential remained unexploited in all three countries for a similar reason: the absence of a hegemonic politics.

One of the obvious similarities amongst Italy, Spain, and Romania is that effective universal suffrage occurred in the absence of a strong conservative political organization. In the period immediately prior to the rise of fascism, each of these political systems lacked a well-defined conservative pole. This was partially the result of the political formlessness of the period of oligarchic liberalism. In a context of censitary suffrage, conservatives could gain little political traction. There were also more specific events that led in the same direction. In Spain the systematic destruction of the party system under Primo de Rivera and in Romania the collapse of the conservatives as a consequence of the war were crucial. In any case, in the immediate aftermath of the transition to universal suffrage, there was no well-established conservative party in any of the three countries.

The absence of this crucial counterweight, surprisingly, tended to disrupt the political cohesiveness of the democratic forces. The same friability that had undermined the development of an elite hegemony now weakened the formation of a nonelite counterhegemony. During the early twenties in Italy, the early thirties in Spain, and the late twenties in Romania, the political forces broadly pushing for democracy remained fragmented. They tended to disintegrate into a number of competing factions pursuing incompatible programs. Just as the social elite had failed to establish strong intradominant class hegemony, so did the representatives of nonelites. The urban working class, the peasantry, and the small bourgeoisie of the towns in particular proved incapable of establishing a solid alliance. In Italy the main conflict was between the PPI and the PSI. Had these forces been able to forge an effective political alliance in 1919, they would have possessed an overwhelming majority in the chamber. Instead, they pursued uncoordinated and incompatible programs. In Spain the main split was between the republicans and the socialists. The latter were attached to a doctrinaire program of anticlericalism, while the former, especially their agrarian wing, wanted land reform. A similar lack of coordination characterized the Romanian PNȚ. In some ways the political situation of Romania's democratic forces was more promising than those of either Italy or Spain, because the PNȚ represented an alliance of peasants and the small urban bourgeoisie (the main democratic forces in the country) within a single political organization. Yet the PNȚ was really two parties: a peasantist party led by Ion Mihalache and a "bourgeois" party led by Iuliu Maniu. These wings never adequately coordinated their reformist program, and they lost support by botching land reform. The rise of a fascist movement in each country was connected with the tendency of democratic forces to split and fragment. This tendency, in turn, was the result of the absence of a conservative pole with a strong hegemonic project against which the democratic forces could articulate a counterhegemonic project.

To summarize, the failure of the democratic movement in Italy, Spain, and Romania was connected to the failure of the social elite to establish hegemony. Without a well-defined conservative enemy, which could at least make a plausible claim to national leadership, democrats tended to fragment into a set of mutually contradictory projects. They suffered from the same problems of intraclass fragmentation that had divided the social elites in the period of oligarchic liberalism. This is what explains the connection between the absence of dominant class hegemony and nonelite counterhegemony. Fascism would arise in this political context.

The Crisis of Politics and the Rise of Fascism

Fascist movements arose out of a crisis of politics that affected both elites and nonelites. Neither group was able to constitute itself as a "leading class" in the Gramscian sense. Instead, in the period immediately prior to the rise of fascism, political struggle reverted to a conflict among narrowly defined and fragmented interests. This discredited politics and opened the way to fascism.

Fascism was a fundamentally antipolitical ideology. For fascists, politics was an unnecessary "superstructure" that distorted the real cohesive nation. Rather than reflecting and channeling different interests, fascists argued, politics was responsible for fomenting social divisions. This was plausible only because fascists hypostatized a real national interest that exists without having to be constructed or shaped through political processes. The Italian ideology of national syndicalism is the clearest expression of this idea. For men in this tradition the fundamental problem of the liberal state is the separation of political decision making from other aspects of social life. For the national syndicalists this led to a number of negative consequences, including a lack of concern with the "real" problems of the country and the formation of a parasitic "political class." Arguments like this resonated broadly in the specific political conditions of interwar Italy, Spain, and Romania, where, as a consequence of the failure of hegemony, there existed a crisis of politics.[14]

The antipolitical nature of fascist ideologies also goes some way to explaining the connection between fascism and civil society. As I argued earlier, fascist movements incorporated the rhetoric of civil society as a realm of spontaneous cooperation that had to be liberated from politics. The basic problem of liberal states, from the fascist perspective, was their inability to represent the complex associational structure of contemporary society.[15] Fascist movements aimed at removing the putatively artificial political class and sought to rest the fascist state directly on interest associations.

Given the centrality of civil society to fascist doctrine, these movements cannot be dismissed simply as antidemocratic. On the contrary their leaderships all sought to establish political orders that would be more representative of the people or nation than the corrupt liberal systems against which they struggled. The fascist movements took up democratic demands and used them to attack politics as such. That fascism was an antipolitical movement is clear from all three of the cases discussed in this book. The fascist movement in Italy arose out of a demand for a more representative state raised by returning war veterans. The failure of the PSI to ally with this movement in the postwar period led to its shift to the right and toward authoritarian tactics. In Spain the CEDA, and particularly the Carlist traditionalists, struggled for a traditionalist democracy, including the devolution of power to the regions and greater participation for the peasantry. In Romania, Codreanu's movement, especially after 1935, was a crucial part of the coalition of forces struggling against the emerging royalist dictatorship of Carol II. These movements cannot be understood as antidemocratic. Indeed, it was the fact that they positioned themselves as carrying forward the project of a democracy beyond liberalism that explains much of their popular support. The fascists promised to break with the faction-ridden and blocked politics that characterized both the oligarchic liberalism and the young liberal democracies of their respective countries. Their mass appeal was based on the promise of realizing the democratic potential of a developing civil society. Fascist movements, in sum, were authoritarian democratic movements. They rejected elections and parliaments as appropriate institutions for establishing popular rule, but they championed a political project to create more representative, not less representative, political institutions.

Fascists rejected liberalism because they rejected the notion that modern complex societies could be integrated through political debate institutionalized in a chamber. They argued that the very complexity of these societies meant that they had to be integrated in a nonpolitical way. Fascists did not attempt to eliminate competing interests or their organizations but rather to eliminate their political expression. The first Italian minister of corporations, Giuseppe Bottai was very clear about this, writing that, "when we say that in Italy there is class collaboration rather than class struggle, we certainly do not want to say that the interests that divide individuals and categories do not exist."[16] Fascist politics, therefore, drew on an antipolitical vision of modernity. The basic claim was that politics gets in the way of integrating modern societies. Fascists denied the positive function of political conflict in modern societies. They thought that competing interests could be resolved only through technical means.[17] Indeed, in their enthusiasm to eliminate politics, fascist thinkers sometimes ended up in the self-contradictory position of denying a central role to fascist parties. Fascism, consequently, is best understood as an antipolitical ideology, a denial of politics as such.

The fascist critique of politics was one of the characteristics that allowed these parties to effectively exploit the crisis of politics that developed in Italy, Spain, and Romania in the interwar years. The central political characteristic of these countries was the absence of hegemony either among the social elite or among nonelites. Fascist movements were well adapted to this political terrain, because their ideology was an ambiguous amalgam of leftist and rightist claims turned against the political class. The weakness of political organizations that had previously destroyed conservatives and that undermined more conventionally democratic forces strengthened fascism. Fascist mass movements were success-ful, then, where they could exploit the democratic demands produced by civil society, in the context of a nonhegemonic political system. These movements positioned themselves to take advantage of a crisis of politics. Gramsci grasped this best with his concept of organic crisis, which he defined as a situation of conflict, not between classes, but between "represented and representatives."[18]

Differences between the Gramscian Argument and Prevailing Accounts

How does this account differ from prevailing explanations of fascism? The most general difference between my perspective on interwar fascism and more-estab-lished accounts is that I see fascism as the result of a failure of the development of hegemonic politics rather than as a consequence of elite resistance to demo-cratic pressures from below. This is not to deny that such resistance played a role, but it alone cannot account for the crisis of politics out of which fascism emerged. Fascism was not solely the reaction of a threatened elite but was also the product of a general crisis of politics involving all social groups.

Before explaining in more theoretical terms what this means, it is useful to summarize the main empirical problems with established accounts. Despite their many differences the Moorian, Weberian, and Tocquevillian explanations, broadly speaking, are all top-down explanations of fascism. They emphasize the strength of states and social elites in relationship either to nonelites or society as a whole. Of course their exact arguments differ. Moore argues that fascism was the consequence of an authoritarian coalition between landlords and capitalists. The Weberians emphasize the importance of a strong old regime. Tocquevillians, in an argument that reinforces the Weberian claim, stress social atomization.

However, as I have suggested, there are some serious empirical problems with these accounts: the first group of problems concerns the nature of the social elite in those countries that succumbed to fascism in the interwar period, the second concerns their state structures, and the third concerns the development of civil society. I have discussed these issues in considerable detail, so it is enough here to reiterate the central points.

The basic problem with analyses in the Moore tradition is that fascist regimes tended to develop where labor-repressive agrarians were not particularly strong, at least in political terms. In Italy the southern landed elite was a junior partner in the unification process.[19] In Spain, although the landed elite was strong, it was unable to form a strong alliance with the industrialists. The conflict between centralizing Castilian landowners and Catalan textile producers was a constant feature of prefascist politics in Spain.[20] In Romania the large landholders were decisively weakened after the war, when their land was redistributed and their political organization collapsed.[21]

The evidence for the Weberian argument that links interwar authoritarianism to late absolutism faces serious empirical difficulties as well. The basic problem with this argument is that fascist regimes emerged only where an old regime did not really exist (as in Italy, Romania, and Spain) or where such a regime had been profoundly politically discredited (as in Germany). Parliament, not the monarchy, was the central political institution of unified Italy.[22] The monarchy was more active in Spain, but it was a modernizing liberal force. Smallholders in the north and east of the country constituted the primary social support for an old regime, Carlism, but this political model was defeated in the civil wars of the nineteenth century.[23] Finally, Romania, much like Italy, had no tradition of an old regime, for the simple reason that its only experience as an independent political unit was under a liberal constitution.[24]

There also appears to be little evidence for the Tocquevillian argument. All of the cases discussed in this book experienced a major spurt of civil society development, especially in agriculture, in the years between 1880 and 1914. Further, the evidence permits the conclusion that, in Italy and Spain, fascist movements concentrated in precisely those areas with the greatest levels of civil society development.

In Romania, in part because local authorities constantly repressed fascism, it is hard to establish this firmly. Yet it is suggestive that Romanian fascism did best among relatively independent smallholders in the mountainous regions and was less successful in the grain-growing plains.

Social atomization, in sum, is simply an inadequate description of societies across interwar Europe and, in particular, it does not well describe the areas where fascist movements were most vigorous. There is, however, an important connection between the specific form of civil society development and the type of fascism that emerged in the cases I have discussed. Party fascism, perhaps the paradigmatic form for the Tocquevillian argument, was associated, quite paradoxically, with the development of a civil society that was autonomous from both social elites and the state. Where civil society development was subordinated either to social elites (Spain) or to the state (Romania), party fascism—characterized by the fusion of a fascist movement from below and a fascist regime from above—was not the outcome. In Spain the outcome was traditionalist fascism, and in Romania, statist fascism. In short, the classic party fascist regimes emerged where civil society development was most autonomous from both the state and the social elite. While the development of voluntary associations importantly shaped the type of fascist regime that emerged, it did so in a way that is fundamentally at odds with most Tocquevillian accounts. What are the broader implications of this argument and the critique of existing accounts that I have offered?

Theoretical Conclusions

The argument I have developed has some obvious implications for the concept of civil society. But my analyses also have a more general set of implications about how one should understand the relationship between "politics" and "society." In developing these points it is useful to begin by revisiting and reformulating the Tocquevillian position and then expanding this to a set of more general considerations.

Civil Society, Democracy, Authoritarianism

Political sociologists have become skeptical of the usefulness of civil society as a concept. Increasingly scholars emphasize the potential risks of civil society development in specific political contexts.[25] My analysis shares much with this critical literature, but in certain respects I believe that the critique of the Tocquevillian position can be carried too far. The notion of civil society is both extremely useful for understanding regime variation and more specifically for understanding democracy. I have argued that the core point of the Tocquevillian thesis, that the development of voluntary associations tends to promote democracy, is correct. The basic problem is that neither the critical nor the positive literature on civil society has adequately distinguished liberal democracy from democracy as such.

To simplify a very complex literature, one group of scholars suggests that the development of voluntary associations promotes the functioning of liberal democracy, while a second position suggests that civil society can just as easily promote antiliberal democratic outcomes. In recent discussions fascism has been treated as the quintessential antiliberal democratic civil society movement.[26] Much of this debate fails to distinguish adequately liberalism from democracy and as a result ignores the genuinely democratic elements within fascist movements. Only by distinguishing clearly between liberalism and democracy can fascism be adequately understood, and only if fascism is adequately understood can one begin to develop the important implications of it for theories of civil society and democracy.

It is useful to begin by returning to Tocqueville. In *Democracy in America* Tocqueville argues that voluntary associations have two sorts of positive effects. First, they promote political participation. By cooperating for common purposes in some areas of social life, men and women learn to cooperate to pursue their political interests as well. The analyses presented in this book are full of examples of precisely this type of behavior. For example, the cooperatives that emerged to solve basic economic problems in the Valley of the Po in Italy quickly also became involved in political matters.[27] This might be called the pedagogical effect of civil society.[28]

Tocqueville also held that voluntary associations constitute a structural barrier to the state. By carrying out tasks that would otherwise be the job of the central government, they limit state power. Many of the examples discussed earlier fit well with such an interpretation. After all, many of the voluntary associations analyzed in this book provided basic welfare services that the poor and weak states of Italy, Spain, and Romania could not hope to provide.[29]

Both of these Tocquevillian arguments are quite solid, and there is nothing in the historical evidence I have brought up that challenges them. It is certainly plausible to argue that voluntary associations increase political participation and decrease pressure on central authorities. The theoretical problem is that the link between these two outcomes and liberalism as a set of institutions is much less clear. One can define liberalism as a form of rule in which political decisions are legitimated through discussion.[30] The basic requirement for such a system is a chamber in which men and women can freely exchange views about political matters. For such a system to work, there is little need to have a highly politically mobilized population or one that is self-governing at the local level. In short, liberalism has no clear relationship to democracy in the sense of the participation of the *demos*, or people, in political decision making and therefore little obvious connection with the development of civil society. As fascist ideologues themselves were highly aware, political participation can take many forms apart from voting and petitioning parliament. Further, as the analyses of the prefascist political systems of Italy, Spain, and Romania show, liberal institutions at the national level are perfectly compatible with restricted suffrage, electoral corruption, and coercive rule at the local level.[31]

Democracy, in contrast to liberalism, is a principle of legitimacy or political formula, rather than a set of institutions.[32] A regime is democratic to the extent that its claim to rule rests on a claim to represent the interests of the *people*, rather than the interests of the deity or his terrestrial representative, for example. *Fascist movements were generally democratic movements in this sense, and their attacks on liberalism derived from their democratic character.* Fascist movements promised not less responsive, less representative political organizations but more responsive, more representative organizations than had existed in the preceding liberal period. Given that fascist movements shared much with other democratic movements, it becomes much less surprising that they seem to have benefited from developed civil societies. Like socialism, Catholicism, and peasantism, fascist movements did well where populations were organized, where traditions of social solidarity were strong, and where people participated in the political process. In one sense, then, my argument suggests that, properly understood, fascism poses less of a problem to Tocquevillian arguments than might at first seem to be the case. Strong civil societies in Italy, Spain, and Romania did support democratic movements, as Tocquevillians might expect. But since democratic movements need not be *liberal democratic* movements, the existence of a strong civil society has, under many circumstances, threatened parliamentary states. Indeed, Tocqueville himself was deeply aware of the double-edged nature of democracy. The central problem of his work was precisely how to make it compatible with liberty.[33]

The general lesson of fascism, in sum, is that a developed civil society can promote a democratic movement that is nevertheless antiliberal because it is antipolitical. In these types of movements civil society is not the basis of liberal democracy but an alternative to political representation as such. Civil society is Janus-faced, capable of sustaining both antiliberal and liberal political movements, because democracy itself is Janus-faced. As a principle of sovereignty it can combine with a wide variety of regime forms.[34]

Hegemonic Politics: The Missing Link

It would be deeply unsatisfying to leave the analysis here: to suggest that, while civil society promotes democracy, it has little relationship to liberalism, for this raises the obvious question, why does civil society development in some contexts produce authoritarian outcomes, while in other contexts it clearly strengthens liberal democracy? Gramsci's concept of hegemony, I would argue, provides the missing link between civil society and regime outcomes. As I have argued at some length, the development of hegemony and the development of civil society are independent historical processes. In Italy, Spain, and Romania they clearly did not coincide. In these cases civil society developed, but in the absence of hegemonic politics. Since political struggle was not defined in terms of a relatively consensual national task established prior to associational development, civil society development produced a confusing welter of claims leading to a crisis of politics and ultimately undermining the legitimacy of the liberal systems of Italy, Spain, and Romania.

The fascist critique of liberalism resonated in these countries precisely because of this. Elections here had no relationship to governments, not only because they were corrupt, but also because of the formlessness of political life, which itself was the result of the absence of hegemonic politics. The absence of strongly structured parties among the social elite was transmitted to the party system after universal suffrage. There was neither a clear conservative or counterrevolutionary pole in these countries, nor was there a clear democratic pole. The necessary tension between a clearly defined left and right, which lends meaning to elections, did not exist.

Thus, one major implication of my analysis is that conservatives and progressives are to some extent interdependent; or, to put the point in Gramscian terms, hegemony and counterhegemony depend upon one another. This is true in two ways. First, the internal cohesion of conservative and progressive movements depends on the existence of a well-defined political enemy. In the absence of such an enemy, political movements are always subject to internal fragmentation; in Gramsci's terms, it becomes difficult to establish intraclass hegemony. In my view, a well-defined conservative pole would have greatly aided the formation of a well-defined progressive democratic pole in each of the cases discussed in this book. This basic condition was lacking in Italy in the early twenties, in Spain in the thirties, and in Romania in the late twenties.

This absence of internal cohesion, or intraclass hegemony, also paradoxically makes the formation of interclass hegemony difficult. If a party or group of parties does not constitute its political project against a clearly defined enemy, the boundary between potential allies and those groups, parties, and associations that are not potential allies becomes blurred. This political confusion leads to tactical errors: the attempt to dominate or liquidate rather than lead potential allies. The construction of hegemony, in both intra- and interclass terms, depends, therefore, on the existence of a well-established political opposition between friends and enemies.[35]

A lack of political structure and a corresponding lack of clarity among those groups sincerely struggling to establish a nonauthoritarian democracy in Italy, Spain, and Romania was clearly in evidence in the period of the organic crisis in each of these countries. Consider the political situation in Italy in 1919. The PSI and the PPI together would have had a massive majority in parliament. And yet, instead of working together to achieve the fundamental political and social reforms that the population desperately needed, they fought amongst themselves as well as splitting internally. This was partially the consequence of the weakness of Italian conservatism. A well-defined mass party of the right would have had an enormously positive effect on the coalitional politics of Italy's democrats. Similar conclusions follow from the Spanish Second Republic. In 1931 Spanish conservatism was in complete disarray. But in the absence of pressure from the right, the various factions and parties of the republican coalition immediately began to fight amongst themselves, pursuing policies that turned out to alienate a social group they should at least have been able to neutralize (the smallholders of north-central Spain). Similar remarks can be made about Romanian politics in the late twenties. Here, too, the absence of a conservative pole led to the fragmentation of the democratic pole. Fascism gained ground in each of these countries only because of this lack of political structure.

This suggests a broader set of conclusions about how one should think about political struggle and group formation. Political sociologists from a wide variety of intellectual backgrounds often conceive of group formation as a zero-sum game.

The organization of one social class or group implies the weakness of its adversary. In the Marxian tradition, to which Gramsci belonged, these groups have generally been conceived as social classes. The concept of hegemony suggests a fundamentally different approach to the process of conflict and group formation than more standard formulations. The difference can be grasped from the way that Gramsci approaches the problem of the failure of revolution in Western Europe. The Marxist tradition has generally argued that the stability of capitalism in the advanced West is to be ascribed to its ideological strength. Starting with Lukács, and extending through the Frankfurt school, Marxian scholarship extended the notion of commodity fetishism, arguing that a passive, contemplative, and atomized worldview was an automatic product of capitalist production and exchange and that it produced an economist and reformist working-class movement.[36] Gramsci's approach to this problem was completely different, partly because of the national context in which he wrote. Like other Western Marxists, Gramsci fought against economism and reformism. Yet he saw this not as a result of capitalist production but rather as a consequence of national political traditions: the absence of hegemonic politics. This approach points to a conception of group formation as fundamentally different from the more mainstream versions of Marxism.

A dominant class that establishes its hegemony, that is, which rules in the name of a national project that it partially fulfills, is not only an obstacle or challenge to the formation of a popular opposition; it is also the condition of possibility for the formation of a counterhegemonic, nondominant class. Hegemonic politics is a struggle over which social group "really causes the whole society to move forward, not merely satisfying its own existential requirements."[37] A successfully established hegemony is therefore *not* simply an obstacle to further historical progress. It establishes the basic framework for a counterhegemonic politics. A political tradition of hegemony is a resource that all social groups can use. As the examples of Italy, Spain, and Romania show, what is perhaps much worse than a hegemonic ruling class is a nonhegemonic one.

Hegemonic politics is not, of course, consensual politics. In fact, consent, in the sense of a set of agreements among narrowly defined interests, is quite compatible with an absence of hegemony. Hegemony requires a constant struggle, both over the definition of a broader national interest and over the social coalition that can carry this forward. However, unlike struggles among closed economic corporate groups, hegemonic politics occurs with reference to a collective project of social transformation, the elements of which can shift across class and group boundaries, becoming resources for the formation of counterhegemony.[38] In this sense hegemony and counterhegemony depend upon one another.

Gramsci's concept of hegemony is useful not only for thinking about group formation but also for specifying the role of political struggle in sustaining liberal democratic polities. Political sociologists have often argued that liberalism requires the existence of social agents willing to compromise their interests.[39] This argument is common to cultural approaches that see liberalism as rooted in a set of dispositions, and more materialist arguments that link liberal regimes to a specific social class—usually the "middle class." The problem with such claims, in my view, is that compromise can be established in a variety of different ways, for instance, as a set of back-room deals between preconstituted interests. Liberal democracies do not depend on compromise as much as on institutionalized political struggle. But what is political struggle, as opposed to social struggle in general? Gramsci's concept of hegemonic politics is suggestive here. Hegemonic politics occurs when social struggles transcend the immediate economic interests of a group and are formulated in terms of a national cultural tradition. It is for this reason that "one may speak separately of economics and politics, and speak of 'political passion' as of an immediate impulse to actions which is born on the 'permanent and organic' terrain of economic life but which transcends it, bringing into play emotions and aspirations in whose incandescent atmosphere even calculations involving the individual human life itself obey different laws from those of individual profit."[40] Suggestively, if embryonically, Gramsci gives a positive value to political struggle that is rare not only in the Marxian tradition but also in much of political sociology. In short, Gramsci allows one to recognize the value of real political struggle, of hegemonic struggle, for liberal democracy.

The opposite is also true. Where politics is not sufficiently autonomous from social interests, where there do not exist organizations that provide a clear national program, voters cannot see any relationship between their preferences and government. Coalition governments made up of many parties pursuing narrow interests do not provide an adequate substitute, because they are not elected as governments. Instead, they form in parliament after elections. The absence of well-structured parties thus lent great plausibility to the fascist critique of liberalism. One of the main targets of fascist criticism in all three of the major cases examined in this book was the "political class." Fascists rejected the idea of political interest representation through votes, because in the specific political conditions in which they operated such mechanisms of interest representation did not work.[41] The political circumstances immediately prior to the rise of fascism in Italy, Spain, and Romania show this clearly; in each of these countries the political problem was not so much a high level of polarization between the left and the right as it was political disorganization. This political fact produced, understandably, the widespread view that voting and parliamentary debate had little or nothing to do with democracy in the sense of the rule of the people.

The above analysis, then, while not addressing the connection between civil society and liberal democracy, suggests a new way of thinking about their relationship. Perhaps the central question is, under what political conditions is associational development compatible with liberal rule? In fact, from the perspective of this book, their coincidence no longer appears obvious but imposes itself instead as a problem. To resolve it is the task of another book.

Notes

Introduction to the Second Edition

1. Mayer, *Dynamics of Counterrevolution in Europe, 1870–1956*, 1971: 3; Eley, "The British Model and the German Road," in *The Peculiarities of German History*, 1989: 91; Togliatti, *Lezioni sul fascismo*, 1970 [1935]: 1.

2. Gentile, *Le origini del ideologia fascista (1918–1925)*, 1975: 248; Gregor, *The Ideology of Fascism*, 1969: 6–10; Griffin, "The Palingenetic Political Community," 2002, 24; Mann, "The Contradictions of Continuous Revolution," in *Stalinism and Nazism*, 1997: 142–145; Sternhell, *The Birth of Fascist Ideology*, 1994: 7.

3. Beetham, "Introduction," in *Marxists in Face of Fascism from the Inter-War Period*, 1983: 11; Mayer, *Why Did the Heavens Not Darken?*, 1989: 94; Tasca, *Nascita e avvento del fascismo*, 1950: 537–539.

4. Mandel, *Trotsky as Alternative*, 1995: 107.

5. Ibid.: 112.

6. Trotsky, "What Next? Vital Questions for the German Proletariat," in *The Struggle Against Fascism in Germany*, 2001: 164–165.

7. Sarti, "Fascist Modernization in Italy: Traditonal or Revolutionary?" 1970: 1040–1044; Sarti, *Fascism and the Industrial Leadership in Italy*, 1971: 1–6; Sarti, "I sindicati fascisti e la politica economica del regime," 1972: 746; Tooze, *The Wages of Destruction*, 2006: 114.

8. Paxton, *The Anatomy of Fascism*, 2004: 98.

9. Marx, "The Eighteenth Brumaire of Louis Bonaparte," in *Marx*: 1996: 119–121.

10. Ibid.: 39.

11. Ibid.

12. Arendt, *The Human Conditio*, 1958: 308–312.

13. Gregor, *The Ideology of Fascism*, xii, 40–58.

14. De Felice, *Le interpretazioni del fascismo*, 2000: xiii.

15. Mann, "The Contradictions of Continuous Revolution," 1997: 136; Finchelstein, "On Fascist Ideology," 2008: 32.

16. Gentile, *Le origini del ideologia fascista*, 1975: 312–313.

17. Gentile, *La via italiana al totalitarismo*, 1995: 187.

18. Mann, "The Contradictions of Continuous Revolution," 1997: 142.

19. Pinto, "European Fascism," 2012: 293.

20. Art, "Review: What Do We Know About Authoritarianism After Ten Years?" 2012: 356.

21. Payne, "Foundations of Fascism," 2010: 707.

22. Canfora, *Democracy in Europe*, 2006: 250; Gallie, "Essentially Contested Concepts," 1955: 183–187.

23. A longer version of this analysis appears in *New Left Review* 114.

24. Poulantzas, *Fascism and Dictatorship*, 1974: 17.

25. Eley, "The British Model and the German Road," 1989: 121.

26. Gentile, *Il mito dello stato nuovo*, 1982: 96.

27. Ridolfi, *Il PSI e la nascita del partito di massa*, 1992: 46.

28. Linz, "Political Space and Fascism as a Late-Comer," in *Who Were the Fascists?*, 1965: 154.

CHAPTER ONE: Civil Society and Fascism in Interwar Europe

1. Tenfeld captures the point best: "Among the many developments European societies shared in common during the nineteenth century was one that time and again provoked the astonishment of contemporary observers—the social process of organization." Tenfeld, "Civil Society and the Middle Classes in Nineteenth-Century Germany," 2000: 85. See also Callahan, *The Catholic Church in Spain, 1875–1998*, 2000: 142–148; Eidelberg, *The Great Rumanian Peasant Revolt of 1907*, 1974: 98; Lyttelton, "Liberalism and Civil Society in Italy," 2000: 69–78.

2. Nord, "Introduction," in *Civil Society before Democracy*, 2000: xvii–xviii; Putnam, *Making Democracy Work*, 1993: 137–148.

3. Arato, "Civil Society against the State," 1981; Cohen and Arato, *Civil Society and Political Theory*, 1992; Gellner, *Conditions of Liberty*, 1994; Nord, *The Republican Moment*, 1995; Putnam, *Making Democracy Work*, 1993; Putnam, *Bowling Alone*, 2000; Varshney, *Ethnic Conflict and Civic Life*, 2002.

4. A search on the LexisNexis newspaper and magazine article database revealed 2,400 articles containing the words *civil society* and *democracy* over the period from February 2008 to February 2009.

5. Putnam's opening question in *Making Democracy Work* defines an entire research agenda: "Why do some democratic governments succeed and others fail?" Putnam, *Making Democracy Work*, 1993: 3. This leaves another question unasked: why does civil society sometimes undermine liberalism? See also Howard, *The Weakness of Civil Society in Post-communist Europe*, 2003; 148–152; Kaufman, *For the Common Good? American Civic Life and the Golden Age of Fraternity*, 2002; Putnam, *Bowling Alone*, 2000; Skocpol, "The Tocqueville Problem," 1997.

6. De Felice, *Le interpretazioni del fascisimo*, 2000: xii; Linz, *Fascismo, autoritarismo, totalitarismo*, 2003: 23–24; Mahoney, "Knowledge Accumulation in Comparative Historical Research," 2003: 158.

7. Luebbert, *Liberalism, Fascism, or Social Democracy*, 1991: 3; Moore, *Social Origins of Dictatorship and Democracy*, 1993: 433–452; Stephens, "Democratic Transition and Breakdown in Western Europe," 1989: 1060–1064.

8. Mann, *Fascists*, 2004: 44–48; Payne, *Fascism: Comparison and Definition*, 1980: 14–21; Payne, *A History of Fascism, 1914–1945*, 1995: 462–470.

9. Bruno Spampanato defined fascism as an "authoritarian democracy, inasmuch as the entire 'demos,' that is all of the people, circulates in the state." Ibid.: 46. Giovanni Gentile similarly argued that "the Fascist State … is a popular state, and, in that sense, a democratic State par excellence." Gentile, *Fascismo: storia e interpretazione*, 2002: 28. Horia Sima, who became the leader of the Romanian fascist movement after the death of its founder, Codreanu, distinguished between "democracy" and the "will of the nation" in a way that is very similar to both Gentile and Spampanato: "The will of the people may express itself at a given moment through democracy and parties, but nothing impedes it from also finding other forms of expression." Sima, *Histoire du mouvement légionnaire*, 1972: 101. Although the language is slightly different from that of the Italian fascists, it is clear that Sima, too, argued for a distinction between democracy as the rule of the people or will of the nation and liberalism as an institutional form. In a 1935 speech Hitler stated that "the state is only the organizational form of popular life." Quoted in Diehl-Thiele, *Partei und Staat im Dritten Reich*, 1969: 20. See also Fritzsche, "Did Weimar Fail?" 1996: 634–635; Gentile, *Fascismo: storia e interpretazione*, 2002: 28–29; Gregor, *Mussolini's Intellectuals*, 2005: 150; Sima, *Histoire du mouvement légionnaire*, 1972: 101; Spampanato, *Democrazia fascista*, 1933: 46.

10. Both Bendix and Weber in these passages define legitimacy as an answer to the question: why do men obey? Bendix points out that domination is "a universal condition of all complex societies." Bendix, *Kings or People*, 1978: 16. The decisive question is on what basis that domination is being exercised. Democracy, therefore, means the claim to rule in the name of the people. It is obvious enough that this general claim can be instituted in a variety of ways. Weber, *Economy and Society*, 1978: 212–215.

11. Bottai, *Esperienza Corporativa*, 1928: 100–101; Mann, "The Dark Side of Democracy," 1999: 29; Mann, *Fascists*, 2004: 2; Manoïlescu, *Le siècle du corporatisme*, 1936: 90; Mazower, *Dark Continent*, 2000: 29; Nolte, *The Three Faces of Fascism*, 1966: 104; Rocco, *Scritti e discorsi politici*, 1938: 637–639, 641; Therborn, *What Does the Ruling Class Do When It Rules?*, 2008: 205–209.

12. Linz, *Fascismo, autoritarismo, totalitarismo*, 2003: 576–62.

13. Kelsen, "Foundations of Democracy," 1955: 3; Schumpeter, *Capitalism, Socialism, and Democracy*, 1942: 269.

14. Mosca, *La classe politica*, 1994: 70.

15. In this way liberalism can be understood as one method among others of instituting democracy. The justification for liberalism rests on the idea that consensus emerges through *discussion* in which men change one another's minds. In liberal theory parliament is a constitutive institution, one that converts the interests of individuals, or what Rousseau called the will of all, into a general will. The decisions that legislative bodies emit are, in theory, qualitatively different from compromises reached between

preexisting groups, because they represent the results of a deliberation in which pre-formed opinions have been transformed through debate. The idea that discussion can produce a rationalized consensus is the basis for all other liberal rights, such as the right to free speech and the right of association. These are justified insofar as they make a reasonable discussion about political matters possible. Habermas, *The Social Structural Transformation of the Public Sphere*, 1989: 54–56.

16. Tönnies, "Demokratie und Palamentarismus," 1927.

17. Balakrishnan, *The Enemy: An Intellectual Portrait of Carl Schmitt*, 2000: 69–76; Schmitt, *The Crisis of Parliamentary Democracy*, 1985: 32. The notion that liberal institutions were incompatible with democracy was quite widespread in the interwar period. Carl Schmitt expresses the argument most clearly. The organization of European societies in the latter part of the twentieth century, the emergence of political parties, unions, and organizations of employers, seemed to many thinkers to undermine the constitutive function of parliament: that is, its ability to constitute the general will. These organizations seemed to constrain the freedom of individual representatives to act according to the results of parliamentary deliberation, because the party member is elected on the basis of his commitment to a preexisting political program. Since these political programs were linked to fundamental differences of opinion and interest in the population, they could not be transformed through discussion. This undermined the ability of parliamentary representatives to respond to argument. As a consequence parliaments could no longer represent the general will as opposed to particular interests. Legislative decisions were no longer based on freedom of discussion but rather on compromises between positions that had been fixed prior to the deputy's entry into the parliamentary chamber. According to this line of thought, while liberalism's claim to legitimacy was based on its ability to produce consensus through discussion, its institutions, at least in modern conditions, could not achieve this. Ibid.: 49.

18. Gregor, *Mussolini's Intellectuals*, 2005: 120.

19. Friedrich, "The Unique Character of Totalitarian Society," 1964: 47–60; Gleason, *Totalitarianism*, 1995: 108–120.

20. Mahoney, "Knowledge Accumulation in Comparative Historical Research," 2003: 158.

21. Linz, "An Authoritarian Regime: Spain," 1970: 255.

22. Pombeni, "La rappresentanza politica," 1995: 108–109.

23. Bobbio, *Teoria generale della politica*, 1999: 272; Cohen and Arato, *Civil Society and Political Theory*, 1992; Gellner, "The Importance of Being Modular," 1995; Hall, "In Search of Civil Society," 1995; Keane, *Democracy and Civil Society*, 1988a; Pérez-Díaz, *The Return of Civil Society*, 1993; Warren, *Democracy and Association*, 2001.

24. Kornhauser, *The Politics of Mass Society*, 1959: 74.

25. Armony, *The Dubious Link*, 2004: 24–30; Hegel, *Elements of the Philosophy of Right*, 1991: 270–274; Howard, *The Weakness of Civil Society in Post-communist Europe*, 2003: 34–35; Kornhauser, *The Politics of Mass Society*, 1959: 74; Putnam, *Making Democracy Work*, 1993: 173–175; Tocqueville, *Democracy in America*, 1988: 513.

26. Gellner poses the issue with exemplary clarity: "How is it possible to have atomization without a political emasculation of the atomized man (à la Ibn Khaldun) and to have politically countervailing associations without these being stifling (as in the world of Fustel de Coulange)?" Gellner, *Conditions of Liberty*, 1994: 99.

27. Tocqueville, *Democracy in America*, 1988: 511.

28. Putnam, *Making Democracy Work*, 1993: 111–112; Villa, "Tocqueville and Civil Society," 2006: 227–228.

29. Hall, "In Search of Civil Society," 1995: 8.

30. Tocqueville, *Democracy in America*, 1988: 523.

31. Arendt, *The Origins of Totalitarianism*, 1966: 313.

32. Lederer, *State of the Masses*, 1967; Arendt, *The Origins of Totalitarianism*, 1966.

33. Kornhauser, *The Politics of Mass Society*, 1959: 80.

34. Sartori, *Parties and Party Systems*, 1976: 16–17.

35. Kornhauser, *The Politics of Mass Society*, 1959: 33.

36. Bendix, "Social Stratification and Political Power," 1952.

37. Keane, *Democracy and Civil Society*, 1988a: 49–51; Keane, "Despotism and Democracy," 1988b: 55–62; Keane, *Civil Society*, 1998: 20; Wuthnow, "Tocqueville's Question Reconsidered," 1991: 288.

38. Arendt, *The Origins of Totalitarianism*, 1966: 316.

39. Ibid.: 313.

40. Putnam, *Bowling Alone*, 2000.

41. Paxton, *The Anatomy of Fascism*, 2004: 3.

42. Putnam, *Making Democracy Work*, 1993: 139.

43. Dovring, *Land and Labor in Europe in the Twentieth Century*, 1965: 206; Gide, *La Coopération dans les Pays Latins*, 1926–1927: 5; Putnam, *Making Democracy Work*, 1993: 139–141.

44. Armony, *The Dubious Link*, 2004; Berman, "Civil Society and the Collapse of the Weimar Republic," 1997; Hagtvet, "The Theory of Mass Society and the Collapse of the Weimar Republic," 1980; Koshar, *Social Life, Local Politics, and Nazism*, 1986.

45. Kaufman, *For the Common Good? American Civic Life and the Golden Age of Fraternity*, 2002: 9–10.

46. Armony, *The Dubious Link*, 2004: 206.

47. Putnam, *Bowling Alone*, 2000: 350–363.

48. Diamond, "Civil Society and the Development of Democracy," 1997: 6; Fiorina, "Extreme Voices," 1999: 403.

49. Armony, *The Dubious Link*, 2004: 10–11.

50. Lakatos, "Falsification and the Methodology of Scientific Research Programmes," 1970: 163.

51. Skocpol, "How Americans Became Civic," 1999: 73.

52. Lakatos, "Falsification and the Methodology of Scientific Research Programmes," 1970: 133.

53. Berman, "Civil Society and the Collapse of the Weimar Republic," 1997: 426–427. Ariel Armony expresses well this point of view when he writes of Weimar Germany that "civic engagement then contributed to the fragmentation of society and, in a context of heightened antipoliticism, to give legitimacy to an antidemocratic movement." Armony, *The Dubious Link*, 2004: 70. I believe it is a serious error to dismiss fascist movements as antidemocratic movements, a point that I make in greater detail in the case studies.

54. Putnam, *Bowling Alone*, 2000: 336; Skocpol, "How Americans Became Civic," 1999: 32–33.

55. Putnam, *Bowling Alone*, 2000.

56. Bobbio, "Gramsci e la concezione della società civile," 1969: 85; Rueschemeyer, Stephens, and Stephens, *Capitalist Development and Democracy*, 1992: 49–50.

57. Gramsci, *Selections from the Prison Notebook*, 1971: 2.

58. Bobbio, "Gramsci e la concezione della società civile," 1969: 85.

59. Burawoy, "Marxism as Science," 1990: 788; Gramsci, *Selections from the Prison Notebook*, 1971: 238.

60. Ibid.: 119, 179, 237–238, 243.

61. Anderson, "The Antinomies of Antonio Gramsci," 1976–1977: 20; Bobbio, "Gramsci e la concezione della società civile," 1969; Coutinho, *Il pensiero politico di Gramsci*, 2006: 95–106; Gramsci, *Selections from the Prison Notebook*, 1971: 12, 119, 179, 235, 238, 243; Laclau and Mouffe, *Hegemony and Socialist Strategy*, 2001: 136.

62. Gramsci, *Selections from the Prison Notebook*, 1971: 181.

63. Ibid.: 181.

64. Ibid.: 181.

65. Laclau and Mouffe, *Hegemony and Socialist Strategy*, 2001: 66–67; Lears, "The Concept of Cultural Hegemony," 1985: 568.

66. Gramsci, *Selections from the Prison Notebook*, 1971: 57.

67. Burawoy, "For a Sociological Marxism," 2003: 225.

68. As Gramsci notes: "The precursors of the Revolution were in fact moderate reformers who shouted very loud but actually demanded very little. Gradually a new elite was selected out which did not concern itself solely with 'corporate' reforms, but tended to conceive the bourgeoisie as the hegemonic group of all the popular forces." Gramsci, *Selections from the Prison Notebook*, 1971: 77.

69. Ibid.: 79. There are interesting parallels between Gramsci's analysis of the transition from corporate group to class and William H. Sewell Jr.'s work on the formation of class consciousness in nineteenth-century France. Sewell, *Work and Revolution in France*, 1980: 213. Sewell, like Gramsci, structures his analysis in terms of an opposition between the corporate consciousnesses of the working class rooted in the organizations of the old regime and the emergence of a sense of fraternity among all workers that for him emerged in the 1830s.

70. Anderson, "Problems of Socialist Strategy," 1965: 242; Gramsci, *Selections from the Prison Notebook*, 1971: 77–78.

71. Ibid.: 90; see also Adamson, "Gramsci's Interpretation of Fascism," 1980: 620.

72. This emphasis on politics and culture might seem to place Gramsci's arguments squarely into the mainstream of Western Marxist theorizing, which was centrally concerned with the role of consciousness in class formation. Lukács, *History and Class Consciousness*, 1971: 52. This is a possible interpretation of Gramsci, and there are certainly elements of such an analysis in his work. But it is worth emphasizing that Gramsci's central concept of hegemony differs crucially from other Western Marxist theories of ideology in two respects. First, unlike the concepts of reification, commodity fetishism, or false consciousness, hegemony is not best understood as an "ideology" in the sense of a set of ideas. It refers, rather, to a concrete, historically achieved form of organization. Second, hegemony, unlike more standard Marxian notions of ideology or false consciousness, is not an obstacle to be overcome by a revolutionary organization endowed with a true or correct understanding of society. On the contrary, hegemony

refers to a basic historical achievement of the Western European bourgeoisie comparable to the establishment of the modern territorial state or factory.

73. Huntington, *Political Order in Changing Societies,* 1968: 20.

74. Gramsci, analyzing the political history of the Italian bourgeoisie, hints at the distinction between the first two forms of hegemony, writing, "The formation of this class involved the gradual but continuous absorption, achieved by methods which varied in their effectiveness, of the active elements produced by allied groups—and even of those which came from antagonistic groups and seemed irreconcilably hostile." Gramsci, *Selections from the Prison Notebook,* 1971: 58–59. The absorption of allied groups refers to the process of intraclass hegemony. The absorption of antagonistic groups refers to the process of interclass hegemony. The term *counterhegemony* appears nowhere in Gramsci's work. However, Gramsci insists that the existence of a "national-popular" tradition, particularly a Jacobin tradition available to nonelites, is a consequence of the existence of a hegemonic dominant class. In contrast, the absence of a truly national politics, in this sense, in Italy is one of Gramsci's basic themes.

75. Ibid.: 210; Huntington, *Political Order in Changing Societies,* 1968: 86.

76. Gramsci, *Selections from the Prison Notebook,* 1971: 130–131; Gramsci, *La Questione Meridionale,* 1974: 142; Laclau and Mouffe, *Hegemony and Socialist Strategy,* 2001: 134–136.

77. Gramsci makes this point with exemplary clarity in his remarks at the end of his notes on the intellectuals. Of England, he writes, "The new social grouping that grew up on the basis of modern industrialism shows a remarkable economic-corporate development but advances only gropingly in the intellectual political field." Gramsci, *Selections from the Prison Notebook,* 1971: 18. In other words, the English bourgeoisie is economically strong but not hegemonic.

78. Ibid.: 95–96, 131.

This situation characterizes much of Italian history. Gramsci argues that in Italy, "an effective *Jacobin* force was always missing that in other nations awakened and organized the national-popular collective will, and founded the modern states." Ibid.: 131. In the postunification period this meant that Italy's dominant classes lacked political organizations of national scope within which they could articulate interests and win over substantial popular support. Instead, clienteles, alliances of diverse but narrow interests held together by great personalities, dominated Italian parliament. The archetype of this kind of politics was Giovanni Giolitti, the dominant figure in Italian parliament from 1896 to 1914. Giolitti allied variously with the Catholics, the socialists, the southern agrarians, and northern industry by attempting to satisfy their immediate material interests through tariffs and state largess. Ibid.: 95–96. This situation of hegemonic weakness produced a crisis in the post–World War I period as suffrage expanded. Ibid.: 209–210. But the underlying cause of the crisis of the postwar period is the development of civil society. As both progressive Catholic and socialist organizations developed in the countryside, it became increasingly difficult to co-opt their leaders into the kinds of amorphous governing coalitions that characterized the Giolittian period. What defines the crisis of the period around World War I, from Gramsci's perspective, is the continued attempt at clientalistic rule, that is to say, the application of nonhegemonic political techniques in the context of a developed civil society.

79. Ibid.: 210.

80. Ibid.: 60–61.

81. Gramsci's writings on fascism were highly distinctive in the context of the Marxist debates with which he engaged. In the interwar period there were basically two orthodox Marxist explanations of fascism. One argued that fascism was the typical political form of underdeveloped or late-developing capitalist societies. A second claimed that it was a necessary "stage" in the transition to socialism, somewhat analogous to the role of absolutism in the rise of capitalism. Thus, while the first argument held that fascism should be connected to capitalist underdevelopment, the second held that fascism should be connected to the most developed capitalist societies. These formally incompatible arguments moved within a common framework seeking to link fascism to a specific stage of economic development. Gramsci broke very sharply with this approach, suggesting instead that fascism was the outcome of a political crisis produced by the hegemonic weakness of the ruling bloc in a situation of rapid civil society development. Ibid.: 210. By linking fascism to hegemony and the development of civil society, rather than stages of economic development, Gramsci transcended the economistic framework within which fascism had been addressed hitherto. Laclau, *Politics and Ideology in Marxist Theory*, 1977: 89–90; Poulantzas, *Fascism and Dictatorship*, 1970: 28–29, 32. He offers, therefore, the beginnings of a highly original *political* theory of fascism. This aspect of Gramsci's argument forms the basis of my approach.

82. Emigh, "The Power of Negative Thinking," 1997; Goldstone, "The Study of Revolutions," 2003: 46.

83. Lakatos, "Falsification and the Methodology of Scientific Research Programmes," 1970: 130.

84. Burawoy, "Marxism as Science," 1990: 778; Emigh, "The Power of Negative Thinking," 1997: 656; Emigh, *The Undevelopment of Capitalism*, 2009: 15–17; Riley, "Privilege and Property," 2003: 192–193.

85. Lakatos, "Falsification and the Methodology of Scientific Research Programmes," 1970: 130.

86. Ernst Nolte's analysis of Charles Maurras is useful for understanding this form of fascism. As Nolte says of Maurras's views, "Democracy is the wasting disease from which the goddess [France] suffers, the deadly threat to her existence." The point is to cure the goddess. Nolte, *The Three Faces of Fascism*, 1966: 107.

87. De Felice, *Mussolini il fascista. L'organizzazione dello Stato fascista 1925–1929*, 1995 [1968]: 4; Falasca-Zamponi, *The Aesthetics of Power in Mussolini's Italy*, 1997: 8, 110; Linz, "An Authoritarian Regime: Spain," 1970: 255; Linz, *Fascismo, autoritarismo, totalitarismo*, 2003: 29–32; Payne, *A History of Fascism, 1914–1945*, 1995: 16.

88. Panunzio, *Il fondamento giuridico del fascismo*, 1987: 208.

89. Nolte, *The Three Faces of Fascism*, 1966; De Felice, *Mussolini il fascista. L'organizzazione dello Stato fascista 1925–1929*, 1995 [1968]: 369; De Felice, *Le interpretazioni del fascisimo*, 2000: xiii; Mosse, *The Nationalization of the Masses*, 1975.

90. Gentile, *La via italiana al totalitarismo*, 1995: 31.

91. Togliatti, *Lectures on Fascism*, 1976: 73–86.

92. De Grazia, *The Culture of Consent* 1981: 4.

93. Pradera, *The New State*, 1938: 134–135.

94. González Cuevas, *Acción Española*, 1998: 14.

95. Pradera, *The New State*, 1938: 97.

96. Linz, *Fascismo, autoritarismo, totalitarismo,* 2003: 31; Rodríguez Jiménez, *Historia de Falange Española de Las JONS,* 2000: 283.

97. Manoïlescu, *Le siècle du corporatisme,* 1936: 15.

98. Berman, "Civil Society and the Collapse of the Weimar Republic," 1997; Kaufman, *For the Common Good? American Civic Life and the Golden Age of Fraternity,* 2002.

CHAPTER TWO: Party Fascism

1. Holt, *Risorgimento: The Making of Italy, 1815–1870,* 1970: 38–42.

2. Banti, *Storia della borghesia italiana,* 1996: 52–53; Ragionieri, *Storia d'Italia,* 1976: 44–53; Seton-Watson, *Italy from Liberalism to Fascism, 1870–1925,* 1967: 26, 49.

3. Farneti, *Sistema politico e società civile,* 1971: 228; Ragionieri, *Storia d'Italia,* 1976: 26–27.

4. Adler, *Italian Industrialists from Liberalism to Fascism,* 1995: 6; Banti, *Storia della borghesia italiana,* 1996: 45; Carocci, *Giolitti e l'età giolittiana,* 1971: 10; Chabod, *L'Italia contemporanea (1918–1948),* 1961: 42; Delle Piane, *Gaetano Mosca,* 1952: 33; De Ruggiero, *The History of European Liberalism,* 1959: 341–342; Gaeta, *La crisi di fine secolo e l'età giolittiana,* 1982: 7; Pombeni, "Trasformismo e questione del partito," 1986: 224; Ragionieri, *Storia d'Italia,* 1976: 74–75; Salomone, *Italy in the Giolittian Era,* 1960: 15; Togliatti, *Lectures on Fascism,* 1976: 29.

5. De Ruggiero, *The History of European Liberalism,* 1959: 300; Mack-Smith, *Italy: A Modern History,* 1959: 184.

6. Chabod, *L'Italia contemporanea (1918–1948),* 1961: 42.

Unless otherwise stated, all translations are my own.

7. As Palmiro Togliatti famously puts the point in his *Lectures on Fascism:* "The bourgeoisie had never possessed a strong, unified political organization; it never had an organization in party form. This was one of the characteristics of the Italian situation before the war." Lyttelton, "Liberalism and Civil Society in Italy," 2000: 74; Togliatti, *Lectures on Fascism,* 1976: 29.

8. Jones, *The Italian City State,* 1997: 71, 79, 231.

9. Ammirato, *La Lega,* 1996: 49; Tomassini, "Mutual Benefit Societies in Italy, 1861–1922," 1996: 239; Ridolfi, *Interessi e passioni,* 1999: 155–156; Zangheri, "Nascita e primi sviluppi," 1987: 6, 8, 10–13, 27, 49, 50.

10. Ammirato, *La Lega,* 1996: 66; Ciuffoletti, "Dirigenti e ideologie del movimento cooperativo," 1981: 91–92; Lyttelton, "Liberalism and Civil Society in Italy," 2000: 68.

11. Ciuffoletti, "Dirigenti e ideologie del movimento cooperativo," 1981: 92; Mazzini, *I doveri dell'uomo,* 1945: 97–101, 109, 112.

12. Zangheri, "Nascita e primi sviluppi," 1987: 42.

13. Ciuffoletti, "Dirigenti e ideologie del movimento cooperativo," 1981: 99.

14. Mazzini, *I doveri dell'uomo,* 1945: 117.

15. Ibid.: 17.

16. Ciuffoletti, "Dirigenti e ideologie del movimento cooperativo," 1981: 97–99; Degl'Innocenti, "Geografia e strutture della cooperazione in Italia," 1981: 7; Zangheri, "Nascita e primi sviluppi," 1987: 68.

17. Ciuffoletti, "Dirigenti e ideologie del movimento cooperativo," 1981: 104–105; Zangheri, "Nascita e primi sviluppi," 1987: 24.

18. Ciuffoletti, "Dirigenti e ideologie del movimento cooperativo," 1981: 91; Zangheri, "Nascita e primi sviluppi," 1987: 70.

19. Ammirato, *La Lega*, 1996: 63–64; Degl'Innocenti, "Geografia e strutture della cooperazione in Italia," 1981: 17, 20; Federico, "Italy 1860–1940," 1996: 767; Ridolfi, "La terra delle associazioni," 1997: 303–307, 315–318; Seton-Watson, *Italy from Liberalism to Fascism, 1870–1925*, 1967: 290; Trebilcock, *The Industrialization of the Continental Powers, 1780–1914*, 1981: 303; Zamagni, *The Economic History of Italy 1860–1990*, 1993: 7–8, 16, 48, 55, 69.

20. Zangheri, "Nascita e primi sviluppi," 1987: 60.

21. Degl'Innocenti, "Geografia e strutture della cooperazione in Italia," 1981: 21.

22. Covino, "Dall'Umbria verde all'Umbria rossa," 1989: 524.

23. Zangheri, "Nascita e primi sviluppi," 1987: 97–98.

24. After 1893 this became the Lega Nazionale delle Cooperative (National League of Cooperatives). The founding meeting in 1886 was convened by "a group of Lombard notables led by Luzzatti." Ammirato, *La Lega*, 1996: 67.

25. Ibid.: 67–68.

26. Ridolfi, "La terra delle associazioni," 1997: 283.

27. Emilia-Romagna was also the core region for Italian republicanism. For example, the Republican Association of Cesena, a small town in Romagna, promoted democratic and republican ideas among both elite and nonelite urban groups. Ridolfi, "Sulla Formazione dele Moderne Organizzazioni Politiche," 1984: 316. As I will show in greater detail later in chapter 2, it was also in this region that fascism first took root.

28. Corner, *Fascism in Ferrara*, 1975: 2–3; Preti, *Le lotte agrarie nella Valle padana*, 1954: 4–7.

29. Ciuffoletti, *Storia del PSI. 1*, 1992: 56.

30. Quoted in Zangheri, "Nascita e primi sviluppi," 1987: 114.

31. According to Zangheri the Ministry of Agriculture, Industry, and Commerce recognized the foundation of sixty-five labor cooperatives between 1883 and 1889. Between 1890 and 1894 this same ministry recognized more than four hundred. Zangheri, "Nascita e primi sviluppi," 1987: 106, 108.

32. Degl'Innocenti, "Geografia e strutture della cooperazione in Italia," 1981: 21; Zangheri, "Nascita e primi sviluppi," 1987: 113–115.

33. Quoted in Ministero di Agricoltura, Industria e Commercio (hereafter MAIC), *Saggio statistico sulle associazioni cooperative in Italia*, 1890: 12

34. Ibid.: 12.

35. Ibid.: 12.

36. Zangheri, "Nascita e primi sviluppi," 1987: 127–128.

37. Ibid.: 124.

38. Ibid.: 122.

39. MAIC, *Saggio statistico sulle associazioni cooperative in Italia*, 1890: 13.

40. Ibid.: 14.

41. Degl'Innocenti, "Geografia e strutture della cooperazione in Italia," 1981: 18–19.

42. MAIC, *Saggio statistico sulle associazioni cooperative in Italia*, 1890: 6–7.

43. Ibid.: 6.

44. Degl'Innocenti, "Geografia e strutture della cooperazione in Italia," 1981: 21.

45. Zeffiro Ciuffoletti summarizes the shift, which he dates from 1898, in the following way: "Up until then cooperation had enjoyed the favor of liberal culture and

of the 'free marketers' [*liberisti*] themselves, since it seemed possible through cooperation, to remove the working and peasant masses from the influence of the socialist movement. The picture began to change when the expansion of the cooperative movement became a growth factor of the socialist party and the Catholic movement, and the cooperative movement itself reached economic and organizational levels such as to impact the economic and political reality of the country, so much so that it could no longer be ignored by the forces of the government itself." Ciuffoletti, "Dirigenti e ideologie del movimento cooperativo," 1981: 146.

46. Ibid.: 103; Michels, *Storia critica del movimento socialista italiano*, 1926: 26–30; Ridolfi, *Il PSI e la nascita del partito di massa*, 1992: 27; Zangheri, "Nascita e primi sviluppi," 1987: 123.

47. Quoted in ibid.: 150.

48. Ibid.: 153.

49. Webster, *The Cross and the Fasces*, 1960: 4.

50. Degl'Innocenti, "Geografia e strutture della cooperazione in Italia," 1981: 37.

51. Ciuffoletti, "Dirigenti e ideologie del movimento cooperativo," 1981: 132.

52. Ibid.: 133.

53. Gide, *La Coopération dans les Pays Latins*, 1926–1927: 27.

54. Ciuffoletti, "Dirigenti e ideologie del movimento cooperativo," 1981: 116; Degl'Innocenti, *Storia della cooperazione in Italia*, 1977: 121–122, 145.

55. Gide, *La Coopération dans les Pays Latins*, 1926–1927: 102–104, 118–120.

56. Banti, *Storia della borghesia italiana*, 1996: 90, 169–170; Degl'Innocenti, *Storia della cooperazione in Italia*, 1977: 13; Gaeta, *La crisi di fine secolo e l'età giolittiana*, 1982: 47, 66–69; Seton-Watson, *Italy from Liberalism to Fascism, 1870–1925*, 1967: 167–169, 182, 190.

57. Banti, *Storia della borghesia italiana*, 1996: 38; Lyttelton, "Landlords, Peasants and the Limits of Liberalism," 1979: 105.

Chapter 5 explores this issue more fully.

58. Giolitti's February 1901 speech effectively sums up his view of civil society. He stated there, "I never fear organized forces; I fear rather more inorganic ones because over the [organized forces] one can legitimately and usefully exercise the action of government, against inorganic movements one can use only force." Quoted in Gaeta, *La crisi di fine secolo e l'età giolittiana*, 1982: 106.

59. Carocci, *Giolitti e l'età giolittiana*, 1971: 66; Gaeta, *La crisi di fine secolo e l'età giolittiana*, 1982: 105; Lyttelton, "Liberalism and Civil Society in Italy," 2000: 73.

60. Seton-Watson, *Italy from Liberalism to Fascism, 1870–1925*, 1967: 238.

61. Adler, *Italian Industrialists from Liberalism to Fascism*, 1995: 34; Seton-Watson, *Italy from Liberalism to Fascism, 1870–1925*, 1967: 237–238.

62. Adler, *Italian Industrialists from Liberalism to Fascism*, 1995: 35–36; Banti, *Storia della borghesia italiana*, 1996: 274, 296.

63. Carocci, *Giolitti e l'età giolittiana*, 1971: 147.

64. Gramsci, *Selections from the Prison Notebook*, 1971: 180.

65. Ibid.: 181.

66. Gramsci acutely captures this continuity: "Indeed one might say that the entire State life of Italy from 1848 onwards has been characterized by transformism—in other words by the formation of an ever more extensive ruling class, within the framework

established by the Moderates after 1848 and the collapse of the neo-Guelph and federalist utopias." Ibid.: 58.

67. King and Okey, *Italy Today*, 1901: 21–22; Saladino, "Parliamentary Politics in the Liberal Era," 1974: 47.

68. Aquarone, *Tre capitoli sull'Italia giolittiana*, 1987: 38–39; Ragionieri, *Storia d'Italia*, 1976: 71.

69. Ridolfi, *Il PSI e la nascita del partito di massa*, 1992: 68.

70. Ibid.: 83, 236.

71. Procacci, *The Italian Working Class from the Risorgimento to Fascism*, 1981: 6; Procacci, *La lotta di classe in Italia agli inizi del secolo XX*, 1992: 60, 64.

72. Quoted in Ridolfi, *Il PSI e la nascita del partito di massa*, 1992: 3.

73. Ibid.: 46.

74. Ibid.: 207.

75. Quoted in ibid.: 209.

76. Bonfante, "La legislazione cooperativistica in Italia dall'Unità a oggi," 1981: 197; Degl'Innocenti, *Storia della cooperazione in Italia*, 1977: 241; Degl'Innocenti, "Geografia e strutture della cooperazione in Italia," 1981: 36–37; Galasso, "Gli anni della grande espansione e la crisi del sistema," 1987: 223; Zangheri, "Nascita e primi sviluppi," 1987: 108.

77. Fabbri, "Crescita e natura delle casse rurali cattoliche," 1977: 796.

78. Ibid.: 789.

79. Webster, *The Cross and the Fasces*, 1960: 4, 9, 19. Many observers have noted that one of the major differences between the prefascist Partito Popolare Italiano (PPI) and the postwar Democrazia Cristiana (DC) was their connection to the church. The DC was a confessional party. The PPI was not. Sturzo lucidly identified the difference, saying: "I did not attempt to realize the political unity of the Catholics. My party was only a current of Catholics who founded a party in which non-Catholics could also be militants. I did not care if there were socialist or liberal Catholics as well. The DC has posed for itself instead, as a party, the problem of the political unification of the Catholics." Quoted in Scoppola, *La repubblica dei partiti*, 1997: 113.

80. De Felice, *Mussolini il rivoluzionario 1883–1920*, 1995 [1965]: 110–111, 115; Romano, *Giolitti: lo stile del potere*, 1989: 238–239.

81. Ciuffoletti, *Storia del PSI. 1*, 1992: 409, 416; De Felice, *Mussolini il rivoluzionario 1883–1920*, 1995 [1965]: 127; Ridolfi, *Il PSI e la nascita del partito di massa*, 1992: 88.

82. De Felice, *Mussolini il rivoluzionario 1883–1920*, 1995 [1965]: 200–220; Milza, *Mussolini*, 2000: 179–182.

83. Adler, *Italian Industrialists from Liberalism to Fascism*, 1995: 97; De Felice, *Mussolini il rivoluzionario 1883–1920*, 1995 [1965]: 208–209, 319; Mack-Smith, *Italy: A Modern History*, 1959: 256–257; Morandi, *I partiti politici in Italia*, 1997: 53.

84. Aquarone, *Tre capitoli sull'Italia giolittiana*, 1987: 65.

85. Skocpol, "How Americans Became Civic," 1999: 55.

86. Tasca, *Nascita e avvento del fascismo*, 1950: 19–20.

87. Adamson, *Avant-Garde Florence*, 1993: 217–218; De Felice, *Mussolini il rivoluzionario 1883–1920*, 1995 [1965]: 338, 388–389; Gentile, *Storia del Partito Fascista*, 1989: 70–73, 515; Tasca, *Nascita e avvento del fascismo*, 1950: 20.

There is little systematic evidence on these organizations, although they are clearly very important for understanding the subsequent development of Italian fascism. They had names like the Anti-Bolshevik League, the *Fascio* of Popular Action, the Alliance for Civil Defense, the Committee for Internal Resistance, and the National Italian *Fascio*. According to Emilio Gentile, who refers to them as organizations of the patriotic bourgeoisie, their archetype was the Patto Nuovo founded at Venice in 1918 on the initiative of the Venetian lawyer, and later secretary of the Fascist Party, Giovanni Giurati. Gentile, *Storia del Partito Fascista*, 1989: 71–72. He writes that the "scope was to keep alive the feeling of 'national concord' through 'a new pact' of brotherhood among citizens and classes, 'sealed with blood on the fields of battle, with work in the factory, with the fervor of faith in the work of assistance, aid, and civil propaganda.'" Ibid.: 72. Similar organizations were founded at Cremona and Florence in 1919. Ibid.: 73. Designed to operate outside the framework of the traditional parties, they were understood by their leaders to embody an alliance of national forces.

88. Chiurco, *Storia della rivoluzione fascista*, 1929: 98.

89. De Felice, *Mussolini il rivoluzionario 1883–1920*, 1995 [1965]: 475.

Prefectural documents from the period immediately following the war give a sense of the numerous connections among veterans groups in this period. In January of 1919 Mussolini's name was listed on a prefectural document describing various Milanese patriotic associations that had come together to constitute a Milanese association for the League of Nations. The Italian National League and the Wilsonian Propaganda Group, called the meeting, to which they invited the heads of some twenty-four patriotic organizations: the Liberal Association and its youth section, the Dante Alighieri Society, the Let's Honor the Army Association, the Liberal Popular Association, the Association of Independent Garibaldinians, the Regional Veteran's Committee, the Democratic Liberal Union, the League for the Dissemination of Courage, the Pensioned Officials of Land and Sea, Civil Service and Military Pensioners, the Constitutional Association, the Welfare Committee, the Political Association of Unredeemed Italians, Officials on Leave, the Mobilization Committee, the Constitutional Party, the Pro-Army Association, the Group of Professionals, the Union of Medical Doctors, the Group of Patriotic Associations, the Fatherland Association, and the Trieste and Trento Association. ACS; MI; DGPS; 97; Milan 1919; Document 564. The meeting resolved to found a new association and entrusted a committee to draw up a statute and provide for financing.

In April of 1919 the Committee for the Defense of the Rights of Italy met to decide what kind of relationship it should have to Mussolini's newly formed *fascio di combattimento*. About two hundred people were at the meeting, and there was lively debate, in which the committee decided to cooperate with Mussolini's organization to form propaganda squads. ACS; MI; DGPS; 97; Milan 1919; Document 2524. In May of 1919 Mussolini's organization was cooperating with a larger umbrella group called the *Fascio* of Patriotic Associations. ACS; MI; DGPS; 97; Milan 1919; Document 15933. Fascism as a political movement developed out of densely organized civil society, which had emerged in the Giolittian period and which had been strengthened by Italy's participation in World War I.

90. Bosworth, *Italy, the Least of the Great Powers*, 1979: 393; De Felice, *Mussolini il rivoluzionario 1883–1920*, 1995 [1965]: 230.

91. De Felice, "L'interventismo rivoluzionario," 1968: 281.

92. De Felice, *Mussolini il rivoluzionario 1883–1920*, 1995 [1965]: 266.

93. Ibid.: 283, 296–297, 472; Tasca, *Nascita e avvento del fascismo*, 1950: 21.

94. Buozzi, *Fascisme et syndicalisme*, 1930: 87–89.

95. At this factory, workers were organized under the leadership of the Unione Italiana di Lavoro (Italian Labor Union, or UIL), a revolutionary syndicalist organization close to many of the left-wing nationalist groups. In late February of 1919, the union leadership demanded the eight-hour day, and a half day on Saturday. The owners refused, and on the 16th of March the union decided to occupy the factory. De Felice, *Mussolini il rivoluzionario 1883–1920*, 1995 [1965]: 503; Tasca, *Nascita e avvento del fascismo*, 1950: 46. Both Mussolini and Michele Bianchi (one of the major co-conspirators of the March on Rome) gave speeches to the assembled workers. Mussolini in particular noted with approval the new technique of the "productive strike"—his term for the occupations. "You," he said, "could have struck in the old style, a negative and destructive strike, but thinking of the interests of the people, you have inaugurated the creative strike, that does not interrupt production." Quoted in De Felice, *Mussolini il rivoluzionario 1883–1920*, 1995 [1965]: 506.

96. Many scholars see Fiume as a laboratory for later fascist political techniques, such as speaking to an assembled crowd from the balcony and wearing black shirts. Milza, *Mussolini*, 2000: 272.

97. De Felice, *Mussolini il rivoluzionario 1883–1920*, 1995 [1965]: 553–555.

98. The program, divided into four sections (politics, social policy, military policy, and financial policy), represented an advanced democratic position in each of these areas. Under the first heading the document called for lowering the electoral age to eighteen, the abolition of the unelected senate in favor of a "National Technical Council of intellectual and manual work and industry," and the pursuit of a "dynamic [foreign policy] ... in contrast with that tending to stabilize the hegemony of the current plutocratic powers." Under social policy the fascists called for the eight-hour day, the minimum wage, workers' participation in industry, entrusting the management of industry and public services to workers' organizations, the reorganization of transport, the calibration of old age insurance to the difficulty of work, the obligation of landed proprietors to cultivate their land, and the transfer of land to the cooperatives in case it remained uncultivated. Under the heading of financial policy, the program called for the "partial expropriation of all wealth," the confiscation of all goods belonging to the religious orders and expropriation of 85% of all war profits. Ibid.: 742–743.

99. Tasca suggests that 900,000 immigrants had left Italy in 1913. The door on immigration was suddenly and permanently closed with the outbreak of World War I. Tasca, *Nascita e avvento del fascismo*, 1950: 17.

100. Cammett, *Antonio Gramsci and the Origins of Italian Communism*, 1967: 65; Mack-Smith, *Italy: A Modern History*, 1959: 289; Tasca, *Nascita e avvento del fascismo*, 1950: 17.

101. Maione, "Il biennio rosso: autonomia e spontaneitá operaia contro le organizzazioni tradizionali (1919–1920)," 1970: 827; Tasca, *Nascita e avvento del fascismo*, 1950: 26–27.

102. Ibid.: 117.

103. Maione, "Il biennio rosso: Lo sciopero delle lancette (marzo-aprile 1920)," 1972: 254.

104. Cammett, *Antonio Gramsci and the Origins of Italian Communism*, 1967: 112–113; De Felice, *Mussolini il rivoluzionario 1883–1920*, 1995 [1965]: 503.

105. Corner, *Fascism in Ferrara*, 1975: 63, 89; Zamagni, "Distribuzione del reddito e classi sociali nell'Italia fra le due guerre," 1979–1980: 24.

106. Maione, "Il biennio rosso: Lo sciopero delle lancette (marzo-aprile 1920)," 1972: 265.

107.   Ridolfi, *Il PSI e la nascita del partito di massa*, 1992: 92; Togliatti, *Lectures on Fascism*, 1976: 171.

108.   De Felice, *Mussolini il rivoluzionario 1883–1920*, 1995 [1965]: 590; Elazar, "The Making of Italian Fascism," 1993: 193; Gentile, *Storia del Partito Fascista*, 1989: 45; Ridolfi, *Il PSI e la nascita del partito di massa*, 1992: 72–76.

109.   Quoted in Maione, "Il biennio rosso: Lo sciopero delle lancette (marzo–aprile 1920)," 1972: 279.

110.   De Felice, *Mussolini il rivoluzionario 1883–1920*, 1995 [1965]: 588.

111.   Tasca sees this as the great tragedy of the postwar period. Yet he does not adequately connect it to the tradition of transformism.

112.   Tasca, *Nascita e avvento del fascismo*, 1950: 190–191.

113.   Ibid.: 24, 124, 128.

114.   Gentile, *Il mito dello stato nuovo*, 1982: 13–14.

Gentile speaks of a culture of organization, by which he means the idea that social self-organization would strengthen the Italian state. Ibid.: 13–14.

115.   Gentile, *Le origini del ideologia fascista*, 1975: 42, 208–209; Gregor, *The Ideology of Fascism*, 1969: 82.

116.   Roberts, *The Syndicalist Tradition and Italian Fascism*, 1979: 72.

117.   Gregor, *Mussolini's Intellectuals*, 2005: 73; Perfetti, "Introduzione. Un teorico dello stato sindicale-corporativo," 1987: 27.

118.   Gentile, *Il mito dello stato nuovo*, 1982: 11–12.

119.   Panunzio, *Il fondamento giuridico del fascismo*, 1987: 143.

David Roberts emphasizes the importance of the concept of organization for all of the revolutionary syndicalists: "The syndicalists, even as fascists, never abandoned their heavy emphasis on the value of organizations for radical change in Italy. Organizations seemed a source of both moral development and political consciousness for the atomized, egotistical Italian masses. In organizing, moreover, Italian society seemed to be developing the strength and resilience it needed to stand up to the exploitative state." Roberts, *The Syndicalist Tradition and Italian Fascism*, 1979: 67. Syndicalism was then an ideology of civil society, as I argue more fully later in chapter 2.

120.   Gentile, *Il mito dello stato nuovo*, 1982: 54–60; Roberts, *The Syndicalist Tradition and Italian Fascism*, 1979: 102–103.

121.   Alfredo Rocco began his political career as a deputy in the Radical Party, an organization that stood well to the left of the established liberal politicians of the early twentieth century. In 1907 he presented a platform proposal at the party's congress defending the right of public employees to organize. In 1914 he joined the Italian National Association, and in 1923 joined the Fascist Party as part of the broader fusion of the nationalist association with the PNF. Gentile, *Il mito dello stato nuovo*, 1982: 167, 173, 195.

122.   Rocco, *Scritti e discorsi politici*, 1938: 634, 637.

123.   Ibid.: 637.

124.   Ibid.: 639.

125.   Ibid.: 641.

126.   Ibid.: 645.

127.   Gentile, *Il mito dello stato nuovo*, 1982: 190.

The first step was to turn unions into branches of the state and to make membership in them obligatory. Then a magistrate, a representative of the state who would act in the "general interest," would decide conflicts among these "syndicates." Rocco, *Scritti e discorsi politici*, 1938: 648.

128. Riosa, "Michele Bianchi," 1968: 147–153.

129. Roveri, "Il sindicalismo rivoluzionario in Italia," 1975: 20.

130. Gentile, *Storia del Partito Fascista*, 1989: 36.

131. Roberts, *The Syndicalist Tradition and Italian Fascism*, 1979: 14.

132. Ibid.: 15–16.

133. Germino, *The Italian Fascist Party in Power*, 1959: 38.

134. Bottai, "Prima seduta," 1990: 90.

135. Emilio Gentile makes this point forcefully. As he writes, "The political problem that emerges in the course of the Giolittian period does not turn, then, on the acceptance or refusal of the democratic principle, understood in the broad sense, as the 'participation' of the people in politics, but on the real capacity of the Giolittian system to promote this participation, to represent the needs and aspirations of the collectivity." Gentile, *Il mito dello stato nuovo*, 1982: 48.

136. As one fascist commentator, C. Morisi, put the point, "The elements that prevail in fascism are in large part elements of the bourgeoisie [*borghesia*] and the workers constituted a small minority … the mass in its great majority is hostile and believes us to be the enemies of its interests and aspirations." Quoted in ibid.: 65–66.

137. Corner, *Fascism in Ferrara*, 1975: 111; De Felice, *Mussolini il rivoluzionario 1883–1920*, 1995 [1965]: 6, 590–592, 594; Gentile, *Storia del Partito Fascista*, 1989: 65, 70; Lyttelton, *The Seizure of Power*, 2004: 56–60; Tasca, *Nascita e avvento del fascismo*, 1950: 57–61, 144.

138. The Palazzo Accursio incident in Bologna on November 21, 1920, exemplifies the process. The socialists occupied the municipal building following their electoral victory. A confused struggle ensued in which a nationalist deputy was shot. In response the first waves of fascist violence broke out in the city. De Felice, *Mussolini il rivoluzionario 1883–1920*, 1995 [1965]: 656–657; Gentile, *Storia del Partito Fascista*, 1989: 150.

139. Ibid.: 126; Tasca, *Nascita e avvento del fascismo*, 1950: 184–185.

The main squadrist political technique was the punitive expedition. One example of this activity, among hundreds of possible ones, comes from a small town called Molinella in the Valley of the Po between Ravenna and Bologna. On the 12th of June 1921, a group of fascists gathered at Molinella to consecrate the banner of the new local *fascio*. In the morning they demanded that the local socialist cooperative display the Italian flag. The socialists refused. After an afternoon of struggle, a small group of fascists reached the rooftop of the cooperative, where they hung a flag with the name of their local *fascio* on it. ACS; MI; DGPS; 93; Document 3060. Several days later, again in Molinella, a group of fascists entered the socialist league, stealing furniture and pictures. At the beginning of July the police reported a third incident, in which the fascists invaded a local socialist pub. At basically the same time that these events were occurring, the fascists engaged in more conventional forms of political propaganda. On the 2nd of June the fascists of Molinella held a meeting, where the speaker encouraged "the peaceful penetration and divulgation among the masses of the principles of fascism." ACS; MI; DGPS; 93; Document 2789.

140. Ciuffoletti, "Dirigenti e ideologie del movimento cooperativo," 1981: 181–182; Cordova, *Le origini dei sindacati fascisti*, 1974: 32–43; De Felice, *Mussolini il fascista. La conquista del potere 1921–1925*, 1995 [1966]: 56; Degl'Innocenti, "Geografia e strutture

della cooperazione in Italia," 1981: 51; Degl'Innocenti, *La società unificata*, 1995: 52–53; Fornasari and Zamagni, *Il movimento cooperativo in Italia*, 1997: 118.

141. Roberto Farinacci is exemplary in this respect. He was an ex–railway union organizer who became a notorious squadrist. Violence and organization often went together in the fascist movement. Gentile, *Storia del Partito Fascista*, 1989: 131.

142. Putnam, *Making Democracy Work*, 1993.

143. Gentile, *Storia del Partito Fascista*, 1989: 212–214; Lyttelton, *The Seizure of Power*, 2004: 72–75.

144. Gentile, *Storia del Partito Fascista*, 1989: 164; Lyttelton, *The Seizure of Power*, 2004: 63.

145. Gentile, *Storia del Partito Fascista*, 1989: 218, 278–288.

146. Ibid.: 388.

147. Bottai, *Esperienza Corporativa*, 1928: 89.

148. De Felice, *Mussolini il fascista. La conquista del potere 1921–1925*, 1995 [1966]: 363; Pellizzi, *Una rivoluzione mancata*, 1949: 39–43; Uva, *La nascita dello stato corporativo e sindacale fascista*, 1974: 12–14.

149. Camillo Pellizzi was one of the major exponents of this "fascism without fascists." He analyzed the fascist project as an attempt to root political authority directly in technical competence but complained of the resistance it faced from the political side of the regime. This argument is most fully developed in his postwar book *Una rivoluzione mancata*. Pellizzi, *Una rivoluzione mancata*, 1949: 55. As will become clear in chapter 3, this was precisely the project that Primo de Rivera successfully pursued.

150. Cordova, *Le origini dei sindacati fascisti*, 1974: 175–177; De Felice, *Mussolini il fascista. La conquista del potere 1921–1925*, 1995 [1966]: 601–605; Uva, *La nascita dello stato corporativo e sindacale fascista*, 1974: 13, 16.

151. Fascist syndicalism was more successful in agriculture. In this sector Rossoni was able to establish the fascist employers' organizations as the only one recognized by the Grande Consiglio, largely due to the extremely close relationship that agrarians had to the fascist organizations in the early twenties. Up until early 1922 the agrarians had generously funded the fascist organizations. Cordova, *Le origini dei sindacati fascisti*, 1974: 61; De Felice, *Mussolini il fascista. La conquista del potere 1921–1925*, 1995 [1966]: 122. In return the fascists had crushed the socialist leagues. This cooperation was, however, costly for the agrarians, who by early 1922 were moving away from the fascists, as is indicated by the foundation of the Partito Agrario (the Agrarian Party) in January of that year. The agrarians wanted to get rid of the socialists and "restore order" in the countryside. But they had no interest in facing a monolithic agrarian syndicate. By early 1922 the northern agrarians were looking for political organizations outside the framework of the Fascist Party. Unlike the industrialists, however, the agrarians were not able to preserve their organization, Confagricola, which was replaced by the Federazione Italiana dei Sindacati degli Agricoltori (FISA), the fascist agrarian employers' organization. Cordova, *Le origini dei sindacati fascisti*, 1974: 90.

152. Cordova, *Le origini dei sindacati fascisti*, 1974: 194–195, 168–178; De Felice, *Mussolini il fascista. La conquista del potere 1921–1925*, 1995 [1966]: 386, 404, 614, 617.

153. De Felice refers to it as a "transformistic" operation. Ibid.: 602.

154. As De Felice puts the point, "Seen correctly these attacks were harsh but purely verbal." Ibid.: 615.

155. Cordova, *Le origini dei sindacati fascisti*, 1974: 180; De Felice, *Mussolini il fascista. La conquista del potere 1921–1925*, 1995 [1966]: 615.

156. According to De Felice, Matteotti spoke "against the fascist government, against fascism tout court, but also, and perhaps above all, against the collaborationists of his own party and in the CGL." Ibid.: 618.

157. Ibid.: 618, 622; Lyttelton, *The Seizure of Power*, 2004: 238.

158. Buozzi, *Fascisme et syndicalisme*, 1930: 113, 118.

159. Aquarone, *L'organizzazione dello stato totalitario*, 1995: 45; Cordova, *Le origini dei sindacati fascisti*, 1974: 246, 265; De Felice, *Mussolini il fascista. La conquista del potere 1921–1925*, 1995 [1966]: 667, 676, 714–715, 722–724.

160. Buozzi, *Fascisme et syndicalisme*, 1930: 113–114; Cordova, *Le origini dei sindacati fascisti*, 1974: 273.

In De Felice's words, this was "a real and proper offensive of fascist syndicalism ... against Confindustria and the industrial world in general, it was aimed at the complete fascisticization of these organizations and their subordination to the will of the syndicates." Ibid.: 95. Edmondo Rossoni, the national leader of the fascist syndicates in this period, argued that the strike was the "return of revolutionary syndicalism." De Felice, *Mussolini il fascista. L'organizzazione dello Stato fascista 1925–1929*, 1995 [1968]: 95.

161. Aquarone, *L'organizzazione dello stato totalitario*, 1995: 122; Rosenstock-Franck, *L'economie corporative fasciste*, 1934: 38–39.

162. Melis, "L'amministrazione," in *Storia dello stato italiano*, 1996a: 211, 216–217; Melis, *Storia dell'amministrazione italiana*, 1996b: 363, 368.

163. Aquarone, *L'organizzazione dello stato totalitario*, 1995: 66; Gentile, *Fascismo: storia e interpretazione*, 2002: 176; Pombeni, *Demagogia e tirannide*, 1984a: 459.

164. Germino, *The Italian Fascist Party in Power*, 1959: 34–36.

As Gentile writes here, "The relations between prefects [the local representatives of the central government] and the federals [the local representatives of the party] always remained in a situation of precarious equilibrium, that depended on the personal relations between prefect and federal or on the force of the personality of one or the other." Gentile summarizes here an emerging consensus that places the party at the center of the fascist regime. Gentile, *Fascismo: storia e interpretazione*, 2002: 182–183.

165. Partito Nazionale Fascista (PNF), *Atti del PNF*, 1935 (XIV): 195.

166. This is probably why there are no national lists of party members, a fact often bemoaned in the literature about Italian fascism. Two party statutes, those of 1929 and 1932, stipulate that membership records were kept at the provincial level. The 1929 statute states, "The federal secretary ... directly, or through means of his functionaries, controls the enrollment lists ... and the archives." Document contained in Aquarone, *L'organizzazione dello stato totalitario*, 1995: 509. The 1932 statute states that "[the federal secretary] is personally responsible for the exact maintenance of the files of the enrolled." Ibid.: 523. The enrollment procedures described in the statutes further stipulate that the provincial directorate, not the national directorate, distributed party cards to the local *fascio*. Article 26 of the 1929 statute stipulates, "The administrative secretary of the *fascio* controls the withdrawal of the cards necessary for the enrolled, at the provincial administrative secretary." Ibid.: 512. Thus, these statutes indicate that the provincial federations controlled the emission of cards and kept the membership

lists. The absence of a single national list of PNF members is actually an important fact about Italian fascism.

167. ACS; AF; PNF; DN; S; Series I; Box 830.

168. ACS; AF; PNF; DN; SPEP; Box 3.

169. ACS; AF; PNF; DN; S; Series I; Box 862.

170. ACS; AF; PNF; SPEP; Box 19.

171. Ibid.

172. Ibid.

173. ACS; AF; PNF; DN; S; Series II; Box 96.

174. ACS; AF; PNF; SPEP.

175. ACS; AF; PNF; DN; S; Series II; Box 96.

176. Ibid.

177. This section and the quote are drawn from ACS; AF; PNF; SPEP; Box 1.

178. ACS; AF; PNF; DN; S; Series I; Box 220.

179. ACS; AF; PNF; DN; S; Series I; Box 215.

180. Aquarone, *L'organizzazione dello stato totalitario*, 1995: 146; Bottai, *Esperienza Corporativa*, 1928: 118; De Felice, *Mussolini il fascista. L'organizzazione dello Stato fascista 1925–1929*, 1995 [1968]: 334–335; Podestà and Uckmar, *I contributi sindacali*, 1929: 18; Valiani, "Il movimento operaio sindacale sotto il fascismo," 1959: 60.

181. Rosenstock-Franck, *L'economie corporative fasciste*, 1934: 112–114.

182. De Felice, *Mussolini il duce. Gli anni del consenso 1929–1936*, 1996 [1974]: 197.

CHAPTER THREE: Traditionalist Fascism

1. Heywood, *Marxism and the Failure of Organized Socialism in Spain*, 1990: 5.
They provided political muscle that the new landed elite required to consolidate its holdings. Later, the parties became a key element in supporting the structure of agrarian relations. As Kern points out, the patron-client system allowed landowners to deal with peasant unrest by providing minimal services to peasant clienteles. Kern, *Liberals, Reformers and Caciques in Restoration Spain*, 1974: 16.

2. *Cacique* is an Amerindian term that was brought to Spain from the colonies.

3. Boyd, *Praetorian Politics in Liberal Spain*, 1979: 4; Carr, *Modern Spain, 1875–1980*, 1982: 356–357; Gómez-Navarro, *El Régimen de Primo de Rivera*, 1991: 60; Lyttelton, "El patronazgo en la Italia de Giolitti (1892–1924)," 1973: 98; Payne, *Politics and the Military in Modern Spain*, 1967: 44–45; Payne, *A History of Spain and Portugal in Two Volumes*, 1973: 495; Tusell, "The Functioning of the Cacique System in Andalusia," 1976a: 14; Tusell, *Oligarquia y caciquismo en Andalucia (1890–1923)*, 1976b: 510; Tusell, *Manual de historia de España*, 1990: 32.

4. In the northern smallholding regions, *caciquismo* was based on local notables, who often had control over credit. In the more egalitarian regions, such as Navarre, liberal elites incorporated local respected figures into the system. Kern, *Liberals, Reformers and Caciques in Restoration Spain*, 1974: 44–45. Controlled elections allowed for the development of surprisingly "democratic" reforms. During the "liberal turn," from 1885 to 1890, under the leadership of the Práxedes Mateo Sagasta (1825–1903), the Cortes adopted universal male suffrage, making the country formally more democratic than Britain by 1890. Further, this period saw the passage of remarkably progressive legislation on the

press and voluntary associations. Gide, *La Coopération dans les Pays Latins*, 1926–1927: 143; Payne, *A History of Spain and Portugal in Two Volumes*, 1973: 492; Tusell, *Manual de historia de España*, 1990: 26.

5. This was a major difference between Italian and Spanish liberalism, because Italian liberalism, as I argued in chapter 2, lacked any structure of parties at the national level.

6. With the demise of their top leaders, Cánovas and Sagasta, the former killed by an anarchist attack and the latter politically destroyed as the result of defeat in 1898, the liberals and conservatives broke into competing factions. Serrano, *Alfonso XIII y la crisis de la restauración*, 1969: 59–75. Simultaneous with this process of fragmentation within the parties, corrosion set in from below. After the elections of 1907 the *el turno* parties ceased to exist in Catalonia, having been soundly defeated in open elections by a coalition of regionalists, Carlists, and republicans. Tusell, *Manual de historia de España*, 1990: 63. The system was beginning to soften in urban areas of southern Spain as well. For example, in the circumscription of Sevilla, republican and Catholic candidates were winning a greater majority of the vote than the official *el turno* parties by 1903. Tusell, "The Functioning of the Cacique System in Andalusia," 1976a: 7.

7. Ibid.: 6.

8. By the 1914 elections in Andalusia, the stronghold of Spanish liberalism, the Liberal Party itself had fragmented into followers of García Prieto (1859–1938) and the Conde de Romanones (1863–1950), while the conservatives were divided between old-style conservatives and followers of Maura. Tusell, *Oligarquia y caciquismo en Andalucia (1890–1923)*, 1976b: 545. By 1914 *caciquismo* remained without *el turno*. At the local level proliferating clienteles made greater demands on a fixed number of seats. Ibid.: 544.

9. Vilar, *Cataluña en la España Moderna*, 1987: 15.

10. Balfour, "Riot, Regeneration and Reaction," 1995: 409–410; Carr, *Modern Spain, 1875–1980*, 1982: 473; Garrido Herrero, *Treballar en comú*, 1996: 49–50; Tusell, *Manual de historia de España*, 1990: 43.

11. Balfour, "Riot, Regeneration and Reaction," 1995: 410; Heywood, *Marxism and the Failure of Organized Socialism in Spain*, 1990: 1, 15; Morales Muñoz, "Los espacios de la sociabilidad radical democrática," 2001–2002: 168–177; Simpson, *The Long Siesta*, 1995: 18; Tusell, *Manual de historia de España*, 1990: 119–120, 153.

12. Baro, *Historia de la cooperacion catalana*, 1974; Garrido Herrero, *Treballar en comú*, 1996: 61–62; Pan-Montojo, "Las Asociaciones Rurales y el nacimiento del Sindicalismo Agrario en España, 1834–1907," 2000: 45; Vilar, *Cataluña en la España Moderna*, 1987: 77.

13. Lannon, *Privilege, Persecution, and Prophecy*, 1987: 3; Callahan, *The Catholic Church in Spain, 1875–1998*, 2000: 4, 27, 61.

14. As Lannon puts the point, "Where welfare—or in the idiom of the time charity—was concerned, central and local government relied absolutely on the religious congregations to staff as well as supplement their institutions." Lannon, *Privilege, Persecution, and Prophecy*, 1987: 74.

15. Ibid.: 74; Callahan, *The Catholic Church in Spain, 1875–1998*, 2000: 52, 191.

16. According to Callahan they were funded predominantly by the "country's wealthy Catholic elite." Ibid.: 191.

17. Ibid.: 191; Garrido Herrero, *Treballar en comú*, 1996: 48–49.

Lannon gives a number of examples. The Society of the Sacred Heart in Madrid opened its house on an estate that was a gift of the Duke of Pastrana. A female order called the

Daughters of the Cross opened an orphanage in Bilbao, where they had been invited to come from France by a group of "the most distinguished and influential ladies." Ibid.: 67. A wealthy industrialist's widow, Dorotea de Chopitea, established several foundations in Barcelona. A wealthy landowner gave an entire hill to the Salesians in 1886. Lannon, *Privilege, Persecution, and Prophecy*, 1987: 68.

18. Tusell, *Historia de la democracia cristiana en España*, 1974: 37.

19. Garrido Herrero, *Treballar en comú*, 1996: 52.

20. Quoted in Montero, *La* CEDA. *El Catolicismo Social y Politico en la* II *Republica*, 1977: 69.

21. Callahan, *The Catholic Church in Spain, 1875–1998*, 2000: 67, 143; Castillo, *Proprietarios muy pobres*, 1979: 16.

22. Callahan claims that they were "largely self-financed through modest contributions of their members." Callahan, *The Catholic Church in Spain, 1875–1998*, 2000: 140.

23. Ibid.: 140–141; Terrón Muñoz, *Las Cajas rurales españolas*, 1987: 111.

24. According to one of the leaders of the movement, the syndicate was "a stable association, formed by proprietors, tenants, field workers, and all persons who exercised professions linked with agriculture, for the study, promotion, and defense of agricultural interests." Quoted in Castillo, *Proprietarios muy pobres*, 1979: 25. The syndicates statute of 1934, which was probably similar to those in this earlier period, provided for separate assemblies of workers, owners, and renters to elect representatives to a council, which would then resolve the dispute in such a way as to avoid "class struggle and strikes." Ibid.: 30.

25. Callahan, *The Catholic Church in Spain, 1875–1998*, 2000: 142; Castillo, *Proprietarios muy pobres*, 1979: 80; Cuenca Toribio, *Catolicismo social y politico en la España contemporánea (1870–2000)*, 2003: 53; Garrido Herrero, *Treballar en comú*, 1996: 60–61; Pan-Montojo, "Las Asociaciones Rurales y el nacimiento del Sindicalismo Agrario en España, 1834–1907," 2000: 49; Tusell, *Historia de la democracia cristiana en España*, 1974: 40.

26. Cuenca Toribio, *Catolicismo social y politico en la España contemporánea (1870–2000)*, 2003: 45; Garrido Herrero, *Treballar en comú*, 1996: 69, 75.

27. Cuenca Toribio, *Catolicismo social y politico en la España contemporánea (1870–2000)*, 2003: 45; Garrido Herrero, *Treballar en comú*, 1996: 83–86.

28. Castillo, *Proprietarios muy pobres*, 1979: 32–33; Montero, *La* CEDA. *El Catolicismo Social y Politico en la* II *Republica*, 1977: 82.

29. Quoted in Garrido Herrero, *Treballar en comú*, 1996: 56.

30. Quoted in ibid.: 56.

31. Ibid.: 56.

32. Callahan, *The Catholic Church in Spain, 1875–1998*, 2000: 142; Garrido Herrero, "El primer cooperativismo agrario español," 2003: 37–41.

According to the development ministry, agrarian syndicates expanded from 972 in 1908 to 2,067 in 1914. The treasury registers a similar trend, with the numbers expanding from 739 in 1908 to 4,316 by 1919. The department of agriculture collected statistics on the basis of questionnaires sent to registered syndicates in 1907, 1908, 1910, 1915, 1916, and 1918–1933. This evidence shows an initial expansion (433 *sindicatos* in 1907 increased to 1,559 in 1910), followed by a five-year period of stagnation between 1910 and 1915, with a renewed expansion from 1915 to 1922. Garrido Herrero, "El cooperativismo agrario Español del primer tercio del siglo xx," 1995: 119.

33. Ibid.: 135.

34. Carr, *Modern Spain, 1875–1980*, 1982: 489–497; Esdaile, *Spain in the Liberal Age*, 2000: 207; Serrano, *Alfonso XIII y la crisis de la restauración*, 1969: 59–75; Tusell, "The Functioning of the Cacique System in Andalusia," 1976a: 7; Tusell, *Oligarquia y caciquismo en Andalucia (1890–1923)*, 1976b: 544; Tusell, *Manual de historia de España*, 1990: 55, 63, 94–98.

35. Esdaile, *Spain in the Liberal Age*, 2000: 211, 217; Serrano, *Alfonso XIII y la crisis de la restauración*, 1969: 80; Tusell, "La descomposicion del sistema caciquil espanol (1902–1931)," 1973: 81; Tusell, *Manual de historia de España*, 1990: 82–83, 85–87.

36. Carr, *Modern Spain, 1875–1980*, 1982: 492–493; Serrano, *Alfonso XIII y la crisis de la restauración*, 1969: 89–90; Tusell, *Manual de historia de España*, 1990: 87.

37. Esdaile, *Spain in the Liberal Age*, 2000: 226–227, 234.

38. Harrison, "Big Business and the Failure of Right-Wing Catalan Nationalism, 1901–1918," 1976: 912.

39. Boyd, *Praetorian Politics in Liberal Spain*, 1979: 78.

40. Harrison, "Big Business and the Failure of Right-Wing Catalan Nationalism, 1901–1918," 1976: 912; Payne, *A History of Spain and Portugal in Two Volumes*, 1973: 608–609.

41. Esdaile, *Spain in the Liberal Age*, 2000: 237.
Some scholars suggest that the conservative Dato government encouraged the intransigent attitude of the railway company. Esdaile, *Spain in the Liberal Age*, 2000: 237. Others doubt this interpretation: "The social and political tension was sufficiently serious to produce such an outbreak without any provocation." Tusell, *Manual de historia de España*, 1990: 158.

42. Payne, *Politics and the Military in Modern Spain*, 1967: 184; Boyd, *Praetorian Politics in Liberal Spain*, 1979: 76.

43. Boyd, *Praetorian Politics in Liberal Spain*, 1979: 82–85; Brenan, *The Spanish Labyrinth*, 2000: 65–69; Tusell, *Manual de historia de España*, 1990: 159–160.

44. Harrison, "Big Business and the Failure of Right-Wing Catalan Nationalism, 1901–1918," 1976: 913.

45. According to Caroline Boyd, the Spanish military collapse in Morocco "was above all the tragic symbol of the political irresponsibility of the dynastic parties, whose pursuit of cheap glory abroad and political stability at home had led them to abdicate control of the Moroccan enterprise to a defective but ambitious army." Boyd, *Praetorian Politics in Liberal Spain*, 1979: 182.

46. Ibid.: 166–167; Bastarreche, "The Spanish Military from the Age of Disasters to the Civil War," 1988: 232; Esdaile, *Spain in the Liberal Age*, 2000: 250–251; Tusell, *Radiografía de un Golpe de Estado*, 1987: 24.

47. Boyd, *Praetorian Politics in Liberal Spain*, 1979: 184; Tusell, *Radiografía de un Golpe de Estado*, 1987: 15.

48. Javier Tusell's tortured prose gives some idea of the difficulties involved in characterizing the political situation in Barcelona during this period: "In Barcelona, in 1923, there existed a confluence of circumstances which permitted the emergence of a radical and populist nationalism that, although distant from other authoritarian movements in Europe of the same period, was however in a certain way similar, even if only in an incipient phase." Ibid.: 49.

49. The Marquis de Comillas worked, according to Del Rey Reguillo, "with zeal to set up the Barcelona Somatén, conferring a 'new character' on it in which the struggle

against syndicalism became the most important aim." Del Rey Reguillo, "Ciudadanos honrados y somentistas," 1987: 102.

50. Del Rey Reguillo, "Ciudadanos honrados y somentistas," 1987: 102; González Calleja and Del Rey Reguillo, *La defensa armada contra la revolución*, 1995: 55; Winston, *Worker's and the Right in Spain*, 1985: 129.

51. Del Rey Reguillo, "Ciudadanos honrados y somentistas," 1987: 105.

52. González Calleja and Del Rey Reguillo, *La defensa armada contra la revolución*, 1995: 79.

53. Ibid.: 111.

54. Ibid.: 95; Del Rey Reguillo, "Ciudadanos honrados y somentistas," 1987: 116; Winston, *Worker's and the Right in Spain*, 1985: 129.

55. González Calleja and Del Rey Reguillo, *La defensa armada contra la revolución*, 1995: 180.

56. Quoted in ibid.: 180.

57. Ibid.: 119, 147–152.

58. Ibid.: 200.

59. Ibid.: 200.

60. Del Rey Reguillo, "Ciudadanos honrados y somentistas," 1987: 343.

61. Winston summarizes the tension this way: "The radical Carlist spirit that infected the … worker centers was difficult to reconcile with the paternalism, clericalism, and subjection to the dictates of the owners that marked the UPS [the Uniones Profesionales, the Catholic union organizations]." Winston, *Worker's and the Right in Spain*, 1985: 94.

62. As the Libres' most careful and sympathetic historian puts it, "At some point during 1920 a few individual owners (and perhaps the Employers' Federation) decided that the Libres would be a useful tool with which to undermine the hegemony of the CNT." Ibid.: 134.

63. "It would be difficult to exaggerate the extent of *Libre* complicity in Martínez Anido's campaign of counter terror," writes Winston. Ibid.: 141.

64. Tusell, *Radiografía de un Golpe de Estado*, 1987: 50; Tusell, *Manual de historia de España*, 1990: 187; Winston, *Worker's and the Right in Spain*, 1985: 103, 128, 134, 145, 111.

65. The general was an establishment figure with extensive Andalusian estates and a noble title (the Marqués Estella). His family included a number of prestigious military men, especially his uncle Fernando Primo de Rivera (1831–1921), and was intimately connected to the Restoration system. Rial, *Revolution from Above*, 1986: 45; Tusell, *Radiografía de un Golpe de Estado*, 1987: 29. The future dictator had a distinguished military career prior to his emergence as a major political figure. He fought in Cuba in the 1890s and had several stints of duty in Morocco. Ibid.: 29–33. The general was thus very much a political insider who initially sought to pursue a political career within the Restoration system and, indeed, was elected as a conservative candidate to the senate in 1920. Ibid.: 22.

66. As Ben-Ami writes, "The entire administrative machinery remained loyal to the government. Thus the king had to accept Primo for the dictatorship to be successful." Ben-Ami, *Fascism from Above*, 1983: 62. It would, however, be a major error to present Primo de Rivera as a military adventurer without a base of social support. His rise to power is inconceivable without the support of Catalan industrialists, who were deeply concerned about the threat from the left. Ibid.: 33–34.

67. Ibid.: 62; Tusell, *Radiografía de un Golpe de Estado*, 1987: 48, 50, 60.

68. Ben-Ami, *The Origins of the Second Republic in Spain*, 1978: 31, 130–131, 159, 399. Ben-Ami stresses this paradox. On the left of the *el turno* system, he suggests, "many moved towards republicanism." Ibid.: 159. A regime whose raison d'etre was precisely to defend the established monarchical state had thus "created more republicans than the fathers of Spanish republicanism ... put together." Ibid.: 31. The directorate merely exacerbated the political isolation of the monarchy by systematically dismantling the dynastic parties: "Primo had shattered the foundations of the old regime without enthroning a new state, thus leaving behind him a dangerous vacuum of power." Ben-Ami, *Fascism from Above*, 1983: 399.

69. It read in part, "The state of war is confirmed ... ceasing of course in their functions the civil governors of all the provinces, whose posts will be entrusted to the respective military commanders and in case these do not reside in the capital, the post of civil governor will devolve to the highest-ranking military figure with permanent residence in the city." Quoted in Gómez-Navarro, *El Régimen de Primo de Rivera*, 1991: 180.

70. Gómez-Navarro presents evidence on the 109 civil governors who held office during the dictatorship, showing that the proportion of politicians from the dynastic parties holding these positions dropped from roughly one-third to a tenth in the period from 1924 to 1930. The highest proportion of civil governors came from the military and the career bureaucracy, suggesting that the civil governors under Primo de Rivera's rule were largely new men, from outside the dynastic party system. Gómez-Navarro, *El Régimen de Primo de Rivera*, 1991: 191–192.

71. Tusell, *La crisis del caciquismo andaluz (1923–1931)*, 1977: 62.

72. As Ben-Ami describes the *delegados*, "They were the censors of public morality, the guardians of cleanliness in public premises, the champions of more humane treatment of animals, and even the peacemakers among quarrelling couples." Ben-Ami, *Fascism from Above*, 1983: 98.

73. Ibid.: 98; Tusell, *La crisis del caciquismo andaluz (1923–1931)*, 1977: 89, 96–97.

74. Ben-Ami, *The Origins of the Second Republic in Spain*, 1978: 155–156; Ben-Ami, *Fascism from Above*, 1983: 14. Some of the previous dynastic politicians attempted to reconstitute themselves as a Bloque Constitucional (Constitutional Bloc), but this organization remained an elite talking shop with no popular support. Pecharromán, *La segunda republica*, 1989: 15; Payne, *Spain's First Democracy*, 1993: 25.

75. University students formed the center of opposition. This sector was particularly irritated by Primo de Rivera's policy allowing Augustian and Jesuit colleges to confer degrees. The Republican Federation of University Students (FUE) made this policy the center of its struggles. Ben-Ami, *Fascism from Above*, 1983: 351. There are a number of examples of elites turning to the republic. Antonio Maura's son Gabriel had become a republican by the midtwenties. A professor of canon law had declared for the republic. Children's games included struggles between republicans and monarchists, and most ominously for the right, a leader of the Lliga, Vallés i Pujals, claimed that 90 percent of the members of his party were republicans. Ben-Ami, *The Origins of the Second Republic in Spain*, 1978: 29–31.

76. Ibid.: 45; Ben-Ami, *Fascism from Above*, 1983: 375.

77. Gómez-Navarro captures the problem the best: "The regime's system of corporative representation, in permitting to the bosses' organizations a direct path of influence to the organs in which it was supposed that the decisions that affected them were taken,

occasioned an apparent politicization of the bosses' organizations based on the defense of their corporative interests and a real depoliticization of the same to the degree that it made it difficult for them to formulate strictly political problems and to seek or support a political alternative in which these problems could be resolved." Gómez-Navarro, *El Régimen de Primo de Rivera*, 1991: 483.

78. Gómez-Navarro, *El Régimen de Primo de Rivera*, 1991: 251–253, 260.

79. Ben-Ami, *Fascism from Above*, 1983: 245–247, 261; Gómez-Navarro, *El Régimen de Primo de Rivera*, 1991: 248.

80. Ibid.: 412–413; McIvor, *Spanish Labor Policy during the Dictablanda of Primo de Rivera*, 1982: 38–39.

81. Ben-Ami, *Fascism from Above*, 1983: 292–294, 309; Gómez-Navarro, *El Régimen de Primo de Rivera*, 1991: 418–419; Winston, *Worker's and the Right in Spain*, 1985: 264.

82. The socialists, supported by the regime, had acquired "the lion's share of working-class representation in the corporative organization."Ben-Ami, *The Origins of the Second Republic in Spain*, 1978: 109. By the late twenties this made the socialist UGT "the strongest and best organized union in the country," Ibid.: 113. totally eclipsing the right-wing Libres, who languished under the regime.

83. This is not to suggest that there were no costs to collaboration with the dictatorship. Many scholars emphasize how relatively unimpressive UGT and PSOE growth was, given the quasi-official positions of these organizations. Much of this was due to the fact that socialist organizations were excluded from the countryside until the late twenties. The socialists also continued to have difficulty in Catalonia, where workers during the dictatorship preferred the rightist Sindicatos Libres, to the socialist UGT. Ibid.: 116–117; Heywood, *Marxism and the Failure of Organized Socialism in Spain*, 1990: 99.

84. Ben-Ami, *The Origins of the Second Republic in Spain*, 1978: 127; Gómez-Navarro, *El Régimen de Primo de Rivera*, 1991: 442; Malefakis, *Agrarian Reform and Peasant Revolution in Spain*, 1970: 290–292; Preston, *The Coming of the Spanish Civil War*, 1994: 27, 31, 87; Thomas, *The Spanish Civil War*, 1961: 83.

85. Callahan, *The Catholic Church in Spain, 1875–1998*, 2000: 166.

86. There is considerable debate about the influence of fascist Italy on these events. Ben-Ami writes that "Primo, according to his finance minister, Calvo Sotelo, was very much impressed by the Duce's recommendation, conveyed to him through Eduardo Aunós in 1926, that he should lose no time in setting up his own parliament." Ben-Ami, *Fascism from Above*, 1983: 210. In contrast Gómez-Navarro's excellent study states, "The repeatedly cited influence of Mussolini on Aunós, with respect to the origins of the idea of the assembly, must be—in any case—marginal or superficial." Gómez-Navarro, *El Régimen de Primo de Rivera*, 1991: 266. The weight of the evidence seems to support the second position, because Primo de Rivera's parliamentary reforms actually predated Mussolini's. The fascist dictator's 1924 elections operated within the broad constraints of *trasformismo*, as I pointed out in chapter 2. It was not until 1929 that a corporative solution appeared in Italy, and even at that late date the senate remained unreformed.

87. Ben-Ami, *Fascism from Above*, 1983: 219; Gómez-Navarro, *El Régimen de Primo de Rivera*, 1991: 267–268.

88. Ibid.: 271; Ben-Ami, *Fascism from Above*, 1983: 221–222.

89. Ben-Ami, *The Origins of the Second Republic in Spain*, 1978: 18; Ben-Ami, *Fascism from Above*, 1983: 354.

90. Ben-Ami, *Fascism from Above*, 1983: 260–261, 323, 329–332, 342; Gómez-Navarro, *El Régimen de Primo de Rivera*, 1991: 463–469.

91. Ben-Ami, *The Origins of the Second Republic in Spain*, 1978: 14, 22–23, 87–95, 238; Pecharromán, *La segunda republica*, 1989: 27; Preston, *The Coming of the Spanish Civil War*, 1994: 38.

92. Ben-Ami, *Fascism from Above*, 1983: 63; Payne, *Spain's First Democracy*, 1993: 36–37; Pecharromán, *La segunda republica*, 1989: 14.

93. As Preston puts the point, "The Socialists took no significant part in the varied resistance movements to the *Dictadura*, at least until its later stages." Preston, *The Coming of the Spanish Civil War*, 1994: 13–14.

94. Ben-Ami, *The Origins of the Second Republic in Spain*, 1978: 124–125, 127, 130–131; Preston, *The Coming of the Spanish Civil War*, 1994: 13–14.

The policy of collaboration brought enormous organizational benefits to the socialists: "For most of the political groups the fall of the Dictatorship was a starting signal for reorganizing their forces, for the Socialists it was the beginning of a period in which their policy during the dictatorship would bear fruit and would make them the best-organized party in the country and the central axis of the leftist coalition." Ben-Ami, *The Origins of the Second Republic in Spain*, 1978: 127.

95. Malefakis, *Agrarian Reform and Peasant Revolution in Spain*, 1970: 172; Preston, *The Coming of the Spanish Civil War*, 1994: 38.

The agrarian minority, an informal parliamentary group that had been elected by smallholders in Old Castile, and the Basque Autonomist Party, remained minuscule until 1933. Malefakis, *Agrarian Reform and Peasant Revolution in Spain*, 1970: 172.

96. Preston, *The Coming of the Spanish Civil War*, 1994: 61; 177.

97. Malefakis, *Agrarian Reform and Peasant Revolution in Spain*, 1970: 166–167.

98. Ibid.: 168–169; Payne, *Spain's First Democracy*, 1993: 116; Preston, *The Coming of the Spanish Civil War*, 1994: 80–81.

99. Malefakis, *Agrarian Reform and Peasant Revolution in Spain*, 1970: 207, 244–245.

100. Ibid.: 253, 289; Preston, *The Coming of the Spanish Civil War*, 1994: 80.

101. As Malefakis summarizes the results of the reform, "In almost every imaginable way, then, rural economic life was threatened with disruption by the attempt to make the labor supply conform to economically artificial boundaries." Malefakis, *Agrarian Reform and Peasant Revolution in Spain*, 1970: 169.

102. Ibid.: 168–169.

103. Pecharromán, *La segunda republica*, 1989: 34–35; Preston, *The Coming of the Spanish Civil War*, 1994: 91.

104. Payne, *Spain's First Democracy*, 1993: 102–103.

105. Payne, *Spain's First Democracy*, 1993: 113; Preston, *The Coming of the Spanish Civil War*, 1994: 78.

106. Payne, *Spain's First Democracy*, 1993: 74.

As Ben-Ami writes, "An emphasis on trade union issues, and a doctrinal 'anti-collaborationism' with bourgeois parties inherited from the past combined both during the Dictatorship and its aftermath, to jeopardize the Republicans' attempts to harness the Socialist movement to the anti-monarchist effort." Ben-Ami, *Fascism from Above*, 1983: 104.

107. Malefakis, *Agrarian Reform and Peasant Revolution in Spain*, 1970: 353; Payne, *Spain's First Democracy*, 1993: 166–168; Pecharromán, *La segunda republica*, 1989: 61; Preston, *The Coming of the Spanish Civil War*, 1994: 42–43, 45, 55, 65.

The CEDA was a complex organization containing both a conservative and a moderate wing. The social Catholic deputy Manuel Jiménez Fernández (1896–1968) led the moderate wing. He sought to reorient the land reform toward the interests of smallholders. But the CEDA right successfully defeated this position. Malefakis, *Agrarian Reform and Peasant Revolution in Spain*, 1970: 199.

108. Tensions among the monarchists continued throughout the republic. But it was the Carlists in this period who provided the basis of an effective mass organization, not the Alfonsists.

109. Blinkhorn, *Carlism and Crisis in Spain*, 1975: 53, 133.

110. This militia numbered around 10,000 men at the outbreak of the Spanish Civil War and was decisive in the early nationalist victories in north-central Spain. Unlike the other paramilitaries on both sides, which generally limited themselves to shooting revolvers off in cities, the Requeté was "a rurally based, genuine citizen army, well trained in the conduct of war in difficult terrain." Ibid.: 224.

111. Ibid.: 210–211; Callahan, *The Catholic Church in Spain, 1875–1998*, 2000: 166; Castillo, *Proprietarios muy pobres*, 1979: 275–276; Muñoz, *Elecciones y partidos politicos en navarra durante la segunda republica*, 1992: 73, 90.

112. Blinkhorn, *Carlism and Crisis in Spain*, 1975: 74, 116–117, 207–210; Thomas, *The Spanish Civil War*, 1961: 97.

113. "Religion was an issue which could be used to mobilize mass support behind the interests of the oligarchy. Having lost their political hegemony in April 1931, the ruling classes clung all the more to the church as one of their key redoubts of social and economic dominance." Preston, *The Coming of the Spanish Civil War*, 1978: 30.

114. Linz, "The Party System of Spain," 1967: 246; Payne, *Spain's First Democracy*, 1993: 179; Preston, *The Coming of the Spanish Civil War*, 1978: 30.

115. Payne, *Spain's First Democracy*, 1993: 168–169; Preston, *The Coming of the Spanish Civil War*, 1994: 66.

116. Preston, *The Coming of the Spanish Civil War*, 1994: 106–107.

117. Ibid.: 122.

118. Malefakis, *Agrarian Reform and Peasant Revolution in Spain*, 1970: 358.

119. Preston, *The Coming of the Spanish Civil War*, 1994: 205–209.

120. Thomas, *The Spanish Civil War*, 1961: 110.

121. Payne, *Falange*, 1961: 8.

122. Payne, "Spain," in *The European Right: A Historical Profile*, 1965: 188–189.

123. Ibid.: 197.

124. Payne, *The Franco Regime*, 1987: 63.

125. Balcells, *Catalan Nationalism*, 1996: 94.

126. Ibid.: 96; Payne, *Spain's First Democracy*, 1993: 105.

127. Balcells, *Catalan Nationalism*, 1996: 102.

128. Ibid.: 107; Payne, *Spain's First Democracy*, 1993: 205.

129. Balcells, *Catalan Nationalism*, 1996: 107.

130. Payne, *Spain's First Democracy*, 1993: 336.

131. Balcells, *Catalan Nationalism*, 1996: 95.

132. Ibid.: 95.

133. Ibid.: 92.

134. Payne, *Spain's First Democracy*, 1993: 336–337.

135. As Martin Blinkhorn puts the point, "The military conspirators' hopes for an expeditious and bloodless *coup d'état* along the lines of a classic *pronunciamiento* as last executed by Primo de Rivera were thus soon disappointed." Blinkhorn, *Carlism and Crisis in Spain*, 1975: 253. Stanley Payne makes the same point, writing, "A revolt that failed in more than half the national territory can scarcely be called a success. What it achieved was not a successful coup but the establishment of several nuclei of armed power in the north, west, and far south that could be coordinated into a major movement against the leftist regime, creating the conditions for full-scale civil war." Payne, *The Franco Regime*, 1987: 102.

136. Blinkhorn, *Carlism and Crisis in Spain*, 1975: 253–254; Payne, *Falange*, 1961: 117; Preston, *Franco*, 1993: 146, 160.

137. Blinkhorn, *Carlism and Crisis in Spain*, 1975: 253; Preston, *Franco*, 1993: 147; Thomas, *The Spanish Civil War*, 1961: 238.

138. One of the most important generals on the nationalist side, Emilio Mola (1887–1937), initially proposed a military directorate that would then be replaced by a constituent parliament. Rodríguez Jiménez, *Historia de Falange Española de Las JONS*, 2000: 237.

139. Payne, *The Franco Regime*, 1987: 109; Payne, *Fascism in Spain*, 1999: 240; Preston, *Franco*, 1993: 249; Rodríguez Jiménez, *Historia de Falange Española de Las JONS*, 2000: 236–237.

140. Payne, *Fascism in Spain*, 1999: 240–241, 275; Preston, *Franco*, 1993: xviii, 164; Rodríguez Jiménez, *Historia de Falange Española de Las JONS*, 2000: 301.

141. Chueca, *El Fascismo en los Comienzos del Regimen de Franco*, 1983: 148; Payne, *Fascism in Spain*, 1999: 259–272; Rodríguez Jiménez, *Historia de Falange Española de Las JONS*, 2000: 317, 336, 341.

142. Preston conveys the informal style of this regime, writing, "All of Franco's ministers coincide in the recollection that the Generalissimo left them entirely free to pursue their own departmental policies. Their only obligation was to be bound to the general direction of policy agreed at cabinet meetings. The sessions would last for hours with acrimonious debates between the Falangists and the more conservative and usually monarchist, military ministers." Preston, *Franco*, 1993: 298.

143. The April 1938 Labor Charter, or Fuero del Trabajo, officially ratified the FET-JONS's control over the syndicates. Paragraph 4 of article XIII specified that the "hierarchs of the syndicate will necessarily come from the militants of the F. E. T. y de las J.O.N.S." Salaya, *Historia del sindicalismo Español*, 1943: 169. The law of syndical unity of January 1940 made this subordination more explicit, stipulating that all economic interest associations would be "incorporated into the syndical organization of the movement." Selgas, *Los Sindicatos en España*, 1966: 432.

144. Chueca, *El Fascismo en los Comienzos del Regimen de Franco*, 1983: 229; Payne, *The Franco Regime*, 1987: 180–181; Salaya, *Historia del sindicalismo Español*, 1943: 169; Selgas, *Los Sindicatos en España*, 1966: 432.

Payne describes the position of the FET-JONS this way: "The Falange was horizontally cut off from the Council of Ministers and had no direct, organic connection with the policy-making bodies of the national administration. While the conservatives and opportunists largely controlled the upper echelons, the party was left to amuse itself with the gigantic bureaucracy that gorged itself on the Franco spoils system. All government employees were supposed to be FET members, but no party leader of doubtful intension was placed in a position of influence. The only department under Falange control was the Syndical organization, which until 1940 was largely a paper creation." Payne, "Spain," in *The European Right: A Historical Profile*, 1965: 212.

145. Part of the reason for the weakness of the Falange, and especially its union wing, was the absence of an organized working class in the nationalist zone. I showed in chapter 2 how decisive the strike of 1925 was for the establishment of fascism in Italy. In Spain the entire process differed. The syndicates in existence in nationalist Spain were weak and fragmented. Aparicio, *El sindicalismo vertical y la formación del estado Franquista*, 1979: 8–11; Payne, *The Franco Regime*, 1987: 185–186. This meant that national syndicalism in Spain would inevitably be driven by the state. Fernandez Cuesta summarized the difference between the Spanish and Italian models as follows: "In those countries in which the governors have encountered on coming to power as in Italy, a class syndicalism that they could not dismantle, they have seen themselves forced as a lesser evil, to convert it into state syndicalism and afterwards to create supersyndical organs of interconnection and self discipline in defense of the totalitarian interest in production. Those organs are corporations. The corporation, then, had a forced basis in class syndicalism. The vertical syndicate, on the other hand, is both the point of departure and the point of arrival. It does not suppose the previous existence of other syndicates. Broad horizontal structures do not interfere with it." Quoted in ibid.: 185. This process was slow and halting. The main achievement of the first minister, González Bueno, was the construction of Centrales Nacional-Sindicalistas. Aparicio, *El sindicalismo vertical y la formación del estado Franquista*, 1979: 40–41. These institutions were provincial-level bodies headed up by a delegate responsible to the Ministry of the Syndicates and the Falange.

146. Ibid.: 85–86; Payne, *The Franco Regime*, 1987: 290.

147. Callahan, *The Catholic Church in Spain, 1875–1998*, 2000: 347, 351; Lannon, *Privilege, Persecution, and Prophecy*, 1987: 199–200.

148. Castillo, *Proprietarios muy pobres*, 1979: 407, 440–443.

149. Blinkhorn notes that Carlists claimed that their political movement was authentically liberal. "They were," he suggests, "voicing a sincere belief in wide civic participation, popular acquiescence in public policies, lack of governmental authoritarianism, and 'representative' monarchy." Blinkhorn, *Carlism and Crisis in Spain*, 1975: 151.

CHAPTER FOUR: Statist Fascism

1. Seton-Watson, *A History of the Roumanians*, 1963: 312–313; Mitrany, *The Land and the Peasant in Rumania*, 1930: 46–49.

2. Jowitt, *Social Change in Romania, 1860–1940*, 1978: 21.

In 1905, 15,973 voters selected 72 seats in the senate, 34,742 urban voters selected over 79 seats in the chamber of deputies, and another 42,907 indirect voters represented over a million effectively disenfranchised rural voters. In 1911, 101,339 men could vote deputies to the lower house, while only 24,921 could vote for seats in the senate, out of a population of 1,644,302. Heinen, *Die Legion "Erzengel Michael" in Rumänien*, 1986: 64; Janos, "Modernization and Decay in Historical Perspective," 1978: 85–86; Seton-Watson, *A History of the Roumanians*, 1963: 357.

3. Eidelberg, *The Great Rumanian Peasant Revolt of 1907*, 1974: 21; Heinen, *Die Legion "Erzengel Michael" in Rumänien*, 1986: 63.

4. Nagy-Talavera, *The Green Shirts and the Others*, 1970: 16; Roberts, *Rumania: Political Problems of an Agrarian State*, 1951: 20; Seton-Watson, *A History of the Roumanians*, 1963: 357–358.

5. Eidelberg, *The Great Rumanian Peasant Revolt of 1907*, 1974: 19; Heinen, *Die Legion "Erzengel Michael" in Rumänien*, 1986: 63.

6. Seton-Watson, *A History of the Roumanians*, 1963: 357.

As Janos writes, "In order to strengthen this machine, Brătianu then abolished the old first college of great landowners and merged it with the second college, whose members were more sympathetic to bureaucratic objectives, or at least were more susceptible to manipulation." Janos, "Modernization and Decay in Historical Perspective," 1978: 87.

7. Chirot, *Social Change in a Peripheral Society*, 1976: 104–105; Heinen, *Die Legion "Erzengel Michael" in Rumänien*, 1986: 52; Mitrany, *The Land and the Peasant in Rumania*, 1930: 21.

8. Heinen, *Die Legion "Erzengel Michael" in Rumänien*, 1986: 59; Janos, "Modernization and Decay in Historical Perspective," 1978: 83; Stokes, "The Social Origins of East European Politics," 1989: 228.

9. Janos, "Modernization and Decay in Historical Perspective," 1978: 86–87.

10. Heinen, *Die Legion "Erzengel Michael" in Rumänien*, 1986: 72.

11. Seton-Watson, *A History of the Roumanians*, 1963: 371.

12. Heinen, *Die Legion "Erzengel Michael" in Rumänien*, 1986: 49–51; Nagy-Talavera, *The Green Shirts and the Others*, 1970: 47.

13. Mitrany effectively summarizes the situation, writing, "The despair to which their ever growing misery was driving the peasants vented itself in the risings of 1888 and 1891. In their need the peasants had sold themselves hand and foot to the large owners and tenants, pledging their labour for years in advance. Such money as they still could obtain in times of stress they had to get from publicans and usurers, at rates of interest which not infrequently rose to 500 per cent." Mitrany, *The Land and the Peasant in Rumania*, 1930: 376.

14. Eidelberg, *The Great Rumanian Peasant Revolt of 1907*, 1974: 74, 84.

15. There is some debate about how these organizations initially formed. Eidelberg suggests that they arose "spontaneously." Ibid.: 75. Diarmid Coffey, in contrast, emphasizes the role of rural schoolteachers. Coffey, *The Cooperative Movement in Jugoslavia, Rumania and North Italy*, 1922: 45.

16. Ibid.: 45; Eidelberg, *The Great Rumanian Peasant Revolt of 1907*, 1974: 74–75, 92–93; Mitrany, *The Land and the Peasant in Rumania*, 1930: 376–378; Orbonas, *Die genossenschaftsbewegung in Rumänien*, 1930: 13; Roberts, *Rumania: Political Problems of an Agrarian State*, 1951: 78–79.

David Mitrany claims that 711 cooperative banks were established before the law on popular banks in 1903: "That first period saw the establishment of 711 popular banks inside ten years, on the initiative and with the means of the villagers. During this period were laid the foundations of the co-operative essays which were promising to transform village life even in the uncongenial conditions which prevailed before the reform [i.e., the land reform of the post–World War I period]." Mitrany, *The Land and the Peasant in Rumania*, 1930: 378.

17. Eidelberg, *The Great Rumanian Peasant Revolt of 1907*, 1974: 76.

18. Ibid.: 78.

19. Ibid.: 76–77.

20. Ibid.: 67.

21. Ibid.: 75, 79–81; Mitrany, *The Land and the Peasant in Rumania*, 1930: 378–379; Orbonas, *Die genossenschaftsbewegung in Rumänien*, 1930: 14.

22. David Mitrany writes, "The newly established Central Office was not so much a joint institution of the popular banks as a State organization destined to control, to guide, and to provide with funds the popular banks in the villages." Mitrany, *The Land and the Peasant in Rumania*, 1930: 378–379. Roberts echoes this view: "Cooperatives were not really cooperative ventures, but rather official institutions, financed, directed, and controlled by the state." Roberts, *Rumania: Political Problems of an Agrarian State*, 1951: 64.

23. Coffey, *The Cooperative Movement in Jugoslavia, Rumania and North Italy*, 1922: 57; Eidelberg, *The Great Rumanian Peasant Revolt of 1907*, 1974: 80–81; Mitrany, *The Land and the Peasant in Rumania*, 1930: 379, 383–384.

24. Coffey, *The Cooperative Movement in Jugoslavia, Rumania and North Italy*, 1922: 45; Eidelberg, *The Great Rumanian Peasant Revolt of 1907*, 1974: 72, 76, 96.

25. Quoted in ibid.: 103.

26. Ibid.: 133, 156.

27. Chirot, *Social Change in a Peripheral Society*, 1976: 150; Eidelberg, *The Great Rumanian Peasant Revolt of 1907*, 1974: 200; Mitrany, *The Land and the Peasant in Rumania*, 1930: 85; Roberts, *Rumania: Political Problems of an Agrarian State*, 1951: 3.

28. Digby, "Rumania: The State as Co-Operator," 1930: 410.

29. Ibid.: 428.

30. Eidelberg, *The Great Rumanian Peasant Revolt of 1907*, 1974: 96.

31. Ibid.: 102–103.

32. Digby, "Rumania: The State as Co-Operator," 1930: 411; Eidelberg, *The Great Rumanian Peasant Revolt of 1907*, 1974: 75, 78–79, 98; Orbonas, *Die genossenschaftsbewegung in Rumänien*, 1930: 18; Roberts, *Rumania: Political Problems of an Agrarian State*, 1951: 78–79.

33. Eidelberg, *The Great Rumanian Peasant Revolt of 1907*, 1974: 18, 20–21.

34. Mitrany, *The Land and the Peasant in Rumania*, 1930: 74–75, 79. Mitrany evokes the power of the mayors, writing, "Through the instrument of the laws on agricultural contracts the Constitutional guarantees for personal liberty and for the sanctity of domicile could be set aside for 95 per cent of the population, at the will and whim of the village mayor; and this not in exceptional circumstances, but in everyday life, in matters arisen out of the daily work—the only means of subsistence—of the people." Mitrany, *The Land and the Peasant in Rumania*, 1930: 79.

35. Heinen, *Die Legion "Erzengel Michael" in Rumänien*, 1986: 69; Weber, "Romania," 1974: 510.

36. Keegan, *The First World War*, 2000: 308; Nagy-Talavera, *The Green Shirts and the Others*, 1970: 26; Rothschild, *East Central Europe between the Two World Wars*, 1974: 290.

37. Musat and Ardeleanu, *Political Life in Romania, 1918–1921*, 1982: 48, 55–58. Livezeanu nicely summarizes the demise of the Conservative Party: "Already weakened before 1914, the Conservatives fell as a result of their wartime pro-German sympathies and of the land and electoral reform that effectively wiped out the class of large landowners the party had traditionally represented." Livezeanu, *Cultural Politics in Greater Romania*, 1995: 22.

38. Ibid.: 251; Nagy-Talavera, *The Green Shirts and the Others*, 1970: 30.

39. Roberts, *Rumania: Political Problems of an Agrarian State*, 1951: 94–95.

40. Heinen, *Die Legion "Erzengel Michael" in Rumänien*, 1986: 52, 103; Maner, *Parlamentarismus in Rumänien*, 1997: 44–49; Roberts, *Rumania: Political Problems of an Agrarian State*, 1951: 98–99, 102; Rothschild, *East Central Europe between the Two World Wars*, 1974: 297–298.

41. Heinen, *Die Legion "Erzengel Michael" in Rumänien*, 1986: 106; Patrascanu, *Sous trois dictatures*, 1946: 102.

42. Heinen, *Die Legion "Erzengel Michael" in Rumänien*, 1986: 106.

43. Nagy-Talavera, *The Green Shirts and the Others*, 1970: 256.

44. Janos, "Modernization and Decay in Historical Perspective," 1978: 102–103; Roberts, *Rumania: Political Problems of an Agrarian State*, 1951: 122–124.

45. Land purchase and leasing societies "were created for the sole purpose of taking over the land which afterward became the private property of their members." Digby, "Rumania: The State as Co-Operator," 1930: 414.

46. Ibid.: 412–414; Mitrany, *The Land and the Peasant in Rumania*, 1930: 398.

47. Roberts, *Rumania: Political Problems of an Agrarian State*, 1951: 126.

48. Coffey, *The Cooperative Movement in Jugoslavia, Rumania and North Italy*, 1922: 57–58; Digby, "Rumania: The State as Co-Operator," 1930: 411; Mitrany, *The Land and the Peasant in Rumania*, 1930: 391.

49. Roberts, *Rumania: Political Problems of an Agrarian State*, 1951: 139–141; Scurtu, *Istoria partidului national-taranesc*, : 12, 69.

50. The model of Romanian development in this scheme was Denmark, depicted as "a modern agrarian economy with small businesses, held together by cooperatives and equipped with the necessary supplemental industry." Heinen, *Die Legion "Erzengel Michael" in Rumänien*, 1986: 77–78.

51. Ibid.: 77–78; Roberts, *Rumania: Political Problems of an Agrarian State*, 1951: 141–146.

52. Heinen, *Die Legion "Erzengel Michael" in Rumänien*, 1986: 152; Nagy-Talavera, *The Green Shirts and the Others*, 1970: 274–275; Roberts, *Rumania: Political Problems of an Agrarian State*, 1951: 118–119, 131; Rothschild, *East Central Europe between the Two World Wars*, 1974: 301.

53. Beer, *Zur Entwicklung des Parteien- und Parlamentsystems in Rumänien 1928–1933*, 1983: 347–348; Heinen, *Die Legion "Erzengel Michael" in Rumänien*, 1986: 154; Patrascanu, *Sous trois dictatures*, 1946: 107; Roberts, *Rumania: Political Problems of an Agrarian State*, 1951: 157.

54. Roberts argues that these incidents show "the tenacity with which old habits persisted under the new order." Ibid.: 133.

55. As Roberts puts the point, "Maniu's resignation in October, 1930, was a significant event as it marked, when viewed in retrospect, the conclusion of Rumania's brief experiment with responsible government." Ibid.: 135. Patrascanu argues, "It was from the decline of the national-peasant party that the expansion of the movements of the extreme right began." Patrascanu, *Sous trois dictatures*, 1946: 109.

56. Hitchins puts the point well: "This situation arose from the dual nature of the party: Ion Mihalache and his wing had a peasant programme and strove to create a peasant state, while the Maniu, or National Party, wing, whose policies generally prevailed, was middle class in its aims and outlook." Hitchins, *Rumania, 1866–1947*, 1994: 415.

57. Heinen, *Die Legion "Erzengel Michael" in Rumänien*, 1986: 104; Maner, *Parlamentarismus in Rumänien*, 1997: 79; Roberts, *Rumania: Political Problems of an Agrarian State*, 1951: 166, 179–180; Rothschild, *East Central Europe between the Two World Wars*, 1974: 295. Larry Watts points this out clearly in his discussion of the involvement of Iuliu Maniu's family in a shady arms deal with the Czech Skoda firm. Watts, *Romanian Cassandra*, 1993: 121–122.

58. Ibid.: 126–127; Maner, *Parlamentarismus in Rumänien*, 1997: 69–70.

59. Roberts, *Rumania: Political Problems of an Agrarian State*, 1951: 132–135; Patrascanu, *Sous trois dictatures*, 1946: 108; Rothschild, *East Central Europe between the Two World Wars*, 1974: 302–303.

60. "He felt himself chosen to be the leader of a 'new Romania,'" writes Heinen in *Die Legion "Erzengel Michael" in Rumänien*, 1986: 159.

61. Heinen writes, "Carol did not want an absolute monarchy. The idea of plebiscitary bonapartist domination fascinated him, a leadership monarchy, which would be revolutionary only by expanding his own sphere of power." Ibid.: 240–241. Watts shares this view: "Carol himself was determined to be a 'Great Man,' loved by and inspiring the people. Fancying himself a soldier and captivated by the popularity and ceremony of Benito Mussolini and his impressive Blackshirts, he doggedly set about emulating the Duce and the Italian Fascist regime." Watts, *Romanian Cassandra*, 1993: 127. Maner echoes these views, although his monograph is much less hostile to Carol than either Heinen or Watts. He writes that "Carol could not hide his admiration for the 'authoritarian and disciplined rule of Mussolini.'" Maner, *Parlamentarismus in Rumänien*, 1997: 101–102.

62. Janos, "Modernization and Decay in Historical Perspective," 1978: 105; Maner, *Parlamentarismus in Rumänien*, 1997: 94, 101.
This last group included Alexander Movrodi, Felix Wieder, Nicolae Malax, and the Auschnitt brothers, Aristide Blank and Oscar Kaufmann.

63. Heinen, *Die Legion "Erzengel Michael" in Rumänien*, 1986: 173–174; Roberts, *Rumania: Political Problems of an Agrarian State*, 1951: 197.

64. Heinen, *Die Legion "Erzengel Michael" in Rumänien*, 1986: 181; Maner, *Parlamentarismus in Rumänien*, 1997: 107; Manoïlescu, *Le siècle du corporatisme*, 1936: 40.

65. Heinen, *Die Legion "Erzengel Michael" in Rumänien*, 1986: 164–165, 203, 240; Maner, *Parlamentarismus in Rumänien*, 1997: 103–104, 113; Roberts, *Rumania: Political Problems of an Agrarian State*, 1951: 206; Rothschild, *East Central Europe between the Two World Wars*, 1974: 304–305.

66. Heinen, *Die Legion "Erzengel Michael" in Rumänien*, 1986: 162, 203, 237–238; Patrascanu, *Sous trois dictatures*, 1946:107.

67. Roberts, *Rumania: Political Problems of an Agrarian State*, 1951: 189.

68. This perhaps explains why liberals attempted to attract foreign loans (rather than foreign direct investment) to finance industrialization. Ibid.: 122–123.

69. Heinen, *Die Legion "Erzengel Michael" in Rumänien*, 1986: 154–155, 264; Patrascanu, *Sous trois dictatures*, 1946: 29–31; Roberts, *Rumania: Political Problems of an Agrarian State*, 1951: 171.
Heinen links the struggle within the Liberal Party between the young and old liberals to a conflict between banks and heavy industry. Heinen, *Die Legion "Erzengel Michael" in Rumänien*, 1986: 265.

70. Ibid.: 265; Janos, "Modernization and Decay in Historical Perspective," 1978: 103. Roberts suggests that King Carol himself "had a large personal stake in the new industries." Roberts, *Rumania: Political Problems of an Agrarian State*, 1951: 199. Patrascanu states that Carol was heavily involved in metallurgy and had a large interest in the Banca de Credit Roman. Patrascanu, *Sous trois dictatures*, 1946: 42.

71. According to a conversation that Carol had with the Romanian foreign minister in October of 1933, he continued to support Vaida-Voevod even at this late date. Maner, *Parlamentarismus in Rumänien*, 1997: 144.

72. "With their procedures the PNL had now started down a new path and borrowed the methods of the PNȚ from April 1928," writes Maner. Ibid.: 143.

73. In his memoirs Codreanu describes invading a state-owned factory where workers had hung the red flag and removed pictures of the monarch. Codreanu, *For My Legionaries (The Iron Guard*, 1990: 12–13. The opening lines of *For My Legionaries* also suggest the importance of anticommunism. Codreanu describes a meeting at which he posed the question, "What are we going to do if the Bolsheviks invade us?" Ibid.: 3.

74. Anti-Semitism gained support among students in part because of the dire economic position of the highly educated in interwar Romania. In 1925 there were 6.8 students for 1,000 inhabitants, while by 1932 this proportion had increased to 19.7 per 1,000. In 1913–1914 there were 3,500 students at the University of Bucharest. By 1929 this figure was more than 20,000. In the context of an underdeveloped economy that could not absorb a large pool of highly educated labor, this resulted in a crowding of the free professions. Romania had by far the highest concentration of lawyers per inhabitant of any European country in 1931. Heinen, *Die Legion "Erzengel Michael" in Rumänien*, 1986: 397–399.

75. Alexander Cuza was the main figure of Romanian anti-Semitism. According to him, the superficial adoption of liberal democratic institutions from the West was incapable of producing the level of social integration required for the construction of a strong national state. The big question in Romania was not which class would rule, but rather which race. Cuza's anti-Semitism thus derived from the demand to create a unified national community. His early political efforts all aimed to keep Jews out of the professions. The National Christian Union of 1922 was established to "protect the economic, political, and cultural interests of Romanians against Jews." Ibid.: 120. This developed later into the LANC, which would remain the "classic party of Romanian anti-Semitism." Ibid.: 193. Despite his anti-Semitism, Cuza remained committed to a legal road to power. Strangely, as we will see later in chapter 4, anti-Semitism was less central to Codreanu's worldview. Ibid.: 87; Nagy-Talavera, *The Green Shirts and the Others*, 1970: 248.

76. Heinen, *Die Legion "Erzengel Michael" in Rumänien*, 1986: 111, 119, 133, 399, 492; Livezeanu, *Cultural Politics in Greater Romania*, 1995: 261.

77. Codreanu, *For My Legionaries (The Iron Guard*, 1990: 131–132; Heinen, *Die Legion "Erzengel Michael" in Rumänien*, 1986: 121; Livezeanu, *Cultural Politics in Greater Romania*, 1995: 291; Nagy-Talavera, *The Green Shirts and the Others*, 1970: 286.

78. Heinen, *Die Legion "Erzengel Michael" in Rumänien*, 1986: 135–136. "The legion's task was not to seize power but to train men," notes Weber. Weber, "Romania," 1974: 531.

79. Heinen, *Die Legion "Erzengel Michael" in Rumänien*, 1986: 193, 221, 494–495.

80. During the summer of 1932 the LAM had only twenty county organizations. By December of 1933 it was in sixty-six counties and had 28,000 members. Ibid.: 222.

81. Patrascanu grasps clearly the connection: "It is from the decline of the national peasant party that the expansion of the movements of the extreme right begins in Romania." Patrascanu, *Sous trois dictatures*, 1946: 107.

82. Codreanu, *For My Legionaries (The Iron Guard*, 1990: 131–132.

83. Heinen describes Codreanu's behavior as follows: "It had been expected that the legion would judge the rebellion of the workers as an act of Moscow, but this was not the case: Codreanu announced in parliament that he understood the workers' conduct. They were unmercifully sweated by the 'political caste' and the 'foreign' firms, and how else could they defend themselves?" Heinen, *Die Legion "Erzengel Michael" in Rumänien*, 1986: 225.

84. "In November 1933 Carol appointed the Liberal leader Ion G. Duca prime minister, with an understanding that he would manipulate the election and crack down on the burgeoning Legionary Movement," writes Nagy-Talavera. Nagy-Talavera, *The Green Shirts and the Others*, 1970: 281.

85. Heinen, *Die Legion "Erzengel Michael" in Rumänien*, 1986: 279, 305; Hibbeln, *Codreanu und die Eiserne Garde*, 1984: 33; Nagy-Talavera, *The Green Shirts and the Others*, 1970: 286; Weber, "Romania," 1974: 537–538.

86. "In contrast to the NSDAP and the PNF, the legion counted no paramilitary troops. The Iron Guard had at the beginning fulfilled this task, but the legion and the guard had not diverged, since the membership in both organizations was identical. Later military-like activities were forbidden by government decision." Heinen, *Die Legion "Erzengel Michael" in Rumänien*, 1986: 278. The legionary movement, therefore, did not develop a strong paramilitary organization.

87. Ibid.: 169, 208–209, 220, 225, 274, 312; Roberts, *Rumania: Political Problems of an Agrarian State*, 1951: 231; Watts, *Romanian Cassandra*, 1993: 148.

Heinen emphasizes the Iron Guard's rejection of the statist industrialization policies of the liberals. As he writes, "They opposed high protectionist tariffs and thereby at the same time the industrialization of the land. Only when labor and capital could not be productively used in any other way should local, controllable industrial undertakings be established." Heinen, *Die Legion "Erzengel Michael" in Rumänien*, 1986: 209.

88. Quoted in ibid.: 351.

89. Livezeanu, *Cultural Politics in Greater Romania*, 1995: 290.

90. Weber, "Romania," 1974: 531.

91. Carsten, *The Rise of Fascism*, 1982: 187–188; Heinen, *Die Legion "Erzengel Michael" in Rumänien*, 1986: 215; Nagy-Talavera, *The Green Shirts and the Others*, 1970: 290; Weber, "Romania," 1974: 548. According to Watts, "Rather than presenting a growing destructive threat, the Guardists, throughout the 1935–1938 period, were principally occupied in constructive projects." He places most of the blame for anti-Semitic violence in the mid- to late thirties on the paramilitary organizations of the LANC called the *lancieri*. Watts, *Romanian Cassandra*, 1993: 159.

92. Heinen, *Die Legion "Erzengel Michael" in Rumänien*, 1986: 384, 386–389.

93. Ibid.: 393; Patrascanu, *Sous trois dictatures*, 1946: 250.

94. Watts, *Romanian Cassandra*, 1993: 131.

95. Patrascanu underlines how decisive this election was: "A government, in Romania, put into the minority at election time constituted in effect an unknown fact up until that time in the history of our country." Patrascanu, *Sous trois dictatures*, 1946: 112.

96. Heinen, *Die Legion "Erzengel Michael" in Rumänien*, 1986: 357; Maner, *Parlamentarismus in Rumänien*, 1997: 101; Patrascanu, *Sous trois dictatures*, 1946: 112.

97. This was a higher percentage than either of the two classic fascist parties (the NSDAP and the PNF) in the period immediately prior to their respective seizures of power. Heinen, *Die Legion "Erzengel Michael" in Rumänien*, 1986: 382.

98. Heinen emphasizes the tension between the liberals and the king, writing, "Already after the student Congress of Tîrgu Mureş, individual groups of the PNL had sharply criticized the king, since the forwardness with which the extreme right publicly acted could not be innocent." Ibid.: 313.

99. Watts discusses the ambiguous attitude of the monarch, writing, "Throughout 1936, in fact, the Palace continued to support the Iron Guard with the eventual aim of channeling it to Carol's purposes—support that Codreanu mistook for Royal approval of the reform program advocated by the Guard." Watts, *Romanian Cassandra*, 1993: 150.

100. Heinen, *Die Legion "Erzengel Michael" in Rumänien*, 1986: 312, 348; Nagy-Talavera, *The Green Shirts and the Others*, 1970: 288; Watts, *Romanian Cassandra*, 1993: 150–151.

101. Heinen, *Die Legion "Erzengel Michael" in Rumänien*, 1986: 358; Weber, "Romania," 1974: 551. According to Watts, "Carol had deprived 225,000 Romanian Jews of their citizenship." He carried out this policy on his own initiative, not under pressure from the Iron Guard. Watts, *Romanian Cassandra*, 1993: 163.

102. The campaign for the planned elections of March 1938 was, in Nagy-Talavera's words, "A full fledged civil war … between Cuzists and the Iron Guard." Nagy-Talavera, *The Green Shirts and the Others*, 1970: 295.

103. Ibid.: 295–296.

104. Heinen, *Die Legion "Erzengel Michael" in Rumänien*, 1986: 364–368.

105. Larry Watts effectively demolishes this idea, pointing out that by appointing the Goga-Cuza government Carol handed the country to Romania's most violently anti-Semitic party. He also emphasizes that Carol doggedly pursued the goal of a fascist dictatorship at least from 1934: "The greatest danger to democracy and civic society in this period was undoubtedly King Carol II and his ambition to form a populist dictatorship." Watts, *Romanian Cassandra*, 1993: 185.

106. Manfred Killinger, the German ambassador to Bucharest in 1940, writes that Mihail Moruzov, the chief of the Romanian secret services during Carol's dictatorship, requested "advice on various matters, for instance, handling of the Jewish problem, labor peace, organization plans, party guard, etc. I told him that I could comment only briefly on all these questions since, if they were to be discussed thoroughly, it would take me days. I proposed that he invite four experts from Germany for an extended period, who could serve the party in an advisory capacity, one to be a representative for propaganda, one for organizational questions, an SA leader, and a representative of the Labor Front. Moruzov cordially welcomed the proposal. The persons concerned would naturally be guests of the country." This is yet another piece of evidence showing that Carol was determined to establish a fascist regime in Romania. Quoted in ibid.: 231–232.

107. Heinen, *Die Legion "Erzengel Michael" in Rumänien*, 1986: 370–372; Nagy-Talavera, *The Green Shirts and the Others*, 1970: 299–304; Watts, *Romanian Cassandra*, 1993: 303.

108. Patrascanu, *Sous trois dictatures*, 1946: 217; Watts, *Romanian Cassandra*, 1993: 215, 247.

"By the summer of 1939, royally sponsored German penetration of Romania was in full swing," as Watts writes. Ibid.: 215.

109. Nagy-Talavera, *The Green Shirts and the Others*, 1970: 342; Watts, *Romanian Cassandra*, 1993: 313.

110. Ibid.: 263, 267–268.

CHAPTER FIVE: Considering Alternatives

1. Carsten, *The Rise of Fascism*, 1982; Linz, *Fascismo, autoritarismo, totalitarismo*, 2003; Luebbert, *Liberalism, Fascism, or Social Democracy*, 1991; Mann, *Fascists*, 2004; Moore, *Social Origins of Dictatorship and Democracy*, 1993; Payne, *A History of Fascism, 1914–1945*, 1995; Poulantzas, *Fascism and Dictatorship*, 1970; Skocpol, "A Critical Review of Barrington Moore's Social Origins of Dictatorship and Democracy," 1973.

2. Mahoney, "Knowledge Accumulation in Comparative Historical Research," 2003: 138–139; Rueschemeyer, Stephens, and Stephens, *Capitalist Development and Democracy*, 1992: 14.

Moore's argument embodies a strong version of Marxist theory. This differs in crucial respects from a tradition that attempted to link fascism to highly developed capitalist economies. In the most sophisticated non-Stalinist versions of this account, fascism corresponds to a "postliberal" monopoly phase of capitalism in which the state, rather than the market, becomes a major determinant of the rate of profit. This is associated with a decline of liberal institutions. Neumann, *Behemoth: The Structure and Practice of National Socialism, 1933–1944*, 1966: 43–44. Arguments of this type were briefly dominant in the thirties and forties but have generally been a minority position within Marxism. Despite this, many scholars of fascism continue to debate them. Gregor, *Mussolini's Intellectuals*, 2005: 1–17. The argument that fascism is associated with a highly developed capitalist economy is open to the obvious objection that, as an ideology and political movement, it arose first in societies with underdeveloped or unevenly developed capitalist economies. Ibid.: 5. The monopoly capitalism thesis is thus vitiated by the fact that the most developed monopoly capitalist economies (e.g., the United States) have never produced serious fascist movements, let alone fascist regimes.

3. Brenner, "Agrarian Class Structure and Economic Development," 2002: 23; Moore, *Social Origins of Dictatorship and Democracy*, 1993: 25, 260, 419–420, 435; Stephens, "Democratic Transition and Breakdown in Western Europe," 1989: 1028.

Sixteenth-century England is the classic ground of agrarian capitalism, in Moore's analysis: "The English landed aristocracy turned to a form of commercial farming that involved setting the peasants free to shift for themselves as best they could." Moore, *Social Origins of Dictatorship and Democracy*, 1993: 419–420. The paradigmatic example of the formation of a labor-repressive landed elite is the manorial reaction of the fifteenth and sixteenth centuries in Germany. Moore argues that expansion of the holdings of the Prussian nobility and the reduction of much of the population to serfdom was partially the result of increased grain exports. Ibid.: 435. But formal enserfment is not the only possible form of labor repression. In Japan the commercialization of agriculture was associated with the establishment of the "five-man group," in which village families monitored one another to fulfill their obligations to the lord. Ibid.: 260.

4. Ibid.: 435.

5. Ibid.: 437; Stephens, "Democratic Transition and Breakdown in Western Europe," 1989: 1021–1025.

6. Moore, *Social Origins of Dictatorship and Democracy*, 1993: 451.

7. Rueschemeyer, Stephens, and Stephens, *Capitalist Development and Democracy*, 1992: 58; Stephens, "Democratic Transition and Breakdown in Western Europe," 1989: 1026.

8. Hintze, *The Historical Essays of Otto Hintze*, 1985; Tilly, *Coercion, Capital and European States*, 1992; Skocpol, "A Critical Review of Barrington Moore's Social Origins of Dictatorship and Democracy," 1973; Ertman, *The Birth of the Leviathan*, 1997; Downing, *The Military Revolution and Political Change*, 1992; and Mann, *States, War and Capitalism*, 1988; Mann, *Fascists*, 2004.

In some ways this separation is a bit artificial, for elements of the Weberian argument exist in Moore's work as well. For example, Moore emphasizes the importance of a "strong and independent Parliament" in undermining an authoritarian outcome in the late eighteenth and nineteenth centuries in England. Moore, *Social Origins of Dictatorship and Democracy*, 1993: 39. But the emphasis of Moore's argument is clearly on the nature of the landed elite.

9. Skocpol, "A Critical Review of Barrington Moore's Social Origins of Dictatorship and Democracy," 1973: 19–27; Trimberger, *Revolution from Above*, 1978: 41.

10. Mann, *Fascists*, 2004: 74.

11. Ibid.: 75–78.

12. Ibid.: 77.

13. Ibid.: 3.

14. Ertman, "Democracy and Dictatorship in Interwar Western Europe Revisited," 1998: 495; Luebbert, "Social Foundations of Political Order in Interwar Europe," 1987: 458–459; Luebbert, *Liberalism, Fascism, or Social Democracy*, 1991: 63.

15. Blackbourn, "The Discreet Charm of the Bourgeoisie," 1989: 91–97.

16. Bauer, "Wie 'bürgerlich' war der Nationalstaat in Deutschland und Italien?" 2005: 112.

17. Anderson, *Lineages of the Absolutist State*, 1989: 144–147; Jones, *The Italian City State*, 1997: 145; Ginsborg, "Gramsci in the Era of Bourgeois Revolution in Italy," 1979: 42; Manselli, "Egemonia imperiale, autonomia comunale, potenza politica della chiesa," 1992: 122–125; Procacci, *History of the Italian People*, 1968: 17–21.

18. Adrian Lyttelton makes this point well in his brief comparison of Italian and German historical development. He points out that the constitutional struggle between king and parliament in Germany was won mostly by the monarchy when this institution succeeded in gaining control over finance. "In Italy," he writes, "the reverse was true: the 1852 Cavour ministry was virtually imposed by Parliament, and it succeeded in reorganizing the bureaucracy so that it answered to the ministers rather than the Crown." Lyttelton, *The Seizure of Power*, 2004: 5.

19. Banti, *Storia della borghesia italiana*, 1996: 7, 11; Lyttelton, *The Seizure of Power*, 2004: 5.

20. Abbate, *La filosofia di Benedetto Croce e la crisi della società italiana*, 1966: 24–25; Banti, *Storia della borghesia italiana*, 1996: 38; Lyttelton, "Landlords, Peasants and the Limits of Liberalism," 1979: 105–106.

21. Melis, *Storia dell'amministrazione italiana*, 1996b: 37.

22. Both Barbagli and Salvati argue that underemployed northern, educated people were a crucial constituency for Italian fascism. Barbagli, *Educating for Unemployment*, 1982: 33; Salvati, *Il regime e gli impiegati*, 1992: 50–51.

23. Dominant class interests in Italy were diverse, both in agriculture and in industry. This point has not been stressed often enough in work on fascism from the Moore perspective, where analysts tend to refer generally to agrarians without adequately distinguishing among them in terms of their reliance on labor-repressive techniques. Rueschemeyer, Stephens, and Stephens, *Capitalist Development and Democracy*, 1992: 103. For example, Rueschemeyer, Stephens, and Stephens identify Italy as a problem for the Moore thesis, in my view correctly. Ibid.: 103; Stephens, "Democratic Transition and Breakdown in Western Europe," 1989: 1041. Yet their reasons for doing so are debatable. They claim that Italy had a strong "bourgeoisie." It would be more accurate to say that it had a strong class of agrarian capitalists. I think the distortion derives from their tendency to conceive of the industrial bourgeoisie and large landholders as monolithic groups without adequately distinguishing among types of landholders.

24. Lyttelton, "Landlords, Peasants and the Limits of Liberalism," 1979: 105; Seton-Watson, *Italy from Liberalism to Fascism, 1870–1925*, 1967: 290; Zamagni, *The Economic History of Italy 1860–1990*, 1993: 7–8, 16, 48, 55, 69.

25. Ibid.: 7.

26. Zamagni, "Gli attori sociali delle transformazioni produttive dell'agricoltura Italiana," 1997: 31.

27. Corner, *Fascism in Ferrara*, 1975: 4–5; Zamagni, *The Economic History of Italy 1860–1990*, 1993: 62.

28. Davis, "The South, the Risorgimento and the Origins of the 'Southern Problem,'" 1979: 73.

29. Ibid.: 75.

30. Zamagni, *The Economic History of Italy 1860–1990*, 1993: 175.

31. Ibid.: 21–22, 56.

32. Castronovo, *La storia economica. Storia d'Italia*, 1975: 58.

33. Federico, "Italy 1860–1940," 1996: 771–772; Zamagni, *The Economic History of Italy 1860–1990*, 1993: 89, 162.

34. Holt, *Risorgimento: The Making of Italy, 1815–1870*, 1970: 19–20; Lyttelton, "Landlords, Peasants and the Limits of Liberalism," 1979: 106–107.

35. Gentile, *Storia del Partito Fascista*, 1989: 80–81.

36. Anderson, *Lineages of the Absolutist State*, 1989: 66–67; Linz, "The Party System of Spain," 1967: 38.

37. Carr, *Modern Spain, 1875–1980*, 1982: 98–100; Payne, "Spain," in *The European Right: A Historical Profile*, 1965: 170–172.

38. Ibid.: 175.

39. Carr, *Modern Spain, 1875–1980*, 1982: 57.

40. Lannon, *Privilege, Persecution, and Prophecy*, 1987: 59.

41. Kern, *Liberals, Reformers and Caciques in Restoration Spain*, 1974: 16.

42. Riquer i Permanyer, "La faiblesse du procesus de construction nationale en Espagne aux xixe Siécle," 1994: 355.

43. Tortella Casares, *The Development of Modern Spain*, 2000: 51–56.

44. Conversi, *The Basques, the Catalans and Spain*, 1997: 20. For similar analyses, see Carr, *Modern Spain, 1875–1980*, 1982: 158; Kern, *Liberals, Reformers and Caciques in Restoration Spain*, 1974: 3.

45. Carr, *Modern Spain, 1875–1980*, 1982: 214–218.

46. Payne, *Politics and the Military in Modern Spain*, 1967: 25.

47. Ibid.: 14–15.

48. Simpson, *The Long Siesta*, 1995: 13–32; Tortella Casares, *The Development of Modern Spain*, 2000: 67.

49. Simpson, "Los límites de crecimiento agrario en España, 1860–1936," 1992: 108–109.

50. Tortella Casares, *The Development of Modern Spain*, 2000: 56; Trebilcock, *The Industrialization of the Continental Powers, 1780–1914*, 1981: 327–328.

51. Malefakis, *Agrarian Reform and Peasant Revolution in Spain*, 1970: 30.
These differences corresponded to stages of the Reconquista (the reconquest of the Iberian peninsula from Islam between the eleventh to the thirteenth centuries). Peasant warriors who then settled on small plots of land were the driving force behind the early Reconquista, which penetrated only slightly from the northern littoral of the Iberian peninsula on the Bay of Biscay. Malefakis, *Agrarian Reform and Peasant Revolution in Spain*, 1970: 51. A warrior nobility emerged at a later period and established, through conquest, large landed estates in southern Spain, in the process reducing much of the indigenous population to servitude. Ibid.: 60.

52. Heywood, *Marxism and the Failure of Organized Socialism in Spain*, 1990: 4; Malefakis, *Agrarian Reform and Peasant Revolution in Spain*, 1970: 89; Simpson, *The Long Siesta*, 1995: 44.

53. Malefakis, *Agrarian Reform and Peasant Revolution in Spain*, 1970: 107.

54. Simpson, *The Long Siesta*, 1995: 6.

55. Tortella Casares, *The Development of Modern Spain*, 2000: 76, 88, 98.

56. Harrison, "Big Business and the Failure of Right-Wing Catalan Nationalism, 1901–1918," 1976: 904; Tortella Casares, *The Development of Modern Spain*, 2000: 199.

57. The Lliga was a strong local success. From 1901 to 1917 the Catalan industrialists were the only dominant class in Spain able effectively to compete in clean elections. Although the party suffered a split in 1904 as a result of its move to the right, and was defeated twice by the radical republicans, it maintained an impressive organizational presence. With dues-paying membership, a board of directors, and planned electoral campaigns with publicity, it was the most modern political organization prior to the rise of the mass parties of the Second Republic discussed later in chapter 5. The party was eventually able to come to power locally in 1914 under an electoral alliance with the left Catalanists, and it dominated Catalan public life until the rise of Primo de Rivera in 1923. Balcells, *Catalan Nationalism*, 1996: 51–54, 65; Payne, "Catalan and Basque Nationalism," 1971: 25–26.

58. Bengoechea, *Organització patronal i conflictivitat social a Catalunya*, 1994: 24; Harrison, "Big Business and the Failure of Right-Wing Catalan Nationalism, 1901–1918," 1976: 906; Payne, "Catalan and Basque Nationalism," 1971: 25; Sellés i Quintana, *El foment del treball nacional 1914–1923*, 2000: 50.

59. Balcells, *Catalan Nationalism*, 1996: 21.

60. Bengoechea, *Organització patronal i conflictivitat social a Catalunya*, 1994: 26; Payne, "Catalan and Basque Nationalism," 1971: 21.

61. Chirot, *Social Change in a Peripheral Society*, 1976: 42.

62. Ibid.: 48.

63. Ibid.: 49.

64. Eidelberg, *The Great Rumanian Peasant Revolt of 1907*, 1974: 14–15; Nagy-Talavera, *The Green Shirts and the Others*, 1970: 15–16.

65. Mitrany, *The Land and the Peasant in Rumania*, 1930: 51–52.

66. Prior to World War I, Romania was comprised of the two principalities of Moldavia in the north and Wallachia in the south. As a result of the Versaille settlement, the country expanded massively, incorporating Transylvania, Bucovina, and Bessarabia.

67. Chirot, *Social Change in a Peripheral Society*, 1976: 16–17; Chirot and Ragin, "The Market, Tradition and Peasant Rebellion," 1975: 430.

68. Chirot, *Social Change in a Peripheral Society*, 1976: 38; Nagy-Talavera, *The Green Shirts and the Others*, 1970: 3–4.

69. Chirot, *Social Change in a Peripheral Society*, 1976: 42.

70. Chirot and Ragin, "The Market, Tradition and Peasant Rebellion," 1975: 430.

71. Chirot and Ragin, "The Market, Tradition and Peasant Rebellion," 1975: 430.

72. This explains why the high aristocracy rather than town dwellers were the main supporters of constitutional rule. Heinen, *Die Legion "Erzengel Michael" in Rumänien*, 1986: 61.

73. Nagy-Talavera, *The Green Shirts and the Others*, 1970: 13.

74. Chirot, *Social Change in a Peripheral Society*, 1976: 101–102; Heinen, *Die Legion "Erzengel Michael" in Rumänien*, 1986: 57; Mitrany, *The Land and the Peasant in Rumania*, 1930: 27–28; Roberts, *Rumania: Political Problems of an Agrarian State*, 1951: 9.

75. Chirot, *Social Change in a Peripheral Society*, 1976: 125, 132–133.

76. Roberts, *Rumania: Political Problems of an Agrarian State*, 1951: 15.

77. Rothschild, *East Central Europe between the Two World Wars*, 1974: 290.

78. Roberts, *Rumania: Political Problems of an Agrarian State*, 1951: 16.

79. Weber, "Romania," 1974: 508.

80. Heinen, *Die Legion "Erzengel Michael" in Rumänien*, 1986: 58.

81. Ibid.: 59; Roberts, *Rumania: Political Problems of an Agrarian State*, 1951: 3–4; Stokes, "The Social Origins of East European Politics," 1989: 233.

82. Rothschild, *East Central Europe between the Two World Wars*, 1974: 291.

83. Roberts, *Rumania: Political Problems of an Agrarian State*, 1951: 31–39.

84. Rothschild, *East Central Europe between the Two World Wars*, 1974: 290.

85. Roberts, *Rumania: Political Problems of an Agrarian State*, 1951: 39.

86. Ibid.: 52–53. According to Roberts the reform increased two categories of holdings: those under 3 hectares, which were economically unviable, and those between 5 and 20 hectares belonging to relatively well-off peasants. Ibid.: 52–53. The most important consequence of land reform, from the perspective of the argument developed here, is that it strengthened the peasantry. Peasant smallholders, rather than capitalist farmers, replaced the large landed estate. There is no evidence of the emergence of a class of middle tenants employing labor on capital-intensive farms. Indeed, the basic organization of agriculture seems to have remained unchanged. Peasants continued to farm their lands in scattered strips, even after they had achieved ownership. Ibid.: 62–63.

87. Heinen, *Die Legion "Erzengel Michael" in Rumänien*, 1986: 72; Patrascanu, *Sous trois dictatures*, 1946: 99; Roberts, *Rumania: Political Problems of an Agrarian State*, 1951: 52–53.

88. Janos, *The Politics of Backwardness in Hungary*, 1982: 5, 27.

89. Gunst, "Hungarian Agrarian Society from Emancipation (1850) to the End of World War I (1918)," 1998: 126.

90. Nagy-Talavera, *The Green Shirts and the Others*, 1970: 2; Szöllösi-Janze, *Die Pfeilkreuzlerbewegung in Ungarn*, 1989: 46.

91. Janos, *The Politics of Backwardness in Hungary*, 1982: 17–19.

92. Ibid.: 40–41; Janos, *East Central Europe in the Modern World*, 2000: 133.

93. Deák, "Hungary," 1966: 369; Gunst, "Hungarian Agrarian Society from Emancipation (1850) to the End of World War I (1918)," 1998: 131–134; Janos, *The Politics of Backwardness in Hungary*, 1982: 56.

94. Nagy-Talavera, *The Green Shirts and the Others*, 1970: 8.

95. Janos, *The Politics of Backwardness in Hungary*, 1982: 118–120.

96. Ibid.: 94, 107–108, 120.

97. Ibid.: 129–130.

98. Ibid.: 150.

99. Nagy-Talavera, *The Green Shirts and the Others*, 1970: 41.

100. Szöllösi-Janze, *Die Pfeilkreuzlerbewegung in Ungarn*, 1989: 65.

101. Stokes, "The Social Origins of East European Politics," 1989: 219.

102. Schandl, *Quarante Années de la Coopération Hongroise*, 1938: 12, 18–20.

103. Ibid.: 51–55.

104. Ibid.: 76.

105. Ibid.: 61.

106. Ibid.: 76–77.

107. Ibid.: 81.

108. Janos, *The Politics of Backwardness in Hungary*, 1982: 191–192.

109. Deák, "Hungary," 1966: 370; Janos, *The Politics of Backwardness in Hungary*, 1982: 197.

110. Carol II participated directly in the repression of the Hungarian Soviet Republic. Watts, *Romanian Cassandra*, 1993: 111.

111. Janos, *The Politics of Backwardness in Hungary*, 1982: 202; Szöllösi-Janze, *Die Pfeilkreuzlerbewegung in Ungarn*, 1989: 72–73.

112. Janos, *The Politics of Backwardness in Hungary*, 1982: 204; Nagy-Talavera, *The Green Shirts and the Others*, 1970: 50.

113. Janos, *The Politics of Backwardness in Hungary*, 1982: 212; Szöllösi-Janze, *Die Pfeilkreuzlerbewegung in Ungarn*, 1989: 80.

114. Janos, *The Politics of Backwardness in Hungary*, 1982: 212–213.

115. Szöllösi-Janze, *Die Pfeilkreuzlerbewegung in Ungarn*, 1989: 81.

116. Deák, "Hungary," 1966: 375.

117. Ibid.: 375; Janos, *The Politics of Backwardness in Hungary*, 1982: 234; Nagy-Talavera, *The Green Shirts and the Others*, 1970: 59; Szöllösi-Janze, *Die Pfeilkreuzlerbewegung in Ungarn*, 1989: 82.

118. Janos, *The Politics of Backwardness in Hungary*, 1982: 213–224.

119. Vago, *The Shadow of the Swastika*, 1975: 10.

120. Nagy-Talavera, *The Green Shirts and the Others*, 1970: 59.

121. Baktay, *Authoritarian Politics in a Transitional State*, 1982: 30–31.

122. Nagy-Talavera, *The Green Shirts and the Others*, 1970: 115–121.

123. Janos, *The Politics of Backwardness in Hungary*, 1982: 250.

124. Nagy-Talavera, *The Green Shirts and the Others*, 1970: 42, 50.

125. Szöllösi-Janze, *Die Pfeilkreuzlerbewegung in Ungarn*, 1989: 51.

126. Janos, *The Politics of Backwardness in Hungary*, 1982: 249.

127. Nagy-Talavera, *The Green Shirts and the Others*, 1970: 85.

128. Nagy-Talavera, *The Green Shirts and the Others*, 1970: 84.

129. Szöllösi-Janze, *Die Pfeilkreuzlerbewegung in Ungarn*, 1989: 90.

130. In every case of historical fascism the general secretary of the party and the "leader" were different people. Some have suggested that this is connected to the charismatic nature of fascist rule, which rejects institutional constraints on the leader's position. Dates for Marton's life are not available.

131. Nagy-Talavera, *The Green Shirts and the Others*, 1970: 94–95; Szöllösi-Janze, *Die Pfeilkreuzlerbewegung in Ungarn*, 1989: 91–94.

132. Deák, "Hungary," 1966: 385.

133. Nagy-Talavera, *The Green Shirts and the Others*, 1970: 108–109; Szöllösi-Janze, *Die Pfeilkreuzlerbewegung in Ungarn*, 1989: 107.

After leading a failed peasant uprising in 1936 Böszörmény fled to Nazi Germany. In 1945 he petitioned Mátyás Rákosi (1892–1971) to allow him to join the Communist Party.

134. Nagy-Talavera, *The Green Shirts and the Others*, 1970: 109.

135. Nagy-Talavera, *The Green Shirts and the Others*, 1970: 100.

136. Janos, *The Politics of Backwardness in Hungary*, 1982: 289–290.

137. Nagy-Talavera, *The Green Shirts and the Others*, 1970: 107.

138. Szöllösi-Janze, *Die Pfeilkreuzlerbewegung in Ungarn*, 1989: 107.

139. Nagy-Talavera, *The Green Shirts and the Others*, 1970: 115–116.

140. Szöllösi-Janze, *Die Pfeilkreuzlerbewegung in Ungarn*, 1989: 128.

141. Ibid.: 131–132.

142. Nagy-Talavera, *The Green Shirts and the Others*, 1970: 127.

143. Deák, "Hungary," 1966: 388.

144. Janos, *The Politics of Backwardness in Hungary*, 1982: 291.

145. Ibid.: 292.

146. Nagy-Talavera, *The Green Shirts and the Others*, 1970: 150.

147. Szöllösi-Janze, *Die Pfeilkreuzlerbewegung in Ungarn*, 1989: 65.

148. Eley, "The British Model and the German Road," 1989: 40.

149. Blackbourn, *The Long Nineteenth Century*, 1998: 154; Calleo, *The German Problem Reconsidered*, 1978: 60–66; Wehler, *The German Empire, 1871–1918*, 1985: 64.

150. Blackbourn, "The Discreet Charm of the Bourgeoisie," 1989: 243, 254; Neumann, *Behemoth: The Structure and Practice of National Socialism, 1933–1944*, 1966: 4; Wehler, *The German Empire, 1871–1918*, 1985: 52–55, 65–66, 80, 148.

151. Blackbourn, "The Discreet Charm of the Bourgeoisie," 1989: 256–257, 275; Eley, "The British Model and the German Road," 1989: 151.

Indeed, Eley argues that, compared to Spain or Italy, the German parliament was "refreshingly free of clientalism and caciquismo." Eley, "The British Model and the German Road," 1989: 151.

152. Blackbourn, "The Discreet Charm of the Bourgeoisie," 1989: 244.

153. Ibid.: 245.

154. Ibid.: 185.

155. Wehler, *The German Empire, 1871–1918*, 1985: 11.

156. Germany was, in the words of Geoff Eley "the most dynamic capitalism in late-nineteenth and early twentieth century Europe." Eley, "The British Model and the German Road," 1989: 138.

157. Blackbourn, "The Discreet Charm of the Bourgeoisie," 1989: 178–179; Eley, "The British Model and the German Road," 1989: 138; Mann, *Fascists*, 2004.

158. Blackbourn, "The Discreet Charm of the Bourgeoisie," 1989: 182, 233.

159. Calleo, *The German Problem Reconsidered*, 1978: 67; Wehler, *The German Empire, 1871–1918*, 1985: 44.

160. Neumann, *Behemoth: The Structure and Practice of National Socialism, 1933–1944*, 1966: 6.

161. Calleo, *The German Problem Reconsidered*, 1978: 67–68, 81; Neumann, *Behemoth: The Structure and Practice of National Socialism, 1933–1944*, 1966: 6, 209; Wehler, *The German Empire, 1871–1918*, 1985: 44–46.

162. Blackbourn summarizes the relationship between the two wings of the social elite in a characteristically judicious manner: "The new elite that was formed in Germany in the nineteenth century especially in the last decades, continued to have a powerful aristocratic component, as in England and elsewhere. But the bourgeoisie, which constituted the growing part of this elite, did not simply succumb to the aristocratic embrace." Blackbourn, "The Discreet Charm of the Bourgeoisie," 1989: 233.

163. Moore, *Social Origins of Dictatorship and Democracy*, 1993: 436–437.

164. "Alongside its own troops, the army was able to keep a grip on at least 5 million Germans before 1914, i.e., a sixth of all adult males and youths," writes Wehler. Wehler, *The German Empire, 1871–1918*, 1985: 163.

165. Koshar, *Social Life, Local Politics, and Nazism*, 1986: 95–96, 142; Wehler, *The German Empire, 1871–1918*, 1985: 163.

166. Blackbourn, "The Discreet Charm of the Bourgeoisie," 1989: 195, 225.

167. Guttsman, *The German Social Democratic Party*, 1981: 80; Wehler, *The German Empire, 1871–1918*, 1985: 73–83.

168. Eley, "The British Model and the German Road," 1989: 122.

169. Wehler, *The German Empire, 1871–1918*, 1985: 86–89.

170. Maier, *Recasting Bourgeois Europe*, 1975: 57; Neumann, *Behemoth: The Structure and Practice of National Socialism, 1933–1944*, 1966: 12–13.

171. Neumann, *Behemoth: The Structure and Practice of National Socialism, 1933–1944*, 1966: 12.

172. Ibid.: 10.

173. Berman, "Civil Society and the Collapse of the Weimar Republic," 1997: 414.

174. Koshar, *Social Life, Local Politics, and Nazism*, 1986: 151.

175. Carsten, *The Rise of Fascism*, 1982: 39.

176. Ibid.: 115.

177. Broszat, *The Hitler State*, 1981: 20.

178. De Felice, *Mussolini il fascista. La conquista del potere 1921–1925*, 1995 [1966]: 115–117.

179. Berman, "Civil Society and the Collapse of the Weimar Republic," 1997: 418.

180. Ibid.: 422.

181. Hagtvet, "The Theory of Mass Society and the Collapse of the Weimar Republic," 1980: 91.

182. Ibid.: 87.

183. Winkler, *Weimar 1918–1933*, 1993: 390.

184. Broszat, *The Hitler State*, 1981: 141.

185. Ibid.: 141.

186. Ibid.: 170.

187. Ibid.: 36.

CHAPTER SIX: Rethinking Civil Society and Fascism

1. Banti, *Storia della borghesia italiana*, 1996: 52–53; Ragionieri, *Storia d'Italia*, 1976: 44–53; Seton-Watson, *Italy from Liberalism to Fascism, 1870–1925*, 1967: 26, 49.

2. Riquer i Permanyer, "La faiblesse du procesus de construction nationale en Espagne aux XIXe Siécle," 1994: 358.

3. Chirot, *Social Change in a Peripheral Society*, 1976: 105.

4. Farneti, *Sistema politico e società civile*, 1971: 228; Ragionieri, *Storia d'Italia*, 1976: 26–27.

5. Boyd, *Praetorian Politics in Liberal Spain*, 1979: 4; Carr, *Modern Spain, 1875–1980*, 1982: 356–357; Gómez-Navarro, *El Régimen de Primo de Rivera*, 1991: 60; Lyttelton, "El patronazgo en la Italia de Giolitti (1892–1924)," 1973: 98; Payne, *Politics and the Military in Modern Spain*, 1967: 44–45; Payne, *A History of Spain and Portugal in Two Volumes*, 1973: 495; Tusell, "The Functioning of the Cacique System in Andalusia," 1976a: 14; Tusell, *Oligarquia y caciquismo en Andalucia (1890–1923)*, 1976b: 510; Tusell, *Manual de historia de España*, 1990: 32.

6. Heinen, *Die Legion "Erzengel Michael" in Rumänien*, 1986: 64; Janos, "Modernization and Decay in Historical Perspective," 1978: 85–86; Seton-Watson, *A History of the Roumanians*, 1963: 357.

7. Trotsky, *The Balkan Wars, 1912–1913*, 1991: 378.

8. Ciuffoletti, "Dirigenti e ideologie del movimento cooperativo," 1981: 146.

9. Cuenca Toribio, *Catolicismo social y politico en la España contemporánea (1870–2000)*, 2003: 45; Garrido Herrero, *Treballar en comú*, 1996: 69, 75.

10. Digby, "Rumania: The State as Co-Operator," 1930: 412–414; Mitrany, *The Land and the Peasant in Rumania*, 1930: 398.

11. In his preprison essay *The Southern Question*, Gramsci analyzes the Giolittian period as follows: "In the new century the dominant class inaugurated a new politics of class alliances, of political class blocs, that is, bourgeois democracy. It had to choose: or rural democracy, that is, an alliance with southern peasants, a policy of tariff freedom, of universal suffrage, of administrative decentralization, of low prices for industrial goods, or an industrial capitalist-worker bloc, without universal suffrage, for tariff protectionism, for the maintenance of state centralization ... for a reformist policy of salaries and union freedom. It chose, not by chance, this second solution. Giolitti impersonated bourgeois domination, the Socialist Party became the instrument of Giolittian policy." Gramsci, *La Questione Meridionale*, 1974: 146. The only distortion in this otherwise illuminating analysis is that Gramsci downplays the significance of the northern peasantry. As I have shown in chapter 2, this was a central constituency of Italian socialism.

12. Carr, *Modern Spain, 1875–1980*, 1982: 489–497; Esdaile, *Spain in the Liberal Age*, 2000: 207; Serrano, *Alfonso XIII y la crisis de la restauración*, 1969: 59–75; Tusell, "The Functioning of the Cacique System in Andalusia," 1976a: 7; Tusell, *Oligarquia y caciquismo en Andalucia (1890–1923)*, 1976b: 544; Tusell, *Manual de historia de España*, 1990: 55, 63, 94–98.

13. Roberts, *Rumania: Political Problems of an Agrarian State*, 1951: 94–95.

14. Bottai, *Esperienza Corporativa*, 1928: 40–41; Gini, "The Scientific Basis of Fascism," 1927; Roberts, *The Syndicalist Tradition and Italian Fascism*, 1979: 72–73.

15. Gregor, *Mussolini's Intellectuals*, 2005: 79.

16. Bottai, *Esperienza Corporativa*, 1928: 40–41.

17. Pellizzi, *Una rivoluzione mancata*, 1949: 231–232.

18. Gramsci, *Selections from the Prison Notebook*, 1971: 210.

19. Holt, *Risorgimento: The Making of Italy, 1815–1870*, 1970: 19–20; Lyttelton, "Landlords, Peasants and the Limits of Liberalism," 1979: 106–107.

20. Bengoechea, *Organització patronal i conflictivitat social a Catalunya*, 1994: 26; Payne, "Catalan and Basque Nationalism," 1971: 21.

21. Heinen, *Die Legion "Erzengel Michael" in Rumänien*, 1986: 72; Patrascanu, *Sous trois dictatures*, 1946: 99; Roberts, *Rumania: Political Problems of an Agrarian State*, 1951: 52–53.

22. Banti, *Storia della borghesia italiana*, 1996: 7, 11; Lyttelton, *The Seizure of Power*, 2004: 5.

23. Carr, *Modern Spain, 1875–1980*, 1982: 98–100; Payne, "Spain," in *The European Right: A Historical Profile*, 1965: 170–172.

24. Eidelberg, *The Great Rumanian Peasant Revolt of 1907*, 1974: 14–15; Nagy-Talavera, *The Green Shirts and the Others*, 1970: 15–16.

25. Armony, *The Dubious Link*, 2004; Berman, "Civil Society and the Collapse of the Weimar Republic," 1997; Hagtvet, "The Theory of Mass Society and the Collapse of the Weimar Republic," 1980; Kaufman, *For the Common Good? American Civic Life and the Golden Age of Fraternity*, 2002.

26. Armony, *The Dubious Link*, 2004; Berman, "Civil Society and the Collapse of the Weimar Republic," 1997; Riley, "Civic Associations and Authoritarian Regimes in Interwar Europe," 2005.

27. Ridolfi, *Il PSI e la nascita del partito di massa*, 1992: 33.

28. Tocqueville, *Democracy in America*, 1988: 522; Villa, "Tocqueville and Civil Society," 2006: 224–225.

29. Tocqueville, *Democracy in America*, 1988: 515–516.
Tocqueville explains the role of associationism in a democracy as follows: "The tasks of government [in a democracy] must therefore perpetually increase, and its efforts to cope with them must spread its net ever wider. The more government takes the place of associations, the more will individuals lose the idea of forming associations and need the government to come to their help. That is a vicious circle of cause and effect." Associations relieve the government of certain tasks and thereby protect liberty. Ibid.: 515–516.

30. De Ruggiero, *The History of European Liberalism*, 1959: 20; Habermas, *The Social Structural Transformation of the Public Sphere*, 1989: 129–140; Schmitt, *The Crisis of Parliamentary Democracy*, 1985: 40–41.

31. Bobbio, *Il futuro della democrazia*, 1991: 37.

32. Mosca, *La classe politica*, 1994: 69–70.

33. Tocqueville, *Democracy in America*, 1988: 12.

34. Aron, *Démocratie et totaliterisme*, 1965: 57.

35. Gramsci, *Selections from the Prison Notebook*, 1971: 57; Schmitt, *The Concept of the Political*, 1996: 27.

36. Lukács, *History and Class Consciousness*, 1971: 51; Marcuse, *One-Dimensional Man*, 1964: 49.

37. Gramsci, *Selections from the Prison Notebook*, 1971: 60.

38. Laclau and Mouffe, *Hegemony and Socialist Strategy*, 2001: 136.

39. Lipset, "Some Social Requisites of Democracy," 1959.

40. Gramsci, *Selections from the Prison Notebook*, 1971: 140.

41. Gentile, *Il mito dello stato nuovo*, 1982: 58.

Bibliography

Manuscript Sources

Archivio Centrale dello Stato (ACS); Ministero dell'Interno (MI); Direzione generale pubblica sicurezza (DGPS).

————. Archivi fascisti (AF); Partito Nazionale Fascista (PNF); Direttorio nazionale (DN); Servizi (S); Series I–II.

————. Archivi fascisti (AF); Partito Nazionale Fascista (PNF); Direttorio nazionale (DN); Segreteria Politica (SP); Situazione politica ed economica nelle provincie (SPEP).

Published Sources

Abbate, Michele. 1966. *La filosofia di Benedetto Croce e la crisi della società italiana.* Turin: Einaudi.

Adamson, Walter L. 1980. "Gramsci's Interpretation of Fascism." *Journal of the History of Ideas* 41: 615–633.

————. 1993. *Avant-Garde Florence: From Modernism to Fascism.* Cambridge: Harvard University Press.

Adler, Frank. 1995. *Italian Industrialists from Liberalism to Fascism.* Cambridge: Cambridge University Press.

Ammirato, Piero. 1996. *La Lega: The Making of a Successful Cooperative Network.* Aldershot: Dartmouth.

Anderson, Perry. 1965. "Problems of Socialist Strategy." Pp. 221–290 in *Towards Socialism.* Ithaca, N.Y.: Cornell University Press.

————. 1976–1977. "The Antinomies of Antonio Gramsci." *New Left Review* 100: 5–78

————. 1989. *Lineages of the Absolutist State.* London: Verso.

Aparicio, Miguel Angel. 1979. *El sindicalismo vertical y la formación del estado Franquista.* Barcelona: Eunibar.

Aquarone, Alberto. 1987. *Tre capitoli sull'Italia giolittiana.* Bologna: Il Mulino.

———. 1995. *L'organizzazione dello stato totalitario.* Turin: Einaudi.

Arato, Andrew. 1981. "Civil Society against the State: Poland 1980–81." *Telos* 47: 23–47.

Arendt, Hannah. 1958. *The Human Condition.* Chicago: University of Chicago Press.

———. 1966. *The Origins of Totalitarianism.* Cleveland: World Publishing Co.

Armony, Ariel C. 2004. *The Dubious Link: Civic Engagement and Democratization.* Stanford: Stanford University Press.

Aron, Raymond. 1965. *Démocratie et totaliterisme.* Paris: Gallimard.

Art, David. 2012. "Review: What Do We Know About Authoritarianism After Ten Years?" *Comparative Politics* 44 (3): 351–373.

Baktay, William M. 1982. *Authoritarian Politics in a Transitional State: Istvan Bethlen and the Unified Party in Hungary, 1919–1926.* New York: Columbia University Press.

Balakrishnan, Gopal. 2000. *The Enemy: An Intellectual Portrait of Carl Schmitt.* London: Verso.

Balcells, Albert. 1996. *Catalan Nationalism: Past and Present.* New York: St. Martin's Press.

Balfour, Sebastian. 1995. "Riot, Regeneration and Reaction: Spain in the Aftermath of the 1898 Disaster." *Historical Journal* 38 (2): 405–423.

Banti, Alberto. 1996. *Storia della borghesia italiana: L'età liberale.* Rome: Donzelli.

Barbagli, Maurizio. 1982. *Educating for Unemployment: Politics, Labor Markets, and the School System—Italy, 1859–1973.* New York: Columbia University Press.

Baro, Albert Perez. 1974. *Historia de la cooperacion catalana.* Barcelona: Canalejas.

Bastarreche, Fernando Fernández. 1988. "The Spanish Military from the Age of Disasters to the Civil War." Pp. 213–247 in *Armed Forces and Society in Spain Past and Present.* Edited by Rafael Bañon Martínez and Thomas M. Barker. New York: Columbia University Press.

Bauer, Franz J. 2005. "Wie 'bürgerlich' war der Nationalstaat in Deutschland und Italien?" Pp. 107–120 in *Deutschland und Italien 1860–1960. Politische und kulturelle Aspekte im Vergleich.* Edited by Christof Dipper and Elisabet Müller-Luckner. Munich: R. Oldenbourg Verlag.

Beer, Klaus P. 1983. *Zur Entwicklung des Parteien- und Parlamentsystems in Rumänien 1928–1933. Die Zeit der national-bäuerlichen Regierungen. Band 1.* Frankfurt am Main: Peter Lang.

Beetham, David. 1983. "Introduction." Pp. 1–62 in *Marxists in Face of Fascism from the Inter-War Period.* Edited by David Beetham. Manchester: Manchester University Press.

Ben-Ami, Shlomo. 1978. *The Origins of the Second Republic in Spain.* Oxford: Oxford University Press.

———. 1983. *Fascism from Above: The Dictatorship of Primo de Rivera in Spain, 1923–1930.* Oxford: Clarendon Press.

Bendix, Reinhard. 1952. "Social Stratification and Political Power." *American Political Science Review* 46: 357–375.

———. 1978. *Kings or People: Power and the Mandate to Rule.* Berkeley: University of California Press.

Bengoechea, Soledad. 1994. *Organització patronal i conflictivitat social a Catalunya.* Barcelona: Publicacions de l'Abadia de Montserrat.

Berezin, Mabel. 1997. *Making the Fascist Self: The Political Culture of Interwar Italy*. Ithaca: Cornell University Press.

Berman, Sheri. 1997. "Civil Society and the Collapse of the Weimar Republic." *World Politics* 49: 401–429.

Blackbourn, David. 1989. "The Discreet Charm of the Bourgeoisie: Reappraising German History in the Nineteenth Century." Pp. 159–292 in *The Peculiarities of German History: Bourgeois Society and Politics in Nineteenth-Century Germany*. New York: Oxford University Press.

———. 1998. *The Long Nineteenth Century: A History of Germany, 1780–1918*. New York: Oxford University Press.

Blinkhorn, Martin. 1975. *Carlism and Crisis in Spain: 1931–1939*. London: Cambridge University Press.

Bobbio, Norberto. 1969. "Gramsci e la concezione della società civile." Pp. 75–100 in *Gramsci e la cultura contemporanea. Atti del Convegno internazionale di studi gramsciani tenuto a Cagliari il 23–27 aprile 1967*. Edited by Pietro Rossi. Rome: Editori riuniti; Istituto Gramsci.

———. 1991. *Il futuro della democrazia*. Turin: Einaudi.

———. 1999. *Teoria generale della politica*. Turin: Einaudi.

Bonfante, Guido. 1981. "La legislazione cooperativistica in Italia dall'Unità a oggi." Pp. 191–252 in *Il movimento cooperativo in Italia. Storia e problemi*. Edited by Giulio Sapelli. Turin: Einaudi.

Bosworth, R. J. B. 1979. *Italy, the Least of the Great Powers: Italian Foreign Policy before the First World War*. New York: Cambridge University Press.

Bottai, Giuseppe. 1928. *Esperienza Corporativa*. Florence: Vallecchi.

———. 1990. "Prima seduta." Pp. 90–98 in *Il convegno italo-francese di studi corporativi 1935*. Rome: Fondazione Ugo Spirito.

Boyd, Carolyn P. 1979. *Praetorian Politics in Liberal Spain*. Chapel Hill: University of North Carolina Press.

Brenan, Gerald. 2000. *The Spanish Labyrinth: The Social and Political Background of the Spanish Civil War*. Cambridge: Cambridge University Press.

Brenner, Robert. 2002. "Agrarian Class Structure and Economic Development." Pp. 10–63. in *The Brenner Debate: Agrarian Class Structure and Economic Development in Pre-Industrial Europe*. Edited by T. H. Aston and C. H. E. Philpin.

Broszat, Martin. 1981. *The Hitler State*. New York: Longman.

Buozzi, Bruno. 1930. *Fascisme et syndicalisme*. Paris: Librairie Valois.

Burawoy, Michael. 1990. "Marxism as Science: Historical Challenges and Theoretical Growth." *American Sociological Review* 55 (6): 775–793.

———. 2003. "For a Sociological Marxism: The Complementary Convergence of Antonio Gramsci and Karl Polanyi." *Politics and Society* 31: 193–261.

Callahan, William J. 2000. *The Catholic Church in Spain, 1875–1998*. Washington, D.C.: Catholic University of America Press.

Calleo, David P. 1978. *The German Problem Reconsidered: Germany and the World Order*. New York: Cambridge University Press.

Cammett, John M. 1967. *Antonio Gramsci and the Origins of Italian Communism*. Stanford: Stanford University Press.

Canfora, Luciano. 2006. *Democracy in Europe: A History of an Ideology*. London: Blackwell.

Carocci, Giampiero. 1971. *Giolitti e l'età giolittiana*. Turin: Einaudi.

Carr, Raymond. 1982. *Modern Spain, 1875–1980*. New York: Oxford University Press.

Carsten, Francis Ludwig. 1982. *The Rise of Fascism*. Berkeley: University of California Press.

Casas de la Vega, Rafael. 1974. *Las milicias nacionales en la guerra de España*. Madrid: Editora Nacional.

Castillo, Juan José. 1979. *Propietarios muy pobres: sobre la subordinacion politica delpequeño campesino en España: La Confederación Nacional Católico-Agraria, 1917–1942*. Madrid: Servicio di Publicaciones Agrarias.

Castronovo, Valerio. 1975. *La storia economica. Storia d'Italia*. Vol. 4, *dall'Unità a oggi*. Turin: Einaudi.

Chabod, Federico. 1961. *L'Italia contemporanea (1918–1948)*. Turin: Einaudi.

Chirot, Daniel. 1976. *Social Change in a Peripheral Society: The Creation of a Balkan Colony*. New York: Academic Press.

Chirot, Daniel, and Charles Ragin. 1975. "The Market, Tradition and Peasant Rebellion: The Case of Romania in 1907." *American Sociological Review* 40: 428–444.

Chiurco, Giorgio Alberto. 1929. *Storia della rivoluzione fascista*. Vol. 1, *Anno 1919*. Florence: Vallecchi.

Chueca, Ricardo. 1983. *El Fascismo en los Comienzos del Regimen de Franco: Un estudio sobre FET-JONS*. Madrid: Centro de Investigaciones Sociologicas.

Ciuffoletti, Zeffiro. 1981. "Dirigenti e ideologie del movimento cooperativo." Pp. 89–189 in *Il movimento cooperativo in Italia*. Edited by Giulio Sapelli. Turin: Einaudi.

———. 1992. *Storia del PSI. 1. Le origini e l'età giolittiana*. Rome-Bari: Laterza.

Codreanu, Corneliu Zelea. 1990. *For My Legionaries (The Iron Guard)*. Reedy, W.Va.: Liberty Bell Publications.

Coffey, Diarmid. 1922. *The Cooperative Movement in Jugoslavia, Rumania and North Italy: During and after the War*. New York: Oxford University Press.

Cohen, J. L., and A. Arato. 1992. *Civil Society and Political Theory*. Cambridge: MIT Press.

Colarizi, Simona. 1977. *Dopoguerra e fascismo in Puglia (1919–1926)*. Bari: Laterza.

Conversi, Daniele. 1997. *The Basques, the Catalans and Spain: Alternative Routes to Nationalist Mobilization*. London: Hurst & Company.

Cordova, Ferdinando. 1974. *Le origini dei sindacati fascisti: 1918–1926*. Rome: Laterza.

Corner, Paul. 1975. *Fascism in Ferrara: 1915–1925*. Oxford: Oxford University Press.

Coutinho, Carlos Nelson. 2006. *Il pensiero politico di Gramsci*. Milan: Edizioni Unicopoli.

Covino, Renato. 1989. "Dall'Umbria verde all'Umbria rossa." Pp. 507–605 in *Storia d'Italia. Le regioni dall'Unità a oggi. L'Umbria*. Edited by Renato Covino and Giampaolo Gallo. Turin: Einaudi.

Cuenca Toribio, José Manuel. 2003. *Catolicismo social y politico en la España contemporánea (1870–2000)*. Madrid: Union Editorial.

Davis, John A. 1979. "The South, the Risorgimento and the Origins of the 'Southern Problem.'" Pp. 67–103 in *Gramsci and Italy's Passive Revolution*. New York: Barnes & Noble.

Deák, István. 1966. "Hungary." Pp. 364–407 in *The European Right: A Historical Profile*. Edited by Hans Rogger and Eugen Weber. Berkeley: University of California Press.

De Felice, Renzo. 1968. "L'interventismo rivoluzionario." Pp. 273–291 in *Il trauma dell'intervento: 1914/1919*. Florence: Vallecchi.

———. 1995 [1965]. *Mussolini il rivoluzionario 1883–1920*. Turin: Einaudi.

———. 1995 [1966]. *Mussolini il fascista. La conquista del potere 1921–1925*. Turin: Einaudi.

——. 1995 [1968]. *Mussolini il fascista. L'organizzazione dello Stato fascista 1925–1929.* Turin: Einaudi.

——. 1996 [1974]. *Mussolini il duce. Gli anni del consenso 1929–1936.* Turin: Einaudi.

——. 2000. *Le interpretazioni del fascisimo.* Rome: Laterza.

Degl'Innocenti, Maurizio. 1977. *Storia della cooperazione in Italia. La Lega nazionale delle cooperative 1886–1925.* Rome: Editori Riuniti.

——. 1981. "Geografia e strutture della cooperazione in Italia." Pp. 3–87. *Il movimento cooperativo in Italia.* Turin: Einaudi.

——. 1995. *La società unificata. Associazione, sindacato, partito sotto il fascismo.* Rome: Manduria.

De Grazia, Victoria. 1981. *The Culture of Consent: The Mass Organization of Leisure in Fascist Italy.* Cambridge: Cambridge University Press.

Delle Piane, Mario. 1952. *Gaetano Mosca: Classe Politica e Liberalismo.* Naples: Edizioni scientifiche italiane.

Del Rey Reguillo, Fernando. 1987. "Ciudadanos honrados y somentistas. El orden y la subversión en la España de los años veinte." *Estudios de Historia Social* 3–4: 97–150.

De Ruggiero, Guido. 1959. *The History of European Liberalism.* Boston: Beacon Hill.

Diamond, Larry. 1997. "Civil Society and the Development of Democracy." *Center for Advanced Study in the Social Sciences of the Juan March Institute Working Paper 101.*

Diehl-Thiele, Peter. 1969. *Partei und Staat im Dritten Reich: Untersuchungen zum Verhältnis von NSDAP und allgemeiner innerer Staatsverwaltung 1933–1945.* Munich: C. H. Beck.

Digby, Margaret. 1930. "Rumania: The State as Co-Operator." Pp. 404–428 in *Year Book of Agricultural Co-operation 1930.* Edited by the Horace Plunkett Foundation. London: George Routledge & Sons.

Dovring, Folke. 1965. *Land and Labor in Europe in the Twentieth Century: A Comparative Survey of Recent Agrarian History.* The Hague: M. Nijhoff.

Downing, Brian. 1992. *The Military Revolution and Political Change: Origins of Democracy and Autocracy in Early Modern Europe.* Princeton: Princeton University Press.

Eidelberg, Philip Gabriel. 1974. *The Great Rumanian Peasant Revolt of 1907: Origins of a Modern Jacquerie.* Leiden: E. J. Brill.

Elazar, Dahlia Sabina. 1993. "The Making of Italian Fascism: The Seizure of Power, 1919–1922." *Political Power and Social* Theory 8: 173–217.

Eley, Geoff. 1989. "The British Model and the German Road: Rethinking the Course of German History before 1914." Pp. 39–155 in *The Peculiarities of German History.* Oxford: Oxford University Press.

Elster, Jon. 1978. *Logic and Society: Contradictions and Possible Worlds.* New York: Wiley.

Emigh, Rebecca Jean. 1997. "The Power of Negative Thinking: The Use of Negative Case Methodology in the Development of Sociological Theory." *Theory and Society* 26 (5): 649–684.

——. 2009. *The Undevelopment of Capitalism: Sectors and Markets in Fifteenth-century Tuscany.* Philadelphia: Temple University Press.

Ertman, Thomas. 1997. *The Birth of the Leviathan.* Cambridge: Cambridge University Press.

——. 1998. "Democracy and Dictatorship in Interwar Western Europe Revisited." *World Politics* 50: 475–505.

Esdaile, Charles J. 2000. *Spain in the Liberal Age.* London: Blackwell.

Fabbri, Lia Gheza. 1977. "Crescita e natura delle casse rurali cattoliche." *Quaderni Storici* 36: 789–807.

Falasca-Zamponi, Simonetta. 1997. *The Aesthetics of Power in Mussolini's Italy*. Berkeley: University of California Press.

Farneti, Paolo. 1971. *Sistema politico e società civile: saggi di teoria e ricerca politica*. Turin: Giappichelli.

Federico, Giovanni. 1996. "Italy 1860–1940: A Little Known Success Story." *Economic History Review* 49: 764–786.

Finchelstein, Federico. 2008. "On Fascist Ideology." *Constellations* 15 (3).

Fiorina, Morris P. 1999. "Extreme Voices: A Dark Side of Civic Engagement." Pp. 395–525 in *Civic Engagement in American Democracy*. Washington, D.C.: Russell Sage Foundation.

Fornasari, Massimo, and Vera Zamagni. 1997. *Il movimento cooperativo in Italia. Un profilo storico-economico (1854–1992)*. Florence: Vallecchi.

Friedrich, Carl J. 1964. "The Unique Character of Totalitarian Society." Pp. 47–60 in *Totalitarianism*. Edited by Carl J. Friedrich. New York: Grosset & Dunlap.

Fritzsche, Peter. 1996. "Did Weimar Fail?" *Journal of Modern History* 68: 629–656.

Gaeta, Franco. 1982. *La crisi di fine secolo e l'età giolittiana*. Turin: UTET.

Galasso, Giuseppe. 1987. "Gli anni della grande espansione e la crisi del sistema." Pp. 219–494 in *Storia del movimento cooperativo in Italia. La Lega Nazionale delle Cooperative e Mutue. 1886–1986*. Turin: Einaudi.

Gallie, W. B. 1956. "Essentially Contested Concepts." *Proceedings of the Aristotelian Society* 56: 167–198.

Garrido Herrero, Samuel. 1995. "El cooperativismo agrario Español del primer tercio del siglo xx." *Revista de Historia Economica*. 1: 115–144.

———. 1996. *Treballar en comú: el cooperativism agrari a Espanya (1900–1936)*. Barcelona: Edicions Afons el Magnanim.

———. 2003. "El primer cooperativismo agrario español." *Ciriec-España. Revista de Economía Pública, Social y Cooperativa* 44: 33–56.

Gellner, Ernst. 1994. *Conditions of Liberty: Civil Society and Its Rivals*. London: Penguin.

———. 1995. "The Importance of Being Modular." Pp. 32–55 in *Civil Society: Theory, History, Comparison*. Oxford: Polity Press.

Gentile, Emilio. 1975. *Le origini del ideologia fascista (1918–1925)*. Rome: Laterza.

———. 1982. *Il mito dello stato nuovo: dall'antigiolittismo al fascismo*. Bari: Laterza.

———. 1984. "The Problem of the Party in Italian Fascism." *Journal of Contemporary History* 19: 251–274.

———. 1989. *Storia del Partito Fascista: 1919–1922, movimento e milizia*. Bari: Laterza.

———. 1995. *La via italiana al totalitarismo: il partito e lo stato nel regime fascista*. Rome: La Nuova Italia scientifica.

———. 2000. *Fascismo e antifascismo. I partiti italiani fra le due guerre*. Florence: Le Monnier.

———. 2002. *Fascismo: storia e interpretazione*. Rome: Laterza.

Gentile, Giovanni. 2002. *Origins and Doctrine of Fascism*. New Brunswick, N.J.: Transaction Publishers.

Germino, Dante L. 1959. *The Italian Fascist Party in Power: A Study in Totalitarian Rule*. Minneapolis: University of Minnesota Press.

Gide, Charles. 1926–1927. *La Coopération dans les Pays Latins: Amérique Latine, Italie, Espagne, Roumanie*. Paris: Association pour l'enseignment de la cooperation.

Gini, Corrado. 1927. "The Scientific Basis of Fascism." *Political Science Quarterly* 42: 99–115.

Ginsborg, Paul. 1979. "Gramsci in the Era of Bourgeois Revolution in Italy." Pp. 31–66 in *Gramsci and Italy's Passive Revolution*. Edited by John A. Davis. New York: Barnes & Noble.

Gleason, Abbott. 1995. *Totalitarianism: The Inner History of the Cold War*. New York: Oxford University Press.

Goldstone, Jack A. 2003. "The Study of Revolutions." Pp. 41–90 in *Comparative Historical Analysis in the Social Sciences*. Edited by James Mahoney and Dietrich Rueschemeyer. Cambridge: Cambridge University Press.

Gómez-Navarro, José Luis. 1991. *El Régimen de Primo de Rivera: Reyes, dictaduras y dictadores*. Madrid: Catedra.

González Calleja, Eduardo, and Fernando Del Rey Reguillo. 1995. *La defensa armada contra la revolución. Una historia del guardias cívicas en la España del siglo XX*. Madrid: Consejo Superior de Investigaciones Científicas.

González Cuevas, Pedro Carlos. 1998. *Acción Española: teología politica y nacionalismo autoritario en España, 1913–1936*. Madrid: Tecnos.

Gramsci, Antonio. 1971. *Selections from the Prison Notebook*. New York: International Publishers.

———. 1974. *La Questione Meridionale*. Rome: Riuniti.

Gregor, James A. 1969. *The Ideology of Fascism: The Rationale of Totalitarianism*. New York: Free Press.

———. 2005. *Mussolini's Intellectuals*. Princeton: Princeton University Press.

Griffin, Roger. 2002. "The Palingenetic Political Community: Rethinking the Legitimation of Totalitarian Regimes in Inter-War Europe." *Totalitarian Movements and Political Religions* 3 (3).

Gunst, Péter. 1998. "Hungarian Agrarian Society from Emancipation (1850) to the End of World War I (1918)." Pp. 125–175 in *Hungarian Agrarian Society from the Emancipation of the Serfs (1848) to the Re-privatization of Land (1998)*. Edited by Péter Gunst. New York: Eastern European Monographs.

Guttsman, W. L. 1981. *The German Social Democratic Party*. Boston: Allen & Unwin.

Habermas, Juergen. 1989. *The Social Structural Transformation of the Public Sphere: An Inquiry into a Category of Bourgeois Society*. London: Polity Press.

Hagtvet, Bernt. 1980. "The Theory of Mass Society and the Collapse of the Weimar Republic: A Re-Examination." Pp 66–117 in *Who Were the Fascists: Social Roots of European Fascism*. Edited by Stein Ugelvik Larsen, Bernt Hagtvet, and Jan Pettery Myklebust. Oslo: Universitetsforlaget.

Hall, John A. 1995. "In Search of Civil Society." Pp. 1–31 in *Civil Society: Theory, History, Comparison*. Edited by J. A. Hall. Oxford: Polity Press.

Harrison, Joseph. 1976. "Big Business and the Failure of Right-Wing Catalan Nationalism, 1901–1918." *Historical Journal* 19 (4): 901–918.

Hegel, Georg Wilhelm Friedrich. 1991. *Elements of the Philosophy of Right*. New York: Cambridge University Press.

Heinen, Armin. 1986. *Die Legion "Erzengel Michael" in Rumänien. Soziale Bewegung und politische Organisation. Ein Beitrag zum Problem des internationalen Faschismus.* Munich: R. Oldenbourg Verlag.

Heywood, Paul. 1990. *Marxism and the Failure of Organized Socialism in Spain, 1879–1936.* New York: Cambridge University Press.

Hibbeln, Ewald. 1984. *Codreanu und die Eiserne Garde.* Marburg: Erich Mauersberger.

Hintze, Otto. 1985. *The Historical Essays of Otto Hintze.* Oxford: Oxford University Press.

Hitchins, Keith. 1994. *Rumania, 1866–1947.* Oxford: Clarendon Press.

Holt, Edgar. 1970. *Risorgimento: The Making of Italy, 1815–1870.* London: Macmillan.

Howard, Marc Majoré. 2003. *The Weakness of Civil Society in Post-communist Europe.* New York: Cambridge University Press.

Huntington, Samuel P. 1968. *Political Order in Changing Societies.* New Haven: Yale University Press.

Instituto de Reformas Sociales. 1907. *Estadística de la asociación obrera.* Madrid: Imprenta de la Sucesora M. Minuesa.

———. 1915. *Avance al censo de asociaciones.* Madrid: Imprenta de la Sucesora de M. Minuesa.

International Institute of Agriculture. 1919. "Part 1: Co-operation and Association. Spain." *International Review of Agricultural Economics* 10: 437–442.

Jacobson, Stephen. 2006. "Law and Nationalism in Nineteenth-Century Europe: The Case of Catalonia in Comparative Perspective." *Law and History Review* 20: 2.

Janos, Andrew C. 1978. "Modernization and Decay in Historical Perspective: The Case of Romania." Pp. 72–116 in *Social Change in Romania, 1860–1940.* Berkeley: Institute of International Studies.

———. 1982. *The Politics of Backwardness in Hungary, 1825–1945.* Princeton: Princeton University Press.

———. 2000. *East Central Europe in the Modern World: The Politics of the Borderlands from Pre- to Postcommunism.* Stanford: Stanford University Press.

Jones, Philip. 1997. *The Italian City State: From Commune to Signoria.* Oxford: Clarendon Press.

Jowitt, Kenneth. 1978. *Social Change in Romania, 1860–1940: A Debate on Development in a European Nation.* Berkeley: Institute of International Studies.

Kaufman, Jason. 2002. *For the Common Good? American Civic Life and the Golden Age of Fraternity.* New York: Oxford University Press.

Keane, John. 1988a. *Democracy and Civil Society.* New York: Verso.

———. 1988b. "Despotism and Democracy: The Origins and Development of the Distinction between Civil Society and the State, 1750–1850." Pp. 35–71 in *Civil Society and the State.* New York: Verso.

———. 1998. *Civil Society: Old Images, New Visions.* Stanford: Stanford University Press.

Keegan, John. 2000. *The First World War.* New York: Knopf.

Kehr, Eckart. 1973. *Battleship Building and Party Politics in Germany, 1894–1901: A Cross-section of the Political, Social and Ideological Preconditions of German Imperialism.* Chicago: University of Chicago Press.

Kelsen, Hans. 1955. "Foundations of Democracy." *Ethics* 66: 1–101.

Kern, Robert W. 1974. *Liberals, Reformers and Caciques in Restoration Spain: 1875–1909.* Albuquerque: University of New Mexico Press.

King, Bolton, and Thomas Okey. 1901. *Italy Today*. London: J. Nisbet.

Kornhauser, William. 1959. *The Politics of Mass Society*. Glencoe: Free Press.

Koshar, Rudy. 1986. *Social Life, Local Politics, and Nazism: Marburg, 1880–1935*. Chapel Hill: University of North Carolina Press.

Laclau, Ernesto. 1977. *Politics and Ideology in Marxist Theory: Capitalism, Fascism, Populism*. London: New Left Books.

Laclau, Ernesto, and Chantal Mouffe. 2001. *Hegemony and Socialist Strategy: Towards a Radical Democratic Politics*. London: Verso.

Lakatos, Imre. 1970. "Falsification and the Methodology of Scientific Research Programmes." Pp. 91–196 in *Criticism and the Growth of Knowledge*. Edited by Imre Lakatos and Alain Musgrave. Cambridge: Cambridge University Press.

Lannon, Frances. 1987. *Privilege, Persecution, and Prophecy: The Catholic Church in Spain: 1875–1975*. Oxford: Clarendon Press.

Lears, T. J. Jackson. 1985. "The Concept of Cultural Hegemony." *American Historical Review* 9: 567–592.

Lederer, Emil. 1967. *State of the Masses*. New York: Howard Fertig.

Lieberson, Stanley. 1991. "Small N's and Big Conclusions: An Examination of the Reasoning in Comparative Studies Based on a Small Number of Cases." *Social Forces* 70 (2): 307–320.

———. 1994. "More on the Uneasy Case for Using Mill-Type Methods in Small N Comparative Studies." *Social Forces* 72 (4): 1225–1237.

Linz, Juan. 1965. "Political Space and Fascism as a Late-Comer: Conditions Conducive to the Success or Failure of Fascism as a Mass-Movement in Inter-War Europe." Pp. 153–201 in *Who Were the Fascists? Social Roots of European Fascism*. Edited by Stein Ugelvik Larsen, Bernt Hagtvet and Jan Petter Myklebust. Bergen: Universitetsforlaget.

———. 1967. "The Party System of Spain: Past and Future." Pp. 197–282 in *Party Systems and Voter Alignments: Cross-National Perspectives*. Edited by Seymour M. Lipset and Stein Rokkan. New York: Free Press.

———. 1970. "An Authoritarian Regime: Spain." Pp. 251–283 in *Mass Politics: Studies in Political Sociology*. E. A. and S. Rokkan. New York: Free Press.

———. 2003. *Fascismo, autoritarismo, totalitarismo. Connessioni e differenze*. Rome: Ideazione editrice.

Lipset, Seymour Martin. 1959. "Some Social Requisites of Democracy: Economic Development and Political Legitimacy." *American Political Science Review* 53: 69–105.

Livezeanu, Irina. 1995. *Cultural Politics in Greater Romania: Regionalism, Nation Building, and Ethnic Struggle*. Ithaca: Cornell University Press.

Luebbert, Gregory M. 1987. "Social Foundations of Political Order in Interwar Europe." *World Politics* 39: 449–478.

———. 1991. *Liberalism, Fascism, or Social Democracy: The Political Origins of Regimes in Interwar Europe*. New York: Oxford University Press.

Lukács, Georg. 1971. *History and Class Consciousness: Studies in Marxist Dialectics*. Cambridge: MIT Press.

Lyttelton, Adrian. 1973. "El patronazgo en la Italia de Giolitti (1892–1924)." *Revista de Occidente* 127: 94–117.

———. 1979. "Landlords, Peasants and the Limits of Liberalism." Pp. 104–135 in *Gramsci and Italy's Passive Revolution*. New York: Barnes & Noble.

————. 2000. "Liberalism and Civil Society in Italy: From Hegemony to Mediation." Pp. 61–81 in *Civil Society before Democracy*. Edited by Nancy Bermeo and Philip Nord. New York: Rowman & Littlefield.

————. 2004. *The Seizure of Power*. Rev. ed., *Fascism in Italy 1919–1929*. London: Routledge.

Mack-Smith, Denis. 1959. *Italy: A Modern History*. Ann Arbor: University of Michigan Press.

Mahoney, James. 2003. "Knowledge Accumulation in Comparative Historical Research. The Case of Democracy and Authoritarianism." Pp. 131–174 in *Comparative Historical Analysis in the Social Sciences*. Edited by James Mahoney and Dietrich Rueschemeyer. Cambridge: Cambridge University Press.

Maier, Charles S. 1975. *Recasting Bourgeois Europe*. Princeton: Princeton University Press.

Maione, Giuseppe. 1970. "Il biennio rosso: autonomia e spontaneità operaia contro le organizzazioni tradizionali (1919–1920)." *Storia Contemporanea* 1 (4): 825–889.

————. 1972. "Il biennio rosso: Lo sciopero delle lancette (marzo–aprile 1920)." *Storia contemporanea* 3 (2): 239–304.

Malefakis, Edward. 1970. *Agrarian Reform and Peasant Revolution in Spain: Origins of the Civil War*. New Haven: Yale University Press.

Mandel, Ernest. 1995. *Trotsky as Alternative*. New York: Verso.

Maner, Hans-Christian. 1997. *Parlamentarismus in Rumänien (1930–1940): Demokratie im autoritären Umfeld*. Munich: R. Oldenbourg Verlag.

Mann, Michael. 1988. *States, War and Capitalism*. Oxford: Blackwell.

————. 1997. "The Contradictions of Continuous Revolution." Pp. 135–157 in *Stalinism and Nazism: Dictatorships in Comparison*. Edited by Ian Kershaw and Moshe Lewin. New York: Cambridge University Press.

————. 1999. "The Dark Side of Democracy: The Modern Tradition of Ethnic and Political Cleansing." *New Left Review* 1: 18–45.

————. 2004. *Fascists*. Cambridge: Cambridge University Press.

Manoïlescu, Mihaïl. 1936. *Le siècle du corporatisme. Doctrine du corporatisme integral et pur*. Paris: Librairie Félix Alcan.

Manselli, Raoul. 1992. "Egemonia imperiale, autonomia comunale, potenza politica della chiesa." Pp. 61–134 in *Storia d'Italia*. Vol. 4, *Comuni e signorie: istituzioni, società e lotte per l'egemonia*. Turin: UTET.

Marcuse, Herbert. 1964. *One-Dimensional Man: Studies in the Ideology of Advanced Industrial Society*. Boston: Beacon Press.

Marfany, Joan-Lluís. 2004. "Minority Languages and Literary Revivals." *Past and Present* 184: 137–167.

Marx, Karl. 1994. *Selected Writings*. Indianapolis: Hackett.

Marx, Karl. 1996 [1852]. "The Eighteenth Brumaire of Louis Bonaparte." Pp. 31–127 in *Marx: Later Political Writings*. Edited by Terrell Carver. New York: Cambridge University Press.

Mayer, Arno. 1971. *Dynamics of Counterrevolution in Europe, 1870–1956: An Analytic Framework*. New York: Harper and Row.

————. 1989. *Why Did the Heavens Not Darken? The "Final Solution" in History*. New York: Pantheon.

Mazower, Mark. 2000. *Dark Continent: Europe's Twentieth Century*. New York: Vintage.

Mazzini, Giuseppe. 1945. *I doveri dell'uomo*. Turin: Vega.

McIvor, Anthony D. 1982. *Spanish Labor Policy during the Dictablanda of Primo de Rivera.* Ph.D. diss., University of California, San Diego.

Melis, Guido. 1996a. "L'amministrazione." Pp. 187–251 in *Storia dello stato italiano.* Edited by Raffaele Romanelli. Rome: Donzelli.

———. 1996b. *Storia dell'amministrazione italiana: 1861–1993.* Bologna: Il Mulino.

Michels, Robert. 1926. *Storia critica del movimento socialista italiano.* Florence: La Voce.

Mill, John Stuart. 1974. *Philosophy of Scientific Methods.* New York: Hafner Press.

Milza, Pierre. 2000. *Mussolini.* Rome: Carocci.

Ministerio de Trabajo y Previsión. 1930. *Censo corporativo electoral.* Madrid: Imprenta de los hijos de M. G. Hernández.

Ministero di Agricoltura, Industria e Commercio (MAIC). 1890. *Saggio statistico sulle associazioni cooperative in Italia.* Rome: Eredi Botta.

———. 1913. *Statistica delle organizzazioni di lavoratori al 10 gennaio 1912.* Rome: Officina Poligrafica.

Mitrany, David. 1930. *The Land and the Peasant in Rumania: The War and Agrarian Reform.* London: Oxford University Press.

Montero, José R. 1977. *La CEDA. El Catolicismo Social y Politico en la II Republica.* Madrid: Ediciones de la Revista de Trabajo.

Moore, Barrington, Jr. 1993. *Social Origins of Dictatorship and Democracy: Lord and Peasant in the Making of the Modern World.* Boston: Beacon Press.

Morales Muñoz, Manuel. 2001–2002. "Los espacios de la sociabilidad radical democrática: casinos, círculos y ateneos." *Studia Historica. Historia Contemporánea* 19–20: 161–205.

Morandi, Carlo. 1997. *I partiti politici in Italia: dal 1848 al 1924.* Florence: Le Monnier.

Mosca, Gaetano. 1994. *La classe politica.* Bari: Laterza.

Mosse, George L. 1975. *The Nationalization of the Masses: Political Symbolism and Mass Movements in Germany from the Napoleonic Wars through the Third Reich.* New York: Howard Fertig.

Muñoz, Manuel Ferrer. 1992. *Elecciones y partidos politicos en navarra durante la segunda republica.* Pamplona: Gobierno de Navarra.

Musat, Mircea, and Ion Ardeleanu. 1982. *Political Life in Romania, 1918–1921.* Bucharest: Editura Academiei Republicii Socialiste Romània.

Nagy-Talavera, Nicholas. 1970. *The Green Shirts and the Others: A History of Fascism in Hungary and Romania.* Stanford: Hoover Institution Press.

Neumann, Franz. 1957. "Notes on the Theory of Dictatorship." Pp. 233–256 in *The Democratic and the Authoritarian State: Essays in Political and Legal Theory.* Glencoe: Free Press.

———. 1966. *Behemoth: The Structure and Practice of National Socialism, 1933–1944.* New York: Harper Torchbooks.

Nolte, Ernst. 1966. *The Three Faces of Fascism: Action Française, Italian Fascism, National Socialism.* London: Weidenfeld & Nicolson.

Nord, Philip. 1995. *The Republican Moment: Struggles for Democracy in Nineteenth-Century France.* Cambridge: Harvard University Press.

———. 2000. "Introduction." Pp. xiii–xxxiii in *Civil Society before Democracy: Lessons from Nineteenth Century Europe.* Edited by Nancy Bermeo and Philip Nord. New York: Rowman & Littlefield.

Olivetti, Angelo Oliviero. 1984. *Dal sindacalismo rivoluzionario al corporativismo*. Rome: Bonacci editore.

Orbonas, Silviu. 1930. *Die genossenschaftsbewegung in Rumänien*. Hermannstadt, Romania: Archdiöcesan Buchdruckerei.

Ortega y Gasset, José. 1937. *Invertebrate Spain*. New York: Norton.

———. 1960. *The Revolt of the Masses*. New York: Norton.

Pan-Montojo, Juan. 2000. "Las Asociaciones Rurales y el nacimiento del Sindicalismo Agrario en España, 1834–1907." Pp. 27–64 in *Actas 1er Congreso sobre Cooperativismo Español: Tomo II Historia Sociología*. Fundación Garrido Tortosa: Cordoba.

Panunzio, Sergio. 1987. *Il fondamento giuridico del fascismo*. Rome: Bonacci Editore.

Partito Nazionale Fascista (PNF). 1935 (XIV). *Atti del PNF*. Rome: Fratelli Palombi.

Patrascanu, Lucretiu. 1946. *Sous trois dictatures*. Paris: Jean Vitiano.

Paxton, Robert O. 2004. *The Anatomy of Fascism*. New York: Knopf.

Payne, Stanley. 1961. *Falange: A History of Spanish Fascism*. Stanford: Stanford University Press.

———. 1965. "Spain." Pp. 168–207 in *The European Right: A Historical Profile*. Edited by Hans Rogger and Eugen Weber. Berkeley: University of California Press.

———. 1967. *Politics and the Military in Modern Spain*. Stanford: Stanford University Press.

———. 1970. *The Spanish Revolution*. New York: Norton.

———. 1971. "Catalan and Basque Nationalism." *Journal of Contemporary History* 6 (1): 15–51.

———. 1973. *A History of Spain and Portugal in Two Volumes*. Vol. 2. Madison: University of Wisconsin Press.

———. 1980. *Fascism: Comparison and Definition*. Madison: University of Wisconsin Press.

———. 1987. *The Franco Regime: 1936–1975*. Madison: University of Wisconsin Press.

———. 1993. *Spain's First Democracy*. Madison: University of Wisconsin Press.

———. 1995. *A History of Fascism, 1914–1945*. Madison: University of Wisconsin Press.

———. 1999. *Fascism in Spain*. Madison: University of Wisconsin Press.

———. 2010. "Foundations of Fascism." *The International History Review* 32 (4): 707–709.

Pecharromán, Julio Gil. 1989. *La segunda republica*. Madrid: Historia.

Pellizzi, Camillo. 1949. *Una rivoluzione mancata*. Milan: Longanesi.

Pepe, Adolfo. 1989. "Il sindacalismo pugliese nel primo Novecento." Pp. 781–810 in *Storia d'Italia. Le regioni dall'unità a oggi. La Puglia*. Turin: Einaudi.

Pérez-Díaz, Victor. 1993. *The Return of Civil Society: The Emergence of Democratic Spain*. Cambridge: Harvard University Press.

Perfetti, Francesco. 1987. "Introduzione. Un teorico dello stato sindacale-corporativo." Pp. 7–136 in *Il fondamento giuridico del fascismo*. Rome: Bonacci.

Pinto, Antonio Costa. 2012. "European Fascism: The Unfinished Handbook." *Contemporary European History* 21 (2): 287–300.

Podestà, Carlo, and Antonio Uckmar. 1929. *I contributi sindacali. Manuale teorico pratico*. Rome: Il Diritto del Lavoro.

Pombeni, Paolo. 1984a. *Demagogia e tirannide: Uno studio sulla forma-partito del fascismo*. Bologna: Il Mulino.

———. 1984b. "All'origine della 'forma partito' moderna. La vicenda delle organizzazioni politiche in Emilia Romagna (1876–1892)." Pp. 9–33 in *All'origine della "forma partito" contemporanea: Emilia Romagna 1876–1892: un caso di studio*. Edited by Paolo Pombeni. Bologna: Il Mulino.

———. 1986. "Trasformismo e questione del partito: la politica italiana e il suo rapporto con la vicenda constituzionale europea." Pp.215–254 in *La trasformazione politica nell'Europa liberale 1870–1890*. Edited by Paolo Pombeni. Bologna: Il Mulino.

———. 1995. "La rappresentanza politica." Pp. 73–124 in *Storia dello stato Italiano dall'Unità a oggi*. Edited by Raffaele Romanelli. Rome: Donzelli editore.

Poulantzas, Nicos. 1974. *Fascism and Dictatorship: The Third International and the Problem of Fascism*. London: Verso.

Pradera, Victor. 1938. *The New State*. London: Sands & Co.

Preston, Paul. 1978. *The Coming of the Spanish Civil War: Reform, Reaction and Revolution in the Second Republic, 1931–1936*. London: Macmillan.

———. 1993. *Franco*. London: Fontana Press.

———. 1994. *The Coming of the Spanish Civil War: Reform, Reaction and Revolution in the Second Republic 1931–1936*. London: Routledge.

Preti, Luigi. 1954. *Le lotte agrarie nella Valle padana*. Turin: Einaudi.

Procacci, Giuliano. 1968. *History of the Italian People*. New York: Harper & Row.

———. 1981. *The Italian Working Class from the Risorgimento to Fascism*. Harvard: Center for European Studies.

———. 1992. *La lotta di classe in Italia agli inizi del secolo xx*. Roma: Editori Riuniti.

Putnam, Robert D. 1993. *Making Democracy Work: Civic Traditions in Modern Italy*. Princeton: Princeton University Press.

———. 2000. *Bowling Alone: The Collapse and Revival of American Community*. New York: Simon & Schuster.

Ragionieri, Ernesto. 1976. *Storia d'Italia*. Vol. 4, *La storia politica e sociale, Dall'Unita a oggi*. Turin: Einaudi.

Rial, James H. 1986. *Revolution from Above: The Primo de Rivera Dictatorship in Spain, 1923–1930*. Fairfax: George Mason University Press.

Ridolfi, Maurizio. 1984. "Sulla Formazione dele Moderne Organizzazioni Politiche: Il Caso dell'Area Cesenate." Pp. 305–372 in *All'origine della 'forma partito' contemporanea. Emilia Romagna 1876–1892: un caso di studio*. Edited by Paolo Pombeni. Bologna: Il Mulino.

———. 1992. *Il psi e la nascita del partito di massa. 1892–1922*. Bari: Laterza.

———. 1997. "La terra delle associazioni. Identità sociali, organizzazione degli interessi e tradizioni civiche." Pp. 276–371 in *Storia d'Italia: L'Emilia-Romagna. Le Regioni dall'unità a oggi*. Edited by Robert Finzi. Turin: Einaudi.

———. 1999. *Interessi e passioni: Storia dei partiti politici italiani tra l'Europa e il Mediterraneo*. Milan: Bruno Mondadori.

Riley, Dylan. 2003. "Privilege and Property: The Political Foundations of Failed Class Formation in Eighteenth-Century Austrian Lombardy." *Comparative Studies in Society and History* 45: 190–213.

———. 2005. "Civic Associations and Authoritarian Regimes in Interwar Europe: Italy and Spain in Comparative Perspective." *American Sociological Review* 70: 288–310.

Riosa, Alceo. 1968. "Michele Bianchi." Pp. 147–153 in *Dizionario Biografico degli Italiani*. Vol. 10. Edited by Alberto M. Ghisalberti. Rome: Istituto della Enciclopedia italiana.

Riquer i Permanyer, Borja de. 1994. "La faiblesse du procesus de construction nationale en Espagne aux XIXe Siécle." *Revue d'Histoire Moderne et Contemporaine* 41 (2): 353–366.

Roberts, David D. 1979. *The Syndicalist Tradition and Italian Fascism*. Chapel Hill: University of North Carolina Press.

Roberts, Henry L. 1951. *Rumania: Political Problems of an Agrarian State*. New Haven: Yale University Press.

Rocco, Alfredo. 1938. *Scritti e discorsi politici*. Milan: A. Giuffré.

Rodríguez Jiménez, José Luis. 2000. *Historia de Falange Española de Las JONS*. Madrid: Alianza Editorial.

Romano, Sergio. 1989. *Giolitti: lo stile del potere*. Milan: Bompiani.

Rosenstock-Franck, Louis. 1934. *L'economie corporative fasciste: en doctrine et en fait*. Paris: Librairie universitaire J. Gamber.

Rothschild, Joseph. 1974. *East Central Europe between the Two World Wars*. Seattle: University of Washington Press.

Roveri, Alessandro. 1975. "Il sindicalismo rivoluzionario in Italia." *Ricerche storiche* 5: 5–82.

Rueschemeyer, Dietrich, Evelyne Huber Stephens, and John D. Stephens. 1992. *Capitalist Development and Democracy*. Chicago: University of Chicago Press.

Sahlins, Marshall. 1985. *Islands of History*. Chicago: University of Chicago Press.

Saladino, Salvatore. 1974. "Parliamentary Politics in the Liberal Era: 1861 to 1914." Pp. 27–51 in *Modern Italy: A Topical History since 1861*. Edited by Edward R. Tannenbaum and Emiliana P. Noether. New York: New York University Press.

Salaya, Guillén. 1943. *Historia del sindicalismo Español*. Madrid: Editora Nacionale.

Salomone, William A. 1960. *Italy in the Giolittian Era: Italian Democracy in the Making, 1900–1914*. Philadelphia: University of Pennsylvania Press.

Salvati, Mariuccia. 1992. *Il regime e gli impiegati*. Bari: Laterza.

Sarti, Roland. 1970. "Fascist Modernization in Italy: Traditonal or Revolutionary?" *American Historical Review* 75 (4): 1029–1045.

———. 1971. *Fascism and the Industrial Leadership in Italy*. Berkeley: University of California Press.

———. 1972. "I sindicati fascisti e la politica economica del regime." Problemi del socialismo 14: 746–765.

Sartori, Giovanni. 1976. *Parties and Party Systems: A Framework for Analysis*. New York: Cambridge University Press.

Schandl, Charles. 1938. *Quarante Années de la Coopération Hongroise: Travaux et Resultats de la Société Centrale de Crédit Mutuel de Hongrie (OKÁHÁ)*. Budapest: Patria.

Schmitt, Carl. 1985. *The Crisis of Parliamentary Democracy*. Cambridge: MIT Press.

———. 1996. *The Concept of the Political*. Chicago: Chicago University Press.

Schumpeter, Joseph A. 1942. *Capitalism, Socialism, and Democracy*. New York: Harper & Brothers.

Scoppola, Pietro. 1997. *La repubblica dei partiti: evoluzione e crisi di un sistema politico 1945–1996*. Milan: Mulino.

Scurtu, Ioan.1994. *Istoria partidului national-taranesc*. Bucharest: Editura Enciclopedica.

Selgas, Carlos Iglesias. 1966. *Los Sindicatos en España*. Madrid: Ediciones del Movimiento.

Sellés i Quintana, Magda. 2000. *El foment del treball nacional 1914–1923*. Barcelona: Publicacions de l'Abadia de Montserrat.

Serrano, Carlos Seco. 1969. *Alfonso XIII y la crisis de la restauración*. Barcelona: Horas de España.

Seton-Watson, Christopher. 1967. *Italy from Liberalism to Fascism, 1870–1925*. London, Methuen; New York, Barnes & Noble.

Seton-Watson, R. W. 1963. *A History of the Roumanians: From Roman Times to the Complete of Unity*. Cambridge: Archon Books.

Sewell, William H., Jr. 1980. *Work and Revolution in France: The Language of Labor from the Old Regime to 1848*. Cambridge: Cambridge University Press.

———. 2005. *Logics of History: Social Theory and Social Transformation*. Chicago: University of Chicago Press.

Sima, Horia. 1972. *Histoire du mouvement légionnaire*. Rio de Janeiro: Editôra Dacia.

Simpson, James. 1992. "Los límites de crecimiento agrario en España, 1860–1936." Pp. 103–138 in *El desarollo económico en la Europa del Sur. España e Italia en perspectiva histórica*. Madrid: Alianza Editorial.

———. 1995. *The Long Siesta*. Cambridge: Cambridge University Press.

Skocpol, Theda. 1973. "A Critical Review of Barrington Moore's Social Origins of Dictatorship and Democracy." *Politics and Society* 4 (11): 1–34.

———. 1979. *States and Social Revolution: A Comparative Analysis of France, Russia, and China*. Cambridge: Cambridge University Press.

———. 1997. "The Tocqueville Problem: Civic Engagement in American Democracy." *Social Science History* 21: 455–479.

———. 1999. "How Americans Became Civic." *Civic Engagement in American Democracy*. Washington, D.C.: Brookings Institution Press and Russell Sage Foundation.

Skocpol, Theda, and Margaret Somers. 1980. "The Uses of Comparative History in Macrosocial Research." *Comparative Studies in Society and History* 22: 174–197.

Spampanato, Bruno. 1933. *Democrazia fascista*. Rome: Edizioni di "Politica Nuova."

Spirito, Ugo. 1999. *Critica della democrazia*. Milan: Luni.

Steinmetz, George. 1997. "German Exceptionalism and the Origins of Nazism: The Career of a Concept." Pp. 251–284 in *Stalinism and Nazism. Dictatorships in Comparison*. Cambridge: Cambridge University Press.

Stephens, John. 1989. "Democratic Transition and Breakdown in Western Europe: A Test of the Moore Thesis." *American Journal of Sociology* 94: 1019–1077.

Sternhell, Zeev. 1994. *The Birth of Fascist Ideology*. Princeton: Princeton University Press.

Stokes, Gale. 1989. "The Social Origins of East European Politics." Pp. 210–251 in *The Origins of Backwardness in Eastern Europe: Economics and Politics from the Middle Ages until the Early Twentieth Century*. Edited by Daniel Chirot. Berkeley: University of California Press.

Szöllösi-Janze, Margit. 1989. *Die Pfeilkreuzlerbewegung in Ungarn: Historischer Kontext, Entwicklung und Herrschaft*. Munich: Oldenbourg Verlag.

Tasca, Angelo. 1950. *Nascita e avvento del fascismo. L'Italia dal 1918 al 1922*. Florence: La Nuova Italia.

Tenfeld, Klaus. 2000. "Civil Society and the Middle Classes in Nineteenth-Century Germany." Pp. 83–108 in *Civil Society before Democracy: Lessons from Nineteenth-Century Europe*. Edited by Nancy Bermeo and Philip Nord. Boulder: Rowman & Littlefield.

Terrón Muñoz, Federico. 1987. *Las Cajas rurales españolas. Nacimiento, auge y perspectivas de cooperativismo agrario crediticio en España.* Introduction by Manuel Martín Rodríguez.

Therborn, Göran. 2008. *What Does the Ruling Class Do When It Rules?* London: Verso.

Thomas, Hugh. 1961. *The Spanish Civil War.* London: Penguin.

Tilly, Charles. 1992. *Coercion, Capital and European States: A.D. 990–1992.* London: Blackwell.

Tocqueville, Alexis de. 1988. *Democracy in America.* New York: Harper & Row.

Togliatti, Palmiro. 1970 [1935]. *Lezioni sul fascismo.* Rome: Editori Riuniti.

———. 1976. *Lectures on Fascism.* London: Lawrence & Wishart.

Tomassini, Luigi. 1996. "Mutual Benefit Societies in Italy, 1861–1922." Pp. 225–270 in *Social Security Mutualism: The Comparative History of Mutual Benefit Societies.* Edited by Marcel van der Linden. New York: Peter Lang.

Tönnies, Ferdinand. 1927. "Demokratie und Palamentarismus." *Schmollers Jahrbuch fur Gesetzgebung, Verwaltung und Volkswirtschaft im Deutschen Reiche* 1: 1–44.

Tooze, Adam. 2006. *The Wages of Destruction.* New York: Penguin.

Tortella Casares, Gabriel. 2000. *The Development of Modern Spain: An Economic History of the Nineteenth and Twentieth Centuries.* Cambridge: Cambridge University Press.

Trebilcock, Clive. 1981. *The Industrialization of the Continental Powers, 1780–1914.* New York: Longman.

Trimberger, Ellen Kay. 1978. *Revolution from Above: Military Bureaucrats and Development in Japan, Turkey, Egypt, and Peru.* New Brunswick, N.J.: Transaction Books.

Trotsky, Leon. 1991. *The Balkan Wars, 1912–1913: The War Correspondence of Leon Trotsky.* New York: Pathfinder.

———. 2001 [1932]. "What Next? Vital Questions for the German Proletariat." Pp. 164–297 in *The Struggle Against Fascism in Germany.* Edited by George Breitman and Merry Maisel. New York: Pathfinder.

Tusell, Javier. 1973. "La descomposicion del sistema caciquil espanol (1902–1931)." *Revista de Occidente* 127: 75–93.

———. 1974. *Historia de la democracia cristiana en España. Tomo I: Antecedentes y C.E.D.A.* Madrid: Editorial Cuadernos Para el Dialogo Edicusa.

———. 1976a. "The Functioning of the Cacique System in Andalusia." Pp. 1–27 in *Politics and Society in Twentieth-Century Spain.* Edited with an Introduction by Stanley G. Payne. New York: New Viewpoints.

———. 1976b. *Oligarquia y caciquismo en Andalucia (1890–1923).* Barcelona: Editorial Planeta.

———. 1977. *La crisis del caciquismo andaluz (1923–1931).* Madrid: Cupsa editorial.

———. 1987. *Radiografía de un Golpe de Estado: el Ascenso al Poder del General Primo de Rivera.* Madrid: Alianza Editorial.

———. 1990. *Manual de historia de España: Siglo XX.* Madrid: Hermanos Garcia Noblejas.

Uva, Bruno. 1974. *La nascita dello stato corporativo e sindacale fascista.* Rome: B. Carucci.

Vago, Bela. 1975. *The Shadow of the Swastika: The Rise of Fascism and Anti-Semitism in the Danube Basin, 1936–1939.* London: Saxon House.

Valiani, Leo. 1959. "Il movimento operaio sindacale sotto il fascismo." Pp. 39–70 in *Dall'antifascismo alla resistenza.* Milan: Feltrinelli.

Varshney, Ashutosh. 2002. *Ethnic Conflict and Civic Life: Hindus and Muslims in India.* New Haven: Yale University Press.

Vilar, Pierre. 1987. *Cataluña en la España Moderna.* Barcelona: Josep Fontana.

Villa, Dana. 2006. "Tocqueville and Civil Society." Pp. 216–244 in *The Cambridge Companion to Tocqueville.* Edited by Cheryl B. Welch. Cambridge: Cambridge University Press.

Warren, Mark. 2001. *Democracy and Association.* Princeton: Princeton University Press.

Watts, Larry L. 1993. *Romanian Cassandra: Ion Antonescu and the Struggle for Reform, 1916–1941.* Boulder: East European Monographs.

Weber, Eugen. 1974. "Romania." Pp. 501–574 in *The European Right: A Historical Profile.* Berkeley: University of California Press.

Weber, Max. 1978. *Economy and Society: An Outline of Interpretive Sociology.* Vol. 1. Berkeley: University of California Press.

Webster, Richard. 1960. *The Cross and the Fasces: Christian Democracy and Fascism in Italy.* Stanford: Stanford University Press.

Wehler, Hans-Ulrich. 1985. *The German Empire, 1871–1918.* Dover, N.H.: Berg.

Winkler, Heinrich August. 1993. *Weimar 1918–1933. Die Geschichte der ersten deutschen Demokratie.* Munich: C. H. Beck.

Winston, Colin M. 1985. *Worker's and the Right in Spain.* Princeton: Princeton University Press.

Wuthnow, Robert. 1991. "Tocqueville's Question Reconsidered: Voluntarism and Public Discourse in Advanced Industrial Societies." Pp. 288–308 in *Between States and Markets: The Voluntary Sector in Comparative Perspective.* Edited by Robert Wuthnow. Princeton: Princeton University Press.

Zamagni, Vera. 1979–1980. "Distribuzione del reddito e classi sociali nell'Italia fra le due guerre." *Annali dell'Istituto Giangiacomo Feltrinelli* 20: 17–49.

———. 1993. *The Economic History of Italy 1860–1990.* Oxford: Clarendon Press.

———. 1997. "Gli attori sociali delle transformazioni produttive dell'agricoltura Italiana." *Annali della fondazione Luigi Einaudi* 31: 29–46.

Zangheri, Renato. 1987. "Nascita e primi sviluppi." Pp. 5–216 in *Storia del movimento cooperativo in Italia.* Turin: Einaudi.

Index